Global Terrorism

James M. Lutz and Brenda J. Lutz

Routledge
Taylor & Francis Group

LONDON AND NEW YORK

First published 2004
by Routledge
11 New Fetter Lane, London EC4P 4EE

Simultaneously published in the USA and Canada
by Routledge
29 West 35th Street, New York, NY 10001

Routledge is an imprint of the Taylor & Francis Group

© 2004 James M. Lutz and Brenda J. Lutz

Typeset in Century Old Style by
Florence Production Ltd, Stoodleigh, Devon
Printed and bound in Great Britain by
Bell & Bain Ltd, Glasgow

British Library Cataloguing in Publication Data
A catalogue record for this book is available from the
British Library

Library of Congress Cataloging in Publication Data
Lutz, James M.
  Global terrorism / James M. Lutz and Brenda J. Lutz.
    p. cm.
  Includes bibliographical references and index.
  1. Terrorism.   I. Lutz, Brenda J., 1957–.   II. Title.
  HV6431.L88 2004
  303.6′25 – dc22   2003021141

ISBN 0–415–70050–7 (hbk)
ISBN 0–415–70051–5 (pbk)

Dedicated to our daughters, Carol and Tessa,
our Newfoundlands, Sadie and Oliver, and our
St Bernards, Elsie, Barnaby, and Alasdair

Contents

LIST OF ILLUSTRATIONS   xi
PREFACE   xiii

1 Terrorism in the world today and yesterday   1

Terms   6
Further reading   6

2 What is terrorism? Definition and classification   7

Defining terrorism   8
Classification and categories   14
Causes of terrorism   16
Prevalence of terrorism   19
Summary   21
Terms   22
Further reading   22

3 Tactics, weapons, and targets   23

Techniques   24
Weapons   26
Targets   32
Summary   42
Terms   43
Further reading   43

4 State sponsors and supporters of terrorism   45

True state control   46
State support of terrorism   48

Case studies 50
    4.1 Italy and Hungary in Yugoslavia—fishing in troubled waters 50
    4.2 Iraq 52
    4.3 Iran 54
    4.4 The United States and the Contras in Nicaragua 56
    4.5 North Korea 59
Summary 61
Terms 62
Further reading 62

5 Religious justifications for terrorism   **63**
Terrorism and the world's religions 64
Case studies 73
    5.1 The Zealots in Judea 73
    5.2 The Sikhs and Khalistan 74
    5.3 Algeria in the 1990s 78
    5.4 Aum Shinrikyo (Supreme Truth) 80
    5.5 Osama bin Laden and the al Qaeda network 82
Summary 85
Terms 87
Further reading 87

6 Ethnic and national bases of terrorism   **89**
Modernity and ethnic conflict 90
Case studies 95
    6.1 The Boston Tea Party 95
    6.2 The Mau Mau uprising in colonial Kenya 96
    6.3 Basque nationalists in Spain 98
    6.4 Dayaks and migrants on Borneo 100
    6.5 Albanians in Kosovo and Macedonia 103
    6.6 The Palestinian Liberation Organization and the struggle with Israel 107
Summary 111
Terms 112
Further reading 113

7 Terrorism and ideologies of the left   **115**
Ideology and beliefs 116
Dissatisfaction from the left 117
Case studies 124
    7.1 The Baader-Meinhof Gang in West Germany 124
    7.2 The Italian Red Brigades 127
    7.3 17 November Organization in Greece 130
    7.4 The Montoneros in Argentina 132
    7.5 The Islamic Republic of Iran and the Mujahedin-e-Khalq 135
    7.6 The Animal Liberation Front and Animal Rights Militia 137

Summary 139
Terms 142
Further reading 142

8 Terrorism and ideologies of the right   **143**

Right-wing dissatisfaction: Marxism and minorities 144
Case studies 148
     8.1 Stormtroopers in Weimar Germany 148
     8.2 Neo-fascism in postwar Italy 151
     8.3 The American militia/patriot movement 153
     8.4 Neo-Nazis and skinheads in Europe 157
Summary 162
Terms 164
Further reading 164

9 Terrorism and multiple motivations   **165**

Terrorist campaigns with complex causes 166
Case studies 170
     9.1 Insurgency and terror in Malaya 170
     9.2 Leftists and indigenous populations in Peru 172
     9.3 Irish republicanism 175
     9.4 Colombia—regionalism, ideology, and narcotics 179
Summary 182
Terms 184
Further reading 185

10 State use of domestic terrorism and repression   **187**

Government-induced fear and compliance 188
Government complicity in terrorism by non-state groups 189
Genocide and ethnic cleansing 192
Case studies 194
     10.1 Terror in the first years of the French Revolution 194
     10.2 The Cherokee Nation versus the State of Georgia 196
     10.3 Paramilitary militias in East Timor 198
     10.4 Farm invasions in Zimbabwe 200
     10.5 Ethnic cleansing in Bosnia and Herzegovina 202
     10.6 Genocide in Rwanda 204
Summary 208
Terms 210
Further reading 210

11 Countries with multiple crises of terrorism   **211**

The prevalence of multiple crises 212
Waves of violence and terrorism in Sri Lanka 214
Summary 221

Terms   222
Further reading   222

12 Counterterrorism   **223**

Techniques of counterterrorism   224
Weapons of mass destruction and mass casualties   238
Summary   239
Terms   241
Further reading   241

13 Terrorism: a continuing phenomenon   **243**

Why terrorism continues   244
What we know from the historical experience   249

GLOSSARY   251
BIBLIOGRAPHY   267
INDEX   283

Illustrations

Maps

1   India and south Asia   75
2   Indonesia   101
3   Former Yugoslavia   104
4   Peru   174
5   East Africa   205

Tables

2.1   Casualties in international terrorist incidents, 1991–2002   20
3.1   Number of international terrorist incidents by region, 1991–2002   38
3.2   Number of casualties due to international terrorist incidents by region, 1991–2002   39
3.3   Number of deaths due to international terrorist incidents by region, 1998–2002   39
5.1   Number of suicide attacks, 1980–2000   70
8.1   Number of deaths in left-wing and right-wing attacks in West Germany and Italy,
      1968–87   164

Preface

There should be a rule that you should never complain in front of your spouse about the textbooks that are available for courses because there is no answer when you are challenged to write one that you like better. That scenario was indeed the genesis of this textbook, but in this case the normal rule about complaining does not hold since we have been able to collaborate on this textbook and have been pleased with the result. We started writing the textbook before September 11, but the sad events of that day have made the task more important. Our concerns that we had about materials available for academic classes on terrorism have been heightened by the attacks on the World Trade Center and the Pentagon. One of the major problems that we had with existing texts on terrorism was the tendency for there to be an over-emphasis on events and actors in the Middle East. Most American students have the misperception that virtually all terrorists are Arabs (or other Middle Easterners). They also believe that terrorism is a relatively recent phenomenon. In point of fact, terrorism is neither recent nor largely restricted to events in the Middle East, and textbooks should not inadvertently reinforce these misconceptions by focusing overly much on current events. Terrorism is deeply rooted in human history. This book has sought to balance the events in the Middle East by including discussions of events in other parts of the world and terrorist violence in other time periods. As a consequence, before September 11 it was not our intent to focus only on the Middle East, and this intent did not change with the attacks of that day. Of course, much of the discussion of terrorism in this book has to include those events since they are far too important to ignore or to downplay. Recent events in the United States, however, should not be covered to the exclusion of other cases of terrorist violence in the world. Events in the rest of the world are important as well.

This book also attempts to help limit one of the major problems that anyone teaching terrorism has to face. The use of anything but the most recent cases runs into the difficulty that not all the students will be familiar enough with world history (even recent world history) or geography to place the terrorist movements in the appropriate context. The instructor will often spend what seems to be an inordinate amount of time providing the context for the terrorist movement and its goals. The use of the case studies in this volume provides enough background to alleviate this difficulty for most of the cases. If the students have read the material, they will have the appropriate context for the analysis of the particular case or series of cases. The case studies are wide ranging in time and space, but they are very amenable to comparison and analysis in a variety of ways. The background in the chapters should also permit an instructor to incorporate additional cases that she or he considers important, either from the historical past or from new events that have occurred. There are, of course, cases that could have been included but were not, and issues that could have been covered in much more depth. This text, however, leaves scope for the assignment of additional books, articles, and readings to incorporate other topics of interest to the instructor. It is designed to be flexible in that regard, and we think that it has succeeded.

Any effort of this magnitude owes a lot to many different people. Foremost in the list are students who have taken the class on terrorism at Indiana University-Purdue University at Fort Wayne. Their questions have influenced the material that has been included in many ways. Some of the case studies are the direct result of questions they have raised about particular events or groups. At other times, their uncertainty about some issues suggested coverage in the pages that follow. Their questions have also helped us to look at old issues in new ways. This book is written foremost for other students (although we hope that general readers will find it enlightening as well), and they have benefited from the insights, the questions, the doubts, and the interests of those who have gone before.

A number of people deserve our thanks. The document delivery people at the Helmke Library were essential in finding the materials for this book. Even with increased electronic access to source materials, it is still essential to have skilled professionals who can find materials and get them for you. Many colleagues on campus also drew our attention to various materials and happenings. They may notice their suggestions incorporated directly or more indirectly in the pages that follow. The help and suggestions were invariably helpful and always welcome. The external reviewers of the manuscript supplied many useful insights and suggestions for improvement. A special note of thanks is due to Barbara Blauvelt, the secretary of the Department of Political Science at Indiana University-Purdue University at Fort Wayne. Administrative duties could have been overwhelming while this book was being written, but her expertise and skill meant that administration, teaching, and writing could proceed at the same time. Without her able assistance to reduce the time spent on essential tasks, it would have taken much longer for this book to be completed.

We would also like to thank the people at Routledge. Craig Fowlie worked with us from the beginning. He not only shepherded us through the process; he also made excellent suggestions for improvements. Zoe Botterell was always available for technical help with the manuscript and for answering questions. Their assistance made the completion of this project possible. We would like to extend our appreciation to Carol and Byron Hoover, Betty Lutz, Dick and Jane Thomas, Elmer Denman, and Bill and Tracy Wimberly for their friendship, personal interest in our book, and support throughout this entire project.

Finally, a word of direct acknowledgment for those who are mentioned on the dedication page is in order. Our girls, Carol (now nine) and Tessa (now seven), are a constant source of inspiration and wonderment to us. Their presence has cheered our lives and given us an additional incentive to work on this project. Their needs also provide a balance in our lives that has worked well personally and professionally. Their presence has brightened our lives and made writing more worthwhile. In much the same way our five dogs have provided enjoyment and diversion on many occasions for us. Our magnificent Newfoundlands and their loyal St Bernard companions have been entertaining throughout the writing of this book. We would like to say that quiet walks with them have helped us to formulate our thoughts, but the walks were too infrequent and seldom quiet enough for much active thinking or even conversation. Their playfulness, and their interactions with Carol and Tessa, however, helped to invigorate us so that we were able to return to the blank pages with a clearer focus and reinforced purpose.

Chapter 1

Terrorism in the world today and yesterday

Terms   6
Further reading   6

The attacks on September 11, 2001 on the World Trade Center and the Pentagon dramatically demonstrated the importance that terrorist acts can have for citizens and residents of the United States. These deadly attacks reinforced the fact that terrorism had been a significant problem for the rest of the world for a long time. Further, the terrorists involved in these attacks used a new and very deadly way of creating fear and terror in a population when civilian airliners loaded with fuel and passengers became the weapons used in the assaults. This use of airliners to destroy the World Trade Center was the single most deadly terrorist act known to have happened. The nature of the weapon used and timing of the attacks made it very clear that the terrorists intended to cause as many casualties as possible on the ground (in addition to the passengers in the airplanes). The airliner that crashed into the Pentagon was not as deadly in terms of the results, but the intent in this case was to cause massive casualties as well, and many did die in this assault. The fourth airliner that was hijacked did not reach its target, which would appear to have been somewhere in the Washington DC area. While it is doubtful that the intended target for this airliner will ever be known for sure, it is very likely that it was taken over to attack a major government building and/or to cause a large number of deaths on the ground. Its delayed departure from the Newark airport meant that it was taken over later than the other three flights, and passengers on this plane became aware of their likely fate. Evidence suggests that the plane crashed when the passengers attempted to recapture the aircraft and prevent the hijackers from using it as a weapon as had been the case with the other three aircraft. Even if the hijackers had maintained control of the aircraft, however, it is likely that it would have been shot down before it would have been allowed to reach the Washington area since authorities were aware of the fact that the plane was off course and presumed to be under the control of more hijackers.

This coordinated attack on September 11 was very sophisticated in terms of conceptualization and execution. The planning involved indicated that determined terrorists with resources were capable of inflicting great damage on targets in the United States. Four aircraft from three different airports were hijacked pretty much simultaneously soon after they took off. The hijackers of the four aircraft knew how to get past airport security in at least three airports with relatively crude, but effective, weapons. They were also aware of the standard operating procedures for airline crews, which specified that they should cooperate with the hijackers. These procedures reflected that fact that there had been no deaths as a result of hijackings in the United States—a presumption that will no longer be operative for many years to come. The organization behind the hijackers made sure that their own pilots were on board. There had to be someone with sufficient skills to navigate and fly the planes well enough to approach New York and Washington and strike the target buildings since there would be no way that the hijackers could force a pilot at the controls of the airliner to commit suicide by flying into a building filled with people. The one failure in this relatively sophisticated plan was the absence of any contingency procedures providing options for the hijackers on any one of the aircraft if their flight was behind schedule. The fourth aircraft that crashed in western Pennsylvania could have done considerable damage somewhere in the United States if the hijackers on board had attempted to take over the craft sooner or had opted to change targets once it became obvious that the authorities and people on the ground knew what was happening.

As deadly as the September 11 attacks were, they have not been the only significant attacks made against targets involving the United States in recent years. The truck bomb detonated at the Murrah federal office building in Oklahoma City in 1995 has been the most deadly attack linked to domestic terrorists in the history of the United States. This attack demonstrated the type of damage that could be done against a relatively vulnerable target and the types of casualties that could result. It also clearly demonstrated that there was a wide range of potential targets for terrorist attacks that existed within the United States. The bombings of the US embassies in Nairobi in Kenya and Dar-es-Salaam in Tanzania in 1998 were clearly attacks directed against the interests of the United States, even if the hundreds of dead and thousands of wounded were mostly residents of these two African countries. The casualty figures were still high and demonstrated what was possible if mass casualties were desired. The suicide attack on the US destroyer *Cole* in the harbor at Aden in 2000 was significant as well because it was an attack on a US warship, indicating that even military targets could be attacked successfully. Violent attacks directed against the United States had been ongoing for years, and there clearly was a problem to be dealt with.

These examples of attacks directed against the United States from within or abroad have only been part of the global pattern of terrorism in the twentieth and now the twenty-first centuries. Terrorist assaults on targets in many countries have occurred with depressing regularity. Palestine and Israel have been the sites of numerous acts of violence in the twentieth century. Intermixed with the attacks by Palestinians or other Arabs against Israel since the creation of the modern state have been terrorist actions by Jewish extremists seeking to promote their own political objectives in the region. Sri Lanka has been wracked by a deadly civil war for years. This conflict, sometimes with a confusing cast of characters, has included a large number of deadly terrorist actions by the sides involved. Bombings and other kinds of attacks have been present in Northern Ireland, in Algeria, in India, in Indonesia, and in Chechnya in the former Soviet Union. The political violence, terrorism, and atrocities in some cases have claimed thousands and tens of thousands of lives, and many of them give every indication of continuing for many years. The high death tolls in some of these countries have been cumulative ones rather than the result of just one deadly attack, but the casualties are still just as high. Of the other countries in the world, some have suffered from violence and

terrorism for decades while others have had only brief periods during which they have had to deal with terrorism. Other countries have avoided any acts of terrorism so far, but any country could experience such acts in the future.

What is obvious from the above very incomplete list of places where terrorism has been occurring is that violence has not been restricted to the United States. It has affected many other countries in the world, and, in fact, it has heretofore been a more serious problem for a number of other countries than it has been for the United States. What should also be obvious from the list of countries mentioned above or any list of countries that have dealt with major terrorist violence in the last quarter of a century is the fact that terrorism has not just been a problem involving actors from the Middle East. Terrorist violence has occurred widely, including in places that have no connection with problems originating in the Middle East. Many groups in many places have relied on political violence in attempts to achieve their goals. Great care must be taken to avoid stereotyping terrorists as persons from the Middle East who are determined to destroy the West. There are other problems, other causes, and other objectives that organizations have sought to resolve or achieve through the use of political violence. Osama bin Laden has been one important terrorist but he is not the only one who has been active in recent years. There have been many others, and it is important to be aware of them as well.

Some of the recent terrorist attacks have involved the use of potentially deadly new techniques designed to inflict mass casualties. Suicide attacks by fanatic pilots in hijacked airliners are just one example that displays the scope of the damage that is possible. The attacks with nerve gas in the subway system of Tokyo by a domestic Japanese group are another recent use of potential weapons of mass destruction that have become available to terrorists. The use of anthrax in the United States in the aftermath of September 11 provides an additional example of the use of a new kind of deadly weapon. There has also been the fear that nuclear weapons could fall into the hands of terrorists. To date this possibility has been a plot for novels and Hollywood movies, but even as an unlikely possibility it is still quite frightening. Of course, more traditional means of terrorizing populations remain and can be quite deadly, as indicated by ethnic cleansing in what used to be Yugoslavia and in Rwanda.

Much of the focus on terrorism has indeed been on recent events. It has been suggested that the attack on Israeli athletes at the 1972 Munich Olympics was the beginning of modern terrorism (Deutch 1997: 11). While this attack may have introduced some new elements into terrorist practices, it is hardly the threshold between non-occurrence and the occurrence of this type of political violence. In point of fact, terrorism had been ongoing in many areas of the world long before 1972. The first airline hijacking, for example, occurred in Peru in 1931 (Goldberg 1991: 80). What made the 1972 attack noteworthy in some respects was that in took place in a Western country and that it managed to capture world attention. Notwithstanding the importance of this particular event, especially to Israel and Germany, terrorism is hardly that recent a phenomenon. There is greater recent awareness today because of modern mass communications capabilities. Violent terrorism, however, is quite ancient. Some of the most notable examples go back centuries or even a millennium or more. It is important to put the current terrorists' activities in both a historical and a geographical perspective. The current political culture of a country or society, which can reflect events and conflicts centuries old, influences the style of confrontation and the type of violence used. It is important to realize that terrorism is not something new under the sun, and its long history as a political tool by various groups suggests that it will not quickly disappear in the immediate future. The attacks on September 11 are one especially deadly example of a continuing phenomenon, one that occurred within existing geographical or historical perspectives. Without these perspectives, however, it is more difficult to understand

events such as September 11, and an appropriate perspective can also suggest actions that are relevant to dealing with terrorism. Governments in the past have ignored terrorists at their own peril at times. In other cases, the governments have made the wrong decisions or played into the hands of the terrorist dissidents. Government policies have created the conditions in which terrorists have prospered and in other cases policies have weakened whatever support terrorists might have had. Thus, what governments do—and do not do—can be very important for the success or failure of terrorist movements. The knowledge of terrorism becomes important for understanding and dealing with terrorism when and where it appears.

Many theories seeking to explain terrorism have been put forward over the years. Of course, there is no one cause for such a widely occurring phenomenon and anyone who suggests that there is only one cause should be regarded with great care. If there were one simple solution to terrorism it would have been discovered by now. Governments have not been able to determine a set of conditions that lead people to resort to violence so that they can avoid them, and appropriate security measures that will always work have not been discovered. The examples of terrorist movements that will be provided in the following chapters will supply some indications of some of the reasons why dissident political movements form and decide to use violence in their efforts to change the political circumstances in which they find themselves, their groups, or their societies. In general, some group has to think that the government is being manifestly unfair in some way. The key is the perception of unfairness. Things may actually turn out not to be better with different laws or leaders or with different boundaries, but if groups think things can be better, demands for change will occur and if these demands are not met, the potential for violence exists. Similarly, things may be much better than the perceptions of the dissidents indicate, but again it is the perceptions that can provoke recourse to violence. Generally, it is true that terrorist groups that constitute real threats to a society cannot be created in countries where there are no major causes for complaint and where no dissident groups have appeared. There have been too many attempts to establish dissident guerrilla movements or terrorist organizations that have quickly failed for such activities to be created out of thin air. Of course, as noted above, events such as recessions, globalization and modernization, and wars will generate sufficient dissatisfaction for some residents of many societies, and potential dissidents can then find an ample number of persons to draw upon for recruits and support in attacks upon governments.

Terrorism as a topic is complex, but it is clearly important in today's world and will continue to be important. One way to better understand the prevalence of terrorism is to compare different groups and their techniques and analyze the circumstances under which organizations willing to use terror appeared. While not all groups and circumstances are similar, there are common patterns that can be found. Most of the following chapters include case studies that provide some detail on particular terrorist groups and their activities. The case studies also provide enough detail so that the appearance of dissident organizations willing to use terror as a means of achieving objectives can be understood in the context of local circumstances. Some grievance, real or imagined, had to be present to trigger the violence. The case studies make clear what these grievances were, what kinds of actions the dissidents attempted, and how successful they were in their efforts. In some cases it will also be readily apparent how governments were able to deal with the terrorist groups or why they failed to be effective in dealing with the challenge. These case studies are described in some depth for they are essential to comparing, contrasting, and understanding what terrorism is and how it can appear within a political system.

The case studies have been drawn from a wide variety of times and places. A conscious effort has been made to include some historical examples of the use of terrorist violence. The use of historical cases clearly indicates that terrorism as a form of political violence has been around for a long time. More importantly, the most historical of the case studies provide some examples of very successful uses of terrorism, successful at least in the sense of achieving or coming close to achieving the goals of the group responsible for the political violence. Of course, the less successful terrorist undertakings from the past will be much less well known. Quick failures usually do not make it into the history books, especially when the victors write history. Notwithstanding the importance of cases from the past, the focus in the choice of the case studies was on more recent events. In addition to selecting examples from across time, a very conscious effort has also been made to discuss terrorists and dissident organizations that have operated in many parts of the world. Europe, North America, South America, Africa, the Middle East, and the rest of Asia have all been the scenes of significant terrorist movements and bloody terrorist attacks. It is important to realize that terrorism has its roots in many societies around the world and the first step in understanding its prevalence is to realize its extent.

The following chapters will thus provide a rather comprehensive introduction to the phenomenon of terrorism. Chapters 2, 3, and 4 will deal with some necessary definitions, broad concepts, and ways of categorizing particular dissident organizations. The basic groundwork will be laid in these chapters for Chapters 5 through 11 that deal with specific types of terrorist groups. These chapters will all include detailed case studies of particular terrorist groups that have operated in the world, including organizations that have been condoned by governments in power. Chapter 12 will deal with a variety of counterterrorist strategies that have been proposed. Chapter 13 will contain some conclusions and a summary of what governments can do and why terrorism persists. The world changes, political activities change, weapons change, and so does terrorism. An understanding of terrorism in the past, and especially in the recent past, will help us all to better understand terrorism when it occurs in the future.

A list of terms and some suggested additional reading will be presented at the end of each chapter. The key terms will be provided as a means of reinforcing the information contained in each of the chapters. These terms will also be contained in the glossary at the end of the book for easy reference. The list of materials for additional reading will provide a starting point to acquire more in-depth information relevant for the case studies that are included in the chapters. Some of the books, articles, and chapters will also provide additional information on the general topics covered in each of the chapters. The additional readings listed at the end of this chapter, for example, will deal with some books that provide useful general introductions to the topic of terrorism or even compilations of valuable material. All of these materials will be useful supplements for what is discussed in the chapters. Occasionally films will be listed as well if they are particularly good demonstrations of key points. While such films are few in number, they are worth viewing if they can be found. These suggested readings, of course, are only a starting point. The references used in each of the chapters and the bibliography at the end of the book will provide many more sources from which to start to gather additional information. Further, there will be additional materials coming out in the future, so a search of the tables of contents for journals and library catalogues is essential as well.

Terms

Munich Olympics (1972)
Murrah Federal Office Building
USS Cole

Further reading

Crenshaw, M. and Pimlott, J. (eds) (1997) *Encyclopedia of World Terrorism*, Armonk, NY: M. E. Sharpe.

Harmon, C. C. (2000) *Terrorism Today*, London: Frank Cass.

Hoffman, B. (1998) *Inside Terrorism*, New York: Columbia University Press.

Kegley, C. W. Jr (ed.) (2003) *The New Global Terrorism: Characteristics, Causes, Controls*, Upper Saddle River, NJ: Prentice Hall.

Laqueur, W. (1999) *The New Terrorism: Fanaticism and the Arms of Mass Destruction*, New York: Oxford University Press.

Chapter 2

What is terrorism? Definition and classification

Defining terrorism   8

Classification and categories   14

Causes of terrorism   16

Prevalence of terrorism   19

Summary   21

Terms   22

Further reading   22

One person's freedom fighter is another person's terrorist.

The above statement occurs in a variety of forms that all say much the same thing— that terrorism, like beauty, is in the eye of the beholder. But having a useable definition of terrorism is essential for any valid consideration of its occurrence in the world. How do you distinguish a terrorist group from a non-terrorist group? What kinds of terrorism have existed and continue to exist in the world? What are some of the underlying causes of terrorism? How prevalent is terrorism—has it been increasing or has it been on the decline? The current chapter will consider these very contentious issues.

Defining terrorism

Terrorism as a word in its usual usage has a connotation of evil, indiscriminate violence, or brutality. Someone has been terrorized! Thus, to label a group or action as terrorist is to seek to imply that the actors or the violence is immoral, wrong, or contrary to obvious basic ethical principles that any reasonable human being might hold. To use different terms for the violence that may occur, such as freedom fighter, revolutionaries, rebels, resistance fighters, members of the democratic opposition, or national liberation soldiers, however, implies that the group undertaking the violence is motivated by some greater good or higher moral principle. The choice of terms to describe persons undertaking political violence often contains underlying assumptions about the goals of the group. To call a group freedom fighters or resistance soldiers suggests a positive evaluation of the goals of the organization. The victims of the violence are usually supporters of a political system that denies freedom and that seeks to oppress and repress at least part of the population. Innocent bystanders—collateral damage in the new parlance of violence—may be killed or wounded. Of course, the losses among the innocent are ultimately the fault of the

repressive government that refuses to grant the people their rights. It might indeed be possible to argue that a truly repressive government kills or harms more people, especially the innocent, than all the attacks by the groups fighting for freedom or democracy. Better to undergo some loss of life in the short term in order to avoid the greater and continuing loss of life in the future.

Terrorists, on the other hand, attack governments that are legitimate and accepted by the people they govern. They seek to undermine and destroy a political system and even a way of life that is desirable or good. Their attacks are frequently directed against innocent civilians and designed to cause indiscriminate casualties among them. The terrorists in some cases may even be labeled cowardly since they sneak about targeting innocent civilians or unarmed members of the government rather than undergoing the risks that would come with attacks on armed police or military troops who would fight back. In the case of suicide bombings the terrorists have convinced gullible supporters to give up their lives for the cause. These evil terrorists are seeking to overthrow democratic governments or at least reasonably democratic governments in some cases. In other cases, they are seeking to replace less than democratic dictatorial systems with one that is far worse. A relatively benign military dictator or king would be supported in order to avoid radical communists or fanatical religious groups from coming to power—that is, support would be provided for the lesser of two evils.

The difficulty with this approach lies in deciding who gets to decide how to define good government and bad government. Different people value different political goals or have different priorities. For some, it is economic equality. Others may find anything more than the most limited government to be oppressive. Yet others may feel that a good political system must support morality and natural rights. All of these groups, and others as well, will categorize the same political systems differently. Thus, a definition of terrorism needs to be separated as much as possible from evaluations of the groups using violence and their targets. This is not to say, however, that value judgments about governments and groups should not be made. Any thinking person has to weigh the good and bad of a political system and its opponents. Are the actions of some groups attacking governments so evil, or so unrelated to the good that they seek, that they have to be opposed—even to the point of sending military aid to support the government under attack? Alternatively, is the government so bad or evil that all external support should be withdrawn, giving the opposition a greater chance of winning, even with violent attacks? Terrorist attacks by the groups being victimized by the Nazis, for example, would hardly have deserved any negative evaluations. Governments and populations must make decisions about right and wrong in such cases. These decisions, however, can be made without the need to apply different terms to persons who have undertaken basically the same action.

When faced with a definition that is so value-laden and used by governments or others to apply negative labels, social scientists frequently like to create new words that are more value free. Since terrorism as a word is so widely used, such an option is really not available. No special vocabulary is necessary. What is necessary is to provide a working definition, as neutral as possible. What is also necessary is to read and evaluate with care how others use the word. A clear, workable definition of terrorism should cover groups that individuals agree with and groups that they disagree with. The need for neutral definitions does not preclude the necessity of making political judgments and evaluating political organizations on the basis of whatever principles and priorities are most important.

It is not surprising that there have been a multitude of definitions provided for terrorism. Many definitions are exceedingly complex or have far too many elements (Schmid 1983). With such complex and all-inclusive definitions, terrorism could involve individuals, groups, or states; attacks could be random or selective; intimidation or propaganda could be the goal; and the goals themselves could be eccentric, political, or

criminal. Definitions to be useful need to exclude as well as include different kinds of violence. Laqueur (1987) considered terrorism the illegitimate use of force to achieve political objectives. This definition has the virtue of being simpler, but it too involves far too many types of activities. It also avoids a definitional problem with terrorism by shifting the definition problems to a determination of what is legitimate use of force and what is illegitimate. Governments provide definitions, but they are often self-serving at least to some degree. Opponents of the government are defined as terrorists while irregular allies of the government fail to meet the definitional standards as terrorists. Over the years, the United States has had a list of countries that have been considered to be state supporters of terrorism. The countries normally on this list include Iran, Iraq, Syria, Libya, Cuba, North Korea, and the Sudan. All of these countries have supported groups or used their own personnel to attack the United States or its allies. The list, however, has never been a complete one. It has ignored countries supporting terrorist groups that were allies or potential allies, because their inclusion would create problems, or because their actions did not especially concern the United States. South Africa aided groups in Angola and Mozambique that practiced terror, but it was never included. Similarly, Angola supported a guerrilla insurgency, complete with terrorist attacks against the South Africans in what came to be Namibia, but was not included. Pakistani support for insurgent groups in Kashmir had also not been considered important enough to the United States to qualify for the inclusion of that country. The Soviet Union never made the list, primarily because its inclusion would have greatly complicated US diplomatic activities and US foreign policies. The obvious point is that governments make definitions fit their own needs. National concerns over foreign policy take precedence over concerns about dealing with terrorism (Goldberg 1991: 86).

Rather than provide a discussion of some of the possible definitions, it will be simpler to provide a working definition that will be reasonably inclusive and to specify the various elements that are part of the definition. This definition will apply to all practitioners of this type of political violence, regardless of the political goals of the terrorists or the political views of the individuals targeted by the terrorists. The definition that will be used throughout this book is one that is derived from the works of Hoffman (1998), Kushner (1998b), and Claridge (1996), all of whom have definitions incorporating most of what will be included in the definition for this volume. The three approached the issue of terrorism from somewhat different perspectives, but between them they cover the key ingredients involved in terrorist activities. Combining the issues raised by these three works results in the following definition, which has six major components:

> Terrorism involves political aims and motives. It is violent or threatens violence. It is designed to generate fear in a target audience that extends beyond the immediate victims of the violence. The violence is conducted by an identifiable organization. The violence involves a non-state actor or actors as either the perpetrator, the victim of the violence, or both. Finally, the acts of violence are designed to create power in situations in which power previously had been lacking (i.e. the violence attempts to enhance the power base of the organization undertaking the actions).

The first key element of this definition is that the violence is undertaken primarily for political reasons. In fact, terrorism has been considered uniquely political in nature, with terrorism even being considered "the continuation of politics by other means" (Sick 1990: 51). Political goals are a key element that separates terrorist acts from other forms of violence (Long 1990: 5). The violence is not undertaken for financial reasons or because of personal issues. Kidnappings of prominent political leaders or corporate executives to make political statements are different from those kidnappings that serve as criminal ventures to raise money for the abductors. The use of fear to extort money from businesses (the protection rackets of American gangster fame or infamy)

is criminal, not political. Sometimes, of course, opposition groups have used kidnapping or bank robberies to finance their organizations. In these cases, the goals are still generally political because the money received is used to fund subsequent political activities, possibly including more violence, rather than leading to gains in personal wealth. While political objectives are a key for defining terrorism, the goals that are sought by terrorists can fall into a number of categories. The terrorists may be seeking to have a government change its policies—to stop a particular program from being continued or to force the adoption of some new policy. The political objectives may involve an effort to change leaders or the political elite, regarded as corrupt or illegitimate. Goals may go further, seeking to bring about a complete change in the framework of the government—changing from a monarchy to a republic or from a strongly centralized system to a more decentralized one or from a military dictatorship to a theocratic state run by religious leaders. Finally, the terrorists may be seeking to change national boundaries—to detach a region to create a new state, to attach some territory to another state, or to amalgamate existing states into a new country.

The second element of a terrorist action is that violence or the threat of violence is present. Requests for changes, demonstrations, and petitions are not terrorism, no matter how disconcerting they may be to a government. Although massive demonstrations may make a government apprehensive about the future, there is no direct threat of violence. Actual violence is fairly obvious to detect and recognize. The threat of violence is only likely to be effective as a technique with a group that has already demonstrated that it is able and willing to be violent—a political organization that has never undertaken any type of political violence is unlikely to be credible in its threats. Once violence has been used, however, the threat of additional violence may generate the necessary fear that the dissident group desires and lead the government to give in to the demands of the group, whatever those demands might be.

For violence, and even political violence, to qualify as terrorism, it must also affect a target audience beyond the immediate victims and influence such audiences as part of the attempt to gain the political objectives of the organization. The violent acts are intended to have effects beyond the immediate events (B. Jenkins 1990: 29). Terrorism is a form of psychological warfare that intends to influence governments and the general public (Chalk 1996: 13). If a political leader is assassinated with the goal of removing that individual in order to permit the next in line to move up, the death is political violence, but it has no target audience. For an assassination to be a terrorist action, it must involve parties beyond the assassin or assassins and the immediate victim (Schmid 1992a: 10). On the other hand, if a political leader is assassinated in order to send a message to other members of the political elite that they need to change policies or make concessions in order to avoid a similar fate, then that assassination is a terrorist act. Bombings of buildings, with or without casualties, or car bombs in crowded areas are often intended to demonstrate to the general public that they are vulnerable. The resulting fear may lead the public to put pressure on the government to change policies, or it may lead to the weakening of public support for the leaders in power who are seen to be unable to protect the citizens from a small band of dissidents. The need to reach a target audience is one reason why terrorist groups seek publicity. If no one knows of a terrorist act, the goals have not been achieved. If the deaths of government personnel are ascribed to a plane crash rather than a bomb on the aircraft, the target audience will draw the wrong conclusion about threats to the state or to the safety of individuals. The need for publicity is also why some organizations have established pre-set code words with the media so that they can authenticate the claims for the organization when they provide a warning that a bomb is about to go off. It will not be necessary in all cases for particular organizations to claim credit for particular terrorist actions. The local situation and the target will often make it clear that the cause of a particular group of dissidents is behind the activity. If swastikas are painted on a Jewish synagogue, the anti-Semitic message is obvious. If a car bomb goes off at the headquarters of the ruling party, the general population is likely to know whether it is a local minority group or whether it is the political opposition that is behind the attack. Victims of terrorist attacks and target audiences will invariably include civilians or non-military government personnel.

For political violence to be terrorism there must be an identifiable organization. An individual is unable to carry out the actions, reach the target audience, and present the political demands for the changes that are necessary to end the violence. An effective campaign to create change also requires enough actions to be credible, an effort beyond a single individual over time. Effective terrorism rests on the potential for repetition and the systematic use of violence (Badey 1998: 93). Terrorist actions almost inevitably lead to casualties or arrests among the dissidents; thus, a single individual is too likely to be captured or killed. There needs to be an organization in place to continue the political battle. Theodore Kaczynski, the Unabomber, is a classic example of the limitations inherent in campaigns by one individual. His bombings over the years inspired fear, but the target audience was unclear, and it was not obvious what actions the target audience should take. The FBI and other police agencies knew that the bombings were related, due to forensic analyses, but they were unable to establish the link between the victims, nor were they were able to identify the political agenda of the person behind them, though the links were present in Kaczynski's mind in terms of the bombings being protests against modern society. Kaczynski himself did not issue any statements for a long time, further reducing any influence on target audiences. While the US government and the general public would not have given into any demands by Kaczynski, it was impossible to undertake any policy changes since the demands were not known. Interestingly enough, once Kaczynski did attempt to present his political agenda, he was identified and arrested, thus ending the bombing campaign.

While organization is a key element of terrorism, the nature of the way in which dissidents are organized has changed with modern technology. Not all terrorist groups have a permanent organization. Different members may coalesce temporarily for a specific attack and then go their separate ways (Cameron 1999: 283). In other cases the terrorists become, in essence, part-time activists. They may accept central direction on how to proceed, but they are not centrally controlled (Hoffman 1995: 281). Individuals may even participate in what has been termed leaderless resistance, where their actions are in accord with a dissident organization, but they are not directly part of the group. With internet capabilities and instantaneous communication, such terrorist actions within a network or loosely coordinated group are not only possible, they can be very effective (Kushner 1998b: 82–3). These kinds of loosely coordinated groups exist in addition to the more conventionally organized groups; they do not replace them completely. These groups have some advantages for the dissidents. Their amorphous nature means that they are more difficult to detect, to infiltrate, and to destroy (Chalk 1999: 159). The persons actually undertaking the actions will also have relative freedom in making tactical decisions regarding the attacks (Hoffman 2001: 418). The lack of central direction may limit the constraints that normally come with an organizational structure. Without central control, loosely aligned individuals who are not concerned about the long-term effects of their actions or about the best way to use terror to achieve political objectives may be more willing to inflict higher casualties and more willing to use exotic weapons than the conventional dissident groups using political violence (Parachini 2001: 403).

For purposes of the present volume, terrorism will be defined as situations in which either the perpetrators of the political violence, the victims, or both are not states or governments. Actions between states, including war, will not be included.

During wartime or Cold War confrontations, a government and/or its military may consciously seek to generate terror in the enemy's ranks or among the civilian population. The Mongols massacred populations of cities that resisted them in order to convince other cities to surrender and avoid a similar fate. The bombings of Rotterdam and London by the Germans and the bombings of Hamburg, Tokyo, and Hiroshima by the Allies during World War II were all designed to create terror as well. Of course, if both state and non-state actions are defined as terrorism, equality is established between dissident groups and governments. Such arguments, of course, have some legitimacy, but they confuse the issue, and they are often raised to promote the cause of the dissidents. Eliminating state actors from consideration in terrorism may suit a particular political agenda, but including state actors will serve a different political agenda. Limiting a definition of terrorism to exclude actions between states, however, does not excuse or ignore the violence that states undertake. One of the myths about terrorism is that it is exclusive to non-state actors (Stohl 2003: 87). As a consequence, the role of states in furthering terrorist actions will indeed be considered and will be part of the case studies. Governments use terror against segments of their own populations in order to achieve some political goal. Frequently such political violence will involve paramilitary groups or death squads, permitting the government to officially deny any role in the actions but to still benefit from the terror created in a target audience. It is important to note, however, that government repression is not necessarily the same as terrorism. Even in a repressive state, individuals have an opportunity to know what the law is and to avoid actions that would lead to punishment (Sproat 1991: 24). Governmental use of terrorism against its own citizens, however, creates situations in which individuals cannot avoid becoming victims.

The last part of the definition depends on the fact that the terrorist actions are used to improve the power situation of the organization that is using this form of political violence. While the specific agendas of groups using terrorism are quite different, they all share this characteristic. They are attempting to improve their power situation—to increase the probability of being able to influence political decisions. Terrorist campaigns are frequently mounted by organizations that have failed to bring about their desired changes by other means, i.e. they are politically weak. They have failed in democratic elections to gain enough power to bring about change, governments have ignored peaceful protests and appeals, or they have been met by government repression that prevents further efforts at peaceful change. Since they are relatively powerless in the conventional political setting of their own society due to limited electoral appeal or limited support in the face of government repression, they resort to unconventional means in an effort to improve their power base. Terrorism is appealing to weaker groups because it can be undertaken with limited resources and the possible rewards are high (Crenshaw 2003a: 97).

While all six of the above characteristics are necessary for an action to be considered a terrorist act, they are interrelated. Political aims are clearly linked with organizations that choose violence given their relative weaknesses. Political goals and aims also generally involve actions designed to affect either the government or other actors in the political system, and in order for this effect to take place, a target audience is obviously necessary for persuasion or influence. Note also that the definition applies to all groups using political violence to induce fear in an effort to bring about political change in any direction. The definition is not specific to any one group nor does it exclude others.

The above six-part definition is basically one for academic use. It is designed to help in understanding the terrorist phenomenon. It cannot serve as an appropriate definition in a court of law. Governments usually need a more precise legal definition if they are going to use their courts and legal systems to try, convict, and punish individuals who are involved in terrorist actions. Such a legal definition may be necessary for use of special

courts or other special procedures, and it may be essential for a government that has to decide whether or not a person accused of terrorism elsewhere should be extradited (Schmid 1992a: 9). Such necessary legal definitions will often be complex since they are a tool for combating terrorism rather than a method for understanding it. In many cases national legal systems will not require any special definition of terrorism. Hijacking an airplane, setting off a bomb, and killing people are already crimes under national laws, even when the crimes are undertaken for political purposes. If a state wishes to impose stiffer penalties for crimes associated with terrorism, however, then some sort of legal definition becomes important. Similarly, if a national legislature desires to prohibit financial contributions to terrorist groups, then the government has to provide some system for designating which groups are prohibited. The legal basis can be a definition used by the prime minister or some other state agency, or the law may simply indicate that the government can choose which groups are prohibited from receiving support. This latter option may introduce arbitrary elements, but it would provide a flexible procedure for a government to use. The definition used by the US Department of State, for example, is ambiguous, giving officials a great deal of flexibility in its application (Badey 1998: 92).

International definitions of terrorism and terrorists may also be necessary, and such definitions will undoubtedly be different from the one suggested above as well as the definitions used in different countries. An international definition would be useful for the purposes of extradition and return of fugitives. Ideally, it would match national definitions or even an analytical definition. Realistically, it will need to be some minimal definition that most countries will accept. It would probably have to include specific actions and would leave some areas of activity uncovered; but some coverage under international law is better than none at all. Countries that wished to cooperate in the elimination of some other terrorist actions would be free to do so if they wished—guaranteeing extradition and coopera-tion in a wider variety of areas. Of course, for such definitions to work, governments would have to risk the possibility that what they see as freedom fighters might be extradited and convicted along with terrorists. The state may, more awkwardly, have to decide when violent political acts do not constitute terrorism and when persons involved in these actions will not be tried or, more import-antly, not extradited. Governments will have to make the distinction between freedom fighter and terrorist—when the same action is acceptable and when it is not. Politicians will have to decide, and local public opinion will be important in that decision. Public opinion is not necessarily a nega-tive factor to be considered in such a situation, but governments will always be caught between choosing consistent approaches and taking into account special circumstances.

Classification and categories

A working definition of terrorism is an essential first step for studying this type of political violence. Also necessary is some classification scheme for presenting and discussing different terrorist organizations that have been present in the world. Similar organizations need to be consid-ered together. The discussion could be organized geographically, chronologically, or thematically. In this volume, the last approach will be taken. Some efforts have attempted to involve psychol-ogy typologies, defining the organizations by the motivations of the membership (Hacker 1976; Bell 1975). While useful complements to the study of terrorism, it must be noted that such approaches require analysis, even psychoanalysis, of individuals not available for detailed study in many cases. Others define and categorize terrorist organizations by levels and types of activity or by the extent to which terror is a tactical weapon versus a strategic one (J. White 1998). Obviously, these kinds of distinctions could change over time for some groups. The categories utilized will be groups pursuing religious goals, national/ethnic/

linguistic/regional goals, left-wing ideological goals, right-wing ideological objectives, groups whose goals have involved a clear mixture of objectives to the extent that no one predominates, and the use of terrorism by governments, espe-cially in contexts where "unofficial" groups under-take the action rather than government agencies.

Religious dissidents will be the first type to be discussed. This discussion will include groups that use terrorist attacks to attempt to achieve their goals in terms of creating religious freedom for their groups or bringing groups that they see as more theologically correct to power. Virtually all the major religions in the world have at times provided the justification for terrorist violence by some adherents (as well as providing justifications for many wars over the centuries). Many active terrorist organizations have sought objectives related to a particular ethnic group, or linguistic group, or region of the country. These groups seek to liberate themselves and their co-nationals from what they perceive to be a colonial situation or a repressive government. What is essential for the nationalist perspective to dominate the dissident group is this perception of colonialism or domination. The actual level of difference present between two groups may be "objectively" small (for example, their languages may be closely related, or their DNA may be so similar that geneticists would find it difficult to separate members of the two groups on that basis), but it is the perceptions of the members of the organ-ization that drive the actions, not the results of some academic research or debate. Such national situations can obviously include cases of overseas colonialization, but some groups will feel colonial-ized by being included as part of a neighbor-ing country. Others may see a foreign minority controlling their own country. Ideologies have also served to define the political objectives of organizations using terror. There have been both left-wing and right-wing groups that have used terrorist tactics. They will be considered separately in different chapters since the goals and objectives of the two types of groups are so dis-similar, even though at times they have shared the goal of destroying the existing states. In many cases they appear in different contexts, with leftist groups opposing one kind of regime or government and rightist groups opposing a different kind of regime or government. However, both groups have at times operated in the same countries, even at the same time, when they have both been opposed to a middle-of-the road government.

It is not possible for some groups that practice terrorism to specify a dominant cause that has fueled their opposition activities. In an ideal typology, every terrorist movement that ever existed or would exist could be easily categorized. But in the real world this is often not possible. In some of the cases that will be discussed in the earlier chapters, the dominant cause underlying the dissident movement will be easily identifiable. Even where one objective dominates, any terrorist organization can reflect other concerns. The ethnic dissidents may practice a different religion or the ideological dissidents may have greater appeal for some minority group. For example, a national liberation movement will usually be ethnically distinct from the colonial power, and the inhabitants of the colony may be overwhelmingly of a different religion. Religious differences may reinforce the national feelings, but the struggle against the colonial power with associated terrorist activities will be national rather than religious. The religious differences simply reinforce the national ones. There are cases, however, where it is difficult to choose a dominant underlying cause for the terrorist organization because of the significance of more than one group of objectives. These complex cases also involve some of the more interesting and more important cases of active terrorist organizations.

The final type of terrorism described in this book is terrorism undertaken essentially by or on behalf of the government. Generally it will involve unofficial groups that use terror to reinforce governmental policies or deal with dissident groups. Governments will frequently use death squads or other such groups to instill fear rather than relying on the police or the armed forces. What will be discussed with this type of terrorism are activities supported by the government that are similar to the activities of terrorist groups, i.e. violence is used for political objectives, it is directed against not only the victims but also a target audience within the country, and its objective is to enhance the power position of the government.

The above definition and typology does not take into account one distinction that is frequently used with analyses of terrorism. Terrorist actions are often divided into domestic terrorism and international terrorism. International terrorism will usually include situations that involve a target in another country attacked by a group from another, thus creating a situation in which more than one government has an interest. Domestic terrorism is an internal affair and at least in theory less open to the involvement of other states. This distinction between domestic and international terrorism, however, can often be a false one. Domestic terrorist actions may only be possible with foreign support and aid, yet the presence of that support and assistance may not be known for some time, leading to a misclassification of the act. A dissident organization may seek to attack a foreign ally of the government that it opposes in order to have the foreign support reduced. Such an attack would clearly be international in scope, but generally domestic in the objective it seeks. In yet other cases, what passes for an international terrorist act is less distinctive. If Kurdish separatists in Turkey attempt to attack the office of a provincial governor, it is domestic terrorism. If the same separatist group attacks a Turkish consulate in France, then the attack is considered international terrorism since it took place on foreign soil. In both cases, however, the attack represents actions by the same organization against the same government. Whether the attack occurred in Turkey or France is a matter of convenience for the separatists; it does not reflect a significantly different type of action. Similarly, the 1934 assassination of King Alexander of Yugoslavia in France by a Bulgarian in the pay of Croat nationalists was ultimately a domestic terrorist action that arose from the regional and ethnic disunity that plagued Yugoslavia between World War I and World War II (not to mention later years). The assassination occurred in France because the terrorists correctly assumed the king would be more vulnerable in that country. The Bulgarian assassin was wanted in Bulgaria on criminal charges related to his attempt to detach portions of Yugoslavia so that they could be united to Bulgaria, and thus despite his nationality he was linked with the Croat nationalists. He also had Croat collaborators in his attack on King Alexander (Havens *et al.* 1975: Chapter 9). Even the fact that Prime Minister Barthou of France was killed did not make the incident international in scope since Barthou was not the target. He was simply an innocent bystander, albeit a very high ranking one. It should also be noted that this assassination was indeed a terrorist attack. King Alexander represented the ruling elite. His death was not expected to end the dissident activities of this group of Croats—it was simply one action among many. The target audience included other members of the Yugoslav political elite.

Causes of terrorism

Virtually every dissident organization has reasons specific to the group and its circumstances that lead it to the decision to rely on violence to achieve its political objectives. There are, however, some general underlying factors that have been theorized to contribute to the appearance of terrorism in different places and different groups. There have been numerous theories as to the causes of terrorism—included among the possibilities are: government structures and exploitative economic systems; repression and discrimination; relative deprivation wherein a group sees its position in society slip in regard to other groups even if all groups are raising their standards of living; rapid change that disrupts the social and political systems; imperialism and colonialism; and disasters—natural or otherwise—that overwhelm the political society. All of these explanations have at least some validity in some circumstances, but terrorism is such a complex phenomenon that no one theory can be sufficient as an explanation for all occurrences. Regardless of the underlying causes in a social or political system, one factor is virtually universal. Violence is likely when some subgroup in the population has major grievances. The problems can be real or perceived. The basis of problems can be grounded in religious beliefs, ethnic concerns, ideological issues, or from a mixture of these factors. In fact, many persons implicitly identify the causes of terrorism in ethnic, religious, and ideological terms when they use the objectives of the terrorist to categorize the causes of the violence. In a large number of cases it is obvious that disparities in economic well being play a role in the grievances (Howell 2003: 177). Marxist theories in its many variations would clearly accept class differences and economic structures as one key to the appearance of violence. Dissidents see their religious, ethnic, or class group suffering from such disparities and take these disparities as an indication of the presence of a discriminatory and unfair political system that needs to be changed, by violence if all else fails. Rapoport (2003) suggests that there is a link between the historical era and the causes of terrorism. He posits four waves of violence. The first was the anarchist—beginning in the 1880s; the second was anti-colonial—beginning in the 1920s; the third was violence associated with the new left, beginning in the late 1960s; and the fourth was a religious wave that began in 1979.

Not only do the dissidents believe that problems exist, but that violence is the solution to the problems. The dissidents can view as illegitimate the structure of the state, the form of government, or its policies. A resort to violence is seen either as the solution to the problems or as one means of forcing a government to deal more quickly with the problems. Violence may also be fueled by a lack of opportunity for political participation in a society (Crenshaw 2003a: 95). Participation opportunities may be lacking because of government repression or the existence of an authoritarian political system. At the extreme, government repression can be so severe that it directly generates violent struggles to overthrow a dictatorial regime or colonial administration. In other cases the dissidents may simply be unable to mobilize political support, even in a democracy, through the existing political processes. Dissident groups will resort to terrorism in frustration when they cannot achieve their objectives through political and legal channels (Pimlott 1997: 682). The failure to mobilize support through existing channels—or the absence of any channels for participation—can then lead the dissidents to use violence to overcome these disadvantages.

There are some factors that can contribute to the occurrence of terrorist violence in many contexts. What governments do or do not do may be important in some circumstances, but there are times when government policies and practices may not be the key factors that account for the appearance of terrorist actions. Economic globalization has caused inequality among states as well as within countries (Hoffmann 2002: 108). The resulting inequalities have fueled frustrations within states and helped set the stage for appeals for violence by dissident groups. It has been suggested that the spread of market capitalism that accompanies globalization has often destroyed the structure of local economies, further contributing to the conditions that support the appearance of violent responses to change (M. Mousseau 2002/3). Globalization may be generally advantageous for a country, but not every group will gain or gain equally (the issue of relative deprivation). Entering the global economy will mean that some groups face income losses or job losses. In addition, even if the globalization process yields new jobs, it is not necessarily true that the persons who lose their jobs are the same persons who are able to fill the new jobs.

Economic recessions and depressions generate economic anxiety and dissatisfaction that in turn can breed terrorism. When economic problems occur, some groups in a society will lose ground while others may stay at the same level or even prosper. The groups that suffer may think that government favoritism is responsible for the faulty distribution of resources and may ultimately resort to violence when government policies fail to reinstate gains for them. Unfortunately for countries facing disgruntled citizens, individual governments are not normally the cause of recessions even when their policies can have some effect on the severity of economic problems. Some countries are even likely to be victims, often unintentional ones, of economic policies in other countries that contribute to recessions. These countries can do little to mitigate the recessions and can only deal with the consequences of economic dislocation. Virtually all the countries of the world suffered during the Great Depression. In a variety of ways the policies of the United States, the United Kingdom, and France helped set the stage for the economic collapse that affected everyone. Germany was one of the countries hardest hit by the economic dislocations, and popular dissatisfaction with the economic problems led to an increase in support for the Nazi Party and Adolf Hitler. Unfortunately for the democratic government and parties in Germany in 1930, there was little that the German government could do about the Great Depression. One of the effects of severe economic dislocations can be a resort to violence arising from the economic frustration of groups in the society.

In addition to direct economic problems, globalization and modernization can place great stresses on societies in other ways. Societies dealing with changes are inherently vulnerable to the displacement of groups and popular dissatisfaction. Modernization can also disrupt social structures by de-emphasizing old patterns of respect and social interaction as new economic and social elites develop. Individuals moving from the village to the modern city will experience culture shock. Leaving the village and the extended family ties can lead to alienation and marginalization in the new society (Esposito 1995: 16). Not everything that comes with modernization is inherently good, and even the good effects can have adverse consequences for portions of society. It is quite likely that life patterns will be disrupted; some groups will gain and others will lose, not just economically but in terms of status or place in a structured social environment. Modernization and globalization will also affect the structure of values and norms. Belief patterns, including religions, will be faced with the challenges that come with changes. Western culture and values are seen as threatening to local religions and cultures (Hoffmann 2002: 112). The importance of modernization and globalization in contributing to terrorism has been demonstrated by the fact that any symbol of modernization becomes a legitimate target for attack (Klare 2003: 30). Political violence can be one reaction to these challenges and changes, especially if the values or beliefs under attack are important ones to the community or a portion of the community. Finally, modernization also has contributed to terrorism by making economies and societies more vulnerable (Crenshaw 2003a: 93). The terrorism of the late twentieth century has been a manifestation of and a reaction to the process of globalization (Wilkinson 2003: 124).

Wars, like economic problems and globalization, have bred situations that have contributed to terrorism in later years. Wars from the past have effects that carry over into later years. There are groups that are unhappy with some aspect of the peace settlements following wars. Lost territories, new boundaries, different government structures, new ruling elites, and other changes can create problems for future governments. Governments inherit these problems, which can include populations predisposed to distrust the government and rulers in power. Governments of states may even be held responsible for changes that do *not* occur in the aftermath of a conflict (for example, an ethnic or religious group does not get to found an independent state). Even the continuation of the status quo can lead to discontent. Those opposed to the government may be willing to use violence, including terrorism, to redress what they see as past wrongs. The current government then has to deal with the problems from the past. At some level, of course, the policies of individual countries are responsible for wars, but the long-term consequences of warfare will often fall upon different states. Often, refugees have appeared as a consequence of war, and the numbers of displaced persons may overwhelm some countries. Refugees may also become permanent residents and create a minority population where none existed before. At the very least, refugee populations cause a temporary economic strain that can lead to political problems further down the road.

Conflict often breeds more conflict. The Napoleonic Wars helped to lead to the rise of modern nationalism, which in turn contributed to national insurrections and additional conflicts —the war of 1812, the wars against the colonial administrations in the Spanish colonial empire, the wars of German and Italian unification, and the Balkan Wars. Each of these conflicts in turn led to more violence, both domestic and international. Similarly, World War I significantly contributed to the overthrow of the Russian monarchy by a war-weary population. That change in government then permitted Lenin and the Bolsheviks to seize power, and this led to the creation of a communist system that in turn played a role in generating many later conflicts. World War I also resulted in the breakup of the German, Austro-Hungarian, Russian, and Ottoman empires with later consequences for political violence and terrorism among the successor states and populations dissatisfied with the new boundaries. It remains to be seen what Iraq's future is and what problems may (or may not) appear down the road in this area. Thus, the outbreak of wars, in both good causes and bad ones, will have consequences years later, and governments have to deal with these consequences. Ending the causes of war may be a major step towards the elimination of terrorism at some point in time, but political leaders in the present will still have to deal with problems inherited from a past that they cannot change. Thus, for the immediate future the world will still have to deal with the consequences of previous international conflicts, even if no new ones appear in the future.

Prevalence of terrorism

One of the more important issues regarding terrorist attacks involves whether or not terrorism has been on the increase. It is a rare day that the newspaper in any medium-sized US city does not contain information about a violent attack somewhere in the world. The news media in larger cities and those with national audiences that cover events in foreign countries more extensively invariably have information on more than one instance of such violence. Even before September 11, there was clearly the perception that the world has become a more dangerous place, and that terrorists could be anywhere. Of course, the definition of terrorism is an important issue in this regard since different authors and the various groups collecting data use different definitions, making precise comparisons more difficult. Trends within data accumulated by the same author or organization, however, can be more trustworthy for the purposes of detecting trends and general patterns. We clearly have much better information about recent years—and especially the most recent half-century—than we do of earlier times. Information on terrorism by groups in the Greek city-states or the Egypt of the Pharaohs or Tang China is singularly lacking. Our knowledge of political violence or terrorism in the Middle Ages in Europe is less than complete as well. While massive campaigns that involved the use of terror would be more obvious in existing historical materials, more isolated instances would be lost. As a consequence, discussions of changing frequencies of terrorist acts have of necessity to be limited to more recent times.

In considerations of all kinds of terrorism, it is clear that there was an increase in the number of incidents in the 1980s. There were almost four times as many acts in the 1980s as there were in the 1970s (Stern 1993: 393–4). The impression that the West is the frequent target of terrorism is probably somewhat misleading. With a free press, the actions that do occur are widely covered in the media (Schmid 1992b: 16). In other circumstances there may be few reliable media sources for collecting data, as has been the case in the former Soviet Union (Pluchinsky 1998: 121). Further, media coverage of some kinds of terrorist acts or terrorist acts in some countries may be limited if the activities are part of a campaign and do not involve spectacular attacks or new types of targets (Jongman 1992: 46–7). Even if it is assumed that the reporting of terrorism improved as terrorism became a phenomenon worthier of watching and analyzing, the increase is still obvious. When terrorism does occur, it can be for a variety of causes as the previous typology has indicated. This typology would suggest that many acts are domestic, and by far the majority of terrorist acts that do occur are domestics ones. Overall there appears to be an increase over time in such acts, and there have been indications that such domestic terrorism was indeed increasing in the 1980s just as international incidents were (Jongman 1992: 35). Of course, whether or not to define an attack as a terrorist act can become very political, as noted above. Some governments will proclaim any act of opposition to be terrorist violence in order to brand a group with a negative label, and governments facing undeniable ongoing campaigns of terror may be quick to label any violence as terrorism (LeVine 1995).

Another way to view terrorism has been to focus on acts that are defined as international terrorism, even though only a small portion of all terrorist attacks can be classified as international (Wilkinson 2000b: 45). The definition is clearly somewhat arbitrary since many international acts are part and parcel of domestic campaigns, as noted above. A focus on such actions, however, can still prove useful for detecting trends. There have been suggestions that many of these international acts of terrorism were related to the struggles that were part of the Cold War. From the late 1960s to the mid-1980s authoritarian regimes, including the Soviet Union, frequently resorted to terrorism in response to foreign policy defeats at the hands of democratic states (O'Brien 1996). Of course, this approach assumes that there was some kind of network involving local groups and outside supporters or that the CIA and KGB were quite active in promoting actions across borders. With the breakup of the Soviet Union there was a decline in Soviet support for terrorism and thus a decrease in the level of international acts of terrorism (Enders and Sandler 2000). While the end of the Cold War may have played a role in the reduction of such violent incidents, counter-measures in Western states could have been a factor as well (Enders and Sandler 1999). But not all terrorism in the world resulted from conflict among nations, as was obvious on September 11, and not even all terrorist actions that have been supported by state governments were part of the Cold War.

What is probably more important than the sheer number of terrorist attacks that occurs is how deadly they are. Not only did the number of attacks from the 1970s to the 1980s increase, they also became much more lethal. Terrorism has become progressively more violent and more extreme (Chalk 1999: 164). The increase in the numbers of dead and injured was much greater than the increase in the number of incidents (Stern 1993: 393–4). The same finding was true for inter-national incidents of terrorism in the 1980s and 1990s. While there were somewhat fewer attacks,

those that did occur were more deadly (Enders and Sandler 2000: 327–8). The upward trend in the 1980s was clear for international incidents of terrorism in various data collections that followed this phenomenon (Jongman 1992: 33). Table 2.1 contains a summary of the casualties resulting from international terrorist incidents from 1991 to 2002. The number of such incidents peaked in 1991 while the total deaths peaked in 2001 with the September 11 attacks. The years 1998 and 2002 also had significant death totals. Overall, it is clear that casualties have increased per incident since 1995, although there were some years with rela-tively few deaths and injuries in the international setting. Terrorist attacks have become more lethal. Singular incidents at the international level can influence the casualty figures. The 2001 fig-ures clearly represent the many that died in the World Trade Center towers. The 1993 injury fig-ures are high because of the 999 persons injured (though not necessarily severely) in the first attack on the World Trade Center. What is less obvious is the fact that casualties in international incidents are but a small portion of the total vic-tims of all terrorist attacks. More people die in domestic incidents than international ones. In

TABLE 2.1 Casualties in international terrorist incidents, 1991–2002

Year	Incidents	Dead	Injured	Total	Dead/ incident	Injured/ incident	Total casualties/ incident
1991	565	–	–	317	–	–	0.56
1992	363	–	–	729	–	–	2.01
1993	431	–	–	1,510	–	–	3.50
1994	322	314	674	988	0.98	2.09	3.07
1995	440	165	6,291	6,454	0.38	14.30	14.68
1996	296	311	2,654	2,965	1.05	8.97	10.02
1997	304	221	693	914	0.73	2.28	3.01
1998	273	741	6,313	7,054	2.71	23.12	25.84
1999	392	233	706	939	0.59	1.80	2.40
2000	423	405	791	1,196	0.96	1.87	2.83
2001*	355	3,572	2,635	6,207	10.06	7.42	17.48
2002	199	725	2,013	2,738	3.64	10.12	13.76

Source: US Department of State, *Patterns of Terrorism*, various years, online at http://www.state.gov/s/ct/rls/pgtrpt.
*Total casualties for the September 11 attacks on the World Trade Center are preliminary.

1995 more people died in the Oklahoma City bombing than in all the recorded international incidents that year. Ongoing terrorist campaigns have also resulted in cumulative death tolls in the thousands or tens of thousands. It is true that international incidents are becoming more deadly, but the largest number of deaths and injuries still occur in domestic situations.* It has been suggested that the increasingly deadly nature of terrorism, both domestic and international, results from three factors: more terrorist groups are motivated by religious views and values; more amateurs operating alone have launched attacks; and the more professional terrorists have greater knowledge about weapons and greater sophistication in using them (Hoffman, 1997, p. 3). The increase in the level of casualties is more important than the number of incidents. Terrorism has not been on the decline with the end of the Cold War or with other changes in the international system. While there would appear to be variations over time with no consistent trend and while the relative contribution of different kinds of terrorist activities (religious, ethnic, ideological, mixed, or state repression) may change from period to period, the overall level of terrorist violence remains high.

Summary

It is quite important to reiterate that terrorism is not a new phenomenon. The infliction of death and misery by dissident groups seeking to achieve political ends has been going on for millennia as will be demonstrated in at least some of the following chapters. If precise information is not always present, enough indications are available to have an idea of past and present occurrences. Religious differences and ethnic differences have long been sources of conflict. Ideological groups of both the left and the right engaged in the use of terror before and after World War II. The following chapters will help to make clear whether terrorism has been on the increase, not just over the centuries but in terms of trends over recent decades as well. The working definition provided at the beginning of this chapter is a key for all the material to follow. It provides a clear summation of what constitutes terrorism—political objectives, violence or the threat of violence, a target audience, an organization, the involvement of non-state actors, and an effort to increase the power of the terrorist group. Individuals may feel in their own minds that other groups qualify. Individual students will also have to make value judgments as to whether the levels of violence utilized are justified by the actions of the target government or the contents of the policies where change is sought. As stated above, the neutral definition of terrorism is not intended to suggest that persons ignore the contexts in which the violence occurs. Terrorist actions can be undertaken in the pursuit of worthwhile causes as well as objectionable ones. It can even be argued in at least some cases that the death and terror in the present will be less than that which would occur were no dissident violence to take place. The neutral definition simply removes the necessary value judgments from the basic analysis of the phenomenon of terrorism. Similarly, the classification, imperfect as it must be since it deals with real world situations, facilitates the understanding of the complexity of terrorist organizations and their goals—whether these goals are religious, national or ethnic, based on left-wing or right-wing ideologies, composed of more than one major element, or designed to support the government. The first steps in terms of beginning to understand these organizations will begin in the next two chapters where the tactics and weapons used by terrorist groups will be discussed and where the issue of foreign support or control of terrorist groups will be dealt with. Discussions of these elements will help to set the stage for the cases studies in the other chapters.

Terms

Alexander of Yugoslavia, King
CIA
KGB
terrorism
Unabomber

Further reading

Claridge, D. (1996) "State Terrorism? Applying a Definitional Model," *Terrorism and Political Violence*, 8, 3: 47–63.
Goldberg, J. E. (1991) "Understanding the Dimensions of Terrorism," *Perspectives on Political Science*, 20, 2: 78–88.
Herman, E. S. (2000) "The Semantics of Terrorism," *Global Dialogue*, 2, 4: 1–6.

Chapter 3

Tactics, weapons, and targets

Techniques   24

Weapons   26

    Conventional weapons   26

    Weapons of mass destruction   29

Targets   32

    Structures and people as targets   33

    Vulnerability of democratic countries   36

Summary   42

Terms   43

Further reading   43

The definition and typology from Chapter 2 provide an essential starting point for understanding terrorism. There are other elements that can be common to various kinds of organizations that practice political violence, regardless of their religious, ethnic/national, or ideological orientation. The ends may be different, but frequently the means can be similar—not just the initial decision to resort to the use of terrorism but in terms of the types of attacks that are undertaken. Dissident organizations may be similar in the techniques they employ, the types of weapons that they use, and the targets that are selected. Local conditions and circumstances are more likely to determine choices rather than the goals of the dissident group using violence. Available resources (financial and otherwise) may be more important in determining which weapons, tactics, or targets are preferred than the political goals of the organization. All of the selections are ultimately made from possibilities that almost any group with sufficient planning skills, funding, weapons, and manpower may attempt to undertake. Techniques will be discussed first. The weapons that can be used will be discussed next, including a consideration of the possibility of groups using weapons of mass destruction such as nuclear bombs, chemical poisons, and biological agents. Clearly, concerns about the possibilities for the use of these weapons in the twenty-first century have increased. Finally, the possible types of targets that can be and are chosen will be discussed. Included in this discussion will be a consideration of the possibility that democratic countries are more vulnerable to terrorist attacks than non-democratic ones.

Techniques

The same techniques are generally available to all dissident organizations, regardless of the type of government they are fighting or the political goals they seek. Of course, some techniques might be more effective against one government and less effective against another. A brutally repressive government may be less concerned about attacks on civilians than one that is trying to represent its population fairly. Personal attacks of various kinds are a frequently used method of attacking the government. Attacks on individuals can take place with a variety of weapons, but the goal is to indicate to the public and to specific groups that are supporting the government that there is a level of vulnerability or risk present. These attacks do not need to involve sophisticated weapons; very simple weapons may suffice. In some cases the personal assault need not be deadly. The terrorists may only wound their chosen targets, as might occur with breaking bones or shooting people in the legs or kneecaps. Choosing to wound rather than kill targets demonstrates to the population at large that the dissidents are not out to kill people. Such attacks show that the terrorists *could* kill since it is more difficult to get close enough to successfully wound a target. The technique of wounding is thus a display of greater ability and can demonstrate that the terrorist group has an even greater potential to disrupt the political life of the society than if it had simply killed an individual.

Personal assaults are not the only possibility. Kidnappings are another tactic available to any dissident group with sufficient resources to capture and hide the victim. The kidnapping may be designed to embarrass the government by demonstrating the ease with which some prominent individual may be taken. The kidnapping also demonstrates how vulnerable persons in the country may be to the political dissidents. The kidnapping may also be designed to raise funds for the group by ransoming the victim. The government, family, or business may be pressured to exchange money for the victim. In other cases the group may offer to release the kidnapped individual in exchange for imprisoned comrades or for government policy concessions. The publicity, financial gain, or political concessions that result can be very beneficial to any dissident organization. Success demonstrates the capabilities of the dissidents and the weaknesses of the government.

Other techniques are similarly available to all kinds of groups. Bank robberies are commonly used to finance dissident movements in many countries. Not only do they raise money, but they may embarrass the government as well. The robberies qualify as terrorism when the funds are devoted to the organization rather than to the private luxuries of the dissidents. Extortion (revolutionary confiscations) may occur when groups have the opportunity to do so during temporary occupations of buildings or villages. Such action may have a short-term advantage in that necessary finances are generated but could have negative long-term costs if the population is alienated from the dissident movement. If the money is taken from groups that are not likely to ever support the dissidents, the cost in terms of alienated segments of the population will be negligible.

Hijackings and the associated taking of hostages have been used by a wide variety of groups. The key to the takeover is usually not the vehicle in question but the crew and passengers that are on board. These individuals become hostages that can be used in the political struggle between the dissidents and the government they are targeting. They are bargaining chips in any negotiations. For example, the release of the hostages is offered in exchange for the release of imprisoned members of the organization. Many governments, however, have been very hesitant to make such trades since it might encourage further hostage-taking efforts or make the government appear to be weak. Hijackers are also frequently willing to exchange hostages for the publication of demands or manifestos. These demands have normally been met lest the government appear to be indifferent to the lives of the hostages. Such publicity is frequently a goal of the groups as they seek to make their cause known and may be invaluable in attracting support for the dissident cause or weakening support for the government. Hijackings to attract media attention usually end with the release of the hostages and some agreement to permit the hijackers to be transported to some other country. The hijackers have gained their immediate goal by publicizing their cause and demonstrating their ability to successfully

undertake a political action. Frequently, the hijackers themselves are allowed to depart as part of the negotiations that free the hostages.

The occupations of government offices and other buildings with the associated taking of hostages have been similar to hijackings. Such occupations can provide an indication of the strength of the dissidents and the weaknesses of the government. The dissidents can then negotiate with the government for publication of demands or release of persons in prison. Arranging for the safe escape of the terrorists may also be part of the negotiations. While the circumstances are generally analogous to hijacking aircraft or ships, occupying buildings is more difficult. On an aircraft or ship, the hostages are naturally concentrated, and a few terrorists can control access. Buildings have more exits, and they are more difficult to control. Thus, the occupation will require a larger number of activists, risking a larger portion of the human assets of the dissident group. Embassies or consulates are targets at times because the occupation generates greater publicity, but such buildings, *once occupied*, may be easier to control since they are frequently designed for greater security with limited access. Seizing an embassy may also introduce international complications for a government. A repressive government may be indifferent to the fate of its own citizens, whereas when foreign citizens are held hostage the government may have to be somewhat more open in terms of what actions are taken or at least have some willingness to negotiate.

It should be re-emphasized that all the above techniques are available to any dissident organization that chooses to use them. These may be "good" terrorist tactics, or at least tactics that can be judged to be less evil (kidnapping instead of death; hijacking a plane rather than blowing it up), but these tactics remain available to freedom fighters and terrorists alike. No one type of group has a monopoly on any particular technique. Once a particular technique proves to be effective, it is quickly copied by groups elsewhere, including those that have nothing in common with the group originating the technique. Hijacking airliners to publicize a cause (with no intention of using them as bombs) was quickly copied around the world. Hijackings became quite common, almost not newsworthy, and groups used them with a wide variety of political interests. There were even civilian airliners from behind the Iron Curtain that were hijacked and flown to "freedom" in the West. The hijackers in these cases were then considered refugees, and heroes, rather than international criminals. One consequence of widely different groups using the same technique is that it becomes more difficult for any country to enforce absolute rules about never granting landing rights to hijackers or refusing to grant them asylum. Political reality and public opinion can require that countries treat individual hijackers differently, depending upon their political values and the goals that are sought.

Weapons

Weapons and techniques are related, of course, and weapon availability will influence what kinds of actions a terrorist group can even attempt. A dissident group that wanted to eliminate the top leadership in a country all at once would like to have a cruise missile or other type of smart bomb that it could direct to the opening session of parliament or to a meeting of the ruling military council. Such a strike would create the chaos that would give the dissidents greater opportunities to take power or otherwise influence government policy. Fortunately, dissident organizations do not have access to such weapons, forcing them to find other weapons for carrying out their attacks. The consideration of weapons that might be used will first deal with more conventional weapons that are available to dissident organization. Then weapons that have come to be termed weapons of mass destruction will be considered. The possibility that terrorist organizations would gain access to such weapons and use them to inflict mass casualties has been of increasing concern in recent years.

Conventional weapons

Most weapons used by dissident organizations are designed to inflict casualties or disruption on a small scale. Terrorist groups normally have little difficulty acquiring personal weapons. A terrorist could attempt to kill a chosen target with a pistol or knife. Since such weapons are only accurate at close range, the apprehension of the attackers will be easy unless the attack takes place in an isolated location away from other people. Rifles are also readily available in many countries and could be used with precision by a marksman from a distance. Various kinds of automatic weapons and assault rifles have also become increasingly easy to obtain. Use of such assault weapons could lead to higher casualties if the attack occurs where many people are present. The advantage of these weapons is that they require less precision to use and that the intent of the dissidents to attack the government can be readily demonstrated. The cause is publicized and a target audience may become aware of the goals of the terrorist organization. These kinds of weapons can be purchased, stolen from the security forces or police, or captured in raids on armories. Increasingly, lethal weapons have also become available because of the stockpiles of "surplus" arms left over after the end of the Cold War (Chalk 1999: 158). Personal weapons will be necessary not only for attempts to inflict casualties but also for activities such as kidnappings, extortion, and bank robberies.

Various kinds of bombs have been a mainstay of terrorist groups for many years. Typical cartoons from the latter part of the nineteenth and into the twentieth century portrayed the terrorist as a bearded, scruffy individual with a lighted bomb in hand. Bombs can range from simple devices, such as a grenade or a Molotov cocktail that is thrown at the target, to more sophisticated devices that can be detonated by remote control or by timers. The more sophisticated devices can be used more selectively against particular targets. A mine that can be detonated by remote control, for example, can be used against a particular vehicle, whereas a regular land mine will detonate when the first vehicle of sufficient weight passes over it. Terrorists, of course, can still use the normal type of land mine since the intent might be to disrupt the transport system, to demonstrate to the general population that the government is unable to provide protection, or to target a particular region or particular group. With increasingly compact explosives, letter bombs and package bombs can be used to attack individuals. If all letters or packages in the national mail system become suspect, the terrorists have already succeeded with one of their desired effects on behavior: inducing widespread fear.

Some kinds of bombs can be especially deadly. Bombs that are intended to go off in planes in the air are obviously designed to kill people. In the past, these bombs usually involved timers, but the bombs sometimes detonated prematurely on the ground due to rough handling. In other cases because of flight delays or because the luggage was misdirected (i.e. lost), the bomb exploded while still on the ground, causing minimal damage. With access to modern technology, the bombers came up with newer methods. The newer bombs were pressure sensitive so that they would go off when the air pressure in the cargo hold of the airliner decreased to a particular level. Such a pressure sensitive device might even be linked to a timing device so that the countdown started at a particular altitude but the plane was over the ocean before detonation. Security agencies for airliners or airports, in turn, developed machinery to simulate this reduced pressure level so that luggage with suspicious materials could be tested on the ground. The development of bombs and detection mechanisms is an ongoing contest between terrorists (and criminals) and the security agencies. As one type of potential attack is rendered ineffective, a new weapon is developed. The battle between bombers and security will go on. As technology provides more opportunities to inflict damage, it will also provide better mechanisms to detect explosives before they can kill and destroy.

Car bombs have been a relatively recent addition to the armory of terrorist groups. Vehicles packed with explosive can do considerable damage and kill and wound many people. The thirteen vehicle bombs that were set off in Bombay, India, in February 1993 killed more than 400 people and injured over 1,000 people (Hoffman 2001: 421). In some cases such car bombs have been driven into targets on suicide missions, as happened in Lebanon to US marines and French paratroopers trying to end the Lebanese civil war. In other cases the vehicles have been left with a timer or to be detonated by remote control. The first bombing of the World Trade Center in New York City in 1995 utilized a bomb with a timer, as did the bomb used against the federal building in Oklahoma City. Car and truck bombs have been used with some regularity in the Middle East and Northern Ireland for many years. Car and truck bombs came to be more extensively used when the techniques for using large amounts of fertilizer to produce a massive blast became available and widely known. Terrorists no longer needed to access high-grade explosives when a ton of fertilizer could easily be obtained. Car bombs have one particular advantage for terrorists in that one vehicle can easily blend with a large number of similar vehicles on a street, in a parking facility, or in a parking area. It will be impossible for local authorities to continuously check all such vehicles. Using civilian airliners as flying bombs has increased the potential for casualties. Suicide bombings are relatively recent phenomena that have increased casualties as well, whether it be by driving a car into a building, by crashing an airplane, or by an individual exploding a bomb on his or her person in a crowded street. Suicide attacks provide an advantage over other bombs since the explosives can more readily be delivered to a location that might otherwise be inaccessible, and the timing of the detonation can be more effectively controlled too (Dolnik 2003: 20). Suicide bombings are also a relatively low-cost method (except to the bomber or driver or pilot) of inflicting damage on opponents.

Modern technology has also provided potential terrorists with many more options. Surface-to-air missiles can be used against commercial aircraft

BOX 2.1 Civilian airliners as bombs in suicide attacks

The use of airliners as suicide vehicles in peacetime was seen as a unique occurrence when it happened on September 11, 2001. The plans for the attack were well thought out. Four airliners were hijacked at virtually the same time. All four were chosen because they were flying from the East Coast to the West Coast and thus their fuel tanks were full given the distances involved. The additional fuel was intended to add to the destruction when they crashed into the buildings. The total destruction of the World Trade Center towers was much more than bin Laden had apparently anticipated, although he was not upset by the more extensive damage (Robbins 2002: 357–8). There had been earlier indications that hijacked airliners might be used in this fashion. In 1986 a TWA plane was seized in Pakistan with the hijackers reportedly intending to have the plane fly to Israel where it would be crashed in the center of Tel Aviv (Hoffman 2002: 306). The plane never had the opportunity of leaving the ground after refueling, but it is unlikely that it could have successfully made the long flight to Israel to launch the attack. In 1994 Algerian dissidents hijacked an Air France flight. They intended to crash the plane in Paris, perhaps with the Eiffel Tower as a specific target. The goal of the attack was to force the French to stop supporting the government in power in Algeria. The effort was short-circuited when French commandos recaptured the plane while it was on the ground in Marseille (Shapiro and Suzan 2003: 81). It is not known at present how much information al Qaeda might have had about these earlier operations.

as well as military ones. The roof of any building along the flight path for an airport could become a site for the launching of such missiles. The successful firing of such a missile is not as simple as it might appear, but the necessary training can be acquired; consequently, such an attack remains a dangerous possibility. There have been over twenty-five attacks using these missiles against aircraft. Most, but not all, of the targets have been military. About 60 percent of the attacks have been successful (Wilkinson 2000b: 214). Many of these missiles are now in national arsenals and could become available to terrorist groups (Chalk 1999: 161). A Russian missile brought down a civilian airliner in Sri Lanka (Hoffman 2002: 312). Civilian airliners have been brought down by guerrillas in the former Rhodesia and the Sudan. The United States attempted to re-acquire the Stinger missiles that it had channeled to the Afghan rebels to minimize future uses of such weapons. In 1982, Italian police found four powerful ground-to-air missiles when they raided a terrorist hideout (R. Drake 1989: 145). Security

forces in Turkey also found Stinger rockets in an arms cache of a Kurdish dissident group (Criss 1995: 29). The biggest disadvantage of these weapons for terrorists is that while opportunities to acquire them do appear, it is difficult to get them in sufficient quantities to permit members of the terrorist group to practice by actually firing the weapons.

The use of sophisticated devices to launch attacks has been on the increase. In 1991 the IRA managed to use a remote control mortar to attack Number 10 Downing Street, the residence of the British prime minister. John Major, the prime minister at the time, and the rest of the cabinet were in a meeting when the attack occurred. The mortar tubes had been hidden in a van parked in the vicinity. The shells landed harmlessly in a courtyard, but the attack demonstrated what was possible, and it might have killed the British prime minister and many cabinet ministers. The persons involved in the attack were able to escape undetected. It does seem to be inevitable that these kinds of weapons and the knowledge about how to use them cannot be kept from terrorist organizations. Formulas for explosives, directions for building bombs with fertilizer, instructions for creating remote control devices, and materials on other ways of creating havoc are all readily available in books and on the internet. The spread of knowledge has also included the spread of the necessary information for creating terror.

There are some additional possible weapons that reflect technical sophistication. Computer systems have become increasingly central for many activities in modern states. Breaking into a computer system and changing commands or introducing a virus could create havoc, and such attacks might even lead to loss of life. These kinds of weapons have been referred to as weapons of mass disruption given the scope of dislocations that could occur. Computers programmed to provide incorrect information could not only create economic difficulties but could also take a long time to fix. Interference with computers or other electronic elements of the modern world could become a very effective terrorist weapon (Bunker 2000). These types of attacks could even result in significant deaths, if for example, a hospital's records were disrupted or an air traffic control system suddenly went off line. Such attacks are a possibility for the future even if there is not an imminent threat of such attacks (Denning 2000: 36).

Weapons of mass destruction

There has been increasing concern recently that terrorists might begin to use weapons of mass destruction to inflict large numbers of casualties on their targets as a means of attempting to obtain their political objectives. Such weapons have generally included biological and chemical weapons, and even nuclear devices. To date there has been no evidence that any terrorist organization has gained access to nuclear devices or to weapons grade uranium or plutonium. One fear has been that with the breakup of the old Soviet Union such weapons would be more readily available since there were doubts about the quality of

security measures and safeguards at Soviet nuclear stockpiles (B. Jenkins 1998: 234). There was a fear that some well funded organization might purchase a nuclear device from one of the successor states. The security guards, currently underpaid (if paid at all), might be susceptible to bribes to let a nuclear device "disappear" (Schmid 2000). The rumors that terrorist groups obtained nuclear weapons from the old Soviet stockpiles have proven to be false so far (Cameron 1999: 289). As knowledge of how to make nuclear weapons spreads, the danger of some sort of nuclear device making its way into the hands of a terrorist organization will increase. There has also been concern that some of the other countries with possible nuclear capabilities, such as Iraq and North Korea, might supply a nuclear device to a dissident group under the right circumstances. For the present, the greatest nuclear danger might be an assault on a nuclear power facility that is designed to create conditions that would lead to a meltdown or a heat explosion similar to the Chernobyl disaster in the old Soviet Union. In fact, nuclear hoaxes or contamination with radioactive materials seem much more likely than the use of nuclear weapons by terrorists (B. Jenkins 1998: 233).

Chemical and biological weapons have generated even more concern. Some observers have considered these emerging weapons to be the weapons of the future for terrorists. Terrorists using such weapons would be able to spread fear and chaos and cause massive casualties. This fear has been particularly great among the policy makers who would have to deal with such attacks (Dishman 2001: 304). Concern has increased because there have now been recent cases of both biological and chemical attacks. In 1995 there was an attack on the Japanese subway with a chemical nerve agent, which resulted in a few fatalities and many more hospitalized. In 2001 in the aftermath of the September 11 attacks in the United States, letters containing anthrax were sent to members of Congress and to persons involved in the news media. Less than a dozen people died in these attacks, but potentially many more could have been affected. The source of the anthrax and the purpose behind the attacks have yet to be determined. While it was initially presumed that the mailings were from someone associated with the Osama bin Laden group, analyses of the anthrax used indicated that the material was likely to have originated in the United States.

While the use of nerve gas and anthrax demonstrate the possibilities of biological and chemical weapons, they have also demonstrated the limitations. Chemical weapons may not be especially lethal. For example, it would take a ton of sarin nerve gas released by aircraft under ideal weather conditions to kill 3,000 to 8,000 people in an urban area (Sokolski, 2000, p. 211). Disseminating a ton of the gas, however, would be difficult even under ideal circumstances. Similarly, biological agents or chemicals released into water systems are unlikely to work because of existing filtration systems and chlorination (Tucker 1996: 174). Tons of chemicals or biological agents would be required to effectively contaminate a municipal water supply given the dilution that would occur in the lake or reservoir (Gurr and Cole 2000: 65). Anthrax is actually quite limited as a biological weapon because it is not contagious. It cannot be spread by human contact, so even though it can be deadly in some forms, it cannot start an epidemic. The more deadly type of biological weapon would be one that was both deadly *and* contagious. The 2001 anthrax attacks did lead to disruptions in mail delivery, and they shut down government offices for various periods of time. They also spread fear throughout the United States, particularly coming so soon after the attacks on New York City and Washington DC. The loss of life, however, was no greater than might have occurred with letter bombs or package bombs left in corridors of government offices or other places. Letter bombs might have had a similar effect in terms of generating fear, but the anthrax scare was probably more effective since it was a new weapon and less well understood by the general public.

— In fact, the threat of chemical and biological weapons may well be exaggerated. Tucker (2000b) collected fifteen cases dealing with various efforts or presumed efforts to use biological or chemical weapons by persons knowledgeable about the individual incidents and the groups involved. Out of the fifteen cases, in only three instances were such weapons actually used on targets. One was the case of the use of nerve gas in Japan that has already been mentioned. A second involved the use of a biological weapon in a very localized setting. The followers of a cult in Oregon attempted to spread food poisoning among the local population just before an election for local officials. Members of the cult hoped to incapacitate enough voters so that the members of the cult living in the religious compound could dominate the election. The sect members spread botulism in local restaurants, causing an outbreak of food poisoning and discomfort, but they still lost the election (Carus 2000). The group abandoned the scheme when it became clear that their candidate was not going to win in any event (Stern 1999: 66). Members of the group were eventually caught and convicted for their use of a biological weapon. The third case of an actual attack with biological weapons occurred even earlier. Immediately after World War II, a group of Jewish Holocaust survivors poisoned the bread given to members of the German SS being held in a prisoner-of-war camp. The goal was to kill as many of the prisoners as possible in retaliation for the death camps run by the Nazis. The attack led to illnesses for many prisoners and some deaths. The authorities were not even aware that the illnesses were intentional since many of the former soldiers were suffering from the long-term effects of malnutrition, wounds suffered during the war, and other physical weaknesses (Sprinzak and Zertal 2000). The attack was successful up to a point. There were deaths, but they were not in the large numbers that the Holocaust survivors had hoped to achieve. The attack does not really qualify as a terrorist act since there was no target audience. The goal was to kill as many as possible in revenge for Nazi atrocities during the war. However, the limited success of the effort does demonstrate the limitations of biological and chemical weapons such as poisons.

There has been one additional case involving the use of a chemical weapon. A guerrilla and terrorist group in Sri Lanka used chlorine gas as part of an attack on a military post. In this case, the use of the gas appeared to reflect the fact that these dissidents lacked sufficient conventional weapons at the time. They were improvising by necessity. The rebels have since acquired plenty of conventional weaponry and have not resorted to chemical warfare again (Parachini 2001: 390–1).

Tucker's collection of fifteen cases of possible chemical and biological weapons is very informative in other ways. It is clear that in twelve cases groups either never reached the stage of actively pursuing the production of chemical or biological weapons or if they did they failed in the efforts. Such weapons have been considered easy to create, but the evidence would suggest otherwise (Rosenau 2001: 297). In the three cases where such weapons were used, mass casualties did not result. In the case of Oregon, the cult was not seeking to kill people. The food poisoning scheme was actually a very appropriate weapon to attempt to use to dominate a local election. In the Japanese case there was intent to cause mass casualties, but it failed. The groups responsible might have been better off using conventional weaponry in its attacks. In the case of the prisoner-of-war camp, too, mass casualties did not result as desired. The recent anthrax attacks in the United States similarly have not led to mass casualties. As a consequence, it is easy to agree with the assessment that known uses of chemical and biological weapons have been infrequent, and none of the ones intended to be weapons of mass destruction has been successful (Tucker 2000a: 253). As with nuclear weapons, credible hoaxes rather than actual use may be the greatest threat associated with biological and chemical weapons (Veness 2001: 409).

While biological weapons have not been effective weapons of mass destruction in the past, their lethal potential exists. The use of a biological agent that is contagious raises its own set of problems. The biological agent may be slow acting. This may make it easier for the terrorists to escape detection (Tucker 2000a: 264), but such slow acting weapons also do not generate the media attention that terrorists often desire. The greatest difficulty with a biological weapon is that it can quickly get beyond the control of the dissident group that used it, and the dissidents could then become victims as well. Handling such weapons is also dangerous, and the terrorists could become victims before the rest of the population if there was an accident or if isolation mechanisms were ineffective. Such weapons might become more deadly if they were used as part of a suicide attack. It is also thought that biological weapons could be used in economic attacks on agricultural systems or livestock in a target country. The disruption of the food system is likely to result in significant economic losses rather than mass casualties (Foxell 2001: 113–14).

Any attempt to use biological and chemical weapons faces other difficulties as well. The political demands of the terrorist organization must be communicated to a government or a public audience, yet doing so means facing possible retaliation. A government facing a rampant plague might be willing to take extreme measures to punish the dissidents and would be unlikely to compromise. A group that has caused massive casualties in the population is likely to be in a poor bargaining position to achieve its objectives (Claridge 2000b: 142). If, however, the attack is intended to paralyze, disrupt, and disorient the government and general population so that some other political goals can be achieved more readily, then a group need not specifically acknowledge its role in causing a large number of deaths. In such circumstances, a group might well be tempted to use a biological or chemical weapon if it is available. Organizations that are seeking or willing to accept a large number of dead or even mass casualties might do so. Groups that have been willing to use conventional weapons to cause many deaths might be tempted to use biological or chemical weapons, especially if the weapon could be controlled.

Pragmatic concerns probably provide the most important reasons why terrorists have refrained from using biological and chemical weapons

(Laqueur 1998: 50). The use of chemical or biological weapons has not spread because terrorists frequently prefer the familiar, tried-and-true weapons (Cameron 1999: 279). The knowledge for building bombs, simple or sophisticated, is known. If the bomb explodes, even in the wrong place, it is a success since the government and the public will not know the intended target (B. Jenkins 1998: 243). There is little incentive to try to develop new weapons, which may or may not be effective and which may or may not be controllable. Investing in new unproven weaponry could stretch the resources of many dissident organizations (Claridge 2000b: 143), although some groups have been willing to invest in labs to try to produce biological and chemical weapons, albeit not very successfully. The use of hijacked airliners in the destruction of the World Trade Center towers and the assault on the Pentagon has demonstrated that terrorist groups can cause mass casualties with familiar techniques used in a new way.

While the use of biological and chemical weapons of mass destruction is not as likely as some have predicted, the threat is still present (Geiger 2001: 709). Efforts to make such weapons have occurred. A wide variety of terrorist organizations have apparently sought to acquire such weapons, including al Qaeda, the Palestinian Liberation Organization (PLO), the Red Army Faction in West Germany, Hizballah in Lebanon, the Kurdish Workers' Party in Turkey, and neo-Nazi groups in Germany (Cronin 2002/3: 48). The danger that a terrorist organization can successfully manufacture or acquire such weapons is likely to increase. The focus on the possible use of such weapons of mass destruction may even have encouraged terrorists to think about obtaining them (Merari 2000: 64). Terrorist groups may be unwilling to use these weapons because of technical difficulties or expense, but clearly some groups are willing to inflict mass casualties. Thus, while gaining operating weapons remains difficult, there are groups that will be more willing to use them once they are acquired (O'Neil 2003: 110). With the passage of time there will be a learning curve, which will probably lead to greater knowledge of the problems involved with the development and use of such weapons—but also to solutions to these problems. Any such weapons will become more effective as terrorist groups learn from their own past mistakes and the mistakes of others and as the knowledge and technology for the use of such weapons diffuse even further. Terrorists do emulate each other, and the successful use of weapons of mass destruction by one group could trigger similar attacks by others (Stern 1999: 74). There is also a continuing possibility that a government might make effective biological or chemical weapons available to a dissident organization. However, most governments are unlikely to supply such weapons to terrorist groups because of a fear of retaliation if the weapons were to be traced back to them; the Iraqi government was probably most likely to use any weapons of mass destruction it may have had once it had been attacked and was facing defeat rather than before it had been attacked (Betts 2003). Providing such weapons might generate significant risks for the country, but if the country or its government is already facing a major crisis or the threat of defeat in war, it might be willing to gamble on being able to avoid retaliation.

Targets

One of the most significant choices that any dissident group has to make is the selection of targets for a terrorist attack. Where will the attack take place? Should the targets be human or simply physical objects? Should the targets include buildings or people associated with foreign countries? Should the targets be chosen on the basis of their symbolic value or because they are representative units of a larger group defined in political, social, or economic terms by the terrorists? What is very rare is the situation in which targets are chosen at random, despite the common misperception that terrorists do not care who or what the targets are. Terrorist groups are very rational in their choice of targets, evaluating strengths and weaknesses, costs and benefits (Long 1990: 139).

Target choice is rarely indiscriminate (C. Drake 1998: 53). The targets that are chosen have at least some linkage with the goals and objectives of the terrorist groups.

Structures and people as targets

Terrorist organizations will at times restrict themselves to efforts to damage property. In fact, the vast majority of terrorist incidents are not directed at people. Between 1968 and 2001, there were no fatalities or only one fatality in almost 96 percent of international incidents (Stohl 2003: 86). Bombs will be set off in buildings at times when it is expected that they will be unoccupied. The building may have a very specific connection with the political concerns of the dissident group. It could be a government office, or a party headquarters in a one-party state or even in a democracy where the party in question is considered to be closely tied to the establishment. It could be a religious building associated with the dominant group or a minority religion that is seen to be a threat to the majority. The offices of a particular business could be the target because of its links to a group or party in power. Newspapers, labor union offices, radio stations, professional associations, and other buildings could all be potential targets in a particular national context. The target possibilities with buildings are legion, but they will vary according to local circumstances and the political goals of the organization that has opted to use violence. The numbers involved will usually be far too many to be effectively guarded by police, troops, or private security personnel.

Some targeted buildings or structures could have symbolic value. National monuments would be a case in point. Their damage or destruction would indicate that any part of a society is vulnerable. If a highly regarded national monument can be successfully attacked, then almost any property or building would be considered to be in danger. If a government cannot protect obvious targets, it will not seem likely that it will be able to guard the less obvious ones. Of course, attacks on symbolic national monuments are not equally likely from all kinds of terrorist groups. A separatist group or a national liberation movement would have the most incentive since likely supporters would be indifferent to the loss of someone else's national monument. A non-separatist group, however, would be less likely to attack such a symbolic target since it would alienate potential supporters.

A terrorist group concerned with global or national capitalism or simply globalization in general could target a particular corporate office or regional headquarters that is a symbol of the free enterprise system (Ford, Coca-Cola, British Petroleum, IBM, Microsoft, Volkswagen, Phillips, or Nestlé). Any government building might be bombed to indicate the vulnerability of such offices. A stadium, a statue, or a building project associated with a particular ruling party, leader, or group would have such high salience that the symbolism would be obvious. The two attacks on the World Trade Center in New York, even though designed to cause large numbers of human casualties, also represented a symbolic target. The World Trade Center served as a symbol of American economic might, the global importance of US capitalism, and of all the changing contexts that go with modernization. The symbolism was even greater for the second attack in 2001. The first attack on the building was largely a failure. Casualties and damage were few; the building did not collapse; the center continued to operate. The second attack demonstrated that even if a building survived one attack, it could succumb to a second. Similarly, the attack on the Pentagon targeted an important symbol of the United States. Most other countries also have structures with similar symbolic values as targets—Westminster Abbey, the Eiffel Tower, the Taj Mahal, the Colosseum in Rome, the Parthenon in Athens, the Imperial Palace in Japan, or the Hermitage in St Petersburg. Attacks on such symbolic buildings would spread the fear that many terrorist groups seek and generate the media attention that is often so essential for broadcasting their message to the world.

While terrorist organizations may restrict their attacks to property as a means of demonstrating their concern for the population and to try to maintain popular support, most organizations will eventually move on to attacks on people. It is a rare circumstance in which property attacks alone will be sufficient to force a government to change policies, to create a democracy, or to allow a region to become independent. If a dissident group perceives conditions to be so oppressive that attacks on property are required, graduation to attacks on people is likely. The human targets can be specific, symbolic and more general, just as property attacks can be.

Specific attacks on individuals may be undertaken because of their particular action as individuals. Assassinations of especially unpopular individuals may also serve the positive benefit of creating support for the terrorists and reaffirming the support of members of the organization (C. Drake 1998: 54). Of course, eliminating an extremely unpopular individual may be counterproductive since one source of popular irritation with the government has been removed. A judge may be killed or wounded because he sentenced members of the group to death or to long prison terms. A member of the security forces with a reputation for torture is killed as punishment for his activities. For the assassination to be terrorism, however, there does have to be a target audience, which could include other judges or police officials. A police official or judge may be targeted because of their positions supporting the (oppressive) legal system of the states. Any police official or judge could be chosen as representatives of their groups. Similarly, a member of the national legislature could be the victim because he is a member of a class of politicians who are refusing to make the appropriate changes in government policy. Business executives, labor leaders, journalists, government workers and teachers, and officials of political parties could also be chosen if they are perceived to be representatives of groups that are supporting or collaborating with the government. The wide range of potential targets provides dissidents with a major advantage. There are far too many individuals to be effectively protected. Some attacks will be successfully made sooner or later, although effective security agencies may be able to track down the persons involved once they have struck. Human targets may be chosen for their symbolic value. Members of a royal family may have no political power or influence, but they may symbolize the nation or institutions under attack. High ranking clerics or media personnel, actors or musicians, or others may also have similar symbolic value. When an IRA bomb killed Lord Mountbatten near his country home in the Republic of Ireland, it was a symbolic attack. Mountbatten was a hero from World War II, and a cousin of Queen Elizabeth II. He played no role in policy making in the United Kingdom, and he was actually retired. He did, however, symbolize the long-standing British presence in Ireland.

The potential target group can be even larger. If ethnic, linguistic, or religious differences separate a society, any members of groups that the terrorists oppose may be considered targets. The attacks could be intended to eliminate group support for disliked policies or government leaders or even to convince members of these groups to leave a particular region of the country or even the country altogether as part of a policy of ethnic cleansing. The general population can serve as potential targets for the terrorists to publicize their goals and to seek to change the government. Actions causing significant casualties and disruptions will be intended to indicate to the population at large that the existing government cannot protect them. The government will have failed to provide security, a primary function of government (Chalk 1998b: 376). Even though it will be dissidents who set off the bombs, it may be the government that is held doubly responsible for the carnage. First, the government is seen as either creating the situation that led to the creation of the terrorist group or allowing a situation to continue that led to the violence. Second, the government is seen to be unable to stop the violence. The violence will end when the general population stops supporting the government in power, and asks the existing government to change its policies or permits the dissidents to establish a new government.

None of the above situations involves random violence. The attacks are designed to inflict casualties on a particular group, and the groups may indeed be an entire national population. The violence and death is not undertaken to inflict pain for the pleasure of doing so but to send specific messages to target audiences. If an entire population begins to fear, the goals of the terrorist may have been achieved. At times the victims will simply be average citizens in the wrong place at the wrong time when a car bomb explodes in a shopping area. If average citizens are the chosen targets, it would indicate that the terrorists are seeking to induce fear in as large a portion of the population as possible to indicate that virtually no one will be safe. Compromise by the government or even surrender becomes more credible to the population if fear becomes widespread. Since many terrorist groups have failed in their political objective, the loss of life may indeed be pointless, but these circumstances do not mean that the attacks are random.

Attacks on foreign interests can also be part of a logical campaign to undermine a domestic government. Like other terrorist attacks, these attacks will not be random but part of a planned effort. External countries may be providing significant support to the government in power, perhaps even making it possible for the regime to survive (Byman 1998: 161). The aid might be as direct as providing arms, anti-terrorist equipment for the police, training in interrogation techniques, and the gathering of intelligence data on dissidents living aboard. Attacks against the foreign interests may persuade the foreign government to cease support because they realize there is real domestic opposition or simply because it thinks its local ally is incompetent. Personnel involved in the provision of economic aid could also be likely targets for two reasons. First, economic aid is likely to strengthen the government in its struggles with dissidents by increasing its capacities to offer resources to wavering groups or to appease

the population in general with items such as subsidized food or fuel prices, increased wages, or new infrastructure projects in a politically volatile region. Thus, economic aid can be a direct threat to the dissident organization. It can also be an indirect threat as well. Some foreign countries will not supply military aid to a government; they limit aid to economic projects in an effort to avoid increasing the military or repressive capacity of the government. Every million dollars of economic aid, however, may permit a government to divert a million dollars of locally raised revenues to buy arms or increase the size of the security forces. As a consequence, economic aid projects that simply seek to help the people may, in fact, provide benefits to the government in terms of its ability to coerce or defeat internal dissidents. When the hand of the government security forces is strengthened in this fashion, it is much more difficult for the internal dissidents to achieve their goals.

For similar reasons, foreign economic activity may become a target for terrorists. Terrorist attacks can lead to reductions in foreign investment, especially when attacks are directed at foreign facilities (Enders and Sandler 1996). Foreign workers in key industries may be targets as well. If selective attacks on technicians or other workers can disrupt key industries or the extraction of natural resources, then the tax base of the government and the revenues available will be reduced. Tourists have become targets in some countries. The attacks on tourists have sometimes been seen as random and to be a reflection of the fact that the terrorists enjoy violence. These attacks, however, have a clear purpose. Any successful attack, and even unsuccessful ones, severely hurts the tourist industry. In some countries tourism brings in badly needed foreign exchange and provides additional revenue. A successful attack leads to tour cancellations and a drop off in revenues (Enders *et al.* 1992). The resource base of the government is hurt and a political message is sent to the world at large. An economy dependent on tourist revenues could be crippled by terrorist campaigns (Enders and

Sandler 1991: 57). The bombing in Bali in Indonesia clearly had such an effect, even if the principal reason for the attack was anti-Western. Attacks against tourists by Muslim groups in Egypt have had exactly these kinds of effects on government revenues (Shultz 1994: 295). Tourism in Egypt declined by 53 per cent in the wake of such attacks with the obvious negative consequences for obtaining foreign currency (Gurr and Cole 2000: 88). The frequency of such attacks rather than their severity has so far had the greatest negative impact on tourism (Pizam and Fleischer 2002: 339).

It has also been logical for groups to launch attacks abroad in many cases—to internationalize the terrorism. In national liberation struggles it makes sense to carry the battle to the colonial power whenever possible. Attacks in other countries may also be logical in other circumstances. When a foreign government is supporting the local domestic regime, attacks abroad can be part of the effort to change polices. Such attacks could be upon government offices, commercial targets, or the population in general. The violence sends a message to a target population, in this case a general audience in the foreign country. It is also possible for the attacks against the foreign supporter of the domestic regime to be undertaken in third, "neutral" countries. Thus, a dissident movement in Country A may regard Country B as an important supporter of the domestic elite in power in Country A. They may then launch at attack against a corporate office of a company from Country B or a consulate of Country B in Country C to send the message to the target audience that Country B is vulnerable around the world and will be forced to pay a price for supporting the regime in Country A. Country C may be chosen for the attack because of the presence of local supporters, because of limited security for the target, because of the minimal security and intelligence forces in Country C, or other factors. The choice of Country C for the attack is simply a matter of convenience for the dissidents. Dissidents in exile could also provide a local support network and local information for

attacks in a foreign country, or the terrorist group may also have established links with a like-minded group in that country.

Vulnerability of democratic countries

Terrorist attacks may be launched in some countries more frequently than others, either by groups of domestic dissidents or by foreign groups seeking to attack their regime in more convenient locations. It has been suggested that democratic countries are more vulnerable to terrorist attacks than other kinds of political systems (Posen 2001/2: 41). Democratic countries with a commitment to civil liberties and basic rights find it more difficult to gather intelligence on citizens, to arrest, to interrogate, and to extract information. The effectiveness of the courts can also be undermined by the intimidation of witnesses or other illegal actions (Schmid 1992b: 19). The whole range of protections generally available in democracies makes both prevention of terrorist actions and the apprehension of terrorists after the fact more difficult. Even when alleged terrorists are arrested, convictions are not automatic. Rights accorded to the accused may mean that there will be insufficient evidence for a conviction. It is also possible that it may be easier to acquire the weapons or explosives needed for a terrorist action in a democracy, although the international market in weapons is often sufficient to supply the needs of many groups. All of these factors may make democracies a more suitable setting for groups initiating violence.

In non-democratic countries, dissident organizations are more constrained. In a totalitarian system where the government has comprehensive security agencies and informers everywhere, opposition is much more difficult to organize. Once suspicion focuses on an individual or a group of individuals, their activities can be monitored, mail opened, phone lines tapped, etc. Persons can be arrested on suspicion and questioned indefinitely. Searches can be arbitrary and undertaken at any time. Torture and drugs can be used to extract information from persons in custody. The investigation and arrest of suspects can proceed with relatively few limitations. Once the official agencies become convinced of the guilt of a particular individual, a conviction will be arranged (unless the state sees no need for a trial). If the dissidents themselves cannot be readily caught, the government has other options. It can retaliate against family members and friends or hold them hostage or use other similar measures to convince terrorists to surrender or go into exile (Chalk 1998b: 386). Groups considering political violence will be limited under these circumstances, and the likelihood of surviving to conduct a long campaign of political violence is very low. The casualties among the group members are likely to be very high as well.

The deterrents that are present in totalitarian systems are fairly obvious in a number of cases. In the old Soviet Union, ethnic tensions such as those present in Chechnya today were not possible. The desires for autonomy and independence were clearly present, but the Soviet system had the capabilities to deal with any dissent quickly and effectively. Many of the successor states to the old Soviet Union are now dealing less effectively with dissident groups that are organized on the basis of nationality and ethnic differences or in terms of different religious backgrounds from the regime elite or the majority of the state. Similarly, the violence in what used to be Yugoslavia did not occur until after the national communist regime collapsed. Prior to that time ethnic differences had been contained by the power of the central government and the security apparatus at its disposal. Opposition groups in Iraq since Saddam Hussein came to power have been very ineffective. Attacks on the regime have been difficult to organize, and when they have occurred, that have not been very successful. Admittedly, the opposition groups have been badly divided among themselves but the regime in power has maintained a significant capacity to control dissidents and eliminate opposition before it can become effective, let alone undertake a terrorist campaign.

Authoritarian governments may have similar state capacities to control dissidents. If the security forces are active and well run, it will be difficult for opponents of the regime to use violent actions successfully. If they do so, they are likely to be caught. But not all authoritarian systems have the resources to detect and capture terrorists with ease. In a poor country, there may simply be too few resources to fund an effective security apparatus. Poverty, however, is no guarantee against efficient security forces. Haiti while governed by François Duvalier ("Papa Doc") was one of the poorest countries in the world and one in which dissidents and opponents were never permitted to organize (or to live). In poorer countries dissidents may have one advantage in that there are likely to be relatively isolated areas or limited transport and communications facilities available. Thus, a terrorist group might be able to retreat into the countryside and survive for at least a period of time sufficient to mount attacks against the government. In other cases, the authoritarian regimes may be unwilling to use sufficiently harsh measures to control dissidents, and thus they will open themselves up to terrorist attacks. Authoritarian regimes, as a consequence, may be very capable of dealing with potential terrorist threats in some cases, and less effective in others. Egypt would qualify as a mildly authoritarian system that has been unable to eliminate Islamic domestic opponents. Syria, a somewhat more repressive authoritarian system, has been more effective in dealing with disgruntled domestic opponents.

Democracies face major difficulties in dealing with terrorism. The limited possibilities for surveillance and detention all combine to encourage terrorist actions on their soil. In dealing with terrorist threats, democratic societies have to be careful to maintain the essence of their system—the rights of individuals. There are dangers of overreaction and deciding that expedited justice is necessary. Democracies face a great dilemma. If the government yields to the terrorists, they are inept. If the government overreacts to the threat and suppresses civil liberties, it risks weakening democracy (Sacopulos 1989: 163). Democracies need to take care in dealing with violent dissidents since the costs may include not only lives and money but potentially the loss of political liberties as well (Cuthbertson 2001/2: 33). A society facing terrorist attacks may develop a siege mentality and permit actions that are contrary to the whole democratic system. Military tribunals with lesser standards for convicting terrorists may be instituted (Chalk 1998b: 377). The country may also adopt procedures to provide for detention of suspects for lengthy periods of time without the filing of formal charges, and overreactions by the government may even increase support for the dissidents (Reinares 1998: 363, 368–9). There can also be cases of rushes to judgment where suspects are poorly treated and confessions are coerced and other rights bypassed (Lutz *et al.* 2002). Even with problems such as these, however, the legal systems in democracies give suspected terrorists more rights than other systems.

There is some evidence that democracies have been more likely to be the locations of terrorist attacks (Weinberg and Eubank 1998). A geo-graphic breakdown of incidents of international terrorism indicates that some democratic areas are prone to terrorist incidents while others have normally been immune (see Table 3.1). North America has the fewest such incidents among the various regions. There has only been an average of two per year. Western Europe, on the other hand, often has a large number of incidents. From 1968 to 1989 there were more incidents in Western Europe than in any other region (Chalk 1996: 174). In many of the years since 1990 the region has had one of the larger figures for number of incidents. Latin America is the only region that has often had more incidents than Western Europe. The Eurasian countries (the former communist countries of Eastern Europe and the successor states of the Soviet Union) had relatively few incidents in the early 1990s but more in later years. These figures demonstrate the relative immunity of strong authoritarian states and the greater vulnerability of countries in transition.

When the casualties inflicted by these incidents are considered, Asia most consistently had high levels, although it is obvious that any region could have a high level in a given year (see Table 3.2).

TABLE 3.1 Number of international terrorist incidents by region, 1991–2002

Year	Region							
	Africa	Asia	Eurasia*	Latin America	Europe	Middle East	North America	Total
1991	3	48	6	199	229	78	2	565
1992	10	13	3	113	143	79	2	363
1993	6	37	5	185	97	100	1	431
1994	25	24	11	88	58	116	0	322
1995	10	16	5	272	92	45	0	440
1996	11	11	24	121	84	45	0	296
1997	11	21	42	128	52	37	13	304
1998	21	49	14	110	48	31	0	273
1999	52	72	35	121	85	25	2	392
2000	55	98	31	193	30	16	0	423
2001	33	68	3	201	17	29	4	355
2002	5	99	7	50	9	29	0	199

Source: US Department of State (various years) *Patterns of Terrorism*, online at http://www.state.gov/s/ct/rls/pgtrpt.
*Former Communist countries of Eastern Europe and successor states of the Soviet Union.

TABLE 3.2 Number of casualties due to international terrorist incidents by region, 1991–2002

Year	Region							
	Africa	Asia	Eurasia*	Latin America	Europe	Middle East	North America	Total
1991	3	150	7	68	56	33	0	317
1992	28	25	0	374	65	236	1	729
1993	7	135	1	66	117	178	1,006	1,510
1994	55	71	151	329	126	256	0	988
1995	8	5,639	29	46	287	445	0	6,454
1996	80	1,507	20	18	503	837	0	2,965
1997	28	344	27	11	17	480	7	914
1998	5,379	635	12	195	405	68	0	6,694
1999	185	690	8	9	16	31	0	939
2000	102	898	103	20	4	69	0	1,196
2001	150	651	0	6	20	513	4,091	5,341
2002	12	1,281	615	52	6	772	0	2,738

Source: US Department of State (various years) *Patterns of Terrorism*, online at http://www.state.gov/s/ct/rls/pgtrpt.
*Former Communist countries of Eastern Europe and successor states of the Soviet Union.

The total casualty figures can be somewhat misleading. Western Europe had moderate numbers of casualties in most years while in North America there were either massive casualties or virtually none. A breakdown of casualties between dead and wounded between 1998 and 2002 indicates that fatalities are more likely in some areas. Western Europe, Latin America, and Eurasia generally had fewer deaths, while North America had virtually none with the obvious exception of 2001 (see Table 3.3). While terrorists may often stage attacks in the democratic countries of Western Europe to generate publicity for their causes, they normally do not seek to kill large numbers of people. In the case of North America, the attacks have been different. The figures for North America (which in this case means the United States) are the most deceptive of all in these tables. In most years there are no international incidents. In 1993, there was only one incident: the first attack on the World Trade Center, with 1,006 casualties, but only seven of these were deaths. In

TABLE 3.3 Number of deaths due to international terrorist incidents by region, 1998–2002

Year	Region							
	Africa	Asia	Eurasia*	Latin America	Europe	Middle East	North America	Total
1998	336	98	8	74	29	27	0	572
1999	76	267	4	3	1	8	0	359
2000	73	72	12	19	1	19	0	196
2001	90	281	0	2	3	62	3,235	3,673
2002	8	327	245	13	0	132	0	725

Source: US Department of State (various years) *Patterns of Terrorism*, online at http://www.state.gov/s/ct/rls/pgtrpt.
*Former Communist countries of Eastern Europe and successor states of the Soviet Union.

2001, however, there were many deaths, but the figures understate the number of wounded in the attack against the World Trade Center and the Pentagon. It needs to be remembered, of course, that none of these tables includes domestic terrorism. Deaths from domestic terrorism in a number of democracies have been high, exceeding any damage resulting from international incidents. The 1995 truck bombing in Oklahoma City was much more deadly than the first attack on the World Trade Center, but it does not appear in the statistics since it was a domestic terrorist act.

The figures in the various tables actually understate the importance of the United States as a target. While incidents on American soil have been rare, US interests abroad are often targeted. The attacks against the US embassies in Kenya and Tanzania in 1998 are a prime example. These car bombings explain the large casualty figures and number of deaths for Africa in 1998, yet the target of the attacks was clearly the United States and not the local African countries. Terrorism has negatively affected Americans abroad for many years. In the 1980s and the 1990s there were 666 Americans killed in incidents of international terrorism—most of them in attacks launched abroad—while 190 died from domestic terrorism (Pillar 2001: 19).

The fact that democracies are more frequently the sites where terrorist attacks occur does not necessarily mean that the democracy itself is the target. A terrorist group from another country could choose to mount an attack in a democratic society against its home authoritarian or totalitarian government because security is weaker in the democracy. Western Europe has served as a convenient site in this regard. Embassies, businesses connected to the home government such as national airlines, or persons from the home country have all been potential targets. Bombing a building, kidnapping a business leader, or the assassination of a diplomat will occur in the democracy because it is easier to make the attack there than it would be in the home country. The same logic can hold true for mounting attacks on

targets in weaker authoritarian systems. The bombing of the two US embassies in Kenya and Tanzania reflected such calculations. Tanzania was a fairly democratic country while a single party with a pretense of democracy governed Kenya. Neither country had special ties with the United States nor would they be considered allies, and neither of them was on bad terms with the Muslim world. In fact, Tanzania had a substantial Muslim population of its own. Both, however, had relatively limited security services available, making any early detection of the bombing operations very unlikely. Both countries also had citizens of Middle Eastern descent in their populations, making it easier for the persons involved in the attacks to blend in with the population. In effect, these two countries were chosen for the attacks because they were convenient for the terrorist organization in question. Some other terrorist group with a grudge against the United States or with a desire to bring about a change in US policy could just as easily have chosen embassies in some other country with limited security and intelligence services.

Other political systems face danger as well. Long established authoritarian regimes where control mechanisms begin to loosen may be especially susceptible (Schreiber 1978: 28). Another type of political system that might be more likely to be chosen as the location for attacks, at least in the short term, would be a country in transition— one in which one type of ruling group is being replaced by another (Weinberg and Eubank 1998: 114). Even a transition from one type of authoritarian regime to another could leave a country temporarily vulnerable. Once the changeover is complete, however, the new authoritarian regime may be quite capable of dealing with challenges to its legitimacy. An authoritarian system shifting towards becoming a new democracy could be subject to attacks as well. While all democracies have indeed been more vulnerable to some types of terrorism, the newest democracies have been the most vulnerable (D. Mousseau 2001). In the case of a political system in the process of changing, if the old security forces have been discredited and eliminated with the fall of the old system, terrorists could have some important temporary advantages. Even if these weaker authoritarian system or systems undergoing transformation are not the targets of terrorist attacks as such, they could still be chosen for attacks against embassies or symbolic targets of other countries since their security apparatuses are likely to be quite weak. Ineffective security arrangements in democracies and weaker authoritarian systems have, in fact, been considered to be a permissive cause (rather than an underlying cause) of increased terrorism (Crenshaw 2003a: 94).

There are some additional reasons why democracies or weaker authoritarian systems might be chosen for attacks. Terrorist groups seek an audience, and it is imperative that knowledge of their actions reaches that audience. If the group is attempting to reach potential supporters among citizens living abroad in exile or the population of the home country, information on the attack has to be disseminated. A totalitarian or strong authoritarian system might be able to repress or control the news if the attack occurs within its own boundaries, limiting the effective influence of even successful terrorist actions. Activities by anti-Soviet groups in the USSR after World War II were not broadcast, and the dissidents operated in isolation and were eventually eliminated. Thus, the attacks never reached the audience they sought to mobilize. In some countries, the news of the assassination of a local official in a state where news is controlled can officially become a traffic fatality or a heart attack. Other incidents can be ascribed to a variety of causes rather than political violence, effectively limiting the public attention that the terrorist action was designed to gain. The government will know the truth, but potential supporters of the dissident organization will remain in the dark. If the action is undertaken in a democratic society, however, the media attention will not be controlled since freedom of the press is present (Schmid 1992b: 16). The incident may only be minor news—hence the tendency of groups to undertake more noteworthy actions—

but it will not be suppressed. If the action is spectacular enough, the media attention is likely to bring the political goals or the demands of the dissidents to public attention. With such press attention the group may be able to raise funds abroad and to begin to pressure the government back home to change policies, at least by threatening to create global embarrassment or to indicate to the world at large that not all citizens are happy to live in a controlled, non-democratic setting. In the world of today with fax machines, the internet, and 24-hours-a-day news broadcasts via satellites in orbit, it is even possible that potential dissidents *within* the authoritarian or totalitarian state will become aware of the presence of like-minded people and what appears to be the existence of an effective dissident group.

Democratic states provide one more advantage for dissidents. Fundraising opportunities may be more easily undertaken there. Civil rights and liberties will often make it difficult for the government to restrict such efforts, especially if the fundraising is undertaken in conjunction with supposed charitable operations. If funds are being raised locally, symbolic attacks may be launched in that country as well to spur the effort. If the dissident group continues to be successful, it will receive funds from exiles, as it becomes the centerpiece to opposition to the regime at home. If the organization is successful, a democracy (or weak authoritarian system) may provide a situation in which the group can levy "taxes" on exiles to fund the effort back home. Funds could even be extorted by selective kidnappings to send a warning to other exiles. The kidnappings themselves can only be marginally considered terrorist activities, but they are being undertaken in the democratic society to pursue the political violence at home. For these efforts to succeed, publicity would again be a key.

While all democracies may be particularly good targets for attacks by terrorists, the United States is particularly appealing to a wide variety of dissidents. The United States has the dubious distinction of being the most favored target of international attacks (Wilkinson 2003: 110). Most of these attacks have been undertaken outside the United States since they are easier to undertake in those locales, but there is no doubt that the United States and its interests are the targets. There are a variety of reasons for the targeting of the United States. It is a media center, so if publicity is important, the effect is greater if US interests are somehow involved if the attack is on a smaller democracy. The United States is also symbolic of the West, modernization, democracy, capitalism, and multinational corporations. The United States' long-standing tradition of distrusting government has meant that tracking "suspicious" individuals is difficult, even in the wake of the attacks of September 11. There is no national ID card, and while social security numbers have been used in that capacity, Americans are not typically required to present their social security card. National government agencies are limited by law in their ability to exchange information among themselves. Literally, the right hand does not know what the left hand is doing much of the time, nor can the right hand legally find out. The CIA and the FBI, the most important national investigatory agencies (Homeland Security could perhaps now be added), lack any institutional base for working together. While many governments separate the tasks of domestic counterespionage from foreign operations, the two are linked more closely than the CIA and FBI. In the United Kingdom, MI5 deals with domestic threats while MI6 (of "M" and James Bond fame) undertakes foreign operations. In this case, however, MI stands for Ministry of Intelligence and the numbers are specific sections. While the two sections may disagree and have different agendas, there is some central control. Further, even the American system of federalism limits the effective responses that can be undertaken in some cases. A handful of national agencies, the state police of the fifty states, and countless thousands of local police forces must cooperate, a process that can be difficult at best and tremendously inefficient at worst.

The United States as the only superpower also becomes a more appealing target for some terrorists. Attacking the only surviving superpower in the world is a means of demonstrating the potential of the dissident organization and its abilities, and the threat to target audiences is greater as a consequence. The United States as a superpower becomes a target because it is involved in political situations throughout the world. Terrorist organizations will attack because of US foreign policy decisions. In some regions the antagonism toward the United States as the symbol of the West is so high than any US activity is seen as having some malignant purpose (M. Mousseau 2002/3: 23). What terrorists believe the United States is doing is very important, and mistaken beliefs are not easily changed by modifications in US policy (Pillar 2001: 67). In other cases, terrorist organizations will target the United States because it fails to take any action. In effect, whatever the United States does or does not do can make it a target. Not all decisions of the US government in any given time period are always the best, but even decisions to undertake an action that is appropriate or decisions to stay uninvolved that are wise can generate adverse reactions by a dissident group. Groups that the United States fails to aid may target US interests, even if the United States does nothing to help the opposing side. The question as to whether the US government made the right decision is, of course, tremendously important, but equally important is the view of dissident groups abroad. If they disagree with US actions, for good reasons or bad, they can choose to launch attacks against the country.

Summary

Clearly the tactics, targets, and weapons available to terrorists can be very varied. An organization that is willing to risk its existence and its members in attacks will always be able to attempt violence. Sophisticated weaponry is not essential to begin a struggle, even if it would be of great value. The range of potential targets is very great; the resources of the terrorist organization and existing security measures will often influence the choice (Drake 1998: 54). Ultimately, "terrorists always have the advantage. They can attack anything, anywhere, at any time. We cannot possibly protect everything all of the time" (Jenkins 2001: 323). If the weapons available are limited, if the planning is poor, or if the security and intelligence forces are on their toes, initial attacks will fail and the organization will be crushed. If the attacks succeed, then the organization may gain strength, gaining additional funds and adherents to strike again. Many more terrorist efforts fail than succeed, for terrorism is a weapon of the weak, and acts of terrorism are designed to change the balance of power between the government and the challengers. If dissident organizations were stronger, they would be able to try to utilize other avenues to create change. Some groups have been successful in bringing about changes, while others ultimately failed when the state opted for repression rather than compromise. A terrorist group that has some initial successes will have more scope to make choices. The choice of targets will have to continue to be non-random if the group is going to continue to be successful. Choices about weapons, techniques, and targets will become important in these contexts. Poor choices could result in the organization losing its momentum and eventually failing, even after a promising start.

Terms

anthrax
Chechnya
Duvalier, François
bin Laden, Osama
Mountbatten, Lord
weapons of mass destruction
weapons of mass disruption

Further reading

Enders, W. and Sandler, T. (1996) "Terrorism and Direct Foreign Investment in Spain and Greece," *Kyklos*, 49, 3: 331–52.

Tucker, J. B. (ed.) (2000b) *Toxic Terror: Assessing Terrorist Use of Chemical and Biological Weapons*, Cambridge, MA: MIT Press.

Weinberg, L. B. and Eubank, W. L. (1998) "Terrorism and Democracy: What Recent Events Disclose," *Terrorism and Political Violence*, 10, 1: 108–18.

Chapter 4

State sponsors and supporters of terrorism

True state control   46

State support of terrorism   48

Case studies   50

    4.1 Italy and Hungary in Yugoslavia—fishing in troubled waters   50

    4.2 Iraq   52

    4.3 Iran   54

    4.4 The United States and the Contras in Nicaragua   56

    4.5 North Korea   59

Summary   61

Terms   62

Further reading   62

One area of contention that has surfaced in regard to terrorism has been the extent to which foreign countries have sponsored such activities. In many cases it is foreign governments that have been considered responsible for bombings, hijackings, and assassinations. It is argued that without the involvement of these foreign sponsors, terrorist threats to domestic peace and security in another country would disappear. Defining a problem as a foreign policy issue presupposes that the solution lies in the area of foreign policy. Diplomatic pressure, economic threats, or even military force might be used to encourage the foreign government to cease their involvement. If one of these methods fails, then another can be tried if the international situation is conducive to some other action. In addition, counterintelligence agencies can be used to deal with the foreign operations in a particular country and to deal with their local collaborators. Ultimately, if foreign sponsorship is the cause of domestic terrorism, it can be defeated abroad. If foreign sponsorship is not responsible for domestic terrorism then efforts directed against foreign nations will be much less successful. Foreign support of terrorist organizations can be direct, but much more often it is indirect.

True state control

The truest form of state sponsorship of violence in other countries for political ends are situations in which intelligence agencies actively plan the actions, train the operatives, issue orders, and then send them off to carry out these orders. This kind of state sponsorship of violence is part and parcel of the ongoing conflict between states that occurs at the covert level and really do not meet the definition of terrorism as provided in Chapter 2 since the activities are state to state ones. Most such actions are designed for intelligence gathering purposes, but they can also include sabotage, economic disruption, bombings, and assassinations. Governments have accepted that this type of activity is one of the normal consequences of being involved in international policies.

Some violent activity is carried out by state agencies. During the Cold War the CIA and KGB were quite active in violent activities. Sometimes, the actions involved agents of allied states. Radio Free Europe relied on refugees and dissidents from Eastern Europe to serve as analysts and broadcasters for sending news and propaganda to various parts of Eastern Europe and the Soviet Union behind the Iron Curtain. In 1978 in London, members of the Bulgarian secret service assassinated a number of these employees in the finest James Bond tradition. Special umbrellas with deadly poison (ricin) in the tips were used to jab these individuals in the leg on crowded London streets or in the subways. These assassinations were clearly state sanctioned and directed, and not just by Bulgarian authorities. Any special operations such as these using special poisons had to be approved by the KGB advisors who ran the Bulgarian secret services. The use of Bulgarian personnel as surrogates, however, technically distanced the Soviet Union from the attacks in case of exposure (and the British authorities did determine what was occurring).

Israel has been active in both direct and indirect use of violence to achieve objectives, for example, by undertaking foreign assassinations against selected targets. Israeli agents tracked down most of the members of Black September involved in the 1972 Munich Olympic attacks and killed them (Partrick, 1997a, p. 307). Israel even used "false flag" operations. In 1954 sympathetic Jews in Egypt used bombs and arson against US installations. The objective was for local Arab radicals to receive the blame for the attacks in order to prevent improved US–Egyptian relations (Arian 1998: 111). In 1978 Israel was alarmed at Iraq's efforts to build a nuclear reactor. After diplomatic efforts failed to deter firms from supplying parts to Iraq, Israel resorted to more direct measures. Parts bound for Iraq were sabotaged. Attacks were made on Italian and French companies that were providing the parts for the reactor, and their employees were threatened—all as part of an effort to stop shipments. When both diplomacy and covert operations failed, Israeli aircraft launched a surprise raid on the reactor in 1981, only months before it was due to become operational (Stern 1999: 115). This direct attack was very successful in eliminating the reactor. Israel also assassinated a member of the Iraqi Atomic Energy Commission and Gerald Bull, an English munitions expert, who were attempting to develop a super long-range gun for Iraq (Richelson 2002: 249). The kinds of operations undertaken by Israel are typical of the actions that governments can undertake. The targeting of private companies and their employees was clearly an effort not only to disrupt the supply of parts to Iraq but also to intimidate and terrorize a target audience into compliance with the wishes of the Israeli government. Another example of such direct state sponsorship was the bombing of Pan Am Flight 103 over Lockerbie, Scotland, in 1988. It was planned and carried out under the orders of the Libyan government, and the bombing would not have occurred without the action of that government. Using the camouflage of a terrorist attack was important for deniability by the government since open acknowledgment of the attack was not possible.

While some activity is directly undertaken by the intelligence agencies of various countries, more frequently state sponsorship has been used to refer to a situation in which a country trains, funds, and controls domestic groups that are involved in political violence in another country. The groups in these circumstances are indirect agents of a foreign power. This type of sponsorship implies that if the foreign country withdraws its support, either because of policy changes, shifting alliances, or a threat of retaliation, the domestic terrorist group would collapse. Both direct and indirect state sponsorship have important implications for domestic terrorist activities. If groups are indeed funded and controlled from outside, the government has not failed in its domestic programs. These foreign sponsors serve as convenient scapegoats for domestic violence that could be the direct consequence of ill-considered government programs or policies.

There are examples of situations where foreign support has been highly important for the continued existence of opposition groups that have resorted to violence. There are other cases where a foreign government has effectively controlled political groups that were willing to undertake violent activities even when the groups had a base in their local societies. The National Socialist (Nazi) Parties in Austria and Czechoslovakia in the late 1930s were prominent examples. They were reflections of right-wing discontent within the Austrian and Czech governments. They were clearly not an invention of the Nazi Party of Germany, nor did they exist solely due to external support. On the other hand, they did respond to directives from the Nazi Party in Germany and after 1933 the German government. Protests, political activity, and violence increased or decreased in response to outside directions. In these cases the local terrorist activities did reflect outside sponsorship in a fairly clear way.

Similarly, in the period before and after World War II various national communist parties around the world took their cues directly from the Soviet Union while that country existed, even though very real national domestic problems and concerns for the plight of the working class existed, but the rise of local communist parties also reflected the fact that workers in many countries faced problems. After World War II, local communist parties frequently underwent contortions in terms of changing their policies to support or attack different governments on the basis of their relationships with the Soviet Union. The Egyptian Communist Party, for example, was called upon to support the government of Nasser when Egypt become an ally of the Soviet Union, even though Nasser was in the process of repressing the Egyptian Communist Party and arresting its members. These communist parties were clearly accepting foreign direction and foreign support, and they undertook at least some violent actions at foreign direction. These parties, however, would have continued to survive without foreign support, even though they would have been less effective in some cases.

State support of terrorism

Most charges of state involvement in terrorist activities have involved situations in which foreign governments have aided terrorist groups that already existed in some other country. One of the myths of terrorism is that governments always oppose action by non-state organizations (Stohl 2003: 87). In fact, they often support terror, and such state support can be very important in increasing the capacity of terrorist groups, expanding the geographical range of possible actions, and making their attacks more lethal (Veness 2001: 409). Governments have been quick to take advantage of opportunities to weaken their enemies or potential enemies, including the provision of support to dissident political movements. If a political movement appeared that caused problems for an enemy or potential enemy, then it was seen as appropriate to assist and encourage that political movement. If the dissident political group resorted to violent attacks and terrorism, then it made sense, from the government's point of view, to provide weapons, money, and a safe refuge. Governments might also train members of dissident groups in the use of weapons and provide expert training for the construction and detonation of bombs. State aid to dissident groups could also include use of diplomatic pouches for communications or arms or the provision of false passports, or even diplomatic passports (Rathmell 1997e: 655–6). Such support would be a relatively inexpensive foreign policy tool. In addition, from the government perspective, these groups were expendable and support could be stopped with little disadvantage if governmental foreign policy should change. Even so, it is important to note that these groups would have existed before they received foreign support and would continue to exist if the foreign support was withdrawn. Any dissident political group capable of undertaking an extended political campaign of terror must be grounded in its own society (Rubenstein 1987: 63). External aid is useful and even important, but it is not essential. Further, foreign governments do not control these groups. The groups themselves

determine their political agendas. They might consult with their foreign allies, and even take their interests into account, but they do not take orders from them. This lack of control is another factor that clearly sets state support for terrorist groups in the form of weapons or money from abroad apart from state terrorism or state sponsorship.

Examples of foreign governments "fishing in troubled waters" in the above fashion abound through the ages (Shultz 1994: 282). During the long Peloponnesian Wars, Sparta and Athens regularly intervened in the internal politics of other Greek city states. Sparta supported aristocratic factions against more popular groups in efforts to separate allies or satellites from Athens, while Athens supported more democratic factions against aristocrats in an effort to convert Spartan allies to its side. The Roman Empire at its height frequently supported a rival claimant to a throne in order to weaken a potential enemy or as a preparatory move to invasion and annexation. Such rival claimants, however, had to have some domestic support to be useful to Roman plans. Such intervention in supporting royal pretenders, separatists, and potential heirs was practiced by many states and empires in later eras as well. In other cases, governments have supported violent groups in states that they have sought to weaken. The Black Hand and the Serbian government were linked in the early 1900s. The goal of the Black Hand was independence for Slavs located in other states. The group was especially interested in detaching areas inhabited by Serbs from Austria-Hungary and uniting them with Serbia. The Black Hand, and indirectly the government of Serbia, supported political dissidents in their violent attacks, the most important case being the aid that was made available for the assassination of Archduke Franz Ferdinand, heir to the Austro-Hungarian throne, in Sarajevo in 1914. This assassination triggered the outbreak of World War I, a conflict in which Serbia itself was defeated and occupied, paying the price for attempting to weaken a threatening neighbor. Notwithstanding the presence of support from Serbia, the

BOX 4.1 **Counterproductive foreign sponsorship**

There are times when foreign support can be counterproductive to dissident groups. After World War II the US and British governments supported nationalists who were opposed to Communist and Russian domination of their regions. Individuals were trained, equipped, and then sent to Eastern Europe and the Ukraine to conduct sabotage and other actions. Soviet security forces quickly captured these operatives, as well as their contacts and supporters. The British and American intelligence communities initially thought that the Soviet counterintelligence forces were very effective, and that the local supporters and national-ist groups had poor security and gave themselves away. As it later became apparent, the quick appre-hension of the nationalist infiltrators was due to the presence of Soviet agents in the British intelligence community. Kim Philby, Guy Burgess, and Donald McLean had been passing information to the Soviet Union before World War II and continued to do so afterwards. The information included the names of agents sent into the Communist countries. The US and British support was not only ineffective, it actually weakened the anti-Communist forces. Even with this handicap, anti-Soviet movements did persist. There were still Ukrainian units fighting the Soviet regime in 1950 (Reid 1997: 159–60). Without external support the movements would undoubtedly have failed in the long run, but more effective Western support might have lengthened their active life rather than shortening it.

opposition to Austrian or Hungarian states by dissident Slavic groups within the Empire were a result of domestic situations and would have been present even in the absence of external Serbian support.

In Asia the intelligence unit of the Pakistani army has supported Muslim dissidents in Kashmir that have been seeking to attach that province to Pakistan (Mohan 1992: 299). One calculation of active fighters in Kashmir concluded that 40 percent of those opposed to continued Indian rule in the region were Pakistanis or Afghans, who outnumbered the secular Kashmiri groups seeking an independent state (Stern 2000b: 118). Pakistan has aided other dissident groups else-where in India as well (Saikia 2002). It is not surprising that India has covertly provided aid in turn to Pakistani dissidents. There is evidence that the Indian aid has been somewhat effective in destabilizing Pakistan (Laqueur 1999: 153). Again, in these cases terrorism led to additional terror-ism; however, foreign support did not create the opposition movements in either country, although that support clearly exacerbated the violence.

One other type of foreign involvement should be mentioned in passing before discussing the case studies in detail. Dissident political organ-izations that have resorted to the use of violence have often had support in diaspora communities. Diaspora groups can prolong violence by dissi-dents in their home country by contributing funds and extremist rhetoric (Stern 2000b: 121). In addi-tion to giving moral support and financial aid to dissident groups, supporters abroad have applied pressure on other governments to support the dissident causes. If the diaspora community is important enough, foreign governments may find it difficult to interfere with fundraising, recruit-ment, sheltering of key figures involved in the violent movements, or even the purchase of arms. For example, the IRA has been able to more or less openly raise funds in the United States, and the PLO has maintained widespread support among the Palestinian community worldwide (Byman 1998: 161). Kashmiris around the world have supported the dissidents in Kashmir (Mohan 1992: 304). In these types of cases the support by foreign governments was given more indirectly, as a result of their reluctance or inability to inter-fere with the support activities of the communities supporting the dissidents. Inaction can sometimes be as helpful as action. The diaspora community was not responsible for the dissidence or the violence, but the continued assistance may be important for a more successful struggle.

The above examples of state support are very clear cut, but there are other ways in which states may be supportive of terrorist organizations. Countries have managed to avoid arresting a wanted terrorist on their own territory in order to avoid becoming a target for terrorist acts (Long 1990: 9). Prior to the 1980s, for example, France had a doctrine of neutrality in regard to inter-national terrorist groups. As long as there were no attacks on France, the members of the groups would be left alone (Shapiro and Suzan 2003: 69). In 1977 French intelligence agents arrested Abu Daoud, a PLO leader implicated in the planning of the attack at the Munich Olympics. He was wanted in a number of countries, including West Germany and Israel. He was released, however, and quickly left France. The French government facilitated his release since his trial in France or his extradition to some other country would have disrupted French diplomatic and economic links with Arab states and exposed France to the danger of possible retaliation (Schreiber 1978: 55–8). Italy for a long time had a similar arrangement with the PLO. In exchange for Italian non-interference, the PLO agreed not to launch attacks in Italy or to target Italian citizens (Chalk 1996: 11). In addi-tion, when a government does not interfere with fundraising for dissidents in another country and the money raised is used to purchase weapons for dissidents, the government's lack of action might constitute indirect state support for terrorists. Obviously, a wide variety of actions and non-actions by a government can contribute aid in some sense for dissident organizations abroad that have used violence or which may use vio-lence, and questions involving state sponsorship or aid can be quite complicated.

Case studies

There are innumerable examples of countries supporting or sponsoring terrorist groups in addition to the examples mentioned above. Five will be discussed in some detail below to indicate that almost any country may at times use such support or even sponsorship of domestic groups in other countries as part of their foreign policies, even when they ultimately do not control the groups. The first case is more historical and deals with the support given by Italy and Hungary to opposition groups and separatist groups in Yugoslavia in the period between World War I and World War II. The second and third cases involve the support given by Iraq and Iran to various groups involved in terrorist activities, not only in the Middle East but in Europe and elsewhere as well. Both of these countries were on the US list of states sponsoring terrorism. A fourth case is the US support for the Contras in Nicaragua. While the Contras were more involved in a guer-rilla insurgency, there were times when they relied more on terrorist actions. Finally, there is the support given by North Korea for decades to groups seeking to destabilize the government of South Korea, including some spectacular attacks and assassinations.

CASE STUDY 4.1
Italy and Hungary in Yugoslavia—fishing in troubled waters

Yugoslavia was created after World War I by the combination of a number of rather disparate territo-ries. The old kingdom of Serbia served as the core of the new state, which expanded to include other terri-tories, and the royal family of Serbia became the royal family for Yugoslavia. In 1918, Serbia included the Macedonian territories that had been acquired in the First and Second Balkan Wars, as well as some addi-tional territory in this area acquired from Bulgaria in the peace settlements after World War I. The small kingdom of Montenegro was forcibly united with

Serbia in the new state, although not without some opposition in the region (Banac 1984: 285–91). The new kingdom also acquired major territories from the old Austro-Hungarian Empire that disintegrated in the aftermath of World War I. Slovenia, Bosnia, Dalmatia, Croatia, Slavonia and the Banat had been part of the dual monarchy. The disparate nature of the new country was indicated by its first name—the Kingdom of the Serbs, the Croats, and the Slovenes, which was changed only in 1929 to the Kingdom of Yugoslavia (Kingdom of South Slavs).

Internally, Yugoslavia reflected the many differences in the territories that made up the new kingdom. Serbia and Montenegro were both largely inhabited by Serbs who were Greek Orthodox and who used the Cyrillic alphabet. There were also Macedonians (South Serbs was the official terminology) in the southern part of the country in the areas acquired in the Balkan wars and after World War I. The Macedonians were also Greek Orthodox, used the Cyrillic alphabet, and spoke a Slavic dialect that was probably linguistically closer to Bulgarian than to Serbian. There was also an Albanian minority in portions of Yugoslavia bordering on Albania who spoke Albanian (a non-Slavic language at its base) and were largely Muslims in terms of religious background. In the northern parts of the new country the Croats and Slovenes were Roman Catholic, reflecting their history as part of the Austro-Hungarian Empire, and they used the Latin alphabet. Croat was linguistically similar to Serbian, while Slovenian was more distant. In the Bosnian region there was a mixture of Serbs, Croats, and those who had converted to Islam centuries earlier when the region was part of the Ottoman Empire. The Banat region (Vojvodina) north of Belgrade, the capital, was acquired from Hungary. While a majority of the inhabitants were Greek Orthodox Serbs, there were significant German and Hungarian minorities in this area. Thus, the new state was a collection of differing languages, religions, alphabets, and governing traditions.

The new state was built upon the Serbian royal family and on the government institutions that had existed in the old Serbia. The Serbs were also the single largest group in the new country, although not a majority. The constitution for the new country created centralized institutions that favored the Serbs as the largest group in the states, and institutions of local government that would have been dominated by local majorities were abolished (Havens et al. 1975: 87). Serbian officials held most of the key positions in the government, and Serbs dominated the officer corps in the military. As a consequence, there were tensions between the Serbs and the other groups in the country, and there was a perception that Serbs were inordinately powerful in the new country. Parties and politicians from other groups in the country boycotted elections or government institutions at different times to protest against Serbian influences, further disrupting the new state. There was overt opposition to the new government in Macedonia, and Croatian leaders began to seek greater autonomy and even independence from Yugoslavia in reaction to the perceptions of Serb dominance. Opposition in other parts of the country included violence and terrorist attacks. The assassination of Croatian parliamentary leaders in 1928 completely disrupted the political system and directly led to the establishment of a royal dictatorship in 1929 (Dragnich 1992: 55–6; Hoptner 1962: 7–8).

While there were real difficulties that appeared within the state, the dissension within Yugoslavia was exacerbated by disputes over borders with neighboring countries and claims by these neighbors to portions of Yugoslav territory. Serbia had acquired territory in Macedonia in the First Balkan War that Bulgaria hoped to gain, and it had taken additional territory at Bulgarian expense in the Second Balkan War and World War I. Yugoslavia had also gained territory in Dalmatia from the Austro-Hungarian Empire that Italy had expected to receive in return for joining the Allies in 1915. These territories were given to the new country instead to strengthen it, notwithstanding earlier British and French promises to Italy. Similarly, Hungary sought to regain at least some of the territories that it had lost to the new state after World War I. Consequently, at various times, all three of these countries supported the internal dissidents as part of their efforts to weaken the Yugoslav state. They all hoped to eventually acquire the disputed territories when Yugoslavia could not resist or when it collapsed.

Bulgarian efforts at supporting dissidents were largely confined to support for Macedonians seeking to unite their regions with Bulgaria. Hungary and Italy, on the other hand, supported dissident groups in Yugoslavia less directly related to their territorial claims. Their support was more directed toward weakening Yugoslavia and making it more vulnerable. In particular, these two governments supported Croat nationalist groups seeking autonomy or independence. Ante Pavelich was the leader of a local Croat fascist party (Utashe)—one of the major dissident groups and one that was willing to use terrorist tactics. After fleeing the country, he established his headquarters in Italy, protected by Mussolini's regime. Hungary's authoritarian government also supported Pavelich and other Croat nationalist groups as part of efforts to destabilize Yugoslavia for their own purposes. Italy and Hungary provided funds and arms to the Croat nationalists groups and supported their terrorist attacks. They offered safe havens for individuals who had to leave Yugoslavia. They provided training camps for potential terrorists, and the Hungarian and Italian intelligence agencies passed along information to the Croat nationalists as well, and helped in the planning of some of their activities (Havens *et al.* 1975: 89–90). The assassination of King Alexander mentioned in the previous chapter took place with the direct involvement of these two countries, including the provision of funds and intelligence information.

Hungary and Italy did not create, control, or direct the domestic opposition groups. They aided them because it was in their perceived national interests to do so. Such assistance was critical to weakening the Yugoslav state and was important in the successful assassination of King Alexander in France. Without Italian and Hungarian support, however, such an attempt on the monarch's life could have occurred elsewhere. There had been an attempt in 1921 that failed and at least one planned attempt earlier in 1933 that miscarried when the assassin lost his nerve (Havens *et al.* 1975: 89–90). The Croat nationalists benefited from the external support, perhaps especially in their terrorist attacks, but they were not dependent upon that external support to persist in their efforts to gain greater control of at least local

political affairs. The Italian and Hungarian efforts were eventually successful in achieving their goals. The efforts to destabilize Yugoslavia weakened resistance to the German invasion that occurred in 1940. The country was overrun and partitioned. Italy and Hungry acquired much of the Yugoslav territory that they had wanted. The Italian, Hungarian, and Bulgarian gains proved to be short lived since they were on the losing side in World War II and had to return the territories. The Croat opposition groups also benefited. After the Axis invasion, an independent Croatia was established under Pavelich, including not only Croatia and Dalmatia but large portions of Bosnia as well. This state was allied to the Germans under these Croat nationalists, but its life as an independent state was limited. It disappeared with the defeat of Germany in World War II.

CASE STUDY 4.2
Iraq

Iraq has been accused of both sponsoring terrorist activities and supporting terrorist organizations. The United States in particular has focused on Iraqi activities, and Iraqi support for terrorism was one of the reasons used to justify the 2003 invasion. Like virtually all the other Arab countries, Iraq has supported the Palestinians and the PLO as the political spokesperson for the Palestinian people. In the early 1970s the Abu Nidal Organization, one of the most active Palestinian terrorist groups, was headquartered in Iraq where it received help from Iraqi officials. The group later changed sponsors to Syria and then Libya before returning to a home in Iraq in 1990 (Wege 1991: 59–60). The group eventually disappeared from active involvement in terrorist operations. In the early days of Palestinian opposition to Israel the Iraqis did have their preferred organization, the Palestinian Liberation Army, but Iraq and the other countries accepted the amalgamation of various groups into the PLO. When the Ba'ath (Arab Socialist Renaissance) party came to power via a military coup the context for Iraqi involvement in terrorist movements changed. The new Ba'athist regime sent assassination teams to eliminate

Iraqi dissidents elsewhere in the Middle East and in Europe (Sciolino 1991: 91–2). The Abu Nidal group while it was in residence in Iraq paid for assistance by helping to eliminate Iraqi dissidents abroad. When Saddam Hussein assumed power in Iraq the regime became increasingly oppressive domestically, and opponents and dissidents, actual and perceived, were jailed, tortured, or killed. The internal violence was matched by the elimination of dissidents overseas (Terrill 1993). The foreign military adventures undertaken by Iraq under the leadership of Hussein also involved increasing activities with terrorist groups in other countries as a consequence of the long war with Iran and then with the invasion of Kuwait and battles with the coalition that liberated that country.

In the war with Iran, Iraq supported dissident groups in that country, particularly the leftist Mujahedin-e-Khalq (MKO). This group had fought to overthrow the Shah in conjunction with other groups, including the supporters of the Ayatollah Khomeini. The MKO resorted to terrorist attacks against the new Islamic Republic, scoring some spectacular successes. The new Iranian regime, however, was able to defeat this campaign and eliminate many of the members (R. Anderson 1997). Iraq undertook to support the MKO, primarily as a means of weakening Iran, a country with which Iraq had a number of grievances (Rathmell 1997b). During the long war with Iran, the MKO cooperated with Iraq in the hope of establishing itself in power in Iran. When Iran and Iraq agreed to end their war on the basis of the boundaries before the Iraqi invasion, Saddam Hussein abandoned the MKO to its fate, one of the clearest examples of a government only using a dissident group in another country as long as it proved useful to foreign policy goals. Iraq also equipped, supplied, and trained the National Liberation Army (NLA), a group made up of Iranian dissidents that fought alongside Iraqi army units during the long war. These dissidents, like the MKO, were seeking to establish a leftist, non-Islamic government in Iran.

The invasion of Kuwait by Iraqi forces, the pressure to force an Iraqi withdrawal, and the subsequent defeat of Iraq by the forces led by the United States led to more Iraqi support for terrorist groups. Hussein threatened increased terrorist attacks against the

countries supporting the end of the Iraqi occupation. There were over 200 terrorist incidents during the Gulf crisis, mostly against businesses associated with countries that had joined the coalition to force Iraq to relinquish its hold on Kuwait. It is likely that at least some of these incidents involved Iraqi agents, some involved groups supported by Iraq, and others resulted from the independent actions of groups that favored Iraq in the conflict. Iraqi efforts to support terrorist attacks were much more inept than most such activities by national intelligence agencies or even well established terrorist groups (Pillar 2001: 57). Iraqi efforts in this area were further curtailed when embassies were closed and diplomats expelled and when remaining diplomats in other countries were closely watched (Terrill 1993). The Iraqi defeat in Kuwait led Hussein to re-emphasize terrorism as a weapon that could be used against the countries that had opposed him.

The most daring plan was an effort (that was discovered in time) to assassinate former President George Bush with the help of MKO operatives in 1993 (Mylroie 2000: 114). Apparently Saddam Hussein was seeking revenge for US attempts to kill him with Smart bombs during the war to liberate Kuwait (Richelson 2002: 252). Iraq was linked to attempted bombings of US facilities abroad, including the residence of the US ambassador to Indonesia. There have been attacks against Kuwaiti targets and other targets abroad. Iraqi dissidents abroad have also continued to be targets for assassinations. Iraq has provided training, weapons, funding, and passport assistance for some terrorist groups. By 2003, however, there was little evidence of any major Iraqi involvement with foreign terrorist groups. Iraq, like other countries and groups, did help to fund pensions for the families of suicide bombers in Israel and the Occupied Territories, but there has been virtually no evidence of any links with al Qaeda.

It would be hard to argue that Iraq has actually benefited from its support of dissidents abroad. No neighboring state was weakened to the point that Iraqi foreign policy objectives were successful. Withdrawal of support for the MKO did provide a bargaining point in negotiations with Iran for an end to their long war. Elimination of dissidents abroad has no doubt limited internal opposition, but these actions were most clearly undertaken by government agencies rather than terrorist organizations. Iraq has also had to deal with adverse reactions from abroad. The attempt to assassinate President Bush (senior) was counterproductive since it led to a continuation of sanctions and continuing pressure on the regime. Had the assassination succeeded, it might have had propaganda value, but as a failure, it lacked even this possible benefit. There was the fear that Iraq might continue to develop chemical and biological weapons or nuclear weapons in the future and that either Iraq would use such weapons of mass destruction in a terrorist fashion or that it would supply these weapons to dissident organizations willing to use them. Extensive repression of the population by the government and its unwillingness to accept weapons inspections were among the factors that led to the 2003 invasion of Iraq.

CASE STUDY 4.3
Iran

When the Shah was in power, Iran was not a supporter of terrorist groups, although the Iranian government did support Kurdish insurgents in neighboring Iraq as a means of weakening various regimes in that country. It is likely that the Shah would have supported terrorist dissidents in Iraq if such had been available, but the political violence by the Kurds was more in the nature of guerrilla activities and small-scale battles. Eventually the Shah stopped aid to the Kurds in return for Iraqi concessions in other areas. When the Islamic Republic was established in Iran, the government became more involved in supporting terrorist groups. Iran has even been considered to be the most active or among the most active sponsors of terrorist groups in other countries. Iranian involvement has taken a number of forms. The Republic has attacked domestic exiles abroad. It has provided support to groups whose activities might in some way facilitate Iranian foreign policy objectives, and it has aided both fellow Shia co-religionists in other parts of the Middle East and more generally other Islamic groups seeking to force their governments to adopt a more decidedly Islamic form of governance. Training

camps in Iran have been open both to Iranians training for battle (perhaps abroad as well as on the borders) and to members of many terrorist and guerrilla organizations. Iranian charitable organizations and funds for cultural groups have also helped Iran to develop linkages in various countries and to recruit allies and even members for terrorist organizations (Harmon 2000: 118–20).

The attacks on dissidents and former members of the Shah's regime would seem to have been undertaken by agents of the Iranian government. Much like the United States, Iran has maintained members of its intelligence services in its embassies abroad. Members of these intelligence services have coordinated the assassinations of dissidents (Harmon 2000: 118–19). Iranian agents have eliminated a variety of dissidents abroad, including Shahpur Bakhtiar, who was a prime minister when the Shah was in power. Attacks against opponents or potential opponents of the Islamic Republic have occurred in Europe and the Middle East (Hoffman 1998: 190–1, 194). Members of the Kurdish opposition and the leftist Mujahedin-e-Khalq Organization (MKO) have also been successfully assassinated (Rathmell, 1997a). Agents of the state or persons hired for the purpose carried out all of these attacks.

Iranian involvement in terrorism has gone beyond the elimination of potential dissidents abroad (and at home). Iran has supported dissident groups in neighboring states in the region, partially at least in an attempt to increase the strength of Iran and to weaken neighbors, and partially in an attempt to establish governments based on the Shia version of Islam. A special coordinating office (Islamic Revolutionary Council) was formed and training was provided to Iranians and others (Shultz 1994: 284–5). Should such regimes be established, their governments would be more likely to be supportive of Iran. Iraq, some of the smaller monarchies in the Persian Gulf, and parts of Saudi Arabia are particularly vulnerable to this type of activity because of significant Shia minorities or even majorities. Iran has supported groups such as the Organization of the Islamic Revolution in the Arabian Peninsula, the Islamic Front for the Liberation of Bahrain, the Islamic Call Party, and the Supreme Council for the Islamic Revolution in Iraq. Shia terrorists have launched attacks in Kuwait, Saudi Arabia, and Bahrain (Green 1995; Shultz 1994). These kinds of activities reflect state support for particular groups that have goals that are complementary to the state. There is no doubt that Iran has provided funding and support for Shia groups in the Persian Gulf area, but it would appear that the dissatisfaction that Shia residents in these states have with their governments was already present, and Iran has simply taken advantage of the opportunity to further its own interests. Like many other states, Iran was supporting terrorism when it thought it could benefit by doing so (Green 1995: 594).

Almost from the outset of the establishment of the Islamic Republic Iran supported the Shia Muslims in Iraq. The fear felt by the government of Saddam Hussein that Shia groups might undermine the legitimacy of his government was one factor in the Iraqi decision to invade Iran. It probably was not the dominant factor since Iraq has demonstrated its ability to deal with domestic opposition without too much difficulty on numerous occasions. Iranian support for Shia groups was clearly an irritant. Once actual war occurred between Iran and Iraq, support for such groups clearly became an element of direct state policy as one means for weakening a military opponent. As it turns out, the Shia dissidents did not prove to be a very effective military weapon against Iraq, but they were a relatively cheap weapon to employ. Iran's support of Shia dissidents elsewhere in the Gulf region, however, explains much of the Arab support for Iraq in its long war with Iran.

Iranian involvement with terrorist groups went further afield. The Iranians clearly supported a variety of groups involved in the conflicts in Israel and Lebanon. The Islamic Republic took a very hard line in the Israeli–Arab struggles, strongly supporting the Palestinians as fellow Muslims. Iran provided funds and weapons to various Palestinian groups including Hamas, Palestinian Islamic Jihad, and the Popular Front for the Liberation of Palestine-General Command (PFLP-GC). At some point in time these groups have all rejected the idea of recognition of the state of Israel, and they have all been involved in terrorist activities in Israel and the Occupied Territories of Gaza and the West Bank (Combs 2000: 80–1). The Islamic Jihad and PFLP-GC predated the appearance of the Islamic

Republic, and they represented groups among the Palestinians who wanted to continue the struggle against Israel. Iranian funding and weapons strengthened their capabilities, but they did not depend upon Iran for their continued existence. Hamas appeared later and became more prominent after the Islamic Republic had been formed, but it drew its strength from support in the Palestinian community in the Occupied Territories and from Palestinians abroad. Iranian support was welcome, but hardly essential for the continuation of the organization.

Iran also became one of the most important supporters of the Hizballah organization in Lebanon. Hizballah represented the Shia community, which had long been a group at the economic bottom of Lebanese society. In fact, Iran's ambassador to Lebanon at the time was important in the creation of the organization, and Hizballah has been a major recipient of Iranian weapons and funds (Hoffman 1998: 194). While the Shia community of Lebanon had clear grievances with other groups in their own country, they were clearly better able to organize with support from Iran. Iran funded the training camps for Hizballah in Lebanon, and Iran was the principal source of weapons as well. Iranian diplomatic relations with Syria, which have tended to be good, have also been important since Syrian military units have been in control of the Bekaa Valley where the training camps have been located. Iran has also sent thousands of its paramilitary Revolutionary Guards to these camps where they supply support, staff, and training personnel (Harmon 2000: 118). A car bomb that destroyed the Iraqi embassy in 1981 and which killed the Iraqi ambassador and 71 others was a Hizballah action (Kostiner 1986: 116). This attack early in the Iraqi–Iranian war was apparently designed to support the Iranian cause. It is probably true that Hizballah has acted at times in direct accordance with Iranian wishes as it did with the attack on the Iraqi embassy, but at other times it has followed its own priorities.

Iran has also cooperated with the Islamic regime established in the Sudan. Sudan, like Iran, followed Islamic doctrines. The Islamic credentials of the government in power since 1989 have been impeccable. Although Sudanese follow Sunni Islam rather than the Shia version, the relationship has indicated Iran's willingness to work with other Islamic countries, notwithstanding doctrinal differences. Sudan has had training camps for a variety of terrorist groups, including Abu Nidal's organization and Egyptian groups opposed to the relatively secular government of that country, and Iran has provided funds and Revolutionary Guards to help run these camps (Shultz 1994: 286). Iran has also actively supported Sunni Islamic movements in Turkey, Egypt, and Algeria (Rathmell 1997a), indicating that Iranian support for Islamic groups at odds with their secular governments can be wide-ranging. In all these cases Iranian support is important to the groups in question, but such support is not essential to their survival.

With the passage of time Iran has been taking a lower profile in terms of supporting terrorist groups abroad. Iran has reduced its support of terrorism in neighboring countries (Bahgat 1999: 144). There has been a softening of Iranian attitudes towards various countries and an apparent desire to move back into the mainstream of international relations and contacts. While such support has lessened, there continue to be many cases of Iranian support for groups abroad, and collaboration with regimes, such as Syria and Sudan, which themselves have been accused of sponsoring, supporting, or controlling terrorist organizations. There is no reason to expect Iran to forgo the advantages of cooperating with terrorist groups whose actions may help weaken Iranian enemies or otherwise facilitate the achievement of other governmental or national goals. Iran is likely to continue to support groups with an anti-Western orientation, given its own conflicts with the West and concerns about Western influences and the continued presence of the state of Israel in the lands of Islam. Many Iranians would even like to see a massive Islamic state, the bringing together of the peoples of Islam under one government, as is seen to be the ideal for an Islamic society. Iran has consequently utilized groups that have been available because of the dissatisfaction of its members with policies, leaders, or the forms of government in their own societies.

Iranian support for terrorist organizations abroad has had both costs and benefits. The elimination of dissidents abroad has probably most directly benefited Iran since potential centers for opposition have disappeared and others have been cowed into silence. Support for dissident groups in Iran during the war with that country at best offset the disadvantages created by Iraqi support for Iranian dissidents. In other cases, Iran's support probably generated greater costs than benefits. The efforts to establish friendly Islamic governments in the Persian Gulf with Shia leaders being in key positions failed. Not only was Iran not able to help these regimes establish themselves, but Iran antagonized the ruling elites that remained in power. Support for terrorists resulted in international isolation, although the support for these terrorists may have helped to consolidate the new government in Iran itself (Crenshaw 1995b: 23). Iran's connections with attacks on Westerners, including hostage taking by Hizballah in Lebanon, meant that Iraq received support from other countries as well. Concern expressed by the administration of George W. Bush about Iranian support for terrorism is evidence of the continuing costs of these policies. Thus, Iranian support for terrorism abroad has had very real costs.

CASE STUDY 4.4

The United States and the Contras in Nicaragua

In July 1979 the Somoza regime in Nicaragua was overthrown. The broad-based opposition had been led by the Sandinistas, a group with a leftist orientation that took its name from a guerrilla leader who fought against the regime put into place by an earlier US involvement in Nicaragua in the 1920s. The Sandinistas gradually eased out of power the other groups that had participated in the struggle against the Somoza regime, concentrating leadership into their own hands. The United States increasingly came to see the regime in power as a leftist authoritarian regime with links to the Soviet Union and its allies. One disturbing indicator was the fact that the military forces in Nicaragua were linked to the Sandinista party, not the state. Thus, the armed forces were organized as the Popular Sandinista Army, not the Nicaraguan Army, indicating that the primary loyalty

BOX 4.2 Cuba as a state sponsor

Cuba has remained on the US list of countries that support terrorism. Currently there is little evidence that Cuba is actively supporting any terrorist activities. In the 1960s, the government of Fidel Castro aided leftist guerrilla movements throughout Latin America, and these groups at times used terrorism as part of their attacks on the existing political system. The level of support dwindled over time, and by the 1980s Cuba was doing little more than providing a refuge for former guerrillas and dissidents from various parts of Latin America. While the government has no doubt continued to sympathize with leftist groups in Latin America, it has provided no meaningful support. The collapse of communism in the Soviet Union meant that Cuba lost its major backer to supply funds and direction to dissidents in the Western hemisphere. Domestic policies and attitudes in the United States explain why Cuba is still on the list, not the level of actual activity.

of the military would be to the party, not to the state. Many in the Sandinista leadership had determined that a neutral, apolitical army was not possible—the armed forces had to be politically controlled in order to avoid a situation in which the military could threaten the government (Pastor 1987: 199–200). As a consequence, doubts developed about the likelihood that there could be a peaceful transition of power from the Sandinistas to opposition groups should they win an election. In fact, the Sandinistas did win a majority in elections that were held somewhat later than promised in 1984. The government used various means in its power in that election to make it difficult for opposition parties to field candidates, mount campaigns, and have an effective chance of winning.

All of the above characteristics did not really distinguish the Sandinistas when in power from any of the other authoritarian regimes in power in Latin America. US concern was present because the regime clearly had a leftist tinge, and the government in fact proceeded to develop close ties with Cuba and the Soviet Union and its allies. The United States also (with justification) charged the regime in Nicaragua with providing aid to the leftist forces in El Salvador that were fighting against the government of that country. Thus, there appeared to be a danger that the creation of an antagonistic, leftist regime in Nicaragua would lead to increased leftist rebellions and the establishment of more such regimes elsewhere in Central America. As a consequence, the United States was predisposed to support groups attempting to bring about the end of the Sandinista regime.

The initial opposition forces drew heavily upon members of the military under Somoza (Barry *et al.* 1988: 89). As such, they suffered from linkages to the old regime, which had become increasingly brutal and generated such widespread opposition that the effort to remove the regime had had tremendous popular support. Military activities against the Sandinistas were few and largely ineffective. Somoza himself provided the necessary leadership for these forces to undertake any action at all. His assassination in Paraguay in 1980, probably by leftist groups in South America rather than by Sandinista operatives (Pastor 1987: 217), removed a key leader from these forces. The opposition forces were thus in some disarray when President Reagan began his administration. The United States through the Central Intelligence Agency (CIA) began to supply increasing support to the opposition forces that came to be known as the Contras (counter-revolutionaries from the Sandinista perspective, hence Contras). Arms, training, food, medicine, and general funding came to the remaining forces in neighboring Honduras. Events in Nicaragua led to additional groups at least tacitly supporting armed opposition to the government in Nicaragua, and even some persons prominent in the initial uprising against Somoza came over to the Contra side. With increasing

US support the Contras did become a more effective military force. US support was very important for the Contras, but the members of the units drew upon some real dissatisfaction with the Sandinistas, especially from peasants in the countryside (Barry *et al.* 1988: 89; Landau 1993: 61). The Contras engaged in both guerrilla attacks and terrorist activities. In effect, their incursions into the country were a combination of such actions, a fairly common situation in such insurgencies. The incursions proved to be relatively unsuccessful, notwithstanding major US support.

While the Contras were able to draw upon some real opposition to the Sandinistas in Nicaragua, they ultimately damaged their cause by the types of activities they undertook. When the military incursions were frequently ineffective, and the Contras were never able to establish a safe base area within Nicaragua, Contra movements into the country increasingly focused on undermining the Sandinista political structure and on terrorizing the population. They murdered villagers who had any connection to the Sandinistas or who appeared to support the government. Government officials were killed, and torture and rape were routinely used against civilians. Murdered officials included teachers, doctors, relief personnel, and other officials attempting to follow through with reforms in the countryside (Calvert 1997d; Landau 1993: 39–46). The Contras were attempting to demonstrate that the government was incapable of protecting its citizens. The murder of government officials would make it more difficult for the Sandinistas to control the countryside or to rally support by the effective implementation of policies that were popular. Ultimately, these terror tactics were ineffective. The Sandinistas proved to be strong enough to prevent the Contras from controlling the countryside, and news of the atrocities created adverse public opinion in the United States to such an extent that the US Congress enacted laws limiting aid to the Contras.

In the fighting between the Contras and the Sandinista Popular Army and local defense forces, the Contras had one advantage that is normally not present for insurgents fighting against regular military forces. The Contras were provided with sophisticated weapons, and in many cases they were better armed than the Sandinista forces (Kornbluh 1987: 25). While the better weaponry did not permit the Contras to win many battles, it did mean that it was also very difficult for the government forces to win clear-cut victories. The US support created a military stalemate, at least in the short term, where neither side was likely to win. The guerrilla insurgency by the Contras, and the terror associated with it, did destabilize the Sandinista regime. The economic reforms that had been promised with the overthrow of Somoza were in many cases never started or in other cases undercut by the fighting (Conroy and Pastor 1988: 220). The government had to divert resources to the military, and government officials attempting the reforms were often the targets of the Contras. The fighting placed a great strain on an economy already facing difficulties (Calvert 1997d: 443). As a consequence, the government suffered a loss of support due to its inability to deliver on its promises. The reforms may or may not have been productive in the long term, but they never had a chance to succeed or fail. As a consequence, when a reasonably fair election took place in 1990, the Sandinistas fell from power. Their electoral defeat was due to a variety of factors. There had remained groups opposed to the Sandinistas from the beginning and other groups that also became opposed after the Sandinistas had consolidated power in their own hands. Some were willing to vote for a change of government since so many Sandinista programs had not worked. It was clear to many voters that if the Sandinistas were defeated, US support for the insurgency would end, the Contras would de-mobilize, and US aid would be available to repair much of the damage of the war. Another factor of major importance was the decline of the Soviet Union as a major power. With the Soviet withdrawal from Eastern Europe and the manifest problems the Soviet Union was facing, it was unlikely that the Soviet Union could continue to serve as a counterweight to the United States.

The support provided by the United States to the Contras was eventually effective. They remained a military force and a threat to the Nicaraguan regime. Even when they were not launching attacks or when the attacks were defeated, the Sandinistas had to divert resources from other areas of government activity to deal with them. It is also evident that without such US support the Contras would have been much less of a threat to the government in Nicaragua. Since the Contras drew upon concerns and dissatisfaction with the Sandinista government felt by people in Nicaragua, the Contras were not a group that was created by the United States. Without US support, however, the Contras could have faded into relative insignificance since the Sandinistas had sufficient resources to deal with an unsupported insurgency. They had the goodwill and support of much of the population for the overthrow of Somoza, and they also received sufficient external aid from Cuba and the Soviet Union as additional resources. The US support was clearly sponsorship, and US "advisors" had tremendous influence with the Contras (planning some of the missions for them), but the movement fell short of being a US creation (Kornbluh 1987: 25). At a case before the International Court of Justice in The Hague in which Nicaragua brought charges against the United States, a majority of judges ruled in 1986 that the United States was guilty of breaches of international law for its support for attacks against Nicaragua. The court also ruled, however, that the Contras were not just an instrument of US policy (i.e. they had a domestic base in Nicaragua) and that the Sandinistas had indeed been aiding the insurgents in El Salvador (S. Kim 1987; Pastor 1987: 257, 376n).

CASE STUDY 4.5
North Korea

North Korea (Democratic People's Republic of Korea) has been one of the countries consistently included on the list of nations that the United States has considered to be supporting terrorism. In fact, North Korea was considered to be part of an "axis of evil" by President George W. Bush for its support of terrorism. North Korea has generally limited its involvement in terrorism to Asia, and the terrorist actions in question have been largely directed against South Korea (Republic of Korea), a close ally rather than the United States. Over the decades there has been little doubt that the government of the north has been involved in

attacks on the south. The real question is the degree of government involvement in and support for the attacks, some of which have been very successful.

When the North invaded South Korea in 1950, there were guerrillas operating in South Korea that participated in the attack. The North Koreans infiltrated trained operatives behind the lines of UN troops throughout the military action. These kinds of activities, however, were related to combat situations and attacks were generally focused on military personnel and facilities. At the end of the Korean conflict with the boundaries roughly where they were before the start of the war, North Korea had to adopt different techniques for maintaining pressure on the government of South Korea. North Korea moved from conventional warfare to unconventional warfare in the 1960s and later decades, including terrorist attacks. In the early years of what could be termed a Cold War between North Korea and South Korea, the north relied largely on infiltration of trained operatives into the south to engage in sabotage and other actions, including those that could be considered terrorist in nature. The attacks were often against civilians, forcing the government in the south to tighten security and divert resources from other areas (Kirkbride 1994: 63–9). North Korea also maintained extensive tunnel complexes in the demilitarized zone separating the military positions of the north and south to infiltrate personnel into the south. These infiltrators, however, were extensions of the North Korean military and intelligence agencies rather than a reflection of an indigenous dissident movement. In fact, North Korea developed a special division of operatives (the VIII Special Purpose Corps of the army) for "service" in the south (J. Kim 1988: 314).

At the same time, the North provided support when it could to various opposition groups in South Korea. The government in the south, despite the presence of democratic institutions in some time periods, was largely a non-democratic system in the 1950s, 1960s, and 1970s. Instability in the ranks of civilian parties led to frequent interventions resulting in governments led by generals or dominated by the military. The opposition groups sought to democratize the system and protested about the limitation on democratic rights in the country. The continuing pressure from the north via infiltrators and terrorist attacks had the effect of strengthening the role security forces played in South Korean society and making infringements on the rights of South Koreans more likely. The North Korean attacks could be seen as an effort to force the capitalist, military-dominated system to reveal its true repressive colors. North Korea aided the dissidents when possible since their activities could potentially weaken the South Korean government, and there were at least a few agents of the north involved with the political opposition. In these times, the north could always maintain a pretense that their system of government was more open and democratic than that of the south. (In actuality, of course, North Korea was one of the most regimented and least free political societies in Asia.)

By the 1980s, Korea was in the process of making the transition from its largely authoritarian regime resting on the military and the government bureaucracy to a democratic system with open elections where the opposition had the opportunity to contest for and win political office. With these events, support for dissident groups and the general opposition provided less advantage to the north. While terror attacks and sabotage continued (Kirkbride 1994: 69–71), North Korea then shifted to attacks directed against the South Korean leaders and the government in general. There have been a series of assassination attempts directed against South Korean presidents. In August 1974, President Park Chung-hee survived an attack that killed his wife (Nahm 1988: 414–15). In another spectacular action, North Korea detonated a bomb in Rangoon in Burma in 1983 that was directed against the President of South Korea. While five cabinet members were killed in the bomb attack, the president survived (Kirkbride 1994: 73). Burma was a convenient location, with less security, for launching an attack against the political leadership of South Korea.

The most spectacular attack after the bombing in Rangoon was an attack on a Korean airliner in 1987; the plane was destroyed, with all 115 on board being killed. The three people who planted the bomb were all North Koreans, recruited specifically for this operation. One, an actress in the north, was the daughter of a North Korean diplomat. This bombing would have

to qualify as state instigated action carried out by agents of the north, directed, in effect against its neighbor. The goal of the bombing was to discourage attendance at the Seoul Olympics and to limit the benefits that otherwise would come from increased tourism and tourist spending (Harmon 2000: 158–9, 213). The intent was to indirectly weaken the government of South Korea by reducing the economic benefits of hosting the Olympics. Lowered attendance at the games could also be used for propaganda purposes by the north in an attempt to demonstrate that the south had not been accepted within the international community as a secure or well-governed country.

Most of the activities noted above were undertaken by agents of North Korea or southerners who were working in extremely close contact with specific agencies of the government of North Korea. As such, these actions are more examples of state-directed and controlled activities with a relatively small amount of state support for South Korean domestic terrorist groups. North Korea also supported dissident groups from other countries. Approximately thirty training camps for terrorists have been maintained in the north for many years. Over 5,000 individuals from more than 60 countries have passed through these facilities, learning a broad range of unconventional tactics and terrorist techniques (Kirkbride 1994: 71). These camps have provided the individual terrorist with a chance to learn important skills from knowledgeable instructors in relative safety. North Korea had links with the Japanese Red Army group, a leftist terrorist organization that operated throughout the world. This support was part of a general struggle with the Western capitalist countries that provided North Korea intelligence agencies with potentially useful information and access to supportive networks elsewhere in the world.

More recently, North Korea has limited its overt support of terrorist groups in general and reduced its own attacks against the south. The economy of the north has all but collapsed, and North Korea itself has been in need of international aid and humanitarian relief to prevent starvation and famine. As a consequence, in 1995, the government officially repudiated the use of terrorism and support for terrorist groups

(Richardson 2000: 210). Clearly the costs of continued support for terrorism have come to be far larger than the government can currently afford to pay. Since most of the actions that had previously been "supported" originated with the government itself, they were relatively easy to stop. North Korea has forsworn terrorism for the moment, but the government that ordered the previous attacks is unchanged, and its willingness to denounce terrorism may only be a temporary tactical maneuver. What makes potential future support or terrorist activities by North Korea of greater concern is the fact that North Korea has or is close to having a nuclear capability that could make potential attacks in the future more devastating. Nuclear weapons in the hands of North Korea could pose a threat to its neighbors, but there is additional concern that such weapons could be transferred to terrorist organizations. A terrorist group with access to such a weapon of mass destruction could raise the stakes in any terrorist confrontation.

Summary

The above case studies illustrate the range of state support for terrorism that is possible. While non-state actors are involved in an overwhelming percentage of significant terrorist attacks, state involvement in terrorism can still be important (Badey 1998: 102). North Korea has most clearly involved itself in state directed and controlled terrorist activities. The kinds of actions undertaken were similar to the activities of the CIA, the KGB, MI6 (of the United Kingdom), and other agencies during the Cold War. Terrorism became a common aspect of foreign policy during the Cold War, and it continues to be important even with the end of the Cold War (Harmon 2000: 152–3). India and Pakistan continue their Cold War with both aiding terrorist groups in the other country. Israeli efforts to track down and assassinate individuals targeted as terrorists fit into this category as well. Many other nations, including Iran and Iraq, have also used state agents to attack

dissidents abroad as part of strengthening the domestic regime. Some of the support by other countries for various groups was designed to further foreign policy goals, as was the case for the Iraqi and Iranian support of dissidents and terrorists on each other's territory during their long war. Syrian aid for groups during the Lebanese civil war and Libyan support for attacks in Europe, including the bombing of the Pan Am flight over Lockerbie, are other examples of countries using their own agents to pursue policy objectives. It is important to note that such foreign policy objectives can be wide-ranging and include a wide variety of goals, increasing the possibility that state support might be available.

The United States' support for the Contras provides an example of state sponsorship that was important to the continuation of a dissident organization. It is possible that the Contras would have faded into insignificance, especially after the assassination of Somoza. The Contras might have survived for a period even without support since the "counter-revolutionary" movements in Eastern Europe and the Soviet Union managed to survive for a number of years despite the negative consequences of US and British support. The US foreign policy goal of establishing a friendlier regime in Nicaragua was ultimately achieved by its support of the Contras. The examples of Italy and Hungary in Yugoslavia and Iraq and Iran in the Middle East are typical of the willingness of governments to use existing dissident groups to further their foreign policy aims. The dissident groups in Yugoslavia, the MKO in Iran, and the Shia elements in Iraq, for example, already existed. The MKO and the Croat nationalist groups obviously benefited from such foreign aid. Iraq and Iran, as well as most of the Arab countries of the Middle East, have supported the PLO or other Palestinian groups. Their support in terms of funding, arms, and safe havens has been important in many cases, but Palestinian opposition to Israel was never dependent on foreign support for its continuation.

Support by Iran for Shia groups in the Gulf area has been religiously motivated in terms of helping co-religionists. While it is true that Shia Islamic Republics in the Gulf area would have been of some benefit to Iran as a country, the assistance seems to have been determined more by religious similarity than by hopes of any immediate benefits for Iran. Support for the Shi'ites in Lebanon would seem to have been based on the same kind of religious linkage since greater power for Shi'ites in a state as small as Lebanon would be unlikely to be able to provide any significant foreign policy advantage for Iran. Further, support for the Islamic government in the Sudan and for political parties rooted in Islam in many other countries in the Middle East would seem to be religiously motivated rather than grounded in any perception of specific Iranian national interests.

In none of the above cases was state sponsorship or support associated with the use of weapons of mass destruction. Car bombs, bombs on airplanes, and other kinds of attacks do cause high numbers of casualties, but the state supporters would appear to have avoided providing terrorist groups with biological or chemical weapons. Clearly countries do have such capabilities, much more so than dissident or terrorist groups. North Korea is considered to have a nuclear capability while not necessarily having built working nuclear weapons; Iraq has used chemical weapons and has claimed a biological capacity; and the United States, of course, has access to all of these weapons. To provide a dissident organization with such weapons, however, would invite world condemnation for the supporting country and make retaliation possible. The benefits of doing so would normally be outweighed by the costs. As a consequence, to some extent it is possible that state sponsorship provides a check on the worst kinds of attacks by terrorist groups. At the same time, however, lesser types of attacks may still be aided.

Further reading

Dillon, S. (1991) *Comandos: The CIA and Nicaragua's Contra Rebels*, New York: Henry Holt.

Green, J. D. (1995) "Terrorism and Politics in Iran," in M. Crenshaw (ed.) *Terrorism in Context*, University Park, PA: Pennsylvania State University Press, 553–94.

Hoptner, J. B. (1962) *Yugoslavia in Crisis: 1934–1941*, New York: Columbia University Press.

Kirkbride, W. A. (1994) *North Korea's Undeclared War: 1953–*, Seoul: Hollym.

Shultz, R. H. Jr (1994) "Iranian Covert Aggression: Support for Radical Political Islamists Conducting Internal Subversion Against States in the Middle East/Southwest Asia Region," *Terrorism and Political Violence*, 6, 3: 281–302.

Terms

Abu Nidal organization	Macedonia	Sandinistas
Ba'ath Party	Mujahedin-e-Khalq	Shia
Bakhtiar, Shahpur	(MKO)	Somoza, Anastacio
Bekaa Valley	National Liberation Army	Sunni
Black Hand	(NLA)	Utashe
Contras	Pavelich, Ante	
false flag attacks	Popular Front for the	
Hamas	Liberation of Palestine-	
Hizballah	General Council	
Hussein, Saddam	(PFLP-GC)	
Islamic Jihad (Palestine)	Revolutionary Guards	

Chapter 5

Religious justifications for terrorism

Terrorism and the world's religions	64
Case studies	73
5.1 The Zealots in Judea 73	
5.2 The Sikhs and Khalistan 74	
5.3 Algeria in the 1990s 78	
5.4 Aum Shinrikyo (Supreme Truth) 80	
5.5 Osama bin Laden and the al Qaeda network 82	
Summary	85
Terms	87
Further reading	87

With the turmoil and conflict based in the Middle East and attacks against the United States at home and abroad, religiously based organizations using terrorism have been in the spotlight. Religious justifications for violence, however, are among the oldest ones in the world. Religion is one important source of group identity that can provide for unity in a community (Juergensmeyer 1996: 5). Given its ancient roots, it will be discussed first from the types mentioned in the classification in Chapter 2. Before the nineteenth century, religious justifications for violence, including terrorism, were the most frequent (Rapoport 1984: 659). The religious justifications for terrorism, of course, are not only ancient but also contemporary, meaning that such causes underlying the use of violence have been very long lasting in the history of humanity. Religious wars and crusades have been among the most devastating and costly conflicts in history. Loss of life in these kinds of conflicts often was higher because those believing in a different religion could be killed with impunity from any religious sanctions whereas members of the same religion would be better treated in a war situation. In some religious wars the clear intent was to eliminate the other religious group. Conquest or conversion were not seen as real options.

Any list of religious wars would be very lengthy indeed, and there has also been domestic political violence resulting from religious differences. A minority group might fear that a centralizing state could undermine its beliefs and the cohesion of the community (Nandi 1996: 180). Religious discrimination by the majority could very easily result in the violent defense of the minority's beliefs (Fox 1998: 46). In some cases a government might initiate the violence to repress a religious minority that could be seen to be unreliable or a community that could revolt in the future or join with a foreign enemy. In other circumstances minorities might seek to defend their status or even their opportunities to practice their beliefs by launching attacks against adherents of the majority religion in a state. This kind of violence might be designed to secure rights for the minority or to lead to separation of the group from the parent state. In rare cases the violence might even be directed at establishing or re-establishing the minority religion as the dominant one in a society. In England after the establishment of the Church of England, Catholics were viewed as an untrustworthy group likely to serve foreign (i.e. papal) interests and re-establish the former dominant religion.

Terrorism can also involve groups that are part of the dominant or majority religion in a country. Such groups may resort to violence in efforts to reinforce or reinvigorate the purity of the religion or force the government to base domestic laws and actions on religious precepts. Legal systems in virtually all countries reflect the cultural effects of the dominant religious affiliations of their people or their elites, but there may be members of the dominant religion who want to imbed their values more forcefully and more deeply in society. As such, these types of groups are most frequently seeking to change the policies of their political leaders. Sometimes they may desire a change of leadership from the ungodly to the more spiritually worthy as well. Much less frequently, major changes in the form of government to correspond to religious standards may be the key objective of the groups. They may, for example, seek to create a theocratic state where religious leaders have the final word on what is permissible and possible within the country.

Terrorism and the world's religions

More extreme forms of religious attitudes have appeared in many religions, and frequently the phrase religious fundamentalism is used and misused to identify terrorists. Many people in the world would qualify as religious fundamentalists. They follow the precepts of their religions with devotion, they attempt to avoid sin, and they practice virtue according to their religious values. They may also take a literal interpretation of their particular set of holy scriptures. They may seek to convert by example or to be more active in their efforts to spread their faith. They may choose to vote for or support "virtuous" persons in the government or political elite. These religious individuals would qualify as fundamentalists, and they might accept that label as well, but they would not use violence to bring about the imposition of their religious values in society. Among religious groups, leaders and institutions often actually promote inactivity rather than activism among their followers (Fox 1999). Obviously, not all fundamentalists are terrorists or even potential terrorists. Similarly, not all terrorists fighting under a religious banner would need to be fundamentalists. Dissidents seeking to defend their religion from state repression may resort to violence in self-defense. The persons involved in the Warsaw Ghetto uprising against the Germans in 1943 were not all fundamentalists. Further, it would be difficult to regard their revolt as anything other than justified. Extremist—although a word with a negative connotation—might be a more precise term to use with regard to religious terrorists instead of fundamentalist since they are the individuals willing to go to extremes for their beliefs, although violence in self-defense is not really extremism.

Fundamentalist groups opposed to a variety of practices and modern attitudes have appeared within the Christian community. Some of these groups have been willing to use violence to reach their objectives. Many Christian groups have supported anti-abortion protests in the United States. These groups have usually practiced passive resistance and demonstrated in front of clinics offering abortions. The vast majority of the participants in these protests have been opposed to violence, but a handful has been willing to try more active efforts to limit the availability of abortions. Frequently, this activism has taken the form of vandalism and other damage to property. Glue is placed in locks, windows are broken, the automobiles of clinic workers are vandalized, and such like. This kind of vandalism and harassment is designed to make clinic operations more difficult. Some of the protesters have graduated from petty vandalism to the use of bombs, which are intended to cause only damage to property, even though, at times, individuals have been seriously injured by accident. All of these activities have been effective to some extent. Clinics have closed or the hours of operation have been limited. The attempts to limit abortions have succeeded indirectly in some cases. Insurance costs for clinics providing abortions have risen so much that some doctors have ceased to provide the procedure. In other cases, landlords have refused to renew leases for clinics and offices where abortions are performed, or even where abortion counseling is offered, because of the fear of damage to their property (Perlstein 1997: 544). The bombings may have been the most important in this regard since such attacks are the ones most likely to lead to increased costs and generate fear amongst the relevant property owners. In a few cases, the violence has escalated to assaults on individuals. Doctors and other clinic workers have been attacked or murdered. Between 1991 and 1995 there were five murders and eleven attempted murders (Griset and Mahan 2003: 113). This type of violence has been relatively rare, and, when it has occurred, it has been committed by individuals or small groups rather than the large organizations. These attacks have clearly been designed to instill fear in wider audiences. Sometimes, there is an implied threat to all persons involved in providing abortions—you could be next! The persons thought to be involved in such attacks or murders have frequently been difficult to capture, even when they have been identified. It has been apparent in the United States that there have been groups that have been willing to aid the activists in escaping from punishment for the assaults and murders.

Extremist violence has developed within Judaism. Jewish groups in the British mandated territory of Palestine utilized terrorism in their independence struggle, but this struggle was much more of an effort at state creation (i.e. national liberation struggle) than religious terrorism. In Israel today there are political parties that seek to incorporate religious ideas into the

BOX 5.1 Army of God

The Army of God is a rather shadowy, anti-abortion organization in the United States that was apparently founded by the Revd Mike Bray. The group has claimed responsibility for a number of bombings of abortion clinics. Bray himself was involved in some of the bombings and seems to have initiated the use of the name Army of God. He may also be the author of an underground manual on anti-abortion activities with that title, which has been distributed to activist groups. In addition, he has provided justifications for the use of violence to stop abortions, and he has defended bombings, assaults, attempted murders, and murders undertaken to achieve this goal. Several persons associated with Bray have been involved in murders or attempted murders. He has indicated that one important advantage of the violent attacks is that they dissuade persons from offering abortions. The violence should not be retribution but serve as a deterrent to future actions (Juergensmeyer 2000: 21–4). There is no doubt that he has hoped to encourage violence against abortion clinics and providers, and there is a great deal of evidence that he has been successful. There seem to be many anti-abortion activists who have volunteered to serve in the Army of God and who have adopted the terminology. Of course, no formal membership has been required to join. The network of like-minded individuals associated with the Army of God has become a form of leaderless resistance. There are indications of links between the Army of God and more formal organizations. The lack of formal organizations protects the leaders but still permits indirect collaboration and direction (Griset and Mahan 2003: 115). In addition, the impression of an organization gives greater weight to activities and encourages a belief that the group is larger and better supported than it actually might be.

government and legal system and even to create a theocracy based on Jewish religious practices (Pedahzur 2001b). More extreme groups have appeared as well. Members of these organizations see themselves as God's Chosen People with a duty to implement God's law (at least according to their interpretations). This worldview permits them to use a wide range of actions since their goals are in keeping with a divine plan (Hanauer 1995: 251–2). Control of the lands in the region that corresponded to the Biblical Kingdom of Israel are seen as part of this plan since God gave the Jewish People all of the lands, including Judea and Samaria (the West Bank) and the Gaza Strip (Hoffman 1998: 103–4). As a consequence, they are opposed to any arrangements to create a Palestinian state in the territories controlled by Israel. Extremists in the settler movement launched terrorist attacks against Arabs in the Occupied Territories, and some even hoped to stop the Israeli withdrawal from the Sinai Penin-

sula in return for peace with Egypt (Sandler 1997: 144). Gush Emunim, a settler group, has long practiced vigilante violence against Palestinians, justifying these activities as part of a new conquest of the land of Canaan (Sprinzak, 2000: 219). There have been other groups that have planned and launched attacks against Palestinians in the West Bank and Gaza, seeking to force them to migrate from the region (Partrick 1997b).

There was also an attack in 1994 by Baruch Goldstein, a Jewish extremist, on Muslim worshippers at the Mosque in Hebron. Goldstein, who was religiously motivated in his desire to make sure that Israel included the West Bank, killed twenty-nine Muslims and wounded many others before he was killed. The Mosque occupies part of the area of the former Jewish temple from the times of Solomon, and has been a focus of contention and confrontation for decades. Rabbi Meir Kahane, an Orthodox American rabbi from Brooklyn, found political support in Israel for extreme views. He justified violence against both Israeli Arabs and Palestinians since the Arabs were eventually likely to attack Jewish citizens of Israel. He argued for driving all Arabs out of Israel and the Occupied Territories (Hoffman, 1998: 101). His views also had a clear racist tinge since he feared that Arabs would sleep with Jews and defile the Jewish nation as a consequence (Pedahzur 2001b: 29). He formed a political party and won two seats in the Israeli parliament. Baruch Goldstein was a member of the party and a student of Kahane, and he was a candidate on the party list in 1983 (Brownfield 2000: 111).

Kahane's views were so extreme that he was eventually denied his seat in the Israeli Parliament. While back in the United States he was murdered by a Palestinian resident in the country, but parties espousing his views have continued to be represented in the Israeli parliament. Other groups have resorted to violence and terrorism against Israelis in their efforts to preserve the state and to secure it from any possible threat. Israeli protesters against their country's involvement in Lebanon became targets for violent attacks by supporters of the invasion (Sprinzak 2000: 223). The assassination of Yitzak Rabin in 1995 for

BOX 5.2 The Assassins

One early Islamic group that practiced political terrorism as a matter of policy was the Assassin sect. The Assassins were an unorthodox Shia sect that appeared in the eleventh century and flourished into the thirteenth century. As an unorthodox minority in an era where religion was a defining characteristic of individuals they faced periodic repressions due to their beliefs. Given their precarious position, the sect used assassination as a weapon against the rulers who represented the Sunni majority. Rulers or governors that sought to suppress the sect would be targeted for political murder to dissuade the continued attacks. The assassinations were essentially a defensive response to protect the members of the sect (Rapoport 1990: 150). The Assassins were successful in killing a number of high-ranking officials (Andriolo 2002: 737). They were almost always successful because escape for the individual committing the act was not an issue. The Assassin believed that his death in the act of political murder would result in immediate entrance into paradise. The deaths of the rulers, governors, or military officers proved to be effective in protecting the sect, especially with the obvious target audience. Sometimes the potential target was even publicly warned of his impending death. If the targeted official changed policy, so much the better. If the target persisted in the attacks on the sect, he was assassinated and the Assassins appeared to be that much more powerful. It has been suggested that the Assassins also used hashish (assassin is a word originally derived from the term for hashish eater) to bolster their resolve in the assassination attempt. While normally considered to be fact, such a policy would be unlikely since individuals under the influence of a narcotic were unlikely to be very effective in undertaking the attack.

The Assassins are an important example because they were so effective. They preserved their sect against a much larger body of more orthodox Muslims for centuries by the selective use of violence and terror. The public as well as leaders and high officials knew the extent and successes of the assassination campaigns, even in a time when there was no mass communication—the news still spread to the relevant persons. Mass media outlets were not essential for the successful communication of fear to the appropriate audiences (Wilkinson 1997: 674). Religious doctrine was important in strengthening the resolve of the individual members, and religion provided them with a reward in the next world for their sacrifice in protecting their religious community. The power base of the Assassins was eventually undermined by the Mongol invasions, which disrupted many states throughout the Middle East.

making concessions to the Palestinians is the most prominent example of such religion-based terrorism. His assassin used religious views to justify the attack. What was perhaps more disturbing to many was the fact that a number of radical settlers in the Occupied Territories supported the assassin (Rathmell 1997c: 357). There have been other threats against Israeli supporters of Palestinian rights or those in favor of peace negotiations (Rathmell 1997c: 356).

Within the Muslim community religious violence has occurred as well. The division between Shia and Sunni within Islam has led to some violence (see Box 5.2). Most attention recently has been focused on the religious extremism of the Muslim community today directed against the West and the concept of jihad or holy war invoked by various leaders. The focus on jihad as a special form of warfare has obscured the real meaning of the word for Muslims. A more accurate translation of jihad is that of striving. First and foremost, it refers to personal striving to achieve the ideals of Islam as a way of life. Second, it means striving in the sense of improving the religious situation for the community of believers. Finally, it refers to striving in the sense of converting non-Muslims and carrying the word of God to the unbelievers. This last striving can refer to the necessity of using force to convert those who do not believe. Thus, at least in theory and in terms of theology, jihad has limits on what it can justify (Esposito 2002: 157). Of course, there are those within Islam that focus on conversion by the sword and selectively use the Qur'an to justify what they are already predisposed to do. The frequent appearance of jihad in the names of their organizations clearly is intended to indicate their support of violence to achieve their ends, not their support of personal reflection. Thus, while jihad has many meanings, dissident organizations do use it to mean holy war. There are some militants among Muslim clerics who have gone so far as to argue that holy war against non-Muslims is an essential tenet of the practice of Islam (Bouchat 1996: 343). The majority of theologians in both branches of Islam, however,

do not agree that such violence is justified, either between Sunni and Shia or against Christians or Jews. Many Muslim groups, including those that would be considered fundamentalist, do not subscribe to these views and do not participate in the violence. In fact, a majority of all Muslims do not accept the principle that God sanctions violence and the use of terror (Kibble 1996: 362). Of course, it is not necessary for all Muslims or a majority of Muslims to subscribe to the idea that violence is essential or justified. A minority of believers is all that is necessary to supply the recruits for the violent groups that practice terrorism. Two of the factors that have led people to see a connection between Islam and violence are that Muslim societies are seen as more likely to be in the Third World and to be conducting national liberation struggles. These liberation struggles, either against colonial powers or governments perceived to be in alliance with the outside world, led to greater violence (Kennedy 1999: 17). The mobilization of Muslims from around the world to battle against the Soviet troops in Afghanistan was also a spur to Islamic radicalism and the spread of violence as the volunteers returned to their countries after the Soviet withdrawal. The emphasis on religion was particularly important since these volunteers were mobilized on a religious basis rather than an ideological one (Khashan 1997: 8).

Difficulties in Islamic societies have risen when Muslim groups have sought to install the Shariat as the basis of the legal system in the country. The Shariat is based on the Qur'an and the life and examples of the Prophet Muhammad and the early Muslim community of believers. The more fundamentalist political groups seeking to have strict adherence to the Shariat serve as the basic law of the land. All other laws must be in accord with the holy scripture and cannot contradict it. The Shariat has been established as the precise basis for law in the Islamic Republic of Iran, the Sudan, and Afghanistan under the Taliban. Large elements of the Shariat have been directly included in the legal system of Pakistan as well. While it is a significant portion of the law in many other Muslim countries, many governments in power in the Middle East, have frequently relied on legal systems based in part on Western or secular principles. Conflict has thus been created between Muslims who are in favor of strict interpretations of their scriptures and more modern groups in society. These conflicts have resulted in the repression of those out of power (either secular or religious) and violence and terrorism against those in power (either secular or religious).

The religious fervor of Islam has also been associated with suicide bombings, especially by Palestinians and by other Muslims as well. Islam does not directly condone suicide, but it accepts self-martyrdom in the right cause. There has been a tradition of suicidal assaults in the Muslim communities of Southeast Asia. As Muslim territories were incorporated into non-Muslim colonial empires, attacks by individuals occurred in an effort to achieve better treatment for other Muslims at the hands of the foreign occupiers. To some extent these tactics were successful in leading the colonial government and prominent individuals to treat local Muslims more fairly (Dale 1988). Hamas in its struggle with Israel has found suicide bombings to be a very effective weapon given the resources available to the organization (Dolnik and Bhattacharjee 2002). Muslim clerics have argued that this kind of attack is justified because the targets are members of a foreign occupation (Malka 2003: 22). Given the prominence of suicide attacks against non-Muslims today, it is ironic that the first suicide car bombing in Lebanon involved an attack by Muslims against other Muslims (Dolnik 2003: 23).

Other cultures have produced suicide attacks by militant dissidents. Baruch Goldstein surely did not expect to survive his attack on the worshippers at the mosque; furthermore, he left a farewell note (Gorenburg 2000: 204). He has come to be regarded as a hero by militant Jewish groups in Israel (Ranstorp 1996: 42). Early Russian anarchists expected to be killed by their dynamite bombs. Their deaths demonstrated to the public that the attack was political and not criminal (Rapoport 2003: 39). In Romania in the 1930s

select members of the Fascist Iron Guard were part of a group that launched suicidal attacks on those considered as enemies, including opposition political leaders (Berend 1998: 337). Most societies glorify heroic exploits of small groups undertaking military missions against great odds—the aptly named suicide missions. The Spartans at Thermopylae are honored for their bravery in covering the retreat of the other Greeks, even though their decision to stand and fight amounted to suicide. In other armies and other wars the sacrifices of individuals or small units to save comrades are honored rather than being denounced as suicide. Suicidal attacks are not unique to Islamic societies. Modern day examples of suicide attacks are not limited to religious groups. Between 1980 and 2000 more than half of the recorded suicide attacks were launched by the nationalist rebels in Sri Lanka (see Table 5.1). While religious groups have used this tactic, others have as well. The secular, Marxist Kurdish Workers Party has launched more attacks than many of the Islamic religious groups in the news today. More recently, elements of secular, nationalist Palestinian groups have begun to use suicide attacks (Dolnik 2003: 25). These secular groups have even been willing to use female bombers whereas the Islamic religious organizations have not (Nacos 2003: 2). Like other activities, suicide bombings are a technique open to many different types of terrorist groups.

Extreme views have also appeared within Hinduism, and religiously motivated violence has resulted. Violent defenders of the Hindu culture go back to the 1920s when the Rashtriya Swayamsevak Sangh (RSS—National Patriotism Organization) began training paramilitaries. A RSS member assassinated Mohandas Ghandi because he was willing to compromise with non-Hindus on the new state of India (Juergensmeyer 2000: 95). There have been Hindu groups and political parties that have sought to have Hindu practices (Hinduvata) incorporated into national law since a large majority of the population of India is Hindu. The Bharatiya Janata Party that promotes Hindu practices has become the largest religious and

TABLE 5.1 Number of suicide attacks, 1980–2000

Group (Type)	Location	Number of attacks
Liberation Tigers of Tamil Eelam (Ethnic)	Sri Lanka/India	168
Hizballah and pro-Syrian Lebanese (Religious)	Lebanon, Kuwait, and Argentina	52
Hamas (Religious)	Israel	22
Kurdish Workers Party (Ideological/Ethnic)	Turkey	15
Palestinian Islamic Jihad (Religious)	Israel	8
al Qaeda (Religious)	East Africa	2
Egyptian Islamic Jihad (Religious)	Croatia	1
Islamic Group (Religious)	Pakistan	1
Barbar Khalsa International (Religious)	India	1
Islamic Army Group (Religious)	Algeria	1

Source: Radu 2002: 280

nationalist movement in the world (Juergens-meyer 1996: 6). The party moderated its use of Hindu themes in the election campaign of 1998, but it did not offer any real assurances to the religious minorities of increased tolerance (Chandra 1999: 65–6). These efforts correspond to the attempts by Muslims to have the Shariat as the basis of national law or of groups in the United States to have Christian principles more directly incorporated into national and state laws. To them, secularism and equal treatment of all religious groups effectively denies equal treatment for Hindus who are the majority. The cow is a sacred animal for Hindus, and one of their goals has been to have national law prohibit the slaughtering of cows or the eating of beef. Incorporation of this belief and other practices into national law would clearly have effects on other religious communities in India.

Efforts at promoting the Hindu religion have gone further than pushing for incorporation of religious practices into national legislation. There have also been pressures on Christians (Greenway 2001: 90). Efforts have been made to reclaim sacred sites on which other religious groups have established mosques or worship centers. More extreme Hindu groups like the RSS have organized efforts where the buildings of other groups have been torn down and Hindu temples erected in their place. These efforts represent a campaign to remove the evidence of the Muslim presence and rule in Hindu India (Jha 1994: 253). Efforts to demolish the existing buildings have at times generated violence between the Hindu and other religious communities. For the Hindu extremists this violence has had a positive outcome since it has led many Hindus in the region to identify with the Hindu majority and support the religious position of the political leaders (Austin and Gupta 1990: 8). The extremists feel that members of the minority religions should be reabsorbed into the Hindu community (Greenway 2001: 91), and some have carried their actions even further. They have fomented communal violence directed at the religious minorities, sometimes with the support of local authorities. Not only Muslims have been affected by these actions. Christian missionaries have been murdered because they were attempting to convert Hindus. The intent has clearly been to indicate to members of at least some religious minorities that they are not necessarily free to practice their religion and that overt community religious practices are not necessarily going to be permitted. Migration or conversion, rather than persistence in minority religious practices, would appear to be the goals desired by these Hindu groups.

Pressures from religious extremists can generate communal violence in other circumstances. Fighting has broken out between Christians and Muslims in Indonesia and Nigeria. In Indonesia, internal migration has resulted in Muslim migration into largely Christian areas of Sulawesi. Local extremists who have hoped to gain by the dominance of their religious community have stoked competition between religious groups, where the Muslims are the national majority but Christians are often a local majority. The end result has been fighting and massacres and terrorist attacks between the two groups. The violence has actually been exacerbated by the appearance of more democratic processes in Indonesia since officials, who have now been elected locally rather than appointed centrally, control significant government resources that can be important for the different religious communities. At least some individuals on each side have sought to use the attacks to drive out members of the other religious community (Rohde 2001). There has been corresponding violence between Muslims and Christians in the Moluccas Province as well. At least some Muslim organizations elsewhere in Indonesia have sent armed supporters and assistance to the local Muslims (Desker 2002: 387). Members of the armed forces and the bureaucracy in this largely Muslim country have aided the movement of these militants to the areas of fighting (Hefner 2002: 760). Their arrival turned the tide in the favor of local Muslims in at least some cases (Abuza 2002: 447). Nigeria has also faced communal violence through its years as an independent country. The military coups in 1966 and the Biafran civil war were triggered in part by communal violence in the northern portion of the country where the Muslim population attacked the Christian Ibo population. More recently, there has been violence in central Nigeria where the largely Muslim north meets the largely Christian south. Cities with mixed population have witnessed the same kinds of violence that has been occurring in Indonesia.

From the above examples it is clear that extreme or fringe groups within many religious communities have used violence. These religious extremists do have some common attributes that go beyond the use of violence and the religious justifications that they draw upon. Many of the more extreme movements and groups have appeared as a consequence of change in their respective societies. Globalization and changing world conditions have generated stress within societies and led people to place a greater reliance on religion to provide mental and psychological support in a changing world. Religious extremism can be a response to the stresses and change that come with modernization and greater globalization (Fox 1998: 51–2). "[P]oliticized religion can be seen as a response to modernity" (Sandler 1997: 134). A greater commitment to religious values is one means of dealing with the threats and dangers that come with changes, and violence is a method that can be used to deal with the forces that the religious communities and others have come to see as the causes of such unwelcome change.

The perception that change brings threats can be seen in the pronouncements of virtually all religions. Groups hearken back to a time in the past when religion played a greater role in society and a time when the values of the dominant religion defined what was and what was not permissible in society. Such groups also define nationality in religious terms rather than ethnic or geographical ones (Hanauer 1995: 248–9). The terrorists see themselves as soldiers in a spiritual army (Juergensmeyer 1997: 16). The past times are often seen as "golden ages" or better times than the present, and change has not been to the benefit of society. Most extreme religious groups see themselves to be battling with secularism (Pillar 2001: 65). The battles against "secular humanism" in the West and efforts to make the Shariat the basis of law in Islamic countries are such efforts. For many Muslims, Western ideas, including Marxism, seem to reflect a different kind of secular humanism that is designed to undermine the religious and moral values of Islamic society. For Jewish extremists, there is the call for the re-creation of a Jewish state within the boundaries established by the Kingdom of Israel in the Old Testament days, combined in many cases with efforts to make the laws of Israel more closely correspond to the religious precepts of Orthodox Judaism. In the case of the Hindu groups there has been the effort to limit foreign influences, represented especially by Islam and Christianity, and to purify the country by officially establishing Hinduism as the state religions or incorporating distinctly Hindu traditions into state law.

The mobilization of groups to practice violence in reaction to the threat of change from the outside may result in terrorist actions being carried out in third countries or for attacks against foreign targets in their own countries. Foreign actors in the outside "contamination" are often associated with the changes that threaten the local religious values. If the foreign support can be removed, then it will be much easier to force the local, godless elites from power (Juergensmeyer 1997: 181). Foreign elements may even be seen as groups that are attempting to proselytize and convert locals to a foreign religion, thus destroying the position of the domestic religion. Western interactions with countries in the Middle East and India have introduced changes, some of which have conflicted with local religious traditions and practices. Western countries have also frequently been more comfortable with the more secular, "modern" political elites that are in power. Not surprisingly, they have frequently supported the leaders who are bringing their countries "into the twentieth century." Further, Western countries have brought in missionaries who seek to convert local populations to Christianity. As a consequence, foreign targets will frequently seem to be very appropriate to many religious groups in non-Western parts of the world when they resort to political violence.

It has been suggested that religious groups that resort to terrorism may be more willing to inflict mass casualties with their attacks, especially when the population is composed of unbelievers. An analysis of terrorist attacks that resulted in 25 or more fatalities in the 1980s and 1990s found that over half of the attacks were undertaken by groups with religious motivations (Quillen 2002). Religious terrorists may also see themselves as following a higher law that they see as superseding normal rules or behavior (Fox 1998: 49). The "unbelievers" are seen as having placed themselves outside the boundaries of the protected community, and may even be considered potential sources for weakening the belief of others. Members of such religious terrorist groups see themselves engaged in a struggle between good and evil, and any outsider is evil (Cronin 2002/3: 41). Religiously motivated terrorists may also be less likely to appeal to an uncommitted audience since they are less likely to convert or win over that part of the population (Hoffman 1995: 272–3). If the religious terrorists see God as being the audience for their actions, they may be less interested in public reactions to a large number of deaths (Crelinsten 2000: 186). Religious dissident groups may also have beliefs that call for the purification of their society. The rites of purification necessary to re-establish the ideal society may lead to actions that are designed to cause a large number of casualties as part of the process of purification. Such apocalyptical views may require massive rather than selective casualties. However, while groups with clear religious motivations have undertaken some attacks resulting in mass casualties, other such attacks have not been launched by religious groups; furthermore, not all religious terrorist groups seek to inflict mass casualties (Parachini 2001: 399).

Huntington (1993) has suggested that the world may be facing a "clash of civilizations." Religion-based terrorism might be especially deadly because it is likely that the great conflicts of the future will occur between different cultures, and it is the major religions that help to culturally define the dominant civilizations in the world. The current civilizations are based in Western Christianity, Latin Christianity (South and Central America), Orthodox Christianity (Russia and Slavic Europe), Confucianism (China and other Asian countries), Shintoism (Japan), Hinduism

(India), and Islam. Clashes at the borders of these civilizations (fault lines) are more likely than clashes within any one civilization. Further, clashes between civilizations are more likely to be sustained in time and more costly than the clashes that occur within a given civilization. While the clashes between the cultural areas are not strictly religious, different religious values underlie the cultures and civilizations of the world. Militant Islamic rhetoric emphasizes these differences when it proclaims that Islam's value is higher than Western ideas (Khashan 1997: 8). Many (but not all) of the recent conflicts with religious elements can be seen in the regions where two or more civilizations or cultural areas meet— Bosnia (Muslim and Orthodox and Western), Israel (Western and Muslim), Nigeria and the Sudan (Muslim and others), and the Indian subcontinent (Hindu and Muslim among others). Once conflict has broken out in areas where religions and cultures meet, there have been local leaders willing to mobilize populations on the basis of their religions and associated cultures. There have even been some indications that terrorism has shifted from being within the same general cultural area to occurring along the fault lines and between such cultural areas (Weinberg and Eubank 2000: 98–9).

Case studies

Five case studies are presented dealing with religious based terrorist activities. The activities of the Jewish Zealots in the Roman Province of Judea before the revolt in 66 CE is one of the earliest examples of a focused campaign of terror directed towards particular political ends. The other examples are more recent and include the outbreak of religious based violence in Algeria in the 1990s, the terrorist and guerrilla campaign of the Sikhs in India to gain greater autonomy or even an independent state, the activities of the Aum Shinrikyo sect in Japan, and the activities of the al Qaeda network associated with Osama bin Laden.

CASE STUDY 5.1
The Zealots in Judea

Zealot has come to refer to someone who is fanatically committed to a particular cause. The term goes back to the first century of the current era when members of the Jewish community in the province of Judea in the Roman Empire sought to liberate their country from alien rule. These efforts eventually resulted in the Jewish Revolt that lasted from 66 to 71 CE. Although Judea was a small province in a large empire, an earlier revolt under the Maccabees, while Israel was part of the Greek state founded by the successors of Alexander the Great, had succeeded. The intent of the Jewish rebels, who came to be known as the Zealots, was to repeat this victory and to force out the Romans, as well as the Greeks who had come in their wake. The Zealots saw the uprising as a necessary preliminary step to divine redemption. They were "profoundly religious patriots" (Applebaum 1971: 169). The Jewish community had to be mobilized for the revolt to pave the way for a new religious state that would follow (Rapoport 1990: 152–3). The religious, rather than the national, character of the uprising was obvious when the Idumeans, Jewish by religion but not one of the tribes of Israel, were brought in as allies against the Romans (Josephus 1981: 252–63).

The Zealots, as well as other militants known as the Sicarri (daggermen) because of one of their weapons of choice when dealing with opponents, first had to convince the Jewish community to support their intended rebellion. They had to intimidate those who opposed the idea of rebellion or who sought to compromise with Rome. Compromise was in fact quite possible since the Romans were quite willing to defer to local religious sensibilities in this period of time. To achieve the objectives of a unified community in favor of revolt, the militants mounted a *campaign* of assassinations. Moderates in the Jewish community, including priests, merchants, and other members of the elite who had benefited from Roman rule, were assassinated, usually in broad daylight. The choice of open attack, often in crowded surroundings, demonstrated the capabilities of the militants and the vulnerability of those who disagreed with them. The assassins were often able to escape, but they were also willing to suffer the consequences if they were caught. The real targets were the entire Jewish population of the region and potential opponents. As Josephus (1981: 147), who was an observer on the scene at the time, noted: "More terrible than the crimes themselves was the fear they aroused."

The Roman response to the campaign of assassinations was initially subdued as the local provincial authorities sought to avoid inflaming local religious sensitivities. Eventually, however, confrontations between crowds of demonstrators and Roman troops resulted in heightened tensions. Riots and panic resulted, and many Jews lost their lives, further inflaming local opinion (Rapoport 1990: 154–5). Eventually, the rebellion that was sought by the Zealots broke out. The opposition had been silenced and support for the revolt was solidified. When the fighting broke out, there was virtually no opposition from the population or pro-Roman elements. The rebels quickly gained control of Jerusalem and much of Judea, and even defeated the initial Roman force sent against them. The rebellion, however, was crushed. Jerusalem was captured by the Roman legions in 70 CE, and the last strongholds of the militants were taken in 71 CE. Judea was then reabsorbed into the Roman Empire.

The revolt, based in the religious values of the Zealots and the population in general, ultimately failed even though the terror campaign to generate the revolt was quite successful. The rebels could not maintain the independence of the region in the face of the Roman legions. Had the revolt been assured of success, there probably would have been very little opposition among the Jewish population. As it was, the issue was in doubt for at least the first years of the revolt. The relative weakness of Jewish military resources vis-à-vis the Empire eventually became obvious when Rome mobilized sufficient resources to deal with the uprising. Even so, it took a major campaign and a long siege of Jerusalem before the revolt was broken. During this time Rome was experiencing its own internal difficulties. In 68 CE a revolt by the legionary commander in Spain resulted in his overthrow of the Emperor Nero. This new emperor himself was overthrown in 69 CE, and finally Vespasian became the generally accepted emperor. He was in command of the Roman forces subduing Judea and besieging Jerusalem when the troubles began, but his departure for Rome did not disrupt the campaign (Grant 1974: Chapter 7). Had his task been more difficult or had he faced possible defeat, the forces in Judea might have been withdrawn (leaving Judea to be re-conquered at some future time). In later centuries, the civil wars and succession struggles in the Roman Empire or pressures on the imperial frontiers made it possible for provinces to break away permanently or for periods of time. Unfortunately for the Zealots, Roman politics were not sufficiently chaotic at the time of the revolt to permit success.

CASE STUDY 5.2
The Sikhs and Khalistan

India is a very diverse country. There are numerous religious, linguistic, ethnic, and regional groups in the state. When independence came in 1948, British India was divided into Pakistan and India. Communal violence broke out between Muslims and Hindus; this meant that many Muslims relocated to Pakistan and virtually all Hindu residents in areas that became part of Pakistan left those areas. In the new, smaller India, there were still significant numbers of Muslims, who constitute the single largest religious minority in the country. Religious tensions between Muslims and Hindus have been present through the decades, and there have been outbreaks of communal violence between members of the two groups during that time. In addition, there are other religious minorities in the countries, including the relatively small (in percentage terms) Sikh and Christian communities. The many linguistic groups in India have caused problems as well. There are over twenty languages that each have at least 1 million speakers. In the northern part of the country, much of the population speaks Hindi or related dialects and languages. In the southern part of the country, the local languages are Dravidian, a completely different language group that is unrelated to Hindi. There have been efforts to promote Hindi as a national language, and these efforts have naturally generated tensions among the speakers of the other

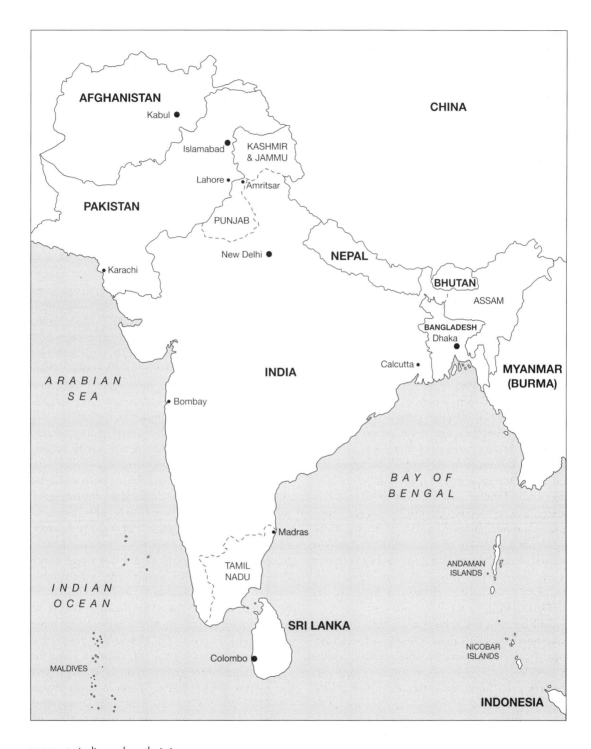

MAP 1 India and south Asia

languages. English remains as an important *de facto* national language that is understood by elites from the different regions, and has the advantage of not providing special advantages to any of the language groups in the country.

Given the tremendous diversity of groups that exists in India, it is not surprising that the country has had to deal with communal tensions and violence. Various groups have provided the personnel for attacks against the government, and in some cases the communities have targeted each other. The Sikhs have been one of the religious groups that for a time presented serious problems for the central government and the preservation of national unity. While the Sikh religion draws heavily upon Hinduism, it has other elements included as well. Most, but not all Sikhs, consider their religion to be distinctive from Hinduism rather than simply a variation within that rather broad religious community. Sikhism is monotheistic, and it never accepted the Hindu caste system (Nandi 1996: 180). Under British rule and the early years of independence, there was little conflict between the Sikh and Hindu communities. In the 1970s, however, problems began to develop, especially in the province of the Punjab. While Sikhs are present in many areas of India, they were geographically concentrated in this province. The cities contained Hindu majorities, but the countryside was overwhelmingly Sikh. Elements of the Sikh community came to see themselves as being marginalized in their own land. Part of the reason for concern among the Sikhs was the increasing demands by some political parties to have Hinduism play a more important part in the country. While this drive to implant Hinduism in the state generated tensions principally between the Muslim and Hindu communities, the pattern was disturbing for the Sikhs as well (Unnithan 1995).

Sikh concerns led to political protests. The Indian government did make some concessions to Sikh feelings. Provincial boundaries were redrawn so that a new, smaller Punjab province had a clear Sikh majority. The Sikhs, however, remained divided amongst themselves—sometimes on the basis of the old caste lines, so the government and other parties were able to divide the Sikh vote to prevent the Sikhs from controlling the province (Nandi 1996: 184). For

example, the government headed by Indira Ghandi and her Congress Party covertly supported Sant Jarnail Singh Bhindranwale who created a new party to challenge the dominant Akali Dal party. Support for this party weakened the Akali Dal, which had cooperated with other parties in opposing the Congress Party (Long 1990: 60). This effort to divide and conquer failed when Bhindranwale became the leader of one of the more important terrorist groups.

In the early 1980s, after he failed to achieve a dominant position in the province through electoral politics, Bhindranwale advocated political violence. He especially attracted as his followers the young and educated, who hoped to re-create the former Sikh periods of glory (Yaeger 1991: 227). His followers began to engage in terrorist actions. A large number of other groups (well over a hundred) appeared and became involved in terrorist actions in the 1980s and the 1990s (Wallace 1995: 357). Many of the groups sought to achieve an independent Sikh Khalistan ("Land of the Pure"), while some appeared willing to accept a de-centralized Indian state in which the Punjab would be dominated by the Sikhs and would have great control over domestic policies. The various groups engaged in typical terrorist operations, including bombings, kidnapping, assassinations, and attacks on the security forces. Among the targets were Hindu inhabitants in the Punjab. The attacks were designed to force other Hindus to flee the area, and in this effort they were somewhat successful, although the terrorist groups never were successful in instigating full-scale communal violence between the two religious communities. Various terrorist groups also attacked moderate Sikhs who were willing to compromise with the government. Bhindranwale and his followers established their headquarters in the compound containing the Golden Temple of Amritsar, the most holy site for the Sikh religion. While Indian authorities knew that members of the terrorist group were present, action was deferred given the religious significance of the temple to all Sikhs. After the failure of negotiations Prime Minister Indira Ghandi ordered a military attack (Operation Blue Star) on the temple compound in 1984. After much fighting and destruction the compound was captured. More than 1,000 persons were killed, including Indian troops, guerrillas, Bhindranwale and members of his organization, and hundreds of Sikh pilgrims who happened to be present at the time of the assault. While the assault was a military success since it eliminated many guerrillas and terrorists and a key leader of the dissidents, it was a political disaster since it alienated many members of the Sikh community who had previously been neutral or even favorably disposed towards the central government.

The assault on the Golden Temple led to additional complications. Later in 1984 Prime Minister Ghandi was assassinated by two of her Sikh bodyguards in retaliation for Operation Blue Star and the sacrilege that it represented. In the aftermath of Ghandi's death, riots broke out in northern India in which Hindus attacked Sikhs and their businesses. Thousands of Sikhs died in the rioting, in many cases while the police did nothing and the military remained in their barracks (Pettigrew 1995: 8–9). These deaths further increased the antagonisms between the Sikh and Hindu communities and drove more recruits into the ranks of the various independence organizations that were practicing terror. The death of Ghandi had another, somewhat indirect, effect. With her demise, the ruling Congress Party lost some of its cohesion, and various opposition parties gained ground. The Congress Party had generally tried, at least to some extent, to generate mass appeal by crossing over ethnic, religious, and regional boundaries. As such it was often a force for integration in India, and it usually, but not always, avoided appeals to specifically Hindu nationalist elements. In the troubled times after Ghandi's death, the party lost ground, and the more parochial Hindu nationalist parties gained strength. The presence of these parties that promoted Hinduism as the national religion in government led many Sikhs to see their religion as being placed in an even more precarious position.

After the assault on the Golden Temple attacks against Hindus escalated. Buses would be stopped and the Hindu passengers would be removed and massacred (Yaeger 1991: 228). Hindus were removed from trains and killed as well (Hoffman 1995: 279). Bombs were set off in New Delhi and other areas of India, taking the battle outside Punjab. Assassinations continued and included the retired general of the Indian Army who had been in charge of Operation Blue Star. Sikhs placed a bomb on an Air India flight in 1985 that exploded over the Atlantic Ocean, killing more than 300 persons. The terrorist attacks in the Punjab also extended to Sikhs who did not support the guerrilla and terrorist organizations and who favored compromise with the government of India. The targets included family members of Punjab police, both Sikh and Hindu. In fact, by the 1990s the targets of the terrorist more frequently included other Sikhs rather than Hindus (Wallace 1995: 355, 399). The leader of the Akali Dal, the large Sikh party favoring "collaboration" with the government, was one of the casualties. The fact that the terrorist groups had shifted their targets to Sikhs in an effort to mobilize support within their own community was one indication of declining support among the very group that they claimed to represent.

The government of India was eventually able to control and contain the worst of the violence in the Punjab, although it has yet to eliminate all the terrorist groups (Wallace 1997: 480). A number of factors came into play in accounting for the eventual success of the government forces. One factor undoubtedly was a certain amount of weariness with the unending violence and uncertainty on the part of the population in general. The government also committed more regular troops and police units to the Punjab, and paramilitary forces were raised to provide some protection against the guerrilla and terrorist forces. Government counter-terrorist techniques also improved. The government relied increasingly on the use of former members of the resistance movements to supply information on their colleagues by either offering rewards or threatening severe punishments. There was also some effort to be more aware of the sensibilities of the Sikh population. A second operation (Operation Black Thunder) to clear the Golden Temple of new concentrations of resistance fighters was undertaken with more care and minimal damage and loss of life to innocent bystanders (Wallace 1995: 398). The government also employed less praiseworthy methods of dealing with the dissidents. There is considerable evidence that the government relied on murders and assassinations (i.e. death squads) to remove leaders and members of the dissident organizations, avoiding the necessity of supplying proof in any judicial setting. There were even questionable deaths among many human rights activists and others who queried the government methods for dealing with the dissident movements in the Punjab (Gossman 2000; Pettigrew 1995: Chapter 1).

The government also attempted to maintain better control on the border with Pakistan. Punjab province borders on Pakistan, and the Indian government long claimed that Pakistan was supplying arms to the organizations opposing the central government (thereby explaining the persistence of the dissident Sikh groups). There was relatively little evidence to indicate that Pakistan consistently supplied arms or major support to the various movements in the Punjab as a matter of policy. On the other hand, looking the other way when Sikhs acquired arms in Pakistan was an effective and inexpensive way of discomforting a potential enemy. A number of Sikh separatist organizations in exile also currently have headquarters in Pakistan (Chima 2002: 33). A more important source of aid for the dissidents over the years came from the Sikh communities in Europe and North America. Sikhs in these areas have provided funds and other aid for the groups opposed to the central government. Such support, while important in the armed struggle, was insufficient to achieve victory or to make continuation of the battle an attractive alternative.

By the mid-1990s the Sikh insurrection and attacks had largely been contained. The violence and efforts to create an independent Khalistan had failed. While immensely disruptive of the ordinary routine of government of the Punjab province, little was ultimately accomplished. Sikh parties returned to the political arena and participated in the usual political exchanges. They bargained with the other large parties, trading their support in the national legislature for projects and other benefits for the Punjab. It was politics as usual, with vote trading and efforts at gaining more national funds for local projects, something that is often the core of political compromise in democracies. Some armed groups still remain, but they largely become bandits rather than groups of political dissidents (Chima 2002: 33). Dissident Sikhs assassinated Punjab's chief minister in 1995 (Juergensmeyer 2000:

91), but the attack did not trigger a new outbreak of violence. Many or most Sikhs could again become concerned about their future or the future of their religion in India. The rise in strength of Hindu nationalist parties, seeking to impose national policies that would limit the religious minorities in the country, or the increase in violence by Hindu fundamentalists could create the necessary concern and foster new violence. Should some dynamic leader arise to unite the frequently divided Sikhs in order to achieve short-term goals such as greater local control of provincial resources or long term goals such as autonomy or even independence, violence could erupt again.

CASE STUDY 5.3
Algeria in the 1990s

Algeria has suffered from political violence and terrorism on two occasions in its recent history. During the struggle for independence from France in the late 1950s and early 1960s, the Algerian National Liberation Front engaged in both guerrilla warfare and terrorism in its efforts to become independent. By 1962 independence was achieved, and a civilian government was installed. In 1965, the military intervened to establish an authoritarian system of government that continued to be dominated by officer corps. Until 1989, Algeria was officially a one party system under a series of presidents, all of whom had been former officers. During this period the higher-ranking officers as a group were really the key decision makers in the country. By the late 1980s, economic problems led to increasing domestic unrest, and Islamic movements appeared that gained support among the groups left behind by modernization. Prices were increasing and there was significant unemployment in the country. Declining prices for petroleum products had led to an economic downturn, and there were also problems with corruption and inadequate provision of services for the population (Fuller 1996: 24–6). In an effort to open the political system to greater input, the government permitted the formation of opposition parties and scheduled elections. One of the more important opposition parties formed to contest the election was the Islamic Salvation Front (FIS). The FIS mobilized support on the basis of structuring the legal system on Islamic principles and promoting an Islamic form of government in contrast to the clearly secular regime of the military and the governing party. The FIS was not unified on all issues. Some leaders adopted a moderate stance on tolerating non-Islamic parties and activities, while others advocated establishing the Qur'an as the state constitution, limiting the role of women in society, and limitations on non-Islamic political activity (Willis 1997: 198–200). The FIS and its allies put many of the more clearly Islamic practices and beliefs into practice when they won control of local institutions of government (Stone 1997: 167–8). Confrontations between the government and the FIS led to a postponement of the elections until 1992. When the elections were held the FIS did extremely well in the first round of elections, and it appeared inevitable that it would win a majority of the seats in the next step when there were runoffs for districts where no candidate had received a majority in the first round. The government proceeded to annul the results of the first round of elections, cancel the second stage of the elections, declare martial law, and ban the FIS.

Faced with government repression and the refusal of the ruling party to abide by the election results, supporters of the FIS and others resorted to violence. The political groups that favored abiding by the election results and a more Islamic form of government came together in the Islamic Army Group (GIA) and the Islamic Movement Army (MIA). While the MIA and later successor groups were linked with the FIS, the FIS did not control the violent dissidents. The GIA shared the Islamic view of the FIS but was an independent organization, and one that at times came into direct conflict with the FIS. These groups that resorted to violence and terrorism recruited members of earlier Islamic movements, and drew upon Algerian veterans of the Afghan war against the Soviet Union, as well as Algerians who had volunteered to fight for Iraq in the Persian Gulf War over Kuwait (Fuller 1996: 38–9; Stone 1997: 180–4). The dissident movements used both guerrilla warfare and terrorism. The guerrilla portion of the struggle occurred in the countryside and consisted of targeting the police, security forces, and the military in an effort to defeat the government in power.

The terrorist campaign that was launched had a number of components. The Islamic groups targeted government leaders, members of the governing party, and individuals working for the government. The president of Algeria was assassinated in June 1992. One view was that it was the Islamic dissidents who planned the attack, while another view is that the Algerian military took advantage of the unrest to eliminate a leader who was not vigorous enough in maintaining the system of government (Willis 1997: 263–6). Other attacks were designed to paralyze government services and to make it impossible for the government to provide services in the country. Other groups quickly became targets. Any individuals seen to be supporting the existing system, including journalists who published accounts favorable to the government, might be killed. In fact, Algeria in the 1990s became the most dangerous country in the world for journalists (van Atta 1998: 70). Academics and schoolteachers who continued to go to work and perform their duties became victims. Liberal and secular members of society became targets, including women who were in positions of some authority or who were public figures. Women in Western dress could be beaten or killed on the streets (Maddy-Weitzman 1997: 182). Even schoolgirls who did not cover their heads in approved Islamic fashion were killed as a warning to others (Crenshaw 1994: 278). A point was even reached where family members of personnel in the security forces were targeted (Stone 1997: 192).

The terrorism widened to include other groups that were considered to be providing challenges to the vision of an Islamic government and society in Algeria. Priests and other members of the Christian clergy became victims (Weinberg and Eubank 2000: 103). The potential targets expanded to include Europeans in general (Kibble 1996: 357). Anyone working for foreign companies or foreign technicians employed by the government of were also included (Willis 1997: 282–4). The attacks against foreign workers threatened key sectors of the economy and made it even more difficult for the government to provide goods and services to the population in general. If economic hardships on the population could be increased, the Islamic groups could gain even greater support. The violence and terrorism spread beyond Algeria itself. The opponents of the government launched attacks in France in an effort to convince the French to end their support of the government in Algeria. These efforts included the effort to use the hijacked Air France plane in a suicide attack on Paris. Such attacks have forced a debate about the French policies towards Algeria and about the policies of the Algerian government (Fuller 1996: 46–7).

The terrorist attacks in Algeria soon included the general population as targets. Car bombs and other attacks have taken place in the cities to demonstrate the weakness of the government and to indicate that the opposition could strike anywhere. The violence now included large numbers of everyday Algerians residing in the countryside. Rebel groups attacked villages with some regularity, massacring the inhabitants. These attacks were carried out with extreme brutality, involving torture, rape, and death. Frequently, women and children were not spared in the attacks. The victims were seen as an offering to God (Chalk 1999: 160). The rationale for the villages that were chosen is often obscure. At times the attacks appeared to be designed to draw military units into ambushes. In other cases there was the possibility that the village was regarded as being pro-government. More generally, the attacks seem to have been designed to indicate to the population at large that the government could not protect them. The only choices for the population were death or active co-operation with the insurgents. The massacres of villagers often involved cutting the throats of the victims in order to create even greater fear in the rest of the population (Laqueur 1999: 130). It is possible that the tactics, which involved such extreme violence, were due to a mixture of a conscious desire to spread fear among the general population and the effects of religious zeal (Stone 1997: 191). One factor that makes it difficult to discern the particular goals of any one set of attackers is the fact that the opposition forces were not a single unified group, and different groups were following different strategies. Particularly violent attacks seem to have been undertaken at times to sabotage any chance of negotiations between the

government and some of the rebel groups (H. Roberts 1995: 242). As a consequence, the reason for one extremely violent attack on a village would not necessarily be the same as the reasons for other attacks. There have been some claims that the government staged the massacres to discredit the insurgents. There is no clear evidence of such a government policy, although there have been some instances of overreaction and active repression by the government forces that have contributed to the death toll in Algeria. In the first five years of fighting over 100,000 Algerians died, a death toll as high as it is because of these kinds of attacks by the dissidents (Barker 1997).

While the government of Algeria received external support, there have been some indications that the Islamic extremists have been receiving some foreign support. Iran and the Sudan and foreign groups in other Arab countries provided some aid (Barker 1997). Algerians who have been living in Europe provided some assistance as well. The nature of the violence and the attacks on foreign workers and the population in general, however, tended to solidify support for the government from countries in the West. The actions of the GIA and other groups have clearly played into the hands of those groups that argue about the dangers presented by Islamic groups. To date the government seems to have survived these attacks. With external support the Algerian government has been able to survive, and to even hold a presidential election. The government, however, has been unable to defeat the insurgents totally. Negotiations between the government and the FIS leadership have reduced the violence, and Islamic parties have won seats in elections for the national legislature. Continuing economic difficulties make the achievement of lasting peace unlikely (Testas 2002: 179). In addition, the GIA has still refused to enter into any negotiations with the government and continues the armed struggle.

CASE STUDY 5.4
Aum Shinrikyo (Supreme Truth)

Japanese domestic terrorism hit the world news in March of 1995 when it was discovered that a religious sect had released sarin nerve gas in the

Japanese subway system in an effort to cause mass casualties. Members of Aum Shinrikyo undertook this attack, resulting in a handful of deaths and the need for medical care for thousands. Had the materials used been more potent and the delivery system better controlled, the death toll could have easily been in the hundreds and might even have been in the thousands. The sect had undertaken earlier attempts at chemical warfare, but they had not been successful. The failure of the earlier attempts was such that the authorities had not even been aware that chemical attacks had been launched.

Shoko Asahara founded Aum Shinrikyo in 1987. It was one of many such sects in Japan, and as a consequence it initially received relatively little attention. Religious sects in Japan are given a great deal of latitude with few restrictions on how they operate. In fact, Aum Shinrikyo was actually the first such sect to undergo rigorous investigation (Szykowiak and Steinhoff 1995: 294). The sect, which claimed more than 40,000 members, most of them in Japan and Russia, was dominated by its founder, who basically made all the rules and set the policy for the group (Schmid 2000: 124). Asahara saw himself as the religious leader who had been sent to save the world and who had acquired the supreme truth necessary to do so (Hoffman 1998: 121–2). Asahara hoped to reinvigorate Japanese society and establish a pure and holy society, and he foresaw a world war that would occur as a necessary form of purification. The world must be destroyed in order to be renewed (Lifton 2000: 203). The use of the chemical weapons and the possibilities of a large number of casualties fit within this framework of ideas, which called for apocalyptic actions and sacrifices to create the new pure society of the future. For Asahara it was necessary to destroy the present government and to create a theocratic state that he would lead in order to save Japan (Watanabe 1998: 95).

While the cult was flourishing and attracting new members, it also began to face problems with former members, including legal action, and disputes related to some of its business practices. The members of the cult began to see themselves as victims of persecution by the government and the general population because they had found the supreme truth; they even-tually came to see non-members as dangerous to the group and its religious mission (Watanabe 1998: 87–9). The sect dealt with former members and other threats to the group by murdering the individuals in question (Raufer 2000: 38). Facing apparent perse-cution, the group increased its efforts to develop chem-ical weapons, and it also sought to acquire a variety of both conventional weapons and biological agents abroad, especially in Russia (Harmon 2000: 97). Such activities eventually led to government interest in the sect. Legal difficulties multiplied, and the group was in danger of being prosecuted for a variety of illegal activities. Violence was seen as one means of deflecting government investigations. The group attempted to incapacitate judges who were hearing a case against the group. Wind-borne chemicals were carried to the hotel and made the judges ill; one of them died. The attack was successful in the sense that it disrupted the trial, although the authorities did not realize at the time that a chemical attack had been launched. There were other unsuccessful efforts to use biological weapons and to launch chemical attacks, which may have been tests of the materials available (Lifton 2000: 39–40, 208–9). The failures kept the movement from being detected as the source of the health problems. Once an attack was reasonably successful, however, the source of the violence was traced and the group was shut down. While these attacks were part of a political agenda, they had a practical goal as well—to deflect government atten-tion away from the activities of the sect. The sarin attacks on the subways occurred at a time when government investigations were beginning to bring unwanted publicity to the activities of the group (Crelinsten 2000: 186). Since the gas was released in the subway system in the heart of Tokyo's govern-ment district, it is possible that government bureau-crats were the targets (Tucker 1996: 167). If large numbers of bureaucrats had been killed, the govern-ment might have found it difficult to cope with everyday issues as well as an investigation of the cult.

The Aum sect was noteworthy in that it was an organization that commanded significant resources. The group had sufficient funds, some of which were attained by the fact that members turned over their assets to the organization. The availability of financial resources meant that the sect could create laboratories and undertake the necessary research to create chemical weapons. The group also attracted a significant number of members who had the appropriate scientific or educational training at graduate or postgraduate level to operate the labs. While Aum was able to produce the chemical weapons that it used with these resources, the materials were not of sufficiently good quality to make them very effective (Leitenberg 2000: 156). It is possible that Asahara was forced to use the low quality materials before he was ready because of the government investigations. With more time the researchers might have been able to come up with much more deadly materials. Even so, with major resources and a period of time during which it did not face government scrutiny Aum Shinrikyo was unable to come up with effective chemical or biological weapons. One problem for the group was that it did not focus on just one project. Instead, resources were shifted from one area to another without achieving truly useful results in any one (Rosenau 2001: 296). The use of the nerve gas by the Aum group remains important, however, because it was the first use of chemical weapons in an attack by an organization in a domestic setting as opposed to open warfare.

While Asahara remains in prison for his role in the subway attacks, the cult has not collapsed. Many secondary leaders of Aum could only be convicted of minor offenses since there was no evidence linking them to involvement in the subway attacks or other acts of violence. The sect is currently regrouping, and there is little evidence that the members feel remorse for the attacks (Kaplan 2000: 225). It remains possible, as a consequence, that the group could again resort to the use of biological or chemical weapons in an effort to achieve its goals. The factors that made Aum Shinrikyo dangerous in the past were its wealth and its belief system that accepted, and even promoted, violence. These circumstances have not changed (Cameron 1999: 301). It is likely that, faced with internal dissention or opposition from outside, the sect could resort to the use of conventional weapons to deal with the disloyal or the unbelievers.

CASE STUDY 5.5
Osama bin Laden and the al Qaeda network

Osama bin Laden and his al Qaeda (the Base) network have become very prominent actors in the international terrorist scene. The organization is multinational in terms of its makeup, and has organizations in many countries that are linked to the network while still operating at the national level. It is estimated that there are between 5,000 and 12,000 members in at least 24 different groups. In addition to undertaking joint operations, the groups share resources, provide local contacts for each other, and aid in money laundering (Abuza 2002: 428–9). The organizational capabilities of this group and the financial resources that it has available have been impressive. The various individuals associated with the network have also displayed extreme dedication, especially among those who have carried out the attacks planned by the group. It is believed that there is a council that reviews and proposes terrorist activities around the globe. Bin Laden has provided important centralized leadership and streamlined the decision making process (Nedoroscik 2002: 72). Bin Laden brought a number of important resources to his terrorism campaign that has made him and the network so dangerous. His personal wealth brought considerable financial resources to his violent political activities. Not only has he provided funding, but he has had access to financial channels that have permitted wealthy supporters that are sympathetic to the activities of the al Qaeda network to transfer funds to the organization. Bin Laden obviously has impressive organizational skills to keep the network of groups in the Middle East functioning and cooperating. The coordination required, and the major attacks attributed to bin Laden, are clear proof of his abilities in this area. Among the other resources that bin Laden has brought to his activities are the face-to-face contacts that he had made in previous years while in Afghanistan that have been so critical to facilitating activities among the different organizations and groups in the network. The network also would appear to use modern technology in terms of the internet and computer access to maintain contact with each other (Ranstorp 1998: 323). Such modern technology obviously has permitted anti-government groups to work together without necessarily always coming together. One other advantage that this particular group has is its loose organization. Destruction of one part by local security forces will not threaten the overall viability of the network. The network is unlikely to be compromised by any single penetration by security forces or informers.

Al Qaeda has been responsible for some major attacks. It has been linked to assaults on US military targets including both the attacks on US forces in Somalia in 1993, the bombing of the US barracks in Dharan, Saudi Arabia, in 1996 that killed 19 US service personnel and wounded over 500, and the suicide attack on the US destroyer *Cole* in 2000 in Aden harbor that killed 17 service personnel and wounded 39 others (Alexander and Swetnam 2001: 33). Bin Laden's network was also responsible for the attacks in 1998 on the US embassies in Nairobi, Kenya and Dar-es-Salaam, Tanzania, which resulted in the deaths of over 200 people and the wounding of thousands, most of whom were the nationals of these countries. There is some evidence that the French embassy was also considered as a target in Nairobi in 1998 (Jacquard 2002: 74). Of course, the most deadly attack was the use of the hijacked airliners against the World Trade Center towers and the Pentagon on September 11, 2001. The network was also probably involved in the recent attack on the Israeli tourists at the hotel outside Mombasa. The bombings that targeted tourist areas in Bali in 2002 were apparently undertaken by groups with links to al Qaeda as well. Cells belonging to the network have been discovered in many countries, and local intelligence agencies, security forces, or the police have prevented the planned actions in a number of other locations. One of the characteristics of al Qaeda is that unlike other dissident groups it has no set style of attack. The various attacks have been innovative, hard to detect, and deadly, making the group much more dangerous (Hoffman 2002: 309).

The genesis of the network goes back to the struggles in Afghanistan against the local communists and the Soviet Union. Bin Laden was one of the many Muslims from around the world who went to Afghanistan to fight on the side of the Afghans. At this time, many countries were supplying arms and funds to the Afghan guerrillas, including Muslim countries out of religious solidarity, China as part of a broader foreign policy, and the United States as the primary Cold War opponent of the Soviet Union. Recruits from Muslim countries all over the world made their way to Afghanistan. There were somewhere between 7,000 and 10,000 such Muslim volunteers (Ranstorp 1998: 321). Many of these fighters received training in camps covertly supported by the United States. Bin Laden was able to meet a substantial number of committed Muslims from many countries—the "Arab Afghans"—at a guest house he established in Pakistan near the border with Afghanistan (Alexander and Swetnam 2001: 4). Such face-to-face contacts are extremely important in Middle Eastern cultures, and the opportunities to interact with such committed Muslims from different countries provided a basis for the network that developed. Many of the fighters in Afghanistan and the members of groups in al Qaeda and other networks are from middle or upper class backgrounds and recruited from the Arab or Muslim diaspora in Europe (Friedman 2001: 98, 101). When the former guerrillas returned to their home countries, they frequently became disenchanted with the political policies and activities of their governments, and they joined local Islamic groups seeking changes in policies or leaders, while in other cases they were attracted to struggles by local Muslims against non-Muslim rulers (Fuller 2002: 53). The linkages that had been formed in Afghanistan have permitted continued cooperation and support among groups in different countries.

After the Soviet withdrawal from Afghanistan, bin Laden saw the West, especially the United States, as the greatest threat to Islam. His negative opinion of US policy had a number of causes. The United States is seen as the primary source for the cultural contamination of the Islamic world (Robbins 2002: 355). Members of the al Qaeda network see themselves as fighting against the evil influences represented by the secular cultures of the West. Bin Laden and others see the United States as being responsible for attacks on Muslim populations in many parts of the world, including Bosnia, Lebanon, and Chechnya (Doran 2002: 28–9). For example the United States was seen to have avoided involvement in Bosnia for so long in order that the Christian Serbs could gain ground at the expense of the local Muslims (Pillar 2001: 68). Bin Laden has also been concerned about US policies that favor the Israelis over the Palestinians. The Persian Gulf conflict that arose after the Iraqi occupation of Kuwait became the trigger that made bin Laden turn against the United States. He opposed the UN sanctions against Iraq as well as the presence of Western troops on the soil of Saudi Arabia where the holy cities of Mecca and Medina are located. Bin Laden has seen all of these activities as part of a Christian–Judeo conspiracy, led by the United States, to weaken Islam. The holy places of Islam are targeted for occupation by the Western forces, a process already begun in 1967 by the Israeli occupation of East Jerusalem, which contains the Mosque of the Dome of the Rock, considered to be the third holiest site in Islam (Ranstorp 1998: 325). These issues seemed to have coalesced to lead bin Laden toward seeking a reinvigorated Muslim community, one that could deal with threats to its holy sites, including those from the West, and one that could defend itself.

There is some evidence that bin Laden attempted to acquire weapons of mass destruction. He used Chechen contacts to try to acquire a nuclear device in the former Soviet Union (McCaffrey and Basso 2002: 215). Such weapons would have made threats and demands upon the United States and its allies more effective and credible (Cameron 1999). Clearly, had an opportunity to acquire chemical, biological, or even nuclear weapons presented itself, bin Laden would have taken it. The financial resources available to him would have made such an acquisition eminently possible. Their use would have been quite probable as well, given the willingness already demonstrated to use deadly conventional weapons to cause mass casualties (Wilkinson 2003: 124).

The various components of al Qaeda all involve fundamentalist groups within individual countries, including the Islamic opposition groups in Egypt and Algeria. The targets for the group have included Western countries and their citizens as symbols of outside contamination of Islam and the local govern-

ments and citizens that cooperate with the intrinsically evil outsiders. Attacks on the West are designed to bring about changes in foreign policy. They would like to see the United States and other Western countries withdraw from the Middle East, end support for Israel, and stop aiding the local governments that do not meet with the favor of the organization. The withdrawal would permit the re-establishing of Islamic values and governments. The governments of secular authoritarian states like Egypt, Algeria, and Iraq would be replaced. The conservative monarchies in the Arabian Peninsula, whose Islamic credentials are somewhat suspect, might also be in line for replacement. The resulting Islamic governments in various parts of the Middle East might even combine into the historical ideal of a unified Muslim community that incorporates believers of different languages, nationalities, and ethnic heritages. Islamic principles and laws would then govern this community.

The religious views of the network also explain why the former Taliban regime in Afghanistan had cooperated with al Qaeda and bin Laden. Al Qaeda and other militant groups are not going to disappear even if bin Laden is captured or killed. Some militant dissident groups have been destroyed by security forces to be replaced by others. Revivalist Islamic movements provide recruits for dissident groups, and as long as existing governments in the Middle East continue to repress opposition groups, including Islamic ones, dissidents will be able to attract the disaffected as well (Khashan 1997: 17). The US and allied attacks against the Taliban regime in Afghanistan destroyed the safe haven that al Qaeda had. The losses sustained in the battles in Afghanistan have clearly hurt the network, but many of the key elements were overseas, operating in their home countries or other areas. There are some indications that many of the surviving leaders of the group have relocated to Southeast Asian countries where they have become increasingly active (Chalk 1998a: 127). While hurt by the expulsion from Afghanistan, al Qaeda has continued to operate.

There has been little indication of external state sponsorship of bin Laden and al Qaeda beyond the activities of the former Taliban regime in Afghanistan, in part because bin Laden's own financial resources

BOX 5.3 Abu Sayyaf group

The Abu Sayyaf group in the Philippines is one of the local Muslim terrorist groups with links to al Qaeda. Somewhere between 300 and 500 Filipinos fought in Afghanistan with the Islamic opposition (Abuza 2002: 440). The southern part of the Philippines has a significant concentration of Muslims in a largely Christian country. Various Muslim dissident groups have appeared seeking autonomy or independence from central authority. Abu Sayyaf is one of the latest groups to appear. It is more extreme than some other dissident groups like the Moro National Liberation Front that have been willing to negotiate with the central government to achieve greater local autonomy. The Abu Sayyaf group has kidnapped foreign tourists in the Philippines and surrounding countries. Many of the victims have been ransomed, providing funds for the organization. The group has also launched attacks against Christian clergy, churches, and the Christian Filipino population in general. The group has suffered numerous casualties in its operations, including the death of key leaders, but it has managed to gain new recruits and to continue the struggle (Filler 2002). The group continues to operate throughout the southern Philippines, taking advantage of weak governmental structures, difficult terrain, a population hostile or indifferent to the government officials, and the availability of aid from abroad as a consequence of linkages with other Islamic dissident groups.

precluded the need for such sponsorship (Cameron 1999: 282). There is no evidence of links between Iraq, Syria, or the Hizballah organization with bin Laden, even though these actors have all been involved in some terrorist actions (Posen 2001/2: 54). The Taliban formerly provided bin Laden with a headquarters, but they have relied on the network for financial and military support in turn. The safe haven was important, but the Afghan regime could provide very little in terms of other support such as financial aid, weapons, the support that normally comes from foreign embassies, and the access to national intelligence agencies. It is possible that bin Laden or the members of the network have links with government officials or members of security agencies in other countries. Such linkages would have proven useful in any number of terrorist actions, and it is highly improbable that there are no individuals in government agencies in any Islamic countries that do not feel some affinity with al Qaeda or one of its component groups. There has been no evidence of official state involvement and support for bin Laden that has come to light so far.

Summary

The cases indicate that the use of terror and violence has had mixed results for the dissidents. The Sikhs and the efforts of Aum Shinrikyo have failed. The dissidents involved in the previous violence, however, have not been eliminated from the scene in their respective countries. Aum has reorganized, and it might again be able to rekindle the global conflagration that it sees as necessary for the triumph of the sect. Similarly, the Sikhs may again attempt to create an independent Khalistan. If Hindu majoritarian efforts at dominance increase, such an outbreak could become more likely. The Zealots came close to achieving their goal of independence. The fact that they might have been victorious under more auspicious circumstances (more severe disruptions elsewhere in the Empire) might account for the Roman response to the Jewish Revolt once it was put down. The Temple in Jerusalem was destroyed and the Jews were dispersed throughout the Empire to limit any danger of a repetition of the revolt. The successes that they achieved led to Roman decisions to make another revolt essentially impossible. Such a response by the state in the case of Japan and India, however, has not been possible. Japan cannot really eliminate or disperse a religious sect in the modern world, and any effort by the Indian government to scatter the Sikh population throughout the country would probably lead to an outbreak of the violence that such dispersal would be seeking to avoid. For the Muslim dissidents in Algeria it is too soon to judge the long-term effectiveness of their attacks. It is possible that the regime could still be toppled by the violence. A more likely outcome is the continued role for at least some of the Muslim groups like the FIS. If changes do occur, then the violence will have been partially successful.

The US response to the attacks of September 11, 2001 has hurt the al Qaeda network. The safe haven in Afghanistan appears to have been eliminated, and other segments of the network have found themselves targets for police forces intelligence agencies and will have to deal with greater attempts at their repression. The success of the attacks, such as the bombings of the East African embassies and of the destruction on September 11, can serve to mobilize support in the future. The attacks have demonstrated what is possible to those seeking a Muslim resurgence and assaults against the West. Revenge attacks for other US policies could be more likely in the future. Other networks have appeared. They join together like-minded Islamic groups, not all of which are necessarily part of al Qaeda (Jones and Smith 2001: 280–1). If the United States had withdrawn from the Middle East, as desired by the attackers, violence against Israel and other governments in the region that the dissidents disliked would have increased. In addition, groups in other regions might have sought to undertake similar spectacular attacks to change US policies that they disliked (Reinares 1998: 355). The launching of the war on terrorism, the efforts to find bin Laden and to destroy al Qaeda, the destruction of the al Qaeda regime in Afghanistan, and the recent invasion of Iraq may increase the chances of revenge attacks, including suicide bombings.

In none of the five cases surveyed was foreign support especially important. The Jewish rebels operated with no external support. Al Qaeda and bin Laden had the safe haven in Afghanistan and what support the Taliban regime could provide, but the group had enough resources of its own. Any support from other countries appears to have been minimal, if present at all. Aum Shinrikyo attempted to purchase biological and chemical weapons abroad, but it was unsuccessful. Foreign governments were unwilling to support the group even when there was a financial profit involved. The Sikhs had some assistance from Pakistan in various periods, but never on a massive scale. The Algerian dissidents would appear to have had the most foreign support, and even that was small.

Casualties from the terrorist attacks and related violence were substantial in the case studies. The example of the Jewish Zealots is one of the oldest known, but the leaders of the revolt dealt with opponents summarily when they were plotting the revolt and continued to do so once in power, so the resulting deaths were substantial in number. The death toll from Aum Shinrikyo was small, but the intent of the cult was to cause massive casualties in the population. The terrorist actions of the Sikhs, the Algerian dissidents, and Osama bin Laden have also resulted in significant death counts. It would appear that suggestions that religious groups are more likely to seek to inflict high casualties has been supported by the above cases.

There are some indications that religious terrorism occurs in agreement with Huntington's thesis that the clash of cultures and civilizations is likely to generate violence of a more severe kind. The Muslim dissidents involved in al Qaeda could succeed in the long run if there is indeed a clash of civilizations between the Western culture and the Islamic culture. Osama bin Laden and the al Qaeda network clearly have sought to prevent the intrusion of external cultural values and the contamination of an outside civilization in the Middle East. Regardless of whether there must be an inevitable clash of civilization, the leaders of al Qaeda have attempted to create one (Blackburn

2002: 3). Bin Laden sees the struggle between Islam and the West as such a clash (Hoffman 2002: 308). Indeed, if Muslim extremists choose to wage war against Western civilization, than a clash of civilizations is already occurring (Howell 2003: 160). The clash of cultures was also evident in the violence in Algeria as the Muslim dissidents, especially the GIA, have sought to drive out Western influences. The Jewish Zealots in their own way and their own time did reflect a clash of cultures. The revolt was designed to drive out the Roman and Greek influences and establish the local religion in the face of the pantheistic beliefs of the outsiders. The example of Aum Shinrikyo is less clear. The sect's origin was in part a reaction to modernity, but the violence was within the same cultural area. The violence between Sikhs and Hindus clearly does not fit within this context of clashing cultures. Sikhism and Hinduism are closely related so this prolonged violence has occurred within the same civilization. Thus not all religiously inspired terrorism occurs along the borders of religious based cultural areas.

Terrorism and violence grounded in the religious beliefs of groups have been present in the world in many circumstances. Such actions are likely to continue. In addition to having millenarian visions, they are often unwilling to compromise or reach accommodations with their opponents (Kelly 1998: 27). Such compromises are not possible since the agreements would run the danger of violating key religious beliefs held by the dissidents. To the extent that such violence is a reaction to changes in the world, it will continue because change will continue. Change and globalization will challenge religions throughout the world, and violence is one form of response to these challenges. The clash of civilizations idea has relevance as well, and the differences between different areas are unlikely to disappear in the immediate future. The fact that state support has been limited in at least some cases is one sign that there might be at least a reduced level of religious violence in the future.

Further reading

Alexander, Y. and Swetnam, M. S. (2001) *Usama bin Laden's al-Qaida: Profile of a Terrorist Network*, Ardsley, NY: Transnational Publishers.

Greenway, H. D. S. (2001) "Hindu Nationalism Clouds the Face of India," *World Policy Journal*, 18, 1: 89–93.

Huntington, S. P. (1993) "The Clash of Civilizations?" *Foreign Affairs*, 72, 3: 22–49.

Lifton, R. J. (2000) *Destroying the World To Save It: Aum Shinrikyo, Apocalyptic Violence, and the New Global Terrorism*, New York: Henry Holt.

Terms

Abu Sayyaf group	Islamic Army Group (GIA)	Rashtriya Swayamsevak
Akali Dal	Islamic Movement Army	Sangh (National
Army of God	(MIA)	Patriotism Organization)
Asahara, Shoko	Islamic Salvation Front (FIS)	sarin
Assassin sect	jihad	Shariat
Aum Shinrikyo	Kahane, Meir	Shia
Bharatiya Janata Party	Khalistan	Sicarri
Bhindranwale, Sant Jarnail	bin Laden, Osama	Sikhs
Singh	Operation Black Thunder	Sunni
Ghandi, Indira	Operation Blue Star	Taliban
Gush Emunim	al Qaeda	Zealots
Hinduvata	Rabin, Yitzak	

Rapoport, D. C. (1990) "Religion and Terror: Thugs, Assassins, and Zealots," in C. W. Kegley, Jr (ed.) *International Terrorism: Characteristics, Causes, Controls*, New York: St. Martin's, 146–57.

Stone, M. (1997) *The Agony of Algeria*, New York: Columbia University Press.

Wallace, P. (1995), "Political Violence and Terrorism in India: The Crisis of Identity," in M. Crenshaw (ed.) *Terrorism in Context*, University Park, PA: Pennsylvania State University Press, 352–409.

Chapter 6

Ethnic and national bases of terrorism

Modernity and ethnic conflict   90

Case studies   95

    6.1 The Boston Tea Party 95

    6.2 The Mau Mau uprising in colonial Kenya 96

    6.3 Basque nationalists in Spain 98

    6.4 Dayaks and migrants on Borneo 100

    6.5 Albanians in Kosovo and Macedonia 103

    *6.6 The Palestinian Liberation Organization and the struggle
        with Israel 107*

Summary   111

Terms   112

Further reading   113

While the popular image of terrorism today is that of a religiously motivated suicide bomber, much of the violence that actually occurs in the world is based in disagreements and dissidence in ethnic and national communities (Byman 1998: 149). Ethnic and nationalist violence is one of the basic causes of the increased levels of terrorism in the world in recent years (Chalk 1999: 152). Ethnic confrontations have become more numerous as groups have sought autonomy or independence or the right to attach themselves to some other country. In multicultural societies where ethnic populations intermingle, communal violence has become more common with opposing groups defining themselves ethnically or racially. Not only have ethnic conflicts become more numerous, they have the additional characteristic of often carrying on for long periods of time. Ethnic rebellions and the related violence are persistent (Tan 2000: 268).

While nationalism does not date back to the first century CE in the conventional sense as an inspiration for violence, it is also not totally new. There were indications of national feeling in the struggles of the Welsh, Irish, and Scots against the English monarchs. Persians, Turks, and Arabs did not always peacefully coexist in various Islamic states. Most conflicts in the first millennium CE and beyond, however, had a religious base rather than a national one or represented struggles between various kings, princes, sultans, dukes and others. By the eighteenth century, the stage was finally set for nationalism to become an important force as the ideas of nations began to become more important. Both the American Revolution and the French Revolution clearly involved the development of national feelings and popular mobilization. Once peoples began to see themselves as nations, the possibility of political violence rooted in feelings of nationalism became more likely. The practice of terrorism then became one of the potential tools for any nationalist group seeking to achieve some sort of political autonomy or independence. Changes in government policies remained among the objectives of such nationalist groups, but local self-governance

was often a key. These new nationalist feelings were often based on a distinctive language, but national feelings could also rely on perceptions of ethnic differences and a cultural or political history, including former golden ages as much as language (Tan 2000: 270). For example, the Scandinavian kingdoms of Denmark, Norway, and Sweden developed with distinctive identities based on their histories. Their languages were similar, their ethnic backgrounds were not tremendously different, all three were overwhelmingly Lutheran, and their cultures had much in common, yet they perceived themselves as separate. The end result was a different national identity for each of these territories, even though provinces could change hands and the populations could be readily assimilated into different kingdoms without too much difficulty, given enough time.

Modernity and ethnic conflict

With modernity, nationalism has emerged more forcibly. It would be useful, of course, to have a clear and precise definition of what constitutes an ethnic or national group, but such precision is not possible. Ultimately, ethnicity or national identification will be self-defined by the groups in question. All that is necessary is that a group sees itself as being unique. And, if a group perceives that it faces disabilities because of ethnic or national differences, the potential for violence, and terrorism, exists. In modern times, the use of terrorism by nationalists has often been associated with national liberation struggles against colonial powers. Terrorism may be the first step in efforts to create the national feeling necessary to force the occupying colonial power to consider giving up control of the territory. In a colony the indigenous inhabitants are almost by definition weaker than the colonizing power, making terrorism one of the few violent techniques available if the colonial power ignores peaceful efforts to change colonial polices. When European colonial empires were being challenged after World

War II, nationalist movements lacked the military power to directly confront the European military and security forces, so they had to rely on guerrilla warfare and terrorism.

There were some significant confrontations as the colonial empires were ending. The fighting at times was accompanied by terrorist campaigns. Beginning in 1954, the French in Algeria faced such a conflict. The French were determined to stay in Algeria in part due to the large number of French settlers who had migrated to the area over the years. Thus part of the struggle was between local French settlers (*colons*), 1 million strong and about 10 percent of the population, and the Muslim inhabitants of Algeria (O'Ballance 1967: 24–5). While the Algerian National Liberation Front used a guerrilla insurgency to force France to begin the negotiations that led to independence, an urban terrorist campaign was an important part of the early campaigns against the French. Attacks with knives and guns as well as bombs were directed at police, local government officials, Algerian collaborators, businesses, and the European *colon* population in general. The French had to bring in military reinforcements when the civilian officials were unable to control Algiers and eventually managed to win the "Battle of Algiers." In the process, however, large segments of the Muslim population were alienated from the colonial administration and France, a goal consciously sought by some of the Algerian leaders. The cycle of bombings and retaliations was designed to eliminate any possibility of compromise and to alienate a majority of Algerian Muslims from the French (Crenshaw 1995a: 487). The struggle for independence had increasing support among the Muslim population. After the Battle of Algiers the insurgents continued to use terrorist attacks to supplement guerrilla attacks in the countryside. While the urban terrorism campaign failed in the short run to oust the French, the battle for the cities did ultimately contribute to the independence struggle. The French defeated the Algerian insurgents militarily, but the continued urban terrorism created insecurity for the colon population and led the

French leaders to conclude that continued control of Algeria would be costly and incomplete (Crenshaw 1995a: 499).

The British also had to face terrorism in their colonial empire. In many colonies peaceful demonstrations sufficed to bring about the negotiations leading to independence. In some cases, however, the nationalists resorted to violence to convince the British to leave. In the case of the British Mandate in Palestine, the colonial administration faced a particularly difficult situation. There was fighting between the Arab and Jewish communities in the Mandate before World War II, and the colonial administration became a target for terrorist actions by Jewish groups that were seeking to establish a national state. This three-sided battle continued after the end of the war. Many of the fatalities caused by such attacks were civilians (Hughes 1997: 280). Later, Count Folke Bernadotte, a UN peace mediator from Sweden was assassinated by members of the Stern Gang, a Jewish terrorist organization, for suggesting that Palestinian Arab refugees be allowed to return to their homes as part of a peace settlement (Cooley 2000: 11). Many Jewish groups viewed the colonial administration as being more favorably disposed to the Arab interests and felt that continued British rule would eventually be to their detriment. The attacks eventually convinced the British to withdraw from the Palestinian Mandate since the cost was too high for any benefits that were received from the colonial position. The British withdrawal led to fighting between the Arabs and the Jews and the establishment of the state of Israel. The attacks on the British were successful in their goal of forcing a withdrawal that was probably favorable to the Jewish community. Soon after, in the mid-1950s, the British faced violent nationalism in Cyprus as the Greek inhabitants of the island colony sought union with Greece. The nationalist movement focused on an urban terrorism campaign rather than a rural guerrilla campaign in part because urban terrorism gave the nationalists access to the media and the resultant publicity for the cause of the Greek Cypriots (Hoffman 1998: 58). The

BOX 6.1 The Quebec Liberation Front (FLQ)

Canada experienced a brief period of separatist terrorism in the later 1960s and early 1970s. The Quebec Liberation Front (FLQ) sought to separate French-speaking Quebec from the rest of Canada. The FLQ developed links with some foreign governments, and some of the members of the group even trained with Palestinians in camps (Ross 1995). The group conducted a small number of terrorist attacks to attain this objective. In 1970, a British official and member of the provincial cabinet in Quebec were kidnapped. The Canadian government implemented heightened security measures, and in retaliation the FLQ killed the provincial minister. The murder resulted in public outrage and in an increase in support for government security measures designed to deal with the terrorist threat. The members of the group holding the British official released him in exchange for safe passage to Cuba (Gurr 2003: 208–9). This violent campaign for an independent Quebec quickly collapsed. Public opposition to the violent methods of the FLQ and the fact that the Canadian political system permitted parties advocating independence for Quebec to compete in elections and to win a considerable number of seats limited the appeal of this violent approach. In fact, the strength of the Quebec separatist parties suggests that normal political activities may be all that is necessary to achieve the goal of an independent Quebec at some time in the future. The political strength of the separatists has been too great for many of them to actively consider a technique of the weak, such as terrorism. Should political support for independence in the province decline or the Canadian government prevent secession by extraordinary means, a reliance on terror could reoccur.

attacks caused enough casualties and problems for the British that independence was negotiated, although the desired union with Greece was not achieved since the British were careful to protect the rights of the Turkish minority on Cyprus that did not desire union with Greece. The terrorism campaign and the resulting cost to the British to maintain the colony had led to the decision to withdraw. The decision to leave Cyprus was strengthened by the fact that Egypt had earlier gained its independence and had assumed control over the Suez Canal, and Cyprus then became less useful as a military base.

While colonial national liberation struggles have frequently resulted in terrorism, other kinds of ethnic or nationalist violence exist. Separatist movements have appeared in a variety of other circumstances. A group that somehow sees itself as distinctive will wish to separate from the larger country. French-speaking inhabitants of Quebec wish for a Quebec that is not part of an English-speaking Canada, and a few of them have been involved in rare instances of terrorist violence (see Box 6.1). The Ibos in Nigeria opted for secession when faced with communal violence directed against Ibo migrants living in the northern region of that country. The Ibos lost the resulting civil war that attempted to create the new state of Biafra. Separatist movements of all kinds can lead to terrorist campaigns or other types of political violence. Kurds in Turkey and Iraq, Chechens in Russia, Croats in Yugoslavia before World War II, various non-Burmese groups in Myanmar, and many others have sought independence, relying on political violence and terror to achieve their aims. Dissidents in these circumstances may engage in terrorism in an effort to force a harsh government response against one community, further dividing the society and creating additional support for the dissidents (Gurr and Cole 2000: 89). All these national groups have sought to gain greater autonomy or to become independent, and

the active members of the struggles have regarded themselves as fighters in liberation struggles. Many of the nationalist struggles current in
the world also have a strong religious element that
strengthens the national feeling, but the dominant
political goals of the groups are separatist or
involve efforts to be united with fellow nationalists
(Hoffman 1995: 272). The struggles of the Jews in
Palestine were nationalist even though religion
separated the Jews from the Arabs and the British.
Similarly, the Muslim Algerians and Greek
Orthodox Cypriots had political goals, but not
religious ones.

Ethnic movements may seek to join themselves to some neighboring country that is populated by members of the same ethnic group as
was the initial goal for the Greek Cypriots. Such
movements may invite support from groups or the
government of this neighboring country. These
irredentist movements do not seek independence
or autonomy but absorption into some other
country. The German minority in Czechoslovakia
engaged in provocative acts in their efforts to be
attached to Germany, and the Austrian Nazi Party
and other groups used terror to try to attach their
state to Hitler's Germany. Similarly, Somalis in
Kenya and parts of Ethiopia in the 1970s and
1980s, Armenians in the Soviet successor state of
Azerbaijan, and Serbs in Bosnia and Croatia have
all sought to be united to some neighboring state.
These groups have been willing to use violence
and at times terrorism to attempt to achieve the
goal of joining their fellow nationals.

Violence can occur between different communities within a state, as different groups struggle for
control in regions where they are intermingled.
The majority may seek to repress the minority and
may even try to ban the use of the minority
language and to forcibly assimilate the minority
group. The minority group may be seen as being
a potentially disloyal element. Ironically, the
efforts at repression or assimilation frequently
encourage the outbreak of the disloyalty that the
actions were designed to avoid. The minority may
resort to violence to safeguard its position in the
society that is under threat. Elements of the

majority may then use violence as well, leading to
outbreaks of violence between different linguistic,
national, or ethnic groups. The entire minority
community may then come to be seen as a legitimate target for terrorist actions (Drake 1998:
65). Of course, the minority community comes
to see the entire majority community as a legitimate target as well. Thus violence among intermingled populations breaks out. Hutu and Tutsi
in Rwanda and Burundi have intermingled
throughout the long history of the two groups.
The intermingling of the populations has exacerbated the periods of communal violence between
these ethnic groups. South Africa with black
African, white, Asian, and Coloured (white–black
persons or Asians mixed with others) populations
intermingled was in a similar situation. Geographical separation of the different groups was not
ultimately possible, although the apartheid system
established by the white minority regime was
designed to achieve social separation. As a consequence, when violence did occur it was likely
to be communal in nature. Indonesia has seen
not only communal violence between religious
groups and separatist movements in various areas
but also communal violence between different
ethnic groups. Obviously outbreaks of violence in
ethnically mixed countries remain possible in the
future and related terrorist campaigns will be
possible as well.

It has been suggested that the end of the Cold
War and the decline of ideological confrontations
have led to the increased salience of ethnic
confrontations and possible outbreaks of violence
and terrorism. With the end of the conflict
between the United States and the Soviet Union,
governments in some countries are no longer
being propped up by one of the superpowers as
worthwhile allies. Violence has become more
likely since the governments of former allies or
satellite countries no longer have the essential
external support to deal with local ethnic groups
seeking independence or autonomy. The breakup
of the German, Russian, Austro-Hungarian, and
Ottoman Empires in the aftermath of World War
I led to a significant number of ethnic conflicts and

BOX 6.2 Terrorism and Armenian history lessons

Ethnic violence and terrorism can even occur in unusual circumstances where neither control of a state nor separation is desired. Among the more unusual terrorist groups to appear after World War II were the Armenian Secret Army for the Liberation of Armenia (ASALA) and the Justice Commandos of the Armenian Genocide (JCAG). While the two groups differed in their political ideologies, they shared the same goals, all related to the attempt of the Ottoman Turks to commit genocide against the Armenians during World War I. Eventually over 1 million Armenians (two-thirds of the population of the Ottoman Empire) perished during this time (Fein 1979: 16). Members of these two organizations sought revenge for the genocide. They wanted the Turkish government to acknowledge the genocide—something no Turkish government had done, and they also wanted the Turkish government to pay reparations. Although the two groups operated separately, they often chose the same types of targets. Both groups undertook a number of assaults against Turkish diplomatic personnel and their families (Hoffman 1998: 77–8). Both ASALA and JCAG were seeking to publicize the past rather than to create an Armenian state or an autonomous Armenian region in Turkey. The Turkish massacres had destroyed the potential territorial base for a nation. Those who were not killed were scattered throughout the Middle East and the world. While the activities of the two groups did generate greater awareness of the fate of the Armenians, none of their demands were realized. By the end of the 1980s, the groups had ceased to operate. The appearance of an independent Armenia as one of the successors of the old Soviet Union gave the Armenians around the world a new focus for their attention. A revival of terrorist campaigns against Turkey does not currently appear likely, barring the outbreak of international disputes between Turkey and the new Armenian state.

outbreaks of violence. Violence within the successor states often had ethnic elements since the intermingling of populations meant that any effort to draw borders on ethnic or linguistic lines was impossible. Population exchanges were at times a possibility, but more frequently assimilation, expulsions, or violence resulted. The breakup of European colonial empires created such problems. The dismantling of the Spanish Empire in Latin America has led to boundary disputes that in some cases have still not been resolved. Most of the boundaries in Africa have been arbitrary and represent borders of convenience for the former European colonizers. As a consequence, many countries became agglomerations of different language groups, ethnic affiliations, or former precolonial states. In many cases such groups have been divided by these borders, leaving groups in one state that may hope to rejoin their fellow nationals in some unified country. The former

Belgian Congo (variously known as Congo-Kinshasa and Zaire) has threatened to break apart on numerous occasions and currently is the scene of separatist efforts in many areas and interventions by its neighbors. The difficulties in the West African countries of Liberia, Sierra Leone, and Guinea have been exacerbated as a consequence of the presence of boundaries that have divided different ethnic groups. The Dutch empire in the East Indies was essentially a combination of different states and cultures that was held together by the colonial administration. The government of Indonesia today is still wrestling with problems resulting from the removal of Dutch control over the entire area.

The possibility for increased ethnic or national conflict has also resulted from the breakup of previous empires, and the Soviet Union is no exception. This breakup and the collapse of communism in Eastern Europe both led to ethnic conflict. In the case of Eastern Europe the collapse of communism removed the strong governments that had held ethnic conflict in check. For example, in Czechoslovakia the antipathy between Czechs and Slovaks resulted in the peaceful separation of the two groups, although Slovakia now has some issues involving the Hungarian minority in the country. In the case of Yugoslavia, the ending of the external threat represented by Soviet style communism resulted in an outbreak of ethnic violence and the splintering of the state along those ethnic lines. The sometimes arbitrary boundaries between republics in the old Soviet Union have left virtually all the successor states facing significant problems with minority populations. The revolt of the Chechens is one of the more dramatic examples. In addition, there has been violence and fighting in Georgia, Azerbaijan, and former Soviet Central Asia among others. The successor states have all been less able to deal with these tensions and violence than the old Soviet system (Holoboff 1997). Before the collapse of communism, ethnic outbreaks were dealt with quickly and severely. None of the new states, either in Eastern Europe or in the territory of the old USSR, has yet been able to match the capabilities that were present before 1990. It has even been suggested that parts of the former Soviet Union could replace the Middle East as future generators of violence and terrorism (Pluchinsky 1998: 140).

Case studies

Terrorism based on ethnicity or nationality has been common. The cases examined in detail below indicate the range that such violence can take. The cases include the attacks on property exemplified by the Boston Tea Party prior to the outbreak of active warfare between colonists and the British, the Mau Mau uprising in Kenya in the 1950s, the ongoing struggle of the Basques in Spain for autonomy and even independence, communal violence in Borneo in Indonesia, the

continuing Palestinian struggle to create a nation, and the efforts of the Albanians in Kosovo and Macedonia to achieve greater control of these regions or greater input into the government.

CASE STUDY 6.1
The Boston Tea Party

The prelude to open warfare between the British Crown and the colonialists during the American Revolution was a period that was filled with high levels of political conflict, including occasional instances of violence. The eventual war itself was an early example of a national liberation struggle. The actual war contained some examples of efforts to instill fear in those on the other side and some instances of cruel and inappropriate actions taken against the military or civilian opponents. There were, however, examples of non-lethal terrorism prior to the outbreak of hostilities at Lexington and Concord. The Boston Tea Party is the best-known example of the type of activities that occurred. The planners of the Boston Tea Party had a number of objectives. First, the dumping of the tea was a clear protest against British laws. The tax on tea and the limitations on trade contained in British regulations (which required that tea be purchased from the East India Company) were seen as illegal and oppressive acts by the Crown. The tea was a highly symbolic target, serving to represent colonial dissatisfaction with other policies. Second, the planners were hoping that the provocation would lead to a response from the Crown that would further unify the colonies. The closing of Boston Harbor and the sending of troops to the city rallied supporters throughout the colonies, especially as many colonialists viewed the punishment as an overreaction. The third objective was to intimidate those Americans who were supportive of the English authorities, which included many persons of wealth and property.

The actions in Boston built upon earlier actions designed to achieve similar results. The Tea Party was designed to intimidate these supporters. Mobs, often organized by the Sons of Liberty, forced officials administering the Stamp Act to resign (Leckie

1992: 49). Because of a fear of violence, customs officials had frequently been afraid to enforce British trade policies or to actively pursue those guilty of smuggling (Bobrick 1997: 62). Agents for the sale of the British tea were similarly induced to resign their positions (Leckie 1992: 79). There were other attacks directed against the property of supporters of the monarchy in colonial America (Division of Archives 1926: 33). Protests and riots over taxation and trade laws had broken out as well. Officials and supporters of the Crown were hanged in effigy and their homes and property were attacked (Bobrick 1997: 75). Supporters of the Crown were also tarred and feathered with some frequency (Rapoport 2003: 37–8). The personal attacks were daunting, of course, but all these actions served to indicate that financial losses could occur for supporting the wrong side. Crown supporters in Boston—and elsewhere—were put on notice that their property was at risk if they continued to oppose the goals of the American "freedom fighters" or supported British efforts to deal with the colonial "terrorists." While political discussions and debates over the appropriate course of action that the colonies should take continued with a remarkable level of toleration given the heightened feelings in the colonies, the Boston Tea Party and other actions elsewhere formed an important prelude to the coming battles and kept the loyalists in the colonies on edge—and probably silenced them on some occasions.

The Boston Tea Party and the other actions are examples of terrorist actions undertaken largely against property. The activities were non-lethal but effective. In the final analysis the Tea Party was a successful terrorist act. Local supporters were cowed, and the British authorities were provoked into retaliation. Closing Boston Harbor to trade led to greater colonial unity, and the increasing tensions in Boston and Massachusetts contributed to the outbreak of hostilities. The British government, of course, had little choice but to respond to the dumping of the tea. Doing nothing would have encouraged the colonial dissidents and completely undercut the possibility of gaining support from those elements favorable to continuation of the colonial administration. Britain had been backed into a corner and had to make a choice from a number of poor options.

CASE STUDY 6.2
The Mau Mau uprising in colonial Kenya

Early in the 1950s the British colony of Kenya was the scene of an early colonial national liberation effort. The Mau Mau uprising, however, only involved a portion of the indigenous Kenyan population, and unlike the efforts of the Jewish inhabitants of Palestine or the Greek Cypriots, this effort at revolt was contained and defeated by the British and the local security forces. At the end of World War II, Kenya was a British colony with a limited measure of self-government for the white settler population while the indigenous African population had virtually no direct say in how the colonial administration was run. The European population was concentrated in the highlands around the capital of Nairobi. This area, also known as the White Highlands, was the region of Kenya in which European settlers could avoid the tropical diseases that made residence in other areas of the colony and Africa more difficult. The settlers had appropriated much of the arable land for themselves at the expense of the native population. As African populations expanded, severe land hunger developed, and many Africans began to regard the land distribution patterns as increasingly unfair. Population densities in some rural areas had reached the limit of agricultural subsistence (Walton 1984: 121). There was simply insufficient land in many areas to support the native African population. In addition, many Africans in the areas reserved for Europeans were squatters and had begun to fear that they would be forced off the land. The Kikuyu tribe in the Nairobi region was one of the groups that was negatively affected by the land pressure, and it was this tribe and the related Embu and Meru that provided the recruits for the uprising that occurred.

The term Mau Mau itself came from the oaths that were administered to the dissidents by established members of the groups using the oaths. Such oathing ceremonies had long been used in the past to bind groups together in African communities, and the dissident groups involved in the uprisings resurrected them. There were general oaths of support that were widely used among the Kikuyu population, and later there were more specific oaths for the persons actively involved in fighting against the colonial government. The general oaths were in effect promises of support and prohibited the oath takers from cooperating with the government. The oaths for the fighters banned surrender and prohibited turning on one's comrades in the struggle. The colonial administration considered the oathing process to be an effective one for the dissidents and consequently used native spiritual leaders to perform ceremonies that cleansed individuals of the effects of the oaths, permitting them to stop supporting the rebels or even to change sides and cooperate with the colonial authorities.

The dissidents resorted to violence in 1952, initially with attacks on European property and cattle (Furedi 1989: 110). The violence soon escalated to attacks on Europeans and native officials. The point of no return occurred when the administration declared a state of emergency in the colony and attempted to arrest the dissidents. The resulting campaign by the dissidents was a combination of guerrilla warfare and terrorism. The field units worked out of forested areas or the rough terrain around the Abedare Mountains. Since the Kikuyu and related groups were in the central areas around Nairobi and the European plantations, there were also opportunities for the use of terrorist tactics. There were attacks on isolated European farms, but the most frequent attacks were on local African officials and villages that were cooperating with the colonial administration (Finlayson 1997). The "elimination of Kikuyu who were collaborating with the government was the first priority of the Mau Mau movement" (Furedi 1989: 114–15). Attacks inside Nairobi were often directed against local Africans as well (Lonsdale 1986: 174). The intent was to deprive the local colonial government of support among the African population. These attacks eventually became counterproductive and the British were able to arm and use African auxiliaries in their campaign against the dissidents. Local chiefs, who had benefited under the colonial system, and practicing Christians were the core of the initial loyalists who supported the British (Maloba 1993: 88).

The Mau Mau uprising was also an early example of a loosely networked organization of dissidents. The resulting campaign lacked central direction; instead, it was a collection of a series of local decisions. While there was often a lack of coordination among different groups, it was not possible for the British to destroy the revolt by capturing the leadership. The colonial administration assumed (wrongly) that prominent African political leaders were involved, so they were arrested. The arrests had no discernible effect on the violence except to silence potential voices of moderation. A coordinating committee was created by the dissidents at one point to provide some structure to the revolt, but its directives and efforts were only advisory since it was the commanders in the field who had the real authority. As a consequence, it was not surprising that when the committee was discovered and its members arrested, it had only a small effect on the revolt.

Eventually, the colonial administration triumphed in defeating the Mau Mau. A variety of factors explain the success. The revolt only involved a portion of the colony, and it never spread outside the central areas of the colony. The security forces did not have to deal with unrest throughout the colony. The British had the necessary military forces available to reinforce the local security personnel, bringing overwhelming power to bear against an outnumbered group of rebels. While the initial counter-insurgency efforts were badly planned, the later British efforts were well led and planned. The British military and security forces were also able to use techniques that had proven effective (at least up to a point) in dealing with the rebellion in southern Ireland after the 1916 uprising. While the British eventually conceded independence, the lessons that had been learned in that struggle could be applied elsewhere (Silvestri 2000: 483). Most importantly, the colonial administration was able to separate the guerrillas and dissidents from the local population. Intelligence gathering was improved significantly, permitting the local supporters to be detained and limiting support from the population, and the guerrillas could not survive separated from the support of the population (Maloba 1993: 90). The home guard units that were established defended villages against both guerrilla attacks and terror attacks. It is perhaps significant that the British were willing to arm and rely on local allies rather than automatically distrusting them.

The threat from the Mau Mau uprising quickly peaked. Since the Mau Mau lacked any external support, they were poorly armed and easier to defeat. The lack of a central organization meant that it took time for the authorities to track down the field forces one by one. African support was essential for the British success, and much of the fighting was within the African community. Less than a hundred Europeans, including soldiers and members of the security forces, died in the Mau Mau uprising. Most of the casualties were African. Over 11,000 rebels died in the conflict, while deaths among loyal Africans were approximately 2,000 (Rosberg and Nottingham 1966: 303). The Mau Mau uprising was not successful in forcing the British out. However, the uprising had some part in persuading British administrators, politicians, and others to at least consider the idea of greater involvement for African peoples in colonial governments.

CASE STUDY 6.3
Basque nationalists in Spain

The Basques in northern Spain bordering on the Bay of Biscay and France have always been somewhat distinct from other groups in the country. The Basque language is unrelated to Spanish and probably represents the modern version of the language of the original inhabitants of the Iberian Peninsula before the arrival of the Celts or the Romans. This distinctive language has always served to set apart the Basque people from other regions in Spain. In the early days of the Spanish state the language difference was not an important one since states and allegiances were not defined on the basis of language but rather on loyalty to the dynasty or ruler. The Basque region did have special rules (the furores) that reflected special privileges that they received from the Spanish crown for their support of the state through the centuries. By the twentieth century the Basques had developed strong regional feelings based on their language and culture. The Basque region also remained a stronghold of Catholicism, which placed the region at odds with the more secularizing elements of the Spanish

state. When the Spanish Civil War broke out between the supporters of the Second Republic and the conservative forces (the Nationalists) led by Francisco Franco, the Basques sided with the Republicans against the Nationalists despite the strong anti-clerical stance of the Republicans. The Basque country, however, was separated from the other Republican areas, and it was one of the first areas conquered by the Nationalists. When Franco came to power at the end of the Civil War he eliminated the special regional status of the Basque region and other areas while imposing a strong centralized structure for Spain. The Basque language was even banned as the Franco regime refused to countenance any weakening of the central state and any possibility of autonomy for the Basque region (or other areas of Spain).

More recent Basque opposition to the Franco regime became organized when Euzkadi ta Askatasuna (ETA)—Basque Homeland and Freedom in Euskara the Basque language—was formed in 1959 to contest the centralization policies of the Spanish government (Corrado 1997: 572). While some ETA members were leftist in their ideology and hoped to unite the Basque and Spanish members of the working class, most were nationalists who hoped to unite Basques of all classes while implicitly or explicitly excluding those of non-Basque background. Notwithstanding the leftist rhetoric sometimes associated with ETA, most of the members of this dissident group joined because of their nationalist feelings and desire for an independent Basque state (Jimenez 1992: 111). Differences have continued to exist to the present time, and splits within the nationalist camp have been frequent, but ETA continued to be the major violent dissident organization for the Basques. The divisions within the nationalist camp have weakened the Basques at times, but it has also provided the region with the opportunity to pursue more than one path to autonomy or special rights by providing the government in Madrid, in effect, with a number of options at various time periods. While a majority of the Basques support nationalism in either the form of independence or autonomy, the majority has not supported terrorism as such (Khatami 1997: 408).

ETA did not initially favor the use of violence against the Franco government, but increasing repression in the Basque region in the 1960s led to the decision to resort to violent tactics. The ultimate goal of ETA is independence for the Basque region, including Euskara speaking inhabitants across the border in France. During the Franco period, ETA frequently targeted members of the political establishment and the security forces. ETA even managed to pull off one of the more spectacular assassinations in the 1970s by killing Franco's prime minister. The attacks in the Basque region itself provoked a violent reaction by the state, resulting in the arrest, imprisonment, and torture of many Basques by the central authorities. One result was that new recruits were attracted to ETA in response to the state repression (Woodworth 2001: 6). In this case the state security forces could not eliminate the violence and actually contributed to violence in the future by helping to alienate segments of the population.

The Franco regime had not succeeded in repressing Basque nationalism when it was replaced with a democratic government. With the appearance of a democratic regime in Spain, nationalist activity did not cease. ETA violence was especially great while the political system was in transition. Since the nationalists were no longer fighting against a dictatorship, their appeal to public opinion was weaker. It could easily be argued that ETA no longer had any reason to continue the struggle. Nevertheless, ETA did continue, arguing in part that the situation of the Basque region still reflected a situation of oppression by the majority (the Spanish) over the minority (the Basques) in their own homeland. As a consequence, ETA was now attempting to end this system of internal colonialism and provide true freedom for the Basque region.

ETA continued its struggle against the Spanish state attempting a variety of maneuvers to increase its appeal among the Basque population and to justify its existence as a dissident organization representing the region and its interests. Attacks were still often focused on the security forces in an effort to provoke the state into massive repression that would be likely to push other individuals into the ranks of ETA (Corrado 1997: 572–3). The Spanish government normally has, however, refrained from taking the bait and not adopted dramatically repressive policies

(Shabad and Ramo 1995). From 1983 to 1987 the Spanish authorities did utilize a special, unofficial squad, the Anti-Liberation Terrorist Group (GAL), to track down and kill Basques suspected of being involved with the different dissident groups or supporting them. Many of the victims were attacked while in France. When the activities of this group came to light, however, it was discontinued (Wilkinson 2000b: 193–4). These extra-legal activities do not seem to have benefited the government in any significant way in the drive against the dissidents, especially once it was discovered that the group was operating. For many Basques they even gave some credence to the idea that the democratic system, like the Franco regime before it, was determined to repress and control the Basque region (Woodworth 2001: 7). Ironically, arrests, trials, and subsequent punishment of ETA activists within the context of normal legal processes often generated public support for the dissidents as martyrs for the cause of Basque freedom. On the other hand, the more successful actions involving violence often alienated the more moderate Basques and drove them away from the group (Byman 1998: 154). Over the years the restraint generally shown by the democratic government has slowly undercut the support for ETA and other violent groups. ETA then shifted to other themes to gain support in the Basque region. It has opposed the creation of nuclear power plants that would threaten the local environment as well as other infrastructure projects that could be environmentally harmful, and even launched attacks on such projects (Khatami 1997: 398). ETA has also launched attacks against foreign tourists, attempting to economically damage the state and to reduce the inflow of income from tourism (Chalk 1998b: 380). Since Spain is a major destination for European tourists, if such attacks were to reduce revenue, it would be noticed. This type of economic warfare was quite successful at times, as there were clear downturns in the number of tourist visits after attacks by ETA (Enders and Sandler 1991). Similarly, terrorist attacks also affected the amount of foreign direct investment in Spain. The drop in such investment resulted in estimates of reductions of over 13 per cent in the total investment between 1976 and 1990 (Enders and Sandler 1996). Since ETA in particular, and other Basque dissidents groups in general, were the major source of terrorist actions, the Basque dissidents were most responsible for this lower level of investment from outside countries. Ultimately, these efforts have all failed to increase support for the group.

ETA did not have any direct source of foreign support. ETA dissidents had some contacts with the PLO and some members trained in their camps, and there were rare opportunities to interact with other nationalist dissidents from other countries. In the 1980s when the control of the border by the French authorities became more effective, ETA lost a valuable sanctuary (Wilkinson 2000b: 193–4). Financial support for the movement was largely self-generated. Members of the Basque community in Spain and France as well as Basques in other countries supplied financial support. ETA also raised funds in some with some of the traditional means available to dissidents. Kidnappings were not infrequent. In some cases ETA collected very substantial ransoms in return for the release of prominent and wealthy individuals (Jimenez 1992: 188). ETA also relied on revolutionary taxes levied on Basques and others to support the cause, and punishment attacks were sometimes undertaken against those who failed to contribute or pay the taxes. The successful kidnappings and the punishment attacks against individuals who did not contribute to the nationalist cause made it relatively easy for ETA to blackmail industrialists and businessmen for funds. In some cases the punishment for failing to provide the requested funds was death (Albin 1989: 202).

ETA has continued to have at least some local support. While the majority of the Basques oppose violence, they are also frequently unwilling to cooperate with the authorities in dealing with members of ETA. ETA has also in a way managed to help the Basque region. Although the demands of ETA have not been met, the central government has granted greater autonomy and local control to the regional government. In effect, the Spanish government and local politicians have used the threat of ETA violence to negotiate for more local control (Shabad and Ramo 1995: 468). Some splinter groups from ETA have been reconciled with the system as a consequence of these concessions. It is unlikely that the government would have conceded as much local autonomy if there

had not been the implied threat that more Basques would have joined ETA or some other violent nationalist organization. Notwithstanding its indirect successes in helping the region to achieve greater autonomy, ETA has not gained its ultimate goal of independence. For ETA other rights granted by the democratic Spanish government are meaningless without the right to independence (Woodworth 2001: 3). Such an outcome is not likely in the future. The Basques no longer constitute a majority in their own region. The hard-core elements have not given up the dream of an independent state, even though ETA "has almost become a terrorist group in exile" (White 1998: 195). To some extent the core of ETA may have become wedded to the violence that they inflict. They have become so immersed in a culture of violence that they cannot give up the struggle. The culture of violence has perpetuated itself (Laqueur 1999: 35). There was a period recently where there were indications that ETA might be willing to settle for a negotiated solution to the future of the Basque region that would lead to the end of the violence (Newman 2000: 37). This willingness to negotiate, however, did not last and the nationalist attacks began yet again. ETA demonstrates that terrorist groups, once established, can survive for a long time with small levels of support, and that it is virtually impossible in the short term to undermine a well-established terrorist organization by negotiation or destroy it completely by police, security, and military measures.

CASE STUDY 6.4
Dayaks and migrants on Borneo

Communal violence can occur in response to government policies without the attacks being directed against the government. The violence can be more directly focused on members of an ethnic community by another group or groups that see the first group as a threat. Such a situation has occurred in the Indonesian provinces on the island of Borneo or Kalimantan (see Map 2). The Dayaks, the local inhabitants of the island, have reacted negatively to the government-supported migration of Madurese to

MAP 2 Indonesia

the Indonesian portion of the island. There has been a great deal of pressure on the land in many parts of Indonesia. The land densities in some parts are extremely high, creating situations where migration to less densely supported areas of the country has been seen as a viable option. The island of Java in particular has faced severe overpopulation. As a consequence, the government has encouraged and fostered migration to other areas (the outer islands from a Javanese perspective) where land has been available. This policy has led to local dissatisfaction in a variety of areas as the migrants have clashed with the local inhabitants. The local dissatisfaction was held pretty much in check while the authoritarian Suharto regime was in power. The return to a more democratic system of government has created a system in transition that is more vulnerable to violent activities than a firmly established governmental system. Javanese migrants have faced opposition from the local populations in Sumatra, including Aceh in the northern portion of that island where a low level guerrilla insurgency has been ongoing for many years (Tan 2000). The migration was also a factor leading to the religious violence that has occurred in Sulawesi and the Moloccus. It has also led to communal massacres in Kalimantan where a large number of Madurese had migrated from an island just off the coast of Java.

The Madurese, with government support, were taking over land and establishing farms in territory that the local Dayak inhabitants naturally regarded as their own. The new migrants in at least some cases were in better positions to dominate commercial relationships in the areas. The differences between the two communities were exacerbated in this case by the fact that many Dayaks are Christian while most of the Madurese are Muslim like the vast majority of the population of Java. The attacks do not appear to be religiously motivated since there is no indication of other Muslim residents of Kalimantan (few in number) being attacked. The violence has been limited to the Madurese. With the loosened control by the central government that came with the demise of the military regime and the creation of a more democratic system, the Dayaks began to attack the Madurese migrants. The violence at first was not noticeably organized and reflected antagonisms between the two

communities, but eventually it came to include a larger element of direction and defined purposes. The attacks on Madurese at times resulted in the massacre of the outsiders by the Dayaks. The Dayaks have not attacked Madurese fleeing from their areas of settlement. The goal of the attacks has been the forced flight of the migrants, not their extermination. The target audience for the violence has extended beyond the immediate to the other migrants. The goal has been the expulsion of the whole migrant community. Survivors of the massacres have been the necessary media to transmit the message of the locals to the Madurese, both on Borneo and Java. The attacks on the Madurese have not required any major changes in government policies, since the policy of supporting Madurese migration to Borneo had been made irrelevant by the violence.

The government has not supported the attacks on the migrants, especially since the migration itself has been a government-supported policy. In a country that is largely Muslim, the government would be more likely to favor the Muslim migrants, especially in a democratic society where the political parties with a strong, Islamic, religious orientation have been especially important for the governments in power. The government, however, has been ill prepared to deal with the violence. Security forces, the police, and the military were present in small numbers and not up to the task of protecting the Madurese. The absence of large security forces has been due in part to the problems in other areas of the country—the need for the military to maintain control for the government in Aceh, the requirements to keep order in East Timor for many years, separatist feelings in Irian Jaya (the Indonesian portion of New Guinea), and the communal violence in Sulawesi and the Moloccus. Police officers have been overwhelmed in the face of the attacks and unable to defend the migrants even if they desired to do so. Providing security for isolated farms is clearly beyond the means of the government when there are insufficient resources to protect the migrants in the towns. The government would have to devote major resources, which are already stretched as noted, to provide even minimal protection in the region. Since the violence has not yet moved toward opposition to the central government as the appropriate political authority on Kalimantan, the government is unlikely to provoke a strong local response and generate even more separatism in the country given the significant demands on government resources that already exist.

At least for the moment, it is difficult to argue that the campaign against the Madurese failed. The tide of migration has been turned at least in part. Many migrants have fled, and new migrants have been discouraged, notwithstanding population pressure on the land and local poverty. While not all the migrants have been driven out, the disruption of the large-scale migration was achieved. For the government to successfully counteract these local successes requires resources unlikely to be available in the near future. At some point in time the consolidation of the democratic system may permit a new attempt at colonization. If local issues in Aceh, Sulawesi, or Irian Jaya are dealt with, the government may even be able to provide the necessary security for such a policy. Of course, if the democratic consolidation means more local autonomy for various provinces, the Dayaks may even prove to have been very successful in the long term in reserving their land for themselves.

CASE STUDY 6.5
Albanians in Kosovo and Macedonia

Kosovo is in the Serbian part of what remained of Yugoslavia after the breakup of that country (see Map 3). The outbreaks of ethnic violence in the area represent some of the classic ethnic issues that generate conflict. The violence also illustrates the very effective use of tactics and techniques by the Albanian dissidents to further their cause. After the violence in Kosovo, the Albanian minority in Macedonia, another successor state from the old Yugoslavia, began to use some of these same techniques and tactics. The similarity of tactics would suggest that the Albanians in Macedonia were quick studies, and had advice from their fellow Albanians in Kosovo—and indeed that some of the same people were involved in the activities in both areas.

For the Serbian population of Yugoslavia the Kosovo region has always had special significance. It

was the heartland of the original Serb state and the later Serbian Empire. It was also the site of two of the most important military defeats suffered by the Serbs at the hands of the Ottoman Turks. The first battle of Kosovo destroyed the Serbian Empire, leading to its subjugation by the Ottomans. The somewhat later second battle of Kosovo resulted in the defeat of the attempt to re-establish Serb independence, which led to the incorporation of the region in the Ottoman Empire for centuries. The Albanians are a non-Slavic people, differing from the Serbs and Macedonians, and their language is not Slavic, so it is easily distinguishable from Serbo-Croat. Although some Albanians were Greek Orthodox, large numbers converted to Islam under Ottoman rule, adding a cultural divide to the linguistic and ethnic one. While religious practices of all kinds were discouraged to some extent in communist Yugoslavia, the cultural milieu that Islam provided for most Albanians set them apart from the cultural setting and history of the Greek Orthodox Serbs.

With the establishment of the Kingdom of Yugoslavia after World War I, Kosovo became an integral part of the new country. In this period the central government encouraged the movement of Serbs into Kosovo (and Macedonia) to change the ethnic balance. Albanians were encouraged to either emigrate or assimilate (Vickers 1995: 127–8). Both before and after World War II the economic centers of Yugoslavia were in Slovenia, Croatia, and the area around the capital of Belgrade. As a consequence of the greater economic opportunities in these regions, Serbs in Kosovo began to leave in increasingly larger numbers. The Albanian population in the area grew both in an absolute sense and as a proportion of the total regional population as they remained behind. By the time the unified Yugoslavia had begun to disintegrate with the collapse of communism, the Albanians had become an overwhelming majority in the Kosovo region.

When Yugoslavia was still united under the communist government headed by Marshall Tito, power was decentralized to a surprising extent for cultural and educational purposes. There were six Republics in the federal Yugoslavia—Slovenia, Croatia, Bosnia and Herzegovina, Serbia, Montenegro, and Macedonia.

MAP 3 Former Yugoslavia

In addition, within the Serbian Republic there were two autonomous provinces in Serbia with special powers—Kosovo with its Albanian majority and Vojvodina (the Banat), which has a Serb majority but large Hungarian and German minorities. Local party organizations were important in governing the six republics and the two autonomous provinces, and the largest ethnic and cultural group invariably dominated the local parties. Thus, local ethnic leaders, even if they were communists, had the opportunity to establish themselves in the various regions, and they catered to the ethnic concerns of local populations to some extent. Even while the communists still ruled in a unified Yugoslavia, tensions appeared between the Albanians and the local Serb population. The Albanians felt that the dominant Serbs treated them poorly. The local Serbian population, on the other hand, felt that the Albanians were doing everything in their power to force out the remaining Serbs from the province and to take over completely. These tensions generated riots and difficulties, although with a strong communist government in power, these tensions were manageable (Vickers 1995: 205–6).

With the breakup of the country, the surviving territory of Yugoslavia consisted of Montenegro and Serbia, which still included Vojvodina and Kosovo. The Serbs were a clear majority, while the Albanians were the largest remaining minority. Under the government of Slobodan Milosevic, a communist turned Serbian nationalist, but authoritarian by nature regardless of ideology, the situation in Kosovo deteriorated. Albanians were treated harshly, and the Yugoslav government sought to repress Albanian aspirations. Local autonomy was withdrawn, while the government encouraged Serbs to migrate back to Kosovo to change the ethnic balance in the province. Albanian dissidents eventually coalesced into the Kosovo Liberation Army (KLA), which began to fight back using both guerrilla and terrorist tactics. Attacks were directed against police, Serb civilians, and Albanians considered to be collaborating with the Yugoslav government (Judah 2000: 137). The Albanian dissidents quickly decided to attempt to provoke an excessive response from the local Yugoslav (i.e. Serb) authorities. They hoped that retaliation would fall upon the local Albanians, alienating them even more from

a repressive state and driving them into the arms of the dissident movement. Army or police patrols would be fired upon from Albanian villages to encourage local security forces to return fire on the villages indiscriminately. Frequently, these tactics were successful. Further, bombs were set off, and assassinations undertaken, including attacks against the local Serb civilian minority. These attacks were intended to provoke retaliations and were also frequently successful. Other methods used by the dissidents to drive a wedge between the local population and the security forces included the torture of prisoners from the security forces or the mutilation of the dead. Serbian police were, in fact, one of the major targets for terrorist attacks (Chalk 1999: 152). It reached the point where Serb police came to regard a transfer or assignment to Kosovo as a virtual death sentence (Macgregor 2001: 97). These techniques used by the Albanian dissidents were successful in provoking government forces to be increasingly repressive, to be high-handed in their methods, and to regard the entire Albanian community as suspect, creating a situation of ongoing and continuous ethnic tensions.

Since the government could not control the territory or the Albanian population, eventually the Yugoslav government decided to attempt to force large segments of the Albanian population out of Kosovo altogether. The government line was that it was expelling post-war migrants into Kosovo and their descendants (Judah 2000: 151–2). A variety of means were used to encourage the Albanians to leave. A large number of the Albanians took the warnings to heart and became refugees, attempting to flee to Montenegrin territory, Albania itself, or Macedonia. The ruthlessness with which the Serbs pursued this policy of forced emigration was ultimately counterproductive. It had extremely negative effects on public opinion in Europe and the United States. The Serbian government was warned to cease its efforts to expel the Albanians or face a military response. When the government failed to yield to the pressure and to withdraw military units from Kosovo, Yugoslavia was subjected to an aerial bombing campaign launched by the United States and other Western countries. The attacks targeted military units, lines of communications, and economic facilities in Serbia proper.

Eventually the Yugoslav military forces were withdrawn from Kosovo, and European and American peacekeeping forces were introduced to protect the Albanians against further repression by the central government.

In the short term the terrorist activities of the KLA were successful. Kosovo had regained its autonomy, and Serbian efforts to control the province and change the ethnic balance in the province had been defeated. Nagging questions about the future of the province remain. The Albanian dissidents would prefer total independence or unity with Albania, options which would be opposed by the central government. Also, since the withdrawal of the Serbian police and military units, the Albanians in power in Kosovo have also not acquitted themselves particularly well. They have used violence against the remaining Serbs in Kosovo and the Gypsies who are assumed to be pro-Serbian. The goal has been to drive both groups out of the province (Judah 2000: 286–90). More than 100,000 Gypsies have fled the province as a consequence of the pressure (Cooper 2001/2: 71). By 1999 an organized campaign of murder and terror was taking place in an effort to drive out the small number of Serb civilians that had remained in Kosovo (Macgregor 2001: 103). Some of these activities might be based on vengeance for past wrongs, but if the remaining Serbs are forced out, independence or unity with Albania becomes a much easier proposition to sell elsewhere in Europe.

There is no indication that there was any external state support for the Albanian dissidents. By the time of the violence in Kosovo, Albania lacked any real functioning national government. The bombing campaign of the Western powers, which ended Serb repression and control, was not state support of terrorist dissidents. While the government of Albania did not provide active military support for the guerrilla insurgency or terrorism of the Kosovo Albanians, members of the KLA did cross over into Albania to get arms. The KLA did maintain supply bases in Albania as well (Pavkovic 2000: 190). The maintenance of these bases was easier once organized government had virtually disappeared in many parts of Albania. It was relatively easy for arms and other forms of support to cross the border between Albania

and Kosovo (Judah 2000: 172–3) even if such movements were not part of any organized state effort.

Once the Serbs had been forced to relinquish control of Kosovo, violence broke out in Macedonia. The Albanian minority in that country began to seek policy changes and greater autonomy for themselves. The National Liberation Army (NLA) was set up to represent the Albanian population. Armed Albanian dissidents began to fire on police patrols, and then on the military, from ethnic Albanian villages. Again the goal appeared to be an effort to provoke a violent response by the Macedonian majority and to drive a wedge between the government and the Slavic Macedonian majority on the one hand and the Albanian minority on the other hand. The tactics that worked in Kosovo were apparently being tried again in Macedonia. The leader of the NLA had previously been active with the KLA in Kosovo (Ash 2003: 63). The situation in Macedonia, however, has yet to get out of hand, even though antagonisms between Albanians and Macedonians have greatly increased. The Albanians control distinct territory and are well armed, and the NLA has received support from Albanian politicians and others in Kosovo. The peacekeeping forces that had been sent to Kosovo to deter the government in Belgrade and other peacekeeping troops that were sent to Macedonia to secure the country from foreign pressure before the outbreak of trouble with the Albanian minority have been able to provide some control over the border areas. These peacekeeping forces have limited contacts between the Albanians in Macedonia and elsewhere, and they have also provided some limitations on the movement of armed Albanian dissidents. Somewhat ironically from the perspective of the Albanian dissidents, the forces initially on the border between Macedonia and Kosovo to help the refugees created by the Serbian efforts as expulsion have provided a deterrent to increased Albanian dissident activities in Macedonia.

To date the success of the dissidents operating in Macedonia has not matched that of the KLA. The Albanians have gained some recognition as a group, and the government has agreed to some concessions and changes, but on the negative side inter-ethnic tensions have been increased. The Albanians have been less able to mobilize European or American public opinion on their behalf in the case of Macedonia than was true for Kosovo. While Milosevic had already weakened his position via-à-vis public opinion by his support for Serbs in their attacks in Bosnia and Croatia and by his own hard line within Yugoslavia, the Macedonian government was democratically elected, and did not have the negative image of the Milosevic government. Also, in the case of Kosovo, the Albanians were very much the majority of the province. The segment of Macedonia that is clearly Albanian has awkward geographic outlines. Activities by dissidents in Macedonia are unlikely to aim towards independence, only towards local autonomy or greater rights for the Albanians. Union with an independent Kosovo or Albania might be a goal for the future, but that is a solution that rewards the dissidents for increasing tensions within Macedonia.

CASE STUDY 6.6
The Palestinian Liberation Organization and the struggle with Israel

The British mandated territory of Palestine was the scene of violence and terrorism in the days prior to World War II and in the years from the outbreak of World War II to the creation of the state of Israel in 1948 by force of arms. The battles that occurred with the British departure between the Israeli forces and the local Palestinians, supported by the armies of neighboring Arab states, involved military actions that sometimes were intended to terrorize the population on the other side (Cooley 1997c). The Israeli leadership actively encouraged Palestinian fears of violence by Jewish forces so that the local Arab population would abandon its lands in the face of advancing Israeli forces. The Palestinian Liberation Organization (PLO) was a nationalist response to the loss of territory. The PLO qualifies as a nationalist organization since the main objective of the organization has been to achieve an independent state for the Palestinian Arabs. While the PLO has not been the first user of terrorism among modern-day political groups that made terror an integral part of their programs for a

significant period of time, the PLO has been one of the more successful and longest lasting organizations of nationalist dissidents.

The PLO, founded in 1964, itself has an umbrella organization that has included through the years many separate groups. Fatah, the group that Yassir Arafat led, was one of the most important groups, and his chairmanship of the umbrella group was one indication of the importance of his organization. At times in the decades since the formation of the PLO groups have dropped out or been expelled for failure to agree with PLO policies. Since the PLO has been composed of many groups and factions, it has sometimes been difficult for it to speak with a truly unified voice. The PLO by conscious choice also has maintained itself as a secular organization, appealing to Muslim, Christian, and non-religious Palestinians. The organization has never stressed Islam as an integral part of the principles of the group. In fact, the failure to stress Islam is one of the things that has led to conflict between the PLO and Hamas.

The PLO was formed as many Palestinians became disenchanted with the prospects of the liberation of their homeland by conventional armed forces of the Arab countries. Israel had defeated the armies of Egypt, Jordan, Syria, Lebanon, and Iraq in 1948, and in 1956 the Israeli army easily dealt with the Egyptian forces in the Sinai. The Palestinians initially formed guerrilla groups to conduct raids and to complement conventional military action by the Arab armies. In the Six Day War in 1967, the Israeli Defense Force decisively defeated the armies of Egypt, Jordan, and Syria, and Israel occupied the West Bank, the Gaza Strip, the Golan Heights, and the Sinai Peninsula. Gaza, formerly administered by Egypt, and the West Bank, which had been part of the Kingdom of Jordan, brought many Palestinian Arabs under direct Israeli rule. The governments of the defeated Arab states now naturally became much more concerned about controlling any Palestinian guerrilla operations in order to avoid military engagements with Israel. As might be expected, they placed their national interests ahead of the Palestinian objective of reclaiming their homeland.

In the aftermath of 1967, the PLO and its component units opted to resort to terrorism. It should be noted

BOX 6.3 Hamas

Hamas (an Arabic acronym for Islamic Resistance Movement) is a Palestinian organization that combines both religious and nationalist appeals. The major objective of the group is an independent Palestinian state that will be an Islamic Republic. The focus on Islam places it at odds with the PLO, which is more secular in its orientation. Israeli authorities actually initially provided some support to Hamas in an effort to weaken the latter organization (Kimmerling 1997: 235). Hamas has also expressed its commitment to a Palestinian state that includes all the territory of the old British Mandate—Israel, the Gaza Strip, and the West Bank. It has refused to recognize the legality of the existence of the state of Israel. The platform of Hamas also calls for the return of the Palestinian refugees and the descendants of the refugees who were forced out in 1948 and 1967 and the expulsion of many of the Jewish inhabitants of Israel. Hamas has gained considerable strength among the Palestinians in the Occupied Territories, especially in the Gaza Strip. This increased strength and the uncompromising objectives of the organization quickly led Israel to withdraw support from the group. Hamas has become an increasingly important political actor in Israel/Palestine, and it has the potential to replace the PLO as the leading Palestinian political group. Hamas, along with Islamic Jihad has attempted to disrupt various peace proposals or negotiations between Israel and the PLO at various times. Both groups initiated attacks by suicide bombers to inflict casualties on the Israeli population and to upset peace talks. At other times, however, the group has been more pragmatic. It has tacitly cooperated with the PLO at times, and it has indicated a willingness to accept truces while negotiations are ongoing. Such pragmatism may reflect a desire to gain some rights for the Palestinian people or even an independent state, where there might be opportunities for political gains in the future. What its future approach to politics would be in an autonomous Palestinian state governed by the PLO is unclear.

that while the PLO was almost always "blamed" or "credited" for terrorist actions, not all terrorist actions were under the control of the PLO. The PLO did at times organize or sanction terrorist attacks. On other occasions it seems reasonably clear that some other independent Palestinian groups undertook actions on their own, contrary to the desires of the PLO leadership. In more ambiguous cases, it would appear that separate organizations undertook actions with the tacit approval or at least the knowledge of the PLO leadership. The leadership had the option, however, of denying involvement if such a denial was beneficial. In general in the period from 1968 to the early 1980s, the PLO was actively undertaking or encouraging terrorist activities as a means of weakening the state of Israel and attracting international attention.

In July 1968, three members of the Popular Front for the Liberation of Palestine (PFLP), a group within the PLO, hijacked an El Al plane en route from Rome to Tel Aviv. El Al as the national airline of Israel was an appropriate target for the Palestinians. The hijackers offered to trade the passengers on the flight for the release of Palestinians imprisoned by the Israelis (Hoffman 1998: 67–8). The publicity that the effort received indicated to the PLO that such operations could generate significant media attention and publicize the cause of the Palestinian people in a way that was not otherwise possible. In fact, the successful hijacking of the plane generated more media attention that any of the battles fought by the Palestinians with the Israeli security forces in their guerrilla incursions (Cooley 1997b: 299). The aftermath of this operation convinced the Palestinians to engage in additional acts of terrorism. In 1969, Yassir Arafat was elected as the chairman. Since Fatah supported the use of terrorism, the election of its leader made it clear that this approach had become the policy of the PLO (Sayigh 1997: 29). While some attacks continued to occur inside Israel, other attacks shifted to other locations. The 1972 Munich Olympics provided an ideal forum to publicize the Palestinian cause when the Black September organization captured Israeli athletes and held them hostage. For days world attention was focused on the hostage situation in Munich, and everyone was aware of the failed attempt by the West Germans to rescue the hostages that resulted in the death of all the Palestinians and the Israeli athletes and coaches. These attacks continued throughout the 1970s and 1980s. The PLO and other Palestinian groups were indisputably the world's most active sources of terrorist actions (Laqueur 1999: 68–9). Some of the activities were relatively spectacular, such as the simultaneous hijacking of four airliners, while other actions included property attacks in the United States and Western Europe, with El Al being a frequent target. There were also assassination attempts against Israeli diplomats abroad. Ultimately, all of these activities generated a tremendous amount of publicity for the Palestinian cause and ultimately for the PLO as well. All of the international attacks and hijackings resulted in a limited number of deaths compared to the attacks within Israel or the Occupied Territories of the Gaza Strip or the West Bank.

The publicity that resulted from these international activities was essential to the Palestinian cause in a number of ways. Every success attracted new recruits from the Palestinians living in the refugee camps and from Palestinians living abroad. The successful attacks also brought in financial support from the Palestinian diaspora. Palestinians in Europe and the United States have been especially important as sources of funds for the PLO and other groups (Kushner 1996: 333). The successes of the PLO also meant that it received financial support from other Arab states including the oil rich monarchies that found it expedient to supply funds to their fellow Arabs (Rubin 1989: 30). The flow of funds from Kuwait or Saudi Arabia neutralized the potential dissident activity from Palestinians residing in their territories and weakened attacks from other non-monarchial Arab states such as Syria and Egypt. The publicity also brought the situation of the Palestinians to world attention and generated sympathy for a people without a land. Prior to these attacks, "few outside the region took any notice of,

much less cared about the Palestinians" (Hoffman 1998: 70). The PLO was ultimately successful to some extent in equating the situation of the Palestinians as a people without a land to that of the Jewish population of the world in 1948 as a people without a land. If the establishment of a Jewish state in Palestine was acceptable, then the establishment of a Palestinian state in the area had gained validity as well.

The PLO survived and grew as the nationalist organization seen to represent Palestinian interests in the Occupied Territories for the Palestinian diaspora. The PLO, unlike most dissident groups, developed a complex organizational structure and developed its own sources of support. The PLO was recognized in an official or semi-official capacity by many governments. In effect, the organization served as an official or unofficial government-in-exile for the Palestinian people with more diplomatic contacts than the state of Israel at one point in time (Hoffman 1998: 75). The PLO even had observer status at the United Nations. Funds from the diaspora, the oil states, and its own businesses permitted the PLO to develop its own financial base.

The PLO did have important external state support at various times in its organizational history. The Soviet Union frequently provided aid, training, and weapons. Soviet support was always related to some extent to Soviet foreign policy objectives and never unconditional (Kushner 1998a: 5). Most other Arab states aided this terrorist organization. They provided the financing or training, bases for striking against Israel, diplomatic contacts, and a variety of other aid that permitted the organization to grow and prosper. The PLO in turn supported other dissident and terrorist groups. PLO training camps in Lebanon were used by more than forty different terrorist organizations (Kushner 1998b: 14). The PLO also frequently had differences with its sponsor states as indicated by the fighting between the PLO and the Jordanian army in September 1971 (the source of the name for the Black September organization that became one of the more notorious Palestinian terrorist groups) or the PLO's participation in some of the fighting in Lebanon. Such state support was critical at times for the PLO.

Slowly the PLO changed its tactics in terms of the confrontation with Israel. The group moved away from its stance of non-recognition of the right of Israel to exist and slowly conceded that the presence of the state of Israel was a fact of life that had to be recognized. The PLO eventually also opened the door for negotiations with the state of Israel and announced its intention to forego further terrorist attacks while still keeping its options open for operations against the Israeli military. The shift towards negotiations had costs. Some groups like the PFLP left the PLO, and Palestinian extremists assassinated moderates in the PLO (Rolef 1997: 260). At this point, it is possible to argue that the PLO as an organization, although not necessarily all the existing Palestinian dissident organizations or all members of the PLO, ceased to qualify as a terrorist organization. Its past terrorist activities had helped consolidate the position of the PLO as a recognized spokesman for the Palestinian people. When the intifada—the uprising against continued Israeli occupation of the West Bank and the Gaza Strip—broke, the PLO became the outside organization that represented the local inhabitants. The uprising, which involved stone throwing, civil disobedience, riots, and low-level violence, resulted from local Palestinian dissatisfaction and distaste for the military occupation. While the PLO did not organize the uprising, it supported it, and an overwhelming majority of the Palestinians considered the PLO to be their representative. The effects of the intifada clearly played a role in the eventual negotiations between Israel and the PLO that led to the creation of the Palestinian Authority with some governmental roles in parts of the West Bank and the Gaza Strip.

The Palestinian Authority was in effect the PLO transformed into a governmental body, even if it was one with limited authority and under Israeli oversight. The PLO had moved from being a dissident organization to a political actor that had to be consulted on at least some issues regarding the Occupied Territories. The PLO had achieved one of its major objectives that it had long fought for. It was recognized as the body representing the Palestinian people and had achieved a position from which it could negotiate with Israel (Kushner 1998b: 21–2). Events in 2001, 2002, and 2003 have led some to argue that the PLO is still a terrorist organization because of continuing terrorist attacks on Israeli targets by some

Palestinians. The PLO is being held responsible for the actions of its citizens as any other state actor might be. Of course, the PLO as a former terrorist organization is being held to a higher standard, but the continuing terrorism cannot be conclusively linked to the PLO as an organization. Many of the recent attacks were launched by Palestinians who not only wanted to force an Israeli withdrawal from the Occupied Territories but who also wanted to displace the leadership group around Yassir Arafat and replace it with different, and younger, individuals (Shikaki 2002: 89). While PLO members may have launched some of the attacks, Hamas, the Palestinian Islamic Jihad, and other groups conducting the attacks are not part of the PLO. The PLO is not automatically responsible for every terrorist attack by a Palestinian Arab any more than the Israeli government is responsible for every terrorist attack by an Israeli Jew on worshippers in a mosque or attacks by hard-line settlers on the West Bank.

The PLO ultimately is an example of a dissident organization that used terrorism successfully to change the balance of power. When it was first formed, the Palestinians were clearly a weaker element in the Middle East equation. They were much weaker militarily than Israel, and the supporting Arab states were quite willing to use them as they saw fit and to sacrifice Palestinian interests for the national interests of the state in question. With the passage of time, the PLO became the representative of the Palestinian people with a sufficient increase in its power and influence to become one of the negotiators of the future rather than a pawn in someone else's game. Public opinion in the world changed to view more favorably the goals of the Palestinians. While many persons in the United States or Europe would continue to favor the interests of Israel, they were now more willing to concede that the Palestinians' demands had at least some merit. (Others, of course, continued to favor either Israel or the Palestinians unequivocally.) With greater international support for the Palestinian cause, the Israelis faced greater pressure to at least consider Palestinian demands. It is highly unlikely that these changes in relative positions would have occurred without the resort to terrorism. It is also instructive that when the PLO was at its weakest it chose to use terrorism, but once it had gained political leverage it was in a position to dispense with it. As a consequence, it is not surprising that the PLO became a model for other ethnic and nationalist groups in other areas that sought to improve their situation or achieve independence (Hoffman 1998: 68–9). The actions of the PLO may yet fail to lead to the creation of a Palestinian state, but even with the violence in the region today, there is a chance that such a state may yet appear.

Summary

Clearly ethno-nationalist terrorism and violence based on language differences has been quite prevalent in the world in recent years. While nationalism first became a dramatic force for change with the American and French Revolutions, it did not immediately result in notable increases in terrorism. The levels of military technology may have been a factor in the lack of terroristic violence in the 1700s and into the 1800s. Arms were not tremendously complicated and could be procured with relative ease. The French revolutionary leaders enrolled mass armies and provided muskets that could be used in large numbers to at least have a chance of defeating the more professional and disciplined armies of the other European states. It thus became possible for hastily assembled and sometimes even poorly equipped citizens' armies to defeat the professional regiments. The possibilities for victory were aptly demonstrated by the ultimate victory of the American colonialists, by the early victories of the French revolutionary armies, and even some of the success of the Irish and Scottish Highlanders in their uprisings against English rule. The lack of sophisticated weaponry in the hands of the national armies meant that the weapons of the weak were conventional arms, sometimes used in set-piece battles with the government forces and sometimes used with guerrilla tactics. Since nationalist causes could usually command widespread popular support, there was little need to resort to terrorism to challenge a foreign, occupying power. Similarly, regionalist forces in the newly independent countries of Latin America had access to the same types of weapons as the armed forces of the central governments. Thus, these dissidents were not forced to rely on terrorism to challenge the government either.

In the twentieth century national groups began to rely much more on terrorism as a tactic to challenge an occupying force. By this time the weapons available to central governments or colonial powers had advanced and become much more deadly. Aircraft, armored cars, and heavy artillery were much less likely to be available to any dissident nationalist group engaging in conventional war. Such weapons, even if captured, require constant maintenance and spare parts and fuel and specialized ammunition. The breakup of the German, Russian, Austro-Hungarian, and Ottoman Empires after World War I resulted in boundaries that were questioned and contested by groups that found themselves on the "wrong" side of a border or groups that thought their nation should have been granted independence. Resorts to terrorism increased after World War II as colonial empires in Asia, Africa, and the Middle East began to collapse. Dissidents seeking independence began to rely on terrorism when confronted with the weaponry of European troops or European led local troops. The Greek Cypriots, the Algerian war of independence, and the Mau Mau uprising in Kenya are some examples of groups forced to rely on terrorism at least in part. Terrorism, sometimes in combination with guerrilla warfare, became the appropriate weapon of the weak.

Problems that came with the end of the colonial empires continue. The Soviet Union and Yugoslavia collapsed, and disputes over boundaries and national affiliations continue to plague the successor states. The ethnic conflicts in the former Yugoslavia resurfaced after more than four decades of firm, centralized rule, indicating that ethnically based violence can indeed persist for lengthy periods of time. The problems in the Balkans today, including those in the former

Yugoslavia, can even be seen as the final stages of conflicts that started with the breakup of the Ottoman Empire (Cronin 2002/3: 36). Ethnic tensions in the Soviet Union resurfaced after more than seven decades of firm control. Successor states to empires continue to face problems as well. The United Kingdom provided unity to India, but that unity collapsed with the separation of Pakistan in 1948, and India has faced other violence since then as well. Indonesia is in danger of losing the unity that was provided by the Dutch. All of these examples indicate that ethnic or nationalist violence can indeed last for long periods of time. Once violence has occurred and communal trust has been broken, like Humpty Dumpty it would seem that not all the king's men or all the king's horses can put it together again.

What will also undoubtedly lead to instances of terrorist violence in the future is the fact that such violence has been successful in the past (Cooley 2000: 12). Terrorism helped convince European powers to abandon many of their colonies. Even in cases where the terrorism and insurgencies failed in the short term, such as Kenya, colonial withdrawal did occur before too many years had passed. The Albanians in Kosovo and perhaps in Macedonia as well in the future have been successful in achieving at least some of their political objectives. Even the activities of ETA in Spain seem to have led the central government to grant a larger measure of autonomy to the region than it might otherwise have been willing to concede. The Dayaks in Borneo managed to reverse a government policy fostering immigration, at least for the immediate future. Finally, the PLO (and its related groups) has used terrorism to create a situation where the possibility of a Palestinian state is at least being considered. The successful Algerian war of independence was a model for Fatah and the PLO (Sayigh 1997: 26). In sum, nationalist or ethnic terrorism will continue because it has been successful in the past.

External state support has not been essential for the success of the nationalist dissidents, even if it has been helpful. In none of the case studies were the dissidents under foreign control. The property terrorism of the colonials in America prior to the actual rebellion also lacked any foreign assistance but was successful in achieving its goals. The Dayaks in Borneo accomplished their major objectives without any external aid. The Basque effort had mixed results in terms of objectives achieved, but there has never been any

Terms

Anti-Liberation Terrorist
    Group (GAL)
Armenian Secret Army for the
    Liberation of Armenia
    (ASALA)
Bernadotte, Count Folke
Biafra
Black September
Chechens
colons
Dayaks
Euzkadi ta Askatasuna (ETA)
Fatah
Franco, Francisco

furores
Gaza Strip
Hamas
Hutu (Bahutu)
Ibos
intifada
Judea and Samaria
Justice Commandos of the
    Armenian Genocide
    (JCAG)
Kikuyu
Kosovo
Kosovo Liberation Army
    (KLA)

Kurds
Mau Mau
Milosevic, Slobodan
Occupied Territories
Palestinian Authority
Palestinian Liberation
    Organization (PLO)
Popular Front for the
    Liberation of Palestine
Quebec Liberation Front
    (FLQ)
Stern Gang
General Suharto
Tutsi (Watutsi)

indication that there was external assistance for ETA or any of its breakaway groups. The KLA and Albanian dissidents also did not have any major foreign backers. Only the PLO had major external support for part of its history. The foreign backers were a mixed blessing since they would often attempt to rein in the Palestinians, and at times were successful in doing so. The fact that the PLO was driven out of Jordan by the Jordanian armed forces and then out of Lebanon by Syria and its local allies is one indication of the ambiguous nature of the foreign linkages. Given the strong roots that the Fatah and other groups, and then the PLO, had in Palestinian society, the foreign support was not essential. The PLO or some representative of the Palestinians was going to exist, and as an initially weak organization in the last half of the twentieth century it would have been likely to use terrorism as a weapon. While foreign links could be important, they were not essential.

Further reading

Byman, D. (1998) "The Logic of Ethnic Terrorism," *Studies in Conflict and Terrorism*, 21, 2: 149–69.

Judah, T. (2000) *Kosovo: War and Revenge*. New Haven: Yale University Press.

Maloba, W. O. (1993) *Mau Mau and Kenya: An Analysis of a Peasant Revolt*, Bloomington: Indiana University Press.

Woodworth, P. (2001) "Why Do They Kill? The Basque Conflict in Spain," *World Policy Journal*, 18, 1: 1–12.

Film

Battle of Algiers (1965)

Chapter 7

Terrorism and ideologies of the left

Ideology and beliefs   116

Dissatisfaction from the left   117

Case studies   124

    7.1 The Baader-Meinhof Gang in West Germany 124

    7.2 The Italian Red Brigades 127

    7.3 17 November Organization in Greece 130

    7.4 The Montoneros in Argentina 132

    *7.5 The Islamic Republic of Iran and the
       Mujahedin-e-Khalq 135*

    *7.6 The Animal Liberation Front and Animal Rights
       Militia 137*

Summary   139

Terms   142

Further reading   142

The two previous chapters dealt with dissident organizations linked with religion and ethnicity —two of the most basic forms of identification available to individuals. Ethnic or national identity is generally difficult to change. Even if one becomes a naturalized citizen, one may still be regarded as foreign, or perhaps just different. In states where communal violence has occurred, shared citizenship has not prevented violence between groups that are perceived to be different. Similarly, religion has formed one of the more basic identifiers for members of a society. While some individuals can and do change religions, most individuals do not. Personal, family, and peer groups may reinforce the religious identity to a sufficient degree as to make conversion relatively rare. Even if individuals are not particularly active in the religion of their group, they will still often have a cultural identification with that religion and be affected by the values that are inherent within it. Of the religious groups discussed in Chapter 5, Aum Shinrikyo was the one exception in this regard since its members voluntarily chose to join and become devoted to the sect and its leader. The followers of Islam, Judaism, Christianity, or Sikhism, on the other hand, are much less likely to be composed of converts or persons who have recently joined, and in religious groups of long-standing members, the newcomers will usually be obvious.

Unlike religion and ethnicity, ideological affiliation involves a much more conscious choice for the followers of the set of political beliefs. Individuals can choose which set of political ideas to value and support, and they can even change their views without necessarily changing other aspects of their lives, such as language or ethnicity. Individuals may even consider these political ideas and values to be worth fighting for. Obviously, if the political ideas are in general agreement with the structure and practices of the governmental system in power, individuals are unlikely to become violent dissidents. On the other hand, if the government in power seems to be antithetical to the cherished ideological concepts and hopes, violence becomes possible for firm believers.

Ideology and beliefs

Ideologies cover virtually all possible political views, solutions to problems or perceived problems, and perspectives. For the most part, political movements that do not involve religious or ethnonationalist elements can be broadly grouped into left and right categories. Leftist ideologies generally proclaim that their ideal state will include the establishment of greater equality and the reduction or destruction of privilege and rank. They are frequently universalistic in that they claim to apply to many, if not all, the peoples and societies of the world. Rightist ideologies usually stress the need for order and hierarchy and the presence of some form of natural ordering of groups in political systems. They may define some natural elite (with definitions varying substantially) that should govern. They can even suggest that there is great value in differences and even in the presence of inequalities. Inequality is considered to be a principle of nature (Bjorgo 1995b: 3). Ideologies of the right often, but clearly not always, involve elements of nationalism, meaning that in many cases they are not really universalistic in their applications. Their prescriptions are seen as being relevant for a particular society or particular group of societies rather than most or all of the societies of the world.

Almost any ideology can be used to support the use of violence and terrorism in the appropriate circumstances. The government may be, or be perceived to be, controlled by an elite following a different or even contradictory ideology. The end result is the followers of one ideology will become dissidents, and just as religious or nationalist dissidents may feel compelled to resort to violence if their views are not being heard or are being ignored, ideological dissidents may feel the need to resort to violence to make their points about policies or the political system. The government in power may also be seen as repressive, and of course it may in fact be a very repressive government. If the government views a particular ideology as being dangerous in terms of circulating ideas that are contrary to the government policy or the structure of the government itself, the groups in power could resort to repression to control the dissidents and generate the violence and the danger that they are seeking to avoid. A dissident group may also resort to violence if they feel there are questions of basic fairness involved in the dispute between themselves and the government. If government policies are seen to be unfairly rewarding one group or penalizing some portion of the population, the unfairness could be used as a justification for violence. If other means of political activity fail to generate the appropriate policies in an ideological sense, groups may resort to violence if their beliefs are strong enough, and the beliefs may be strengthened by the presence of a well developed political ideology that explains why the unfairness is present.

Dissatisfaction from the left

While ideological conflict, like nationalism, is often seen as a nineteenth- or twentieth-century phenomenon, there were occurrences of political violence and even terrorism further in the past that had some of the hallmarks of ideological attacks. Politics in the Roman Republic up to the time of Julius Caesar was often quite violent. Aspirants to public office often used groups of supporters or even paid mobs to intimidate opponents and even to coerce voters. Assassinations were not unknown, and the politicians of Rome often felt that it was necessary to maintain armed retainers and to have bodyguards when traveling in the streets of the city. The assassinations that did occur at times were intended in at least some of the cases not only to remove a political leader who was a threat but to send a message to an opposing group as well. While the various groups in these internal struggles did not think of themselves as being left or right in terms of their ideologies, some of the leaders sought to extend privileges to a larger group of citizens and to reduce the advantages and privileges of the nobility (Grant 1992: 4).

Other examples of violence in centuries past that had ideas and concepts that are related to current leftist ideologies were the peasant rebellions that occurred in Europe in the late Middle Ages, the early Renaissance, and other times as well. These uprisings lacked a coherent ideological basis for the violence that did occur, but the kinship of these rebellions with later leftist campaigns involving violence is obvious. The peasants were attempting to restore greater equality to their society and to reform the practices involved in their working of the land (Desai and Eckstein 1990: 449). The peasant rebellions usually involved violence against the local minor nobility, agents of the upper classes, and other officials. These peasant revolts in the second millennium CE had elements of equalitarian violence, and even included acts of terrorism. The early days of the French Revolution involved political violence and terrorism that took place in urban areas as well as rural ones. The Reign of Terror will be discussed in some detail as a case in Chapter 10. Much of the violence and intimidation in this case was linked to the more radical groups supporting the Revolution, which hoped to change the political system of France even more than the early changes that had already come with the Revolution. Opposition to monarchies and aristocracies was not limited to France. Movements by the middle and lower classes to limit the powers of the governing noble and royal elites in other countries would qualify as movements based on at least implicit ideologies of the left. These movements were opposed to privilege and sought a more equitable distribution of political power (and wealth), even if they did not seek equal political rights for all.

The most important source for ideologies of the left, of course, appeared with the writings of Marx and Engels, which were followed by the writings of later communists such as Lenin and Mao Tsetung. The detailed ideology that developed in the initial writings of Marx provided a critique of the inequality and limitations present in the capitalist societies that existed in nineteenth century Europe, and the ideology provided a blueprint for a better future. Marx's writings also performed the extremely useful purposes of helping to demonize the existing system and providing at least an initial basis to serve as a justification for violence. While theoretical disputes have raged and will continue to rage about whether Marxism is correct, about whether Marxism has ever really been put into effect (communism being considered by many to be a major aberration from what Marx intended), and whether various interpretations and additions to Marx's writings are correct, the ultimate importance of his writings and of others that elaborated and supported his theories is that they have been believed by many adherents. The believers and supporters of anarchism, Marxism, Marxism-Leninism, Maoism, and other variations have been motivated by the theories and have used the theories to encourage others to undertake actions against capitalist political systems or other non-Marxist systems. The theory and its ideals have served to fuel dissidence, and the dissidents have in many cases eventually opted to use violence and terrorism as the only means of defeating exploitive, non-Marxist political systems.

Leftist dissident groups are unlikely to simply seek a change of political leaders when they resort to political violence. Ideologies of the left are usually economically deterministic and indicate that the evils of modern day societies occur when a particular class dominates the system. As a consequence, changing leaders without changing the underlying system is unlikely to make much of a difference. Changes of policies at the very least are likely to be sought by leftist dissidents who resort to violence. The dissidents may seek better conditions for workers, changes in the tax structure so that the wealthy contribute more to society, modifications of economic policies to discourage investment by foreign multinationals and to favor domestic business, changes in trade policy, the end to foreign military alliances or other changes in foreign policy, land reform, or better social services. All of these desired policy changes reflect the leftist ideology and various Marxist interpretations of what ails society, and if

such changes in policy occur, they might be enough for dissidents to end their opposition and their reliance on violence. However, even though changes in policy to remedy injustice may be sought, leftist groups are more likely to seek structural changes in the government, society, and the economy. They believe that true policy reform cannot occur without more far-reaching reforms in the society, and that the capitalist ruling class needs to be deprived of its opportunity to dominate and control the political system. In order for this domination to end, the power base of the class must be destroyed and political institutions changed to permit control by the appropriate classes in society.

The fact that leftist dissidents often see connections between domestic classes and similar groups in other countries can affect their choice of targets. Since both domestic and foreign capitalist groups are seen to be in league to perpetuate the dominance of the local and global system by international capitalism, they are both appropriate targets for violent attack. While dissident leftists may focus more on domestic targets because they are more important for the local population or they are more accessible, they can also select targets that are in other countries. The United States as the center of the capitalist system can always be seen as a legitimate symbolic target and as a key supporter of the local capitalist ruling class. Attacks against foreign interests abroad may do little to mobilize support at home, so dissident groups may have to focus upon targets in their own countries if they hope to mobilize the local population to support them and their objectives. These local targets can include foreign operations in the country. In fact, attacks against foreigners instead of local citizens are often very popular with the local population and may generate support for the group (Laqueur 2001: 223).

One of the first groups of leftists to opt for terrorism as a weapon in the struggle against the oppressive dominating class were the anarchists who began to operate in the nineteenth century. Anarchist doctrine suggested that the ruling classes would be overthrown as a result of a spontaneous uprising by the masses. Although the uprising was to be spontaneous, the anarchists did believe that the masses could be educated about the inferior position that they were relegated to and that they could be inspired to undertake the uprising. One method of informing the common people of their situation and of the need for change was by "propaganda of the word." (Propaganda as initially used simply meant to educate and thus did not originally have the negative connotation of biased information that goes with the term today.) The second form of inspiration and example that could be provided was "propaganda of the deed." The anarchists believed that actions, including violent ones, could be used to mobilize the masses by indicating that the dominating classes and the supporting governmental structure were weak and vulnerable. The government would strike back with repression, driving opponents to more attacks, leading to more repression, and the eventual popular rebellion (Laqueur 2001: 50).

The deed that the anarchists hit upon to serve these purposes was assassination as part of a campaign rather than isolated actions unrelated to each other, even though there was no central planning committee. The anarchists were an early version of a network of terrorist groups. The particular individuals targeted were less important than their value as symbols of the ruling classes. While occasional attacks with bombs were made against legislative bodies, the most frequent targets were heads of state, who were symbolic of the political system. Among the casualties caused by anarchists were President Carnot of France in 1894, Spanish Prime Minister Canova del Castillo in 1897, Empress Elizabeth of Austria-Hungary in 1898, King Umberto of Italy in 1900, and President McKinley of the United States in 1901. Queen Victoria of Great Britain, King Louis Philippe of France, and Kaiser Wilhelm I of Germany were also targeted unsuccessfully (Ford 1985: 208–9, 360). All of these attacks were intended to disrupt the political system and to create the circumstances in which the anticipated uprising would occur. The targets themselves were not chosen for

any particular actions that they had undertaken as indicated by the fact that the Empress Elizabeth was killed instead of the intended target, the French Duke of Orléans, who failed to appear as expected (Ford 1985: 209). The anarchists were poorly trained and lacked external support, and they proved to be easy targets for infiltration and discovery by the security officials of the time (Carr 2002: 149–50). The anarchists did not believe that the assassinations alone would lead to the necessary changes in the political systems. They were designed to be catalysts for changes rather than the causes of the changes. In one sense the anarchists actually did have the catalyzing effect they were seeking, although not when anticipated. They served as an example and impetus for later leftist movements in the twentieth century.

The anarchist campaign of political assassinations became most extensive in Russia with the Will of the People (Narodnaya I Volya) organization. This group attempted to assassinate the Tsar and other high-ranking officials in the government. Over the course of years they managed to successfully assassinate ministers in the government, other officials, and Tsar Alexander II in 1881. The goal of this campaign of assassinations, like the anarchist attacks elsewhere, was to provide examples by propaganda of the deed to the general population and to provoke the government. The group did not believe that any one assassination would lead to measurable change in the political system. They were attempting to deflate the supporting myths of the Russian political system and show that its leaders were human, as well as demonstrate what could be done so that the general population could at least begin to think about attempting to change things (Rubenstein 1987: 145). The group was careful to avoid casualties among bystanders and those not directly connected to the government. In one case an assassin did not use a bomb at one point in the evening because the Grand Duke was in a carriage with his wife and a group of her nieces and nephews. He waited until later in the evening when he could assassinate the Grand Duke without killing the others (Combs 2000: 25). In the short term, these efforts by Russian anarchists failed. The police with the aid of informants managed to break the group, capturing and imprisoning those who were not killed. The autocratic government remained in power, and there was no popular uprising. Of course, it is possible to argue that the repressive response of the government that was provoked by the assassinations did alienate the Russian people even more and did set the stage for the revolutions in February and October of 1917 (old calendar) that destroyed the Russian monarchy and the associated system of government. For example, Vladimir Lenin's older brother Alexander had been executed following a plot against the life of Alexander III (Chamberlin 1935: 123). This defining event early in his life led Lenin to join the Bolshevik party, and his opposition to the regime eventually led to his participation in its overthrow and the establishment of the Soviet Union.

It is worth noting that Marx himself disagreed with the anarchists and their efforts to use propaganda of the deed to mobilize the masses. Marx felt that terrorism as a tactic was likely to be counterproductive in terms of achieving an ideal state in which the capitalist classes had been stripped of their power (Smith and Damphousse 1998: 140). Notwithstanding Marx's view that terrorism was not an appropriate tactic to use in efforts to change the nature of capitalist states, it did become a technique utilized by leftist movements with increasing frequency. After World War I, Marxist groups used terror, conspiracies, and mass uprisings interchangeably in efforts to overthrow existing governments. The creation of the Soviet Union as a communist society provided local Marxist-Leninist parties and groups with external support for both election campaigns and clandestine underground activities. Some of these activities before World War II in effect became state sponsored and state controlled efforts by the Soviet Union to establish friendly regimes in different countries while in other cases the activities of local communists were more autonomous. After World War II, left-wing ideologies served as

the ideological basis for dissident groups in a variety of contexts, and these groups frequently resorted to the use of terrorism. These groups adapted variations of the theories of Marx and Lenin, sometimes claiming affinity with anarchist principles, the ideas of Leon Trotsky, or the ideas of Mao Tse-tung in China. Regardless of the variations in their particular theoretical principles, their justifications for political violence, including acts of terrorism, were usually similar.

While movements based on Marxist-Leninist ideologies have had very little scope for overlapping with dissident movements grounded in religion, the ideas have appeared as an element in national liberation movements because colonies and subject territories have often been seen as part of an international proletariat that is being exploited by the international capitalist classes. Marxist-Leninist groups have broken away from mainstream nationalist groups to create parallel organizations seeking an independent, progressive, and working class (communist) state. The Vietnam War generated a great deal of political dissidence and activity in many countries, much of which was based on the premise of solidarity with the exploited Third World peoples, including the Vietnamese. Anti-war protests in the United States spawned groups like the Students for a Democratic Society (SDS). The most radical elements of the SDS in turn became the Weather Underground or the Weathermen, which used terror attacks, usually confined to property, to challenge the system and US involvement in Southeast Asia. Groups like the Symbionese Liberation Army grew out of the same protest culture of anti-government and anti-system feelings. Concern among leftist students in Europe about capitalism and exploitation of workers and the developing world and the war in Vietnam generated a wide variety of dissident groups that proved to be willing to use violence and terrorism to attempt to achieve their political goals of change in individual countries and in the international system as a whole.

Leftist groups have felt that the violence that they were undertaking could lead to victories for

BOX 7.1 Symbionese Liberation Army

Even though the United States was normally seen as the center of the system of global capitalism and was also held responsible for the Vietnam conflict, domestic violence from the left was relatively subdued in the late 1960s and 1970s. The Weathermen or Weather Underground was not nearly as active as its European or Latin American counterparts. A number of isolated groups with elements of leftist ideology did appear, including the Symbionese Liberation Army (SLA). The SLA combined elements of the black community in the United States, individuals with criminal records, and a few white leftists. The SLA launched a series of violent attacks on US society and the political system, including bank robberies that helped to fund the group. The biggest coup for the organization was the kidnapping of heiress Patricia Hearst. As part of the ransom the SLA demanded that her family distribute food to the poor. This demand, as well as associated political communiqués, clearly established the leftist credentials and objectives of the group. Despite concessions and expenditures from the Hearst family, she was not released; instead, she became an active member of the SLA, either because of fear and intimidation, conversion, or a combination of both factors. Whether or not she was a willing participant in the group is still a matter of some controversy. When the police freed her from the SLA, she was placed under arrest and eventually tried for participating in a bank robbery. She was convicted, and sentenced to a term in jail. The life span of the SLA proved to be relatively short. Most of the members were either killed or captured by the police. A few surviving members of the group went into hiding, but they made no attempt to continue the revolutionary struggle. The SLA quickly became a thing of the past. The group would not have achieved the notoriety that it did without the daring kidnapping of Hearst. The attention that came with the kidnapping gave the SLA tremendous publicity, but it may have been a double-edged sword since it focused special police attention on the SLA, which hastened its end.

the working class in one of two ways. The first way in which they hoped to succeed was by destabilizing the state. If the government failed to deal effectively with the terrorists, it was hoped that popular support for the government would disappear, and the resulting popular discontent could then bring about changes in the government. In such a period of change, dissidents and progressive groups in the society might have an opportunity to gain power after which they could implement change. A non-democratic government might be forced to open up the political process, presenting opportunities for dissident leftists to gain greater power or even to seize control through some form of conspiratorial takeover (e.g. to replicate the Bolshevik seizure of power from a provisional government). The collapse of a parliamentary democratic system could also give

a conspiratorial group or its legal allies an opportunity to gain power in order to establish a more ideal society.

A second objective of such a terrorist campaign is somewhat more indirect in its contribution toward undercutting a capitalist political system. A successful terrorist campaign, especially in a state that has the appearance of being a democratic country, could force the state and the ruling capitalist classes to reveal their true colors. Faced with popular violence and the threat to the security of the state and the ruling classes, the government is likely to become more repressive in its activities as it seeks to destroy the terrorists that threaten to mobilize the population against the status quo. As the government becomes more repressive, it is likely to trample upon the rights of the population since protection of the interests of the ruling capitalist class becomes more important than preserving the façade of democracy that was possible in more peaceful times. This resort to repression should make obvious to the population as a whole the true nature of the regime. If the population is alienated enough by the continued repression, a national uprising could be triggered. This more repressive state would undoubtedly make life for the dissidents much more difficult and hinder their pursuit of their political objectives in the short run, but according to this analysis the overthrow of the system becomes more likely when the people come to realize the true character of the government in power. A terrorist dissident group might even sacrifice itself in this situation since a more repressive state can sometimes deal with terrorist violence more effectively, but it would be helping to create a situation in which a population revolution becomes more likely. The assassination of Tsar Alexander II of Russia may have had such an effect. The Russian anarchists were destroyed by an increasingly repressive state but that state repression (along with other factors) may have increased popular dissatisfaction with the government.

It might appear to be a fantasy that a terror campaign could lead to the fall of a government and create a situation in which it would be replaced by a more repressive political system, yet such has indeed happened. The Tupamaros (officially the Movement of National Liberation) were a Marxist-Leninist group that appeared in Uruguay in 1964. This group, like European leftist groups, was composed largely of students and other young idealists opposed to the inequities present in the supposedly democratic system. The dissidents robbed banks and even took over towns for a few hours to demonstrate their capabilities and to embarrass the politicians in power. Many of their actions, but not all, had characteristics of pranks (Calvert 1997e: 451). They also used some of the funds they acquired to aid the poor in the fashion of latter-day Robin Hoods (Clutterbuck 1975: 36). With time the Tupamaros became more serious, using kidnappings and increasing violence. The

violence weakened the early support that the dissidents had had and eventually alienated the public, which then supported harsher measures for dealing with the terrorists (J. White 1998: 76). However, the activities of the Tupamaros had called into question the competence of the government since the established politicians had proved to be totally unable to deal with the situation. Eventually key military leaders intervened to overthrow the government and install a military government. The Tupamaros had succeeded in creating the desired change of regime. This government opted for harsher and more repressive measures, in effect showing the true colors of the more powerful classes in Uruguay. This new government was much more effective than the previous democratic one. With the necessary disregard for civil rights, procedures, and even the use of death squads, the Tupamaros were defeated (Calvert 1997e: 454). Their members were arrested, imprisoned, or killed. While the predicted repressive government did appear, there was no mass uprising against it. Thus the sacrifice of the Tupamaros was in vain.

Leftist ideologies have included Marxism-Leninism and anarchist strains among others. Terrorism and political violence that originated in social democratic and liberal democratic movements targeting governments that were repressive or extremely conservative could also be considered to be leftist. The efforts led by Sun Yat-sen to create a democracy in China in place of the Manchu dynasty were clearly leftist given the goal (a democracy) and the target (a traditional monarchy). In 1878 in Japan, a senior government official was assassinated by a group seeking a representative national legislature (Angel 1990: 33). This action clearly was leftist in its political objectives given the existing political system. Terrorist campaigns mounted by democratic forces against military dictators and personal tyrants can also be considered leftist in terms of the relative positions of the government and the dissidents. Not all political violence and terrorism based upon ideologies that are left of the government in power is based on Marxist-Leninist concepts.

BOX 7.2 **Japanese Red Army**

The Japanese Red Army (JRA) was a group that attracted young leftists just as its European counterparts did. The group shared the general distaste of the left for global capitalism and joined in the general opposition to the economic and political policies of the United States. Unlike the Red Brigades or the Red Army Faction in Germany, this group undertook its most important attacks on foreign soil. It initially attempted to generate attacks within Japan, which were stymied by the fact that the Japanese authorities proved to be relatively efficient in tracking down and capturing or killing members of the JRA and other violent leftist dissident organizations in the country. As a consequence, the members of the JRA decided to undertake operations outside the country where they would have some chance of surviving to continue the struggle. The group resorted to hijacking airliners flying out of Japan; it also attacked embassies abroad as a means of furthering its Marxist-Leninist agenda, and it gained concessions from the Japanese government in return for releasing hostages (Wilkinson 2003: 117). The JRA has operated with a variety of other dissident organizations over the years in its attacks. A group of members training in a camp in the Middle East cooperated with the Popular Front for the Liberation of Palestine in carrying out an attack at Lod Airport in Tel Aviv, Israel, in 1976. Twenty-five people were killed and seventy-six injured in the assault (Kuramatsu 1997). The members of the JRA found it much easier to smuggle weapons onto the flight than other individuals, especially since no intelligence agencies appear to have been aware of the involvement of Japanese leftists with Palestinian nationalists. This attack was basically a suicide attack since the members of the assault squad had no chance of avoiding death or capture once they opened fire with automatic weapons and grenades. Attacks have been rare in recent years, although the group has attempted to remain active, but like other leftist groups it has gradually faded from prominence. Enough members or former members remain available for the core of a revived organization or for an alliance with other terrorist groups.

One additional kind of ideology that can be considered at least generally leftist involves views dealing with the preservation of the environment and animal rights. While such views are not Marxist in background, the views of the dissidents involved generally attack the political and theoretical premises of the political system from the left rather than the right. While Green parties and defenders of the position of animals in society as part of the necessary ecological balance do have clear differences with Marxist-Leninist groups, they also share some positions. Ecological groups are often concerned with fairness and the equitable distribution of resources to some extent, and ecological and environmental movements are almost inevitably anti-capitalist. Capitalism has hardly been environmentally benign, and pollution and destruction of the natural habitat has often been associated with capitalism. Communist systems were even more destructive of the environment, as can be seen in the ecological disasters that were created by communist regimes in Eastern Europe and the old Soviet Union, but the communist countries did not permit any meaningful environmental protests or resorts to violence. The communist systems are now virtually gone, leaving only unrestrained capitalism to threaten environmental quality. In particular, large multinational companies are often seen as the greatest threats. The idea that small is beautiful almost invariably runs counter to the idea that greater growth is valuable. Frustrated by the lack of progress in defending the environment, groups have resorted to violence and terror, and persons have been injured (Eagan 1996). Much of the violence has been directed against property. Throwing paint on persons wearing furs or splashing corporate executives with the polluted water or earth from their companies' operations are not deadly acts. These types of activities have been designed to publicize the cause and to embarrass rather than to harm. There have also been attacks on ski resorts, new housing, recreational developments, and other property in the United States that threaten the national habitat in some way in the eyes of the attackers (B. Taylor 1998). More recently, large gas guzzlers (SUVs) in the United States have even become targets for environmental violence. There has been a recent increase in the use of violence, which some environmental and ecological groups have become willing to tolerate in their cause. The Unabomber as an individual shared at least some of these concerns given his opposition to modernization and technology. Further, there have been some recent fears that radical environmental groups might endanger food supplies by using biological agents to attack genetically engineered crops or to prevent the inhumane treatment of animals (Foxell 2001: 109).

Case studies

The following six case studies represent clear examples of dissident movements that have both been based on leftist ideologies and that have resorted to the use of terror. Ideology at some level has served as a rationalization for the violence. The cases include examples of three European countries that faced terrorist campaigns from the left in the latter half of the twentieth century, usually involving activities by dissident students. The activities of the Red Army Faction or Baader-Meinhof Gang in the former West Germany, the Red Brigades in Italy, and the 17 November Movement in Greece are representative of activities by younger leftists. The other three cases are more varied. The Montoneros in Argentina, who were eventually destroyed by the military regime

in power, were similar in many ways to the movements in Western Europe in the political goals that they sought. There were leftist groups that unsuccessfully sought to unseat the religious rulers who came to power in Iran after the overthrow of the Shah. The final case involves the Animal Liberation Front in the United Kingdom, which has indicated its willingness to use terror in its efforts to dissuade companies and individuals from violating the rights of animals.

CASE STUDY 7.1
The Baader-Meinhof Gang in West Germany

One of the most infamous of the Marxist-Leninist terrorist groups that appeared in Europe in the 1970s was the Baader-Meinhof Gang, which was also known as the Red Army Faction (RAF). While the group was not the most effective organization that appeared, it did catch the imagination of the press and public opinion. In this sense the group was very effective in broadcasting its message of opposition to the international capitalist system of which West Germany was a part. It developed a rather extensive support system within Western Europe, utilized contacts with East Germany and the Soviet Union to further its activities, and joined in some rather spectacular international efforts. The original group was effectively disrupted by the security forces, but the RAF was succeeded by the June 2nd Movement and the Red Cells as later generations of the same movement.

The RAF was formed in 1968 at the height of the student protests that were sweeping Europe and which seemed, even if only briefly, to have some chance of changing the political systems of the West. The particular motivation for the initial members of the RAF was the death of a student protester at the hands of the police. The student was protesting about a visit of the Shah of Iran to Berlin and he died in the midst of a struggle between the protesters and the police authorities, who were not prepared for the student demonstrations that had begun to appear (Otte 1997b: 552). His death was seen as an integral part of the effort of the capitalists to maintain order and control in their home countries. The Shah was perceived to be a Third World leader who worked hand in glove with Western capitalism. The political system and government of West Germany was seen as a thinly disguised continuation of Nazi Germany (Crenshaw 1995b: 21). The founding members of the RAF drew upon Marxist-Leninist writings to explain current events. The war in Vietnam, the failure of student protests, the poverty in the Third World, and the failure of the Palestinians to achieve their rights were all seen as symptoms of the continuing domination of the world economic system by capitalists. Their ultimate goal was the destruction of international capitalism and imperialism (C. Drake 1998: 71).

The RAF selected a variety of targets in keeping with its anti-capitalist stance. The initial attacks launched by the group were relatively amateurish bombings of buildings, but the group quickly moved on to more violent and deadly attacks. A variety of businessmen, seen as representatives of the oppressive capitalist system, were chosen for personal attacks, letter bombs, kidnapping, or assassination. Their targets included bankers, and occasionally the press and publishing industries. They kidnapped reasonably prominent individuals in a number of efforts to gain the freedom of imprisoned comrades. American military personnel also became targets at times. The RAF managed to detonate bombs on or near American military bases on a number of occasions. The RAF even attempted to assassinate General Alexander Haig, who was then the commander of the NATO forces in Europe (Pluchinsky 1992: 44). The RAF did threaten to launch a chemical attack on one occasion with mustard gas that it claimed to possess. This threat proved to be a hoax. The group apparently learned that the gas was missing and claimed to have acquired it in order to increase pressure on the West German government over an upcoming trial of RAF members. Ultimately, there was no evidence that the group ever did have the mustard gas (Claridge 2000a: 105), but since the RAF had already demonstrated its willingness to use violence to achieve its objectives, such a threat could not be totally ignored.

The original members of the RAF turned out not to be very effective dissidents. Although they launched a

number of successful attacks, and focused attention on the problems that they claimed were present within the system, they were all apprehended and sent to prison. The leaders of the RAF, however, were able to give directions to their followers while in prison, and, in fact, they were somewhat more effective from what would seem to have been a less than ideal location. From prison they served as an inspiration for other leftists to struggle against world capitalism. They became symbols of the struggle against the status quo, and new dissident groups appeared following the example of the RAF. These new organizations even attempted some actions that were designed to free the imprisoned original members of the Baader-Meinhof Gang. These attempts included the kidnapping of a German industrialist and the hijacking of an airliner in 1977. When the hijackers were captured, three of the RAF leaders in prison committed suicide. The members on the outside were convinced that the three had been murdered, and the industrialist was killed in retaliation (Pluchinsky 1992: 46–7). The suicides of the RAF leaders have continued to be considered suspicious by leftists in Germany and elsewhere in Europe, who have regarded them as more victims of the system. Members of leftist groups who were captured in later years followed their example by committing suicide while in custody (Otte 1997b: 554).

The West German dissidents also eventually developed strong connections with the Palestinian opposition groups. The West German dissidents received training in Palestinian camps, learning how to handle arms and weapons. The German dissidents and Palestinians cooperated in a number of major actions. At least one former or present RAF member was involved with the Palestinian groups that were responsible for the hostage situation involving the OPEC oil ministers in Vienna in December of 1975 (Otte 1997b: 555). RAF members were also involved in the hijacking of the Air France flight that was eventually diverted to Entebbe in Uganda—only to be killed when the Israeli commandos struck and rescued the hostages. German and Palestinian terrorists were involved in the hijacking of a Lufthansa airliner flying to Somalia in October of 1977. When special units of the German border police attacked the aircraft on the ground (with the permission of the Somali authorities), the hostages were freed and the hijackers captured or killed (Otte 1997b: 556). The failure of the hijackers to maintain control of the airliner and the hostages was the event that triggered the suicides of the three imprisoned RAF leaders.

One factor that made it possible for the RAF to survive and to continue to mount attacks was the presence of a substantial support network. While the active members of the various groups were relatively few in number, they depended upon a network of supporters to provide them with safe houses, information, to serve as couriers, and to scout locations for attacks. Surviving underground in West Germany was also an expensive proposition. It has been estimated that it cost $50,000 a year for one member of the RAF to survive in German society (Long 1990: 69). Such costs

required a financial support network for the movement to be able to continue. Without the support of other supporters of Marxist-Leninist ideologies, the German revolutionaries would have been much less effective than they were. The RAF was also very successful in its efforts to internationalize its activities. It undertook terrorist attacks, bank robberies, and engaged in confrontations with security forces in Sweden (where it seized the West German embassy), Belgium, Spain, Austria, Italy, Switzerland, the Netherlands, and France. Some of these efforts involved coordination with other leftist dissident groups in these countries. The RAF was in fact the group most important in efforts at forming a broad, leftist, anti-capitalist front throughout Europe (Pluchinsky 1992: 44). This effort at international coordination was never as effective as the organizers hoped, but the combined efforts that

BOX 7.3 Popular Front for the Liberation of Palestine (PFLP)

The Popular Front for the Liberation of Palestine (PFLP) was founded by George Habash, who tied the cause of an independent Palestinian state to Marxist-Leninist theories and the battle against global capitalism. He saw the struggle of the Palestinians as part of the broader struggle of colonial peoples and the working class against global capitalism. The PFLP has cooperated in the Palestinian struggle. It joined the PLO when it was formed, but it never commanded the following of Fatah and Yassir Arafat. The group was very active in airline hijackings. In 1968 it successfully undertook a hijacking to popularize the cause of the Palestinians and to seek the release of imprisoned Palestinians (Hoffman 1998: 67–8). The group also took part in joint actions such as the hijacking of an Air France flight to Entebbe, the assault on oil ministers at an OPEC meeting in Vienna, the Lod Airport attack by the Japanese Red Army, and other attacks. Because of its leftist orientation it was able to develop effective ties with various leftist groups in Europe and Japan that saw the Palestinian struggle as part of a global battle between capitalism and the people.

The PFLP has been among the more intransigent Palestinian groups. It supported the intifada in the Occupied Territories when opposition to the Israelis broke out, joining forces with other local groups. When the PLO decided to renounce terrorism as a weapon, implicitly recognizing the right of Israel to exist, and agreed to open negotiations with the government of Israel, the PFLP left the organization. It joined the Rejectionist Front with other groups that were opposed to any accommodation with Israel. Because of its Marxist-Leninist ideology the PFLP has become somewhat marginalized in the struggle with Israel. The ideology has prevented it from mobilizing on the basis of religion, and it has been less effective than the mainstream PLO groups in competing on the basis of Palestinian nationalism. Like other leftist groups it has suffered from the breakup of the Soviet Union and the end of Communism in so many parts of the world, and like other leftist organizations it has suffered from internal differences and splits within the organization.

did occur were indicative of the importance of the RAF. The RAF and its successors did have external support from East Germany and the Soviet Union. The external support was helpful but not essential for the survival of the group. The members of the RAF were capable of finding arms and building bombs on their own, and they did not have to rely on support from communist countries, even though such help was useful. Probably the most important contribution made by the East Germans was to provide members of various groups with safe havens to relax without fear of arrest or discovery (Pluchinsky 1992: 81). Ten members of the RAF, including the leading surviving members of the RAF were discovered and arrested in East Germany in 1990 after the fall of the communist government in that state (Laqueur 1999: 167).

One facet of the RAF that was relatively unusual was its ability to develop new generations of leaders as members of the current active group that were caught or killed. The RAF was thus able to survive as a group even as its membership changed completely. It was able to overcome losses in personnel and leadership (Pluchinsky, 1992: 44). This continuity was due in significant measure to the well-developed support groups that supplied the active terrorists with material aid and information, and which was also able to supply recruits to replace the lost comrades. The RAF was able to bedevil the West German government for years. The RAF, however, was not prepared for the collapse of communism in the Soviet Union and Eastern Europe (Merkl 1995b: 172–3). The Marxist goals and critiques of the capitalist system became more difficult to put forward with the disintegration of the system that the dissidents claimed to be their ultimate goal. There was a series of attacks and assassinations in 1991, but the group began to reconsider its whole campaign. In a series of communiqués in 1992, the surviving leftists indicated that they were ceasing their activities (Pluchinsky 1993).

CASE STUDY 7.2
The Italian Red Brigades

The Baader-Meinhof Gang/Red Army Faction managed to generate considerable publicity through-

out Europe and the world without having had any major long-term successes in disrupting the German political system. The Italian Red Brigades, however, was a much more potent terrorist group. Its activities in the late 1960s, 1970s, and 1980s generated greater fear and disruptions. The total active membership of the Red Brigades or related groups reached levels that were considerably higher than the levels attained in West Germany. The Italian Red Brigades, however, concentrated almost totally on targets related to the domestic, economic, and political systems throughout its campaigns (although it did kidnap a US general assigned to NATO). The Red Brigades, as well as other leftists in Italy, regarded the parliamentary democratic system that was created after World War II to be simply a continuation of the fascist regime in power under Benito Mussolini. There was a wide range of targets, including business leaders, judges, police officials, union personnel, party leaders, and politicians.

The Red Brigades grew out of the Italian university setting, and most of the members were young and idealistic. They could see the problems that were present with Western capitalism, and they were influenced by the purer versions of Marxism that were typically presented in the universities at the time. They sought to create the socialism of Lenin in the early years of Russia or of the Maoist revolution, not the version of socialism that existed in the USSR in the 1970s (Raufer 1993: 319). Flirtations with leftist ideologies were not unusual for university students in the late 1960s and early 1970s. Many Marxist theories also specified that the intelligentsia, including students, have a key role to play in preparing a society for revolution, so these theories had an additional attraction for young students since it gave them a potentially key role to play. These years were somewhat heady days for young Marxists with the appearance of student protests and demonstrations against the American involvement in Vietnam—and of the explicit or implicit support provided to the United States by its European allies. The leaders of the Red Brigades saw themselves as part of the vanguard of the proletariat. This intellectual vanguard was prepared to do battle with the global system of capitalism in order to liberate the working classes.

The Marxist beliefs of the dissidents and their concern for the working class were obvious in the original choices of targets. The Red Brigades' activities were clearly designed to discredit Italian business leaders. The first actions, while violent, were not lethal. Attacks were on company property and the possessions of local capitalists. Vehicles of prominent capitalists were vandalized or bombed. Brief symbolic kidnappings of executives and labor leaders from the more conservative unions were undertaken. Bank robberies became a mechanism for attacking the system, as well as a means of funding their activities (Rimanelli 1989: 270). Eventually, funding for the organization became easier when an Italian millionaire with a publishing firm, Franco Feltrinelli, joined the dissidents. His personal wealth funded the Red Brigades until he was accidentally killed while planting explosives on a tower for power lines (Rimanelli 1992: 160–1).

The early efforts of the Red Brigades had benefited from a shakeup of the Italian security forces. Many key members of the intelligence services had been dismissed because of their links with members of the extreme right and because they were suspected of planning some sort of coup against the democratic government (della Porta 1995: 117). As a consequence, the security forces were somewhat disorganized at the time that the Red Brigades became a threat. With the passage of time members of the Brigades escalated the violence and began the practice of kneecapping. They would approach targets, which included business executives, union leaders, and journalists who failed to report the truth as defined by the dissidents. The targets would then be shot in both knees. This intentional wounding of targets was a step towards greater violence, but it was still a technique that avoided killing the enemies of the people. Kneecapping was actually inherently more dangerous for the dissidents than simply killing targets, which could be done with a car bomb or letter bomb. Bombs could be detonated from a safe distance by remote control or activated by the pressure of the target entering a car or opening a package, whereas kneecapping required that a member of the organization had to be near enough to the target to be able to cause harm while also being able to avoid killing the target. The use of such a technique also demonstrated to the public at large not only the restraint of the dissidents in not killing their targets but their nerve and their abilities in being able to get near enough to be successful. Kneecappings also demonstrated that the authorities were incapable of protecting persons who were supporters of the system, even though it was clearly impossible for the security forces to protect everyone who could be seen as a representative of the capitalist system. The decision to escalate to kneecapping was thus a very well chosen tactic in many respects. It discredited the state in some ways, and it was effective in terms of instilling fear in a broad audience, while limiting the possibility of alienating the general public by ensuring that killing individuals in ways that virtually guaranteed that the deaths of innocent bystanders would not occur.

Notwithstanding the successes of kneecapping, the members of the Red Brigades graduated toward even more violent activities in efforts to liberate members who had been captured by the police or security forces, including some of the initial leaders of the group. When their trial was approaching in 1977, the Brigades concentrated on disrupting the judicial proceedings. In an effort to prevent the trial from taking place, they began to target judges, prosecutors, and the lawyers who were appointed to defend the captured members of the Red Brigades. They killed a judge, the president of the lawyers' association who had selected the public defenders, and members of the security forces. Their efforts were successful in disrupting the trial and forcing postponements because of the threats to the various participants in the proceedings. The legal system was almost paralyzed for a time. Jurors were afraid to serve because of the fear of retaliation, and not every judge was willing to be a hero (Laqueur 1999: 29). When the trials did resume, the public was treated to the spectacle of 8,000 security personnel being necessary to guard the courthouse in order for the judicial proceedings to begin anew (R. Drake 1997: 562). The Brigades had clearly demonstrated their capacity to undermine the system while demonstrating the inability of the system to function except through the use of massive defensive forces.

In 1978 the terrorist attacks of the Red Brigades became even more lethal. While kneecappings and other types of attacks continued, the dissidents were now much more likely to kill their victims. The highlight of the year for the group came when members of the organization kidnapped the President of the Christian Democratic Party and former Prime Minister Aldo Moro in Rome, killing his five-man security team in the process. He was held captive for almost two months while the authorities were unable to locate him despite massive efforts to do so. The Red Brigades then tried him for crimes against the people. He was convicted and was killed. His body was left in the trunk of a car only a hundred yards from the Christian Democratic Party headquarters in Rome (R. Drake 1997: 562–3). The Moro kidnapping displayed the abilities of the dissidents, but the subsequent execution of Moro turned the political leadership in Italy and the general population against the group (Rimanelli 1992: 151). The Italian authorities now began to make even greater efforts to control the Red Brigades. All the major political parties, including the Communist Party, cooperated in passing enhanced security laws that were designed to control the Red Brigades. Special units were set up to deal with the terrorists, and they proved to be more effective than the regular police. The government also began a policy of providing lighter sentences for members of the group who "repented" of their actions and demonstrated their repentance by providing information on the organization. The captured members were bribed with lighter sentences if they informed on others in the organization. This technique proved to be very effective once enough dissidents had been captured. When the first few opted to accept the reduced sentences, it became possible to capture others. By the mid-1980s the bulk of the dissidents had been captured. The Red Brigades then became a negligible force that was no longer capable of matching the efforts of five years earlier, even though isolated attacks were still to occur. Early in 2002 the Italian Minister of Economics was assassinated by surviving members of the Red Brigades for suggesting that layoffs by companies should be made easier. The threat to political stability and the democratic system, however, had long since passed.

The Italian government ultimately managed to deal with the threat from these dissidents without major limitations on civil liberties. At least some members of the Red Brigades had hoped to force the Italian political elite to support a more repressive state. They thought that greater repression would have helped the general public realize that the government fronted the capitalists and their interests. In this effort they failed, although there was at least some evidence of at least one conspiracy by the extreme right to intervene against the democratic system and to establish a stronger government that would be able to deal with the leftist dissidents. When the security forces began to improve, the Red Brigades were further weakened by schisms within the movement. Like many leftist organizations splits within terrorist groups weakened them. The lack of unity also meant that it was harder for them to mobilize resources since to at least some extent they were competing with each other as well as with the government. The Brigades themselves were divided on the wisdom of killing Moro; thus, his death weakened the movement.

The Red Brigades had some external contacts and support. While the dissidents were organized within Italy and financed locally, there were some contacts with countries behind the Soviet Union. In the case of Italy, Czechoslovakia served as the Soviet surrogate for providing assistance to the leftists. Training, some arms, and some financing were arranged through the Czech government. While logistical support was present from the Czechs, neither the Czechs nor the Soviet KGB played any role in developing the strategy and techniques utilized by the Red Brigades (Rimanelli 1989: 280). The Red Brigades also maintained contacts with other leftist groups in Europe, such as the Red Army Faction. Efforts to generate combined action among the various groups did not come to very much. Notwithstanding the contacts with outside supporters and groups, the Red Brigades remained very much a domestic Italian phenomenon drawing upon Italian circumstances.

The Red Brigades were one of the more successful dissident groups from the left that appeared in Europe. They were the only terrorist groups in Italy that had sufficient organizational capabilities, personnel, and other resources to undertake complex actions

(Rimanelli 1992: 149). The threat that they created to the stability of the Italian political system was very real. The fact that some groups on the Italian right were preparing to create a more authoritarian form of government indicates that the leftists had managed to at least create the possibility that Italian democracy would fall. The targets that they selected demonstrated their ability to attack the capitalist system in all its manifestations. The capitalist executives were among the first, and major business figures were always under threat. Targets went beyond the obvious to include journalists whose stories were either less than flattering to the leftist goals or supportive of the government, union officials who were not active enough in challenging the system, and members of the major political parties which were seen as being part of the system. The Red Brigades also demonstrated a progressive increase in the level of violence when their first attacks were insufficient to achieve their goals. They moved from the attacks on property and the symbolic kidnappings, to kneecapping and wounding targets, and finally to assassinations and murder. Even though the stability of the system was indeed challenged by the left, the attacks were not able either to bring the leftists to power and change government policies to any significant degree or to force the government to become extremely repressive as befitted a state that was simply fascist in disguise.

CASE STUDY 7.3
17 November Organization in Greece

One of the longest-lasting and most intriguing terrorist groups drawing on ideologies of the left has been the 17 November Organization or 17 November Movement in Greece. While not the only leftist dissident organization operating in Greece, it has been the most prominent one over time. The group has had the typical Marxist goal of attempting to create circumstances favorable to a popular insurrection. The dissidents have hoped to discredit the Greek government and political system and trigger a popular uprising through terrorist attacks while avoiding the need to engage in guerrilla warfare (Kassimeris 2001: 206).

The desire to avoid guerrilla tactics might be due to the fact that Greek communist groups attempted such guerrilla warfare in the aftermath of World War II, but the attempts ultimately failed to overthrow the government, partially because of aid supplied by the United States. The group took its name from the date in 1973 when there was a student uprising in Athens against the military regime that was then in power. The military regime easily dealt with the protests and used force that resulted in the deaths of at least 30 people and injuries to another 800. The first terrorist actions by this group began in 1975, and the group remained active and immune to discovery until the summer of 2002. What made the group so unusual was that for nearly thirty years no member of the organization had ever been identified. Even more surprising was the fact that the police had no confirmed fingerprints on the terrorists, and for more than twenty years no blood samples or strands of hair, no samples of clothing, or any other piece of physical evidence that could be used to identify a group member was found (Kassimeris 1995: 74–5). In 1999 police finally acquired a blood sample that was presumed to belong to a member (Kassimeris 2001: 104). The Greek authorities failed to penetrate the organization or learn the identity of its members even when they had the help of the intelligence resources of the United States and other countries. The group was finally exposed when one of its members was injured when a bomb went off prematurely. Once he was in custody, other members of the group became vulnerable and arrests started.

Even though none of the members was initially caught, the leftist orientation of 17 November was clear in two ways. The group usually provided communiqués after its attacks, justifying the action and specifying the logic behind the choice of targets. The language of these communiqués clearly drew upon Marxist-Leninist rhetoric and clearly indicated that the group was opposed to the United States and its policies, as well as Greek membership in NATO and the European Community (later European Union). Second, the targets themselves were typical of those chosen by leftist groups, including US military personnel (reflecting the group's antipathy to US military bases in Greece), a British military attaché, the CIA station chief in Athens, buildings and offices associated with major multinational corporations that were considered to be "stealing from the Greek people," and politicians associated with the conservative parties in Greece as well as supporters of those parties (Harmon 2000: 14). Attacks on Western targets increased during the Gulf War of 1990–1 to indicate the organization's solidarity with the Iraqi people as part of the Third World, although the group's pronouncements never offered support to Saddam Hussein (Corsun 1992: 116). The group later attacked Western targets to indicate its opposition to the bombing of Yugoslavia by NATO countries in support of the Albanians in Kosovo. In other periods the choice of targets shifted to domestic politicians and local Greeks who could be seen to be collaborating with the outside exploiters of the Greek people (Corsun 1992: 93).

The group's activities all seem to have been carefully chosen to encourage opposition to the current Greek political system as part of the world capitalist system while not alienating the population at large. The bombings of buildings were designed to avoid casualties among innocent bystanders. Assassinations were of particular individuals and avoided killing persons other than the targets. Only twenty-three people died as a result of the attacks by the groups in twenty-eight years of activity. Many of the assassination victims were foreign, including US military officers and personnel attached to various Western embassies. In the case of attacks on Greeks, many of them were clearly intended only to wound the targets. The Greek dissidents adopted the Italian technique of kneecapping individuals who were seen to be part of the oppressive system. As was the case for the Italian Red Brigades, getting close enough to wound the target but not to kill the target even when one could obviously do so clearly demonstrated the capabilities and the power of the organization and its members. It also clearly demonstrated the inability of the government to protect its own since the terrorist had got so close to the targets. The one person who died as a consequence of such an attack did so because he received inadequate treatment in a local hospital, a fact that could be taken to demonstrate the inadequacies of the current Greek government and society (Corsun 1992: 102).

Some of the group's activities have a sense of the theatrical, and members of the group have been rather innovative in some of their activities. A bazooka or some other type of rocket-launching mechanism was necessary for one of their attacks. Members of the group entered the national war museum just before closing, overcame the staff and the visitors, and stole World War II vintage weapons to use in their attack. No one at the museum was harmed, and the terrorists escaped without being identified (Corsun 1992: 110). In another example of derring-do, members of the group entered a police station, overpowered the officers present, and escaped with police weapons, all without firing a shot (Gourdoumbas 1997). In yet another case, members of the organization who faced a confrontation with the police managed to elude the police officials and escape by taking a taxi (Kassimeris 1995: 85). Such attacks and escapes, especially when no one was hurt, created a positive image for the terrorists in the public's eye in terms of their abilities. They also highlighted the weaknesses of the government and mocked the government's inability to do anything to stop the group.

The tactics of the group would seem to have been chosen in order to maintain invulnerability to detection. There have been assassinations, bombings, and attacks on buildings. None of these actions, by their very nature, leaves witnesses if the attackers are careful. Wounding and kneecapping of targets expose the dissidents to possibilities of identification, but again with appropriate care, identification can be avoided. The organization has never taken hostages or kidnapped individuals (Gourdoumbas 1997). To do so would place the anonymity of the organization in great jeopardy. A hostage situation would involve negotiations with the government in which the negotiator for the terrorists could be more readily identified. Media pictures and tapes would also be available. With kidnappings it would always be possible, even with the greatest care in the world, for the victim to pick up some bits of information that might provide a lead for the police and security agencies. The group has thus avoided using some of the typical terrorist techniques that might compromise the security of the group. The group also maintained its anonymity by limiting the membership, and there is very little indication that the group sought to increase its membership in any significant way. While the organization has been continuously active for more than a quarter of a century, the small membership and the need to maintain themselves in the community by holding down jobs has meant that the number of such attacks has been limited.

The 17 November group displays some of the strengths and weaknesses of a successful terrorist group. This group and other Marxist-Leninist groups that have existed in Greece have clearly demonstrated that the Greek government has been quite incompetent in terms of dealing with internal threats. At least with some of the other groups, the police have made an occasional arrest, but the overall record of the Greek authorities in this area has been dismal. This weakness has shown up Greece in other areas. Non-Greek terrorist groups that have sought to hijack airliners and undertake actions elsewhere in Europe have often used the airport in Athens as a point from which to penetrate security since the airport has been notorious for its lax security. In Athens individuals have been able to board aircraft with weapons that they then carried with them to other airports, where they boarded the flights that were the real targets for hijackings. The Greek police lack the training, expertise, equipment, and motivation to deal effectively with terrorist threats (Kassimeris 1995: 85).

In fact, the strengths and weaknesses of the organization are related. The group has been eminently successful in keeping the government from gaining any information on its members and activities. It has been one of the most successful clandestine groups in this regard, and it has managed to avoid government discovery by remaining small. As a consequence, while it has been able to humiliate the security forces, it has never been able to disrupt the Greek political system really effectively. Its attacks have constituted a nuisance and an embarrassment to many Greek politicians and the government in power over the years, but they have never been able to cause enough damage or difficulties to really threaten the Greek political system. In order to do so, the organization would have had to increase its membership and seek to undertake more attacks with greater frequency. Such an expansion, of course, would have made it

more likely that eventually the Greek security forces would have captured or at least identified some members of the group. In effect, if the group were really serious about attempting to destroy the Greek political system through the use of terrorism as a stimulus for a popular uprising, it would have had to take a chance on opening itself up to discovery and counter-attack by government forces. The 17 November Organization ultimately failed to undermine the existing Greek political system—just as the Greek authorities failed to catch the terrorists for so long—and the changes that the dissidents sought have not occurred.

CASE STUDY 7.4
The Montoneros in Argentina

The Montoneros was a left-wing movement that arose in Argentina in the late 1960s. The group was similar in some respects to the Marxist-Leninist movements that appeared in Europe at the same time, but there were distinctly Argentine elements that characterized the organization. The persons who joined the movement in the years that it was active were invariably young, middle-class idealists seeking greater equality and justice for all portions of the Argentine population, especially the working class. The government in power at the time of the group's formation was a military regime that had come to power in 1966. These dissidents maintained their opposition to at least some elements of government policies during a number of civilian and military regimes that followed. The Montoneros were initially supporters of former President Juan Perón. They were particularly in sympathy with the redistributive, populist, and nationalist policies that Perón and his wife, Evita, had supported while he was in power (Calvert 1997b: 417). Ironically, Perón himself had come to power through a military coup, although he later built a mass following from the civilian sector. His own policies while in power were a mixture of both conservative and progressive attributes. He did differ from other political leaders with a military background in South America in that he favored workers and labor unions, and some of his strongest support came from this sector, but he also worked closely with the military, business, and the Catholic Church. Perón was able to stay in power as long as his policies favoring the left did not become too irritating to the middle and upper classes, and as long as he was able to institute some policies that the more conservative interests desired. His nationalist policies that discriminated against European and American capital and businesses were popular with both the working classes and the middle classes. He was removed from power in a military coup in 1955 when he was no longer able to balance all of these interests successfully.

Although Perón was overthrown and left the country, he quickly became the most important Argentine political figure. From his exile in Spain he helped to direct his followers and appointed leaders of parties seeking his return. He chose other candidates for office that would be supported by his followers when various governments in Argentina prohibited parties openly supporting Perón from contesting elections. Perón's support was often essential for victory of the candidates, but any effort by civilian politicians to legalize the Peronista party or some version of it led to military intervention. The military would not permit supporters of Perón, or Perón himself, to govern, but the supporters of Perón were able to prevent any other party or president from governing effectively. Perón's followers continued to reflect the contradictions from the past since they included both the left and the right. Labor unions and leftists and conservative groups supported a return of Perón. These contradictions in the Peronista movement were not so obvious when it was in opposition. All the various groups could agree to be opposed to whatever civilian or military government was in power and assumed that if Perón did indeed return, their preferred policies would be implemented. The members of the Montoneros believed that if they were able to rid the country of the military government, they would be able to influence the supporters of Perón and Perón himself to follow the appropriate policies (Wynia 1986: 78–9).

The spark for the organization of the Montoneros from among the left-wing supporters of Perón was a popular uprising in the city of Cordoba in 1969 that united workers and students. The uprising was a protest against the austerity program implemented by the military government then in power (Calvert 1997b: 417). The government was able to put down the uprising, but its suppression generated more opposition throughout the country. The Montoneros was one of the left-wing dissident organizations to appear, and it eventually became the largest one. In 1970 the small group of original members decided to begin violent political action directed against the military regime that was in power. They kidnapped a former President (and general) who had ruled immediately after Perón's ouster. After a trial for crimes committed while he was in office, he was executed for his misdeeds (Wynia 1986:77–8). From this point, the battle lines between the Montoneros and other groups in Argentine society were clearly drawn.

While the government managed to capture most of the original members of the Montoneros, the organization had begun to expand and attract new recruits. It began a campaign against the government based on the use of terror. Efforts to undertake guerrilla insurgencies in Argentina in the past had failed, so the Montoneros, like the contemporary Tupamaros in Uruguay, opted for an urban strategy using their attacks as examples of propaganda of the deed as part of an effort to influence the general public and to bring discredit upon the government (Wynia 1986: 79). The group relied on bombings, kidnappings, assassinations, and other tactics in cities as a means of promoting its political objectives, including the demand that Peronistas be allowed to participate in politics. The violence was not just directed against vulnerable civilians since the attacks included bombs and other attacks against the police and the military. Kidnappings of executives from multinational corporations became an especially effective way of financing the movement since a successful kidnapping not only displayed the ineptitude of the government but also generated the revenues for proceeding with the struggle. One leftist group accumulated $30 million from such kidnappings (Bell 1997b: 239).

The campaign of the Montoneros, the activities of the other supporters of Perón who were more conservative, and the attacks by the People's Revolutionary Army (ERP), a more clearly Marxist movement, were ultimately successful. The military government found it increasingly difficult to govern Argentina and eventually decided to hold free elections in 1973 that were open to all parties. A Peronist candidate won the presidency as a stand-in, and he immediately allowed Juan Perón to return in triumph. He then resigned so that Perón could run for President himself. Perón easily won the new election, completing his return to power. The successful election of Perón, however, brought the differences between the groups that were supporting him to the forefront. Violence between the supporters began, and Perón had to decide which group to favor. He initially moved against the ERP since that leftist group had never been supportive of him. The significance of the attacks to the Montoneros should have been clear in terms of Perón's ultimate choice between his own conservative backers and the more radical groups that had brought him to power. Restrictions were then placed on the political activities of the Montoneros, and Perón was clearly distancing himself from the Montoneros when he died in 1974 (Gillespie 1982: 150–1). The nature of the campaign against the Montoneros changed with Perón's death. His wife, Isabel, who had served as his vice-president, took power, but she quickly demonstrated that she was incapable of dealing with the complexities of governing, especially in a divided society facing assaults on the government from a variety of sources. Her advisors, who were among the most conservative of the Peronistas, used the security forces and para-military groups to launch attacks on the leftists (Poneman 1987: 33). Faced with repression, the Montoneros reverted to their assaults on the government. Their attacks continued when Isabel Perón was replaced by a military coup in 1976.

The new round of violence that began in 1974 was much more intense than the previous fighting. Both the Montoneros and the ERP began targeting police and military officials. Unlike their European counterparts, the Montoneros consciously avoided targeting innocent civilians (Gillespie 1995: 214). When assassinations against members of the military forces increased, the security forces began to retaliate. When the military government took power in 1976, repression of dissidents became more determined. Previously, when members of the leftist groups were captured, they were often tortured for information

before being released or imprisoned. With the new military government they were still tortured for information but they were killed. In addition, the security forces began to use death squads to kidnap and question suspected supporters of the leftist, and most of these persons died as well, becoming the "disappeared ones" from that era of Argentine history. The Montoneros and the ERP were crushed and destroyed as effective dissident organizations in two years. The death toll among the dissidents and other suspect members of the population has never been completely determined, since suspects were killed and no records kept or notifications made. One estimate for the number of dead from the dissidents, presumed sympathizers, and others has been estimated to total somewhere between 15,000 and 30,000 individuals (Fagen 1992: 64). The survivors, few in number, fled the country. The terror campaign from the left had generated severe government repression, but that repression was more than adequate to deal with the challenges that the government faced. The deaths of sympathizers and even innocent persons, however, weakened support for the military regime, and popular dissatisfaction began to erode the public's willingness to acquiesce with the continuation in power of a military government. The seizure of the Falkland Islands by Argentine forces was an effort by the military regime in power to restore public support. The successful seizure was quite popular throughout Argentina, but the failure to prevent the British recapture of the islands resulted in the military turning power over to civilians.

The use of terror by the Montoneros and the other leftist organizations in Argentina had mixed results in terms of their political objectives. They were quite successful in helping to destabilize the military regime that was in power in the early 1970s. As a consequence, their efforts had indeed helped to bring about free elections and the return of Perón. Perón's return, however, did not result in the adoption of their desired policies. Thus, while they were successful in bringing down the old regime, they lacked sufficient support to establish the government and policies that they desired. Once Juan Perón died, the struggle became more intense, and the security forces and the military defeated the Montoneros. Ironically, the Montoneros was not one of the Marxist-Leninist movements that sought to force the government to become more repressive to demonstrate its true character. The Argentine circumstances did not adapt themselves to that approach, and the frequent presence of military regimes in power was a sufficient indication to most that the Argentine government was responsive to conservative and business interests. The terrorism of the Argentine dissident groups, however, did indicate that such campaigns could indeed result in a government adopting measures involving massive repression as theorists had predicted. In this case the repression decimated the dissident organizations. Ultimately, it could be argued that the campaign by the Montoneros and the resulting repression did actually shorten the life of the military regime and that it helped to set the stage for the resumption of free elections and democratic rule, but it came at a high cost.

CASE STUDY 7.5
The Islamic Republic of Iran and the Mujahedin-e-Khalq

Since the Islamic Republic was established Iran has most frequently been viewed as one of the states promoting and sponsoring terrorism around the world. Not only did Iran support dissident groups in Iraq, as might be expected during time of war, but the clerical leadership in Iran supported many other groups that were seeking to create more Islamic governments in the Middle East. The government of the Islamic Republic, however, faced a major domestic terrorist campaign early in its existence that was launched by groups that were opposed to the influence that Islamic religious principles and the clerical leaders had in the new regime. Given the religious nature of the government and the secular nature of the opposition, the opposition would clearly have to be considered as left in terms of its political objectives. The opposition included groups that were avowedly Marxist-Leninist in their ideology but there were other dissidents that were simply secular in their views, including those favoring the creation of a non-religious, liberal democratic government.

When the Shah was still in power, there was a variety of leftist groups that existed. Some operated fairly openly in the political system while others were more clandestine in their activities. There were some acts of terrorism and guerrilla activities by leftist groups under the monarchy, but such activities were sporadic. While some members of these Marxist groups did receive training in PLO camps in Lebanon and South Yemen, they were never able to mount an effective challenge to the Shah (R. Anderson 1997: 387). There were efforts by various organizations or the more militant splinter groups from among them to foment dissent in either the rural areas or the urban centers. None of the efforts lasted very long or were very successful. The secret police and the military proved to be quite capable of dealing with the limited threats that these activities presented, and the leadership of the groups involved was decimated as a consequence (Behrooz 2000: 140). Well placed informants inside various organizations aided the secret police. Further, the dissidents were also rather amateurish in their attempts to resort to armed attacks, and the various leftist groups were often more interested in engaging in ideological disputes among themselves than in cooperating to overthrow the monarchy.

As the Shah's regime began to experience difficulties in maintaining political control in the 1970s, opposition included Islamic clerics led by Ayatollah Khomeini in exile and groups on the left. Members of the Westernized middle class also began to join the agitation for change. This latter group was later to supply many of the Iranians who opposed the religious government that did come to power when the Shah fell. The religiously based opposition to the Shah was relatively unified under the leadership of the Shia Muslim clerics in the country and especially Ayatollah Khomeini from his exile in Paris. While the secular opposition remained divided among a great number of different groups, the religious opposition, the middle classes, and the Marxist groups eventually all did cooperate in overthrowing the monarchy. After the Shah fled the country, the middle class and the leftist groups quickly discovered that they were going to be junior partners in the government if they were allowed to participate at all. The Marxist groups were eliminated from involvement by a policy of divide and conquer. Different organizations were induced to cooperate in working against other Marxists, permitting the clerical government to defeat them in detail (Behrooz 2000: 145–6). The middle classes were similarly prevented from any meaningful participation in government and were targets for attacks as well (Bill and Leiden 1984: 389). These modernists were divided and failed to unite to oppose the dominant role being assumed by the clerics in the new government (Benard and Khalilzad 1984: 112–13). When more and more groups were eliminated from control in the government, and revolutionary guards began to attack those who might be opponents of the government, dissidents from the middle class and from the left—moderates and radicals—came together and formed the Mujahedin-e-Khalq. Failing to displace the clerics from power, the group resorted to a campaign of terror in its efforts to overthrow the Islamic Republic. The government forces responded with repression and violence of their own.

The government was especially vulnerable in its early years. It was clearly a regime in transition, and the clerical leaders of the revolution lacked experience in governing a large country and diverse population. As such it was vulnerable at the time the Mujahedin appeared to challenge the government. The Mujahedin attracted substantial support in the population, both from secular groups and some of the ethnic minorities, including Kurds and Turkish speaking Azeris in the northwestern portion of the country. The government, of course, had the support of many elements of the population, and Islamic parties had managed to dominate the early elections. The government also had the services of the clerics in the country to mobilize its supporters on behalf of the government. The religious leaders, since they had gained early control of the government institutions, were also able to call upon the police, security forces, and Islamic paramilitary groups for support and used laws to undercut the position and activities of the opposition. Notwithstanding the disadvantages that they faced, the Mujahedin mounted some spectacular attacks against the government and groups supporting it. The Speaker of the Parliament and a number of members of the legislature and others were killed with a bomb that exploded at the headquarters of the ruling party.

Assassinations and bombings took their toll elsewhere. Victims included a newly appointed president, a prime minister, a police head, and other officials and government supporters. Somewhere between 1,000 and 2,000 officials and supporters of the government died in the attacks (R. Anderson 1997: 391). The terrorists as individuals were dedicated to their cause, and in many ways were just as dedicated and zealous as the supporters of the government. Members of the Mujahedin even engaged in suicide attacks in their efforts to destroy the regime in power (Bill and Leiden 1984: 388). The dedication of those opposed to the government and the vulnerability of a political system in transition to a new system of government meant that the campaign from the left could not be immediately defeated. The campaign of bombings and assassinations continued for 18 months before the government gained effective control in the country (Green 1995: 579–80). Notwithstanding the dedication of the dissidents in carrying out the battle against the government and the security forces, the Mujahedin were not successful in changing the government of the Islamic Republic. Once the clerics began to learn how to govern and to organize the widespread support that they had, they were able to triumph and to strengthen the domestic roots of the system (Bill and Leiden 1984: 390–1).

When the government of the Islamic Republic had gained effective control, the surviving members of the dissident groups fled the country or lapsed into passivity. Their dissatisfaction with the government had not disappeared, and then the Iraqi invasion of Iran occurred, many of the members of the Mujahedin allied themselves with the secular Iraqi regime against the Islamic leadership of their own country. The Mujahedin tied down Iraqi military forces and undertook assassinations and sabotage inside Iran. They were even able to launch some terrorist attacks in Tehran the capital (Kostiner 1989: 125). With the eventual withdrawal of the Iraqi army from Iran, the Mujahedin-e-Khalq lost the opportunity to change the nature of the government in Iran. As a prerequisite for peace, Iraq was forced to cease support for the Mujahedin, a condition that Iraq largely fulfilled. The Iraqis even arranged for unsupported units of the Mujahedin to be isolated so that they could be destroyed by units of the Iranian armed forces. The Mujahedin still exists in exile, but for the moment it does not constitute any real threat to the government of Iran, especially since it has adopted more moderate policies, and the more extreme religious elements present in earlier days are no longer as influential. Over time, the government has become more pragmatic and more moderate leadership groups have appeared. Elections within the country have been reasonably fair and competitive, and there are many indications of continuing movement toward a more open political society.

CASE STUDY 7.6

The Animal Liberation Front and the Animal Rights Militia

Various organizations have appeared in the Western industrialized countries that have been opposed to using animals as test subjects in situations leading to death or injury. Some groups are opposed to using animals as a food source. While there have been differences among the persons involved in these groups, most of them have been opposed to the killing of animals simply to provide fur that can be made into stylish coats. Animal rights activists have been opposed to the use of animals as subjects to test cosmetics for problems or for research on other products where the animals serve as convenient test subjects. Most activists oppose using animals in cases where it is simply cheaper and more convenient to use animals instead of more expensive lab processes. Some opponents have extended their activities to attempt to prevent the use of animal subjects for medical research. Such research will involve pain since the animals are injured or infected with diseases in order for the necessary tests and research to occur. Not all persons concerned with the welfare of animals, however, share this view since such medical research prolongs human life and helps to facilitate medical breakthroughs. The maximum goal for some of the activists in animal rights groups is the hope that eventually it will be possible to prevent the eating of any meat and that everyone will be required to be vege-

tarian as a matter of state policy, although they realize this objective is unlikely to be achieved at any point in time in the near future.

Persons in favor of animal rights have already had an impact on the activities of private companies and have influenced government policies through peaceful means. Boycotts of cosmetic firms using animals for experiments have led many of them to discontinue the practice and to publicize their commitment to not using animals for such tests. Public pressure has resulted in the passage of laws in many countries that prohibit cruelty to animals. Owners can be fined or imprisoned for ignoring these laws, and they can lose the animals into protective care as well. There are international treaties and conventions prohibiting trade in endangered species or products obtained from endangered species (such as ivory from elephants). In the private sector standards have been established for using animals in films and TV productions, for appropriate care for animals that are used in racing such as horses and dogs, and for housing animals in zoos and similar situations. Groups seeking to protect animals, however, have felt that such peaceful actions have been either too slow or not successful enough and, as a consequence, have resorted to the use of violence to achieve their objectives. One very active group has sunk at least eight whaling ships and rammed others in efforts to protect sea life (Eagan 1996: 5).

Another group that has resorted to violence has been the Animal Liberation Front (ALF) in the United Kingdom. The initiative for the ALF originated in the early 1970s with groups that were opposed to hunts and the attendant cruelty to animals involved in such activities (Monaghan 2000: 160). Sabotage of hunts by friends of animals has a long history in the United Kingdom and a logical connection with a concern for animal rights. The ALF as an organization drew on this tradition of concern and has focused on both short-term and long-term goals in its ongoing struggle for animals. The basic short-term goal has been to prevent obvious animal abuse in its various forms, while the ultimate goal has been an effort to end all animal suffering and abuse and to force the recognition that the rights of animals cannot be sacrificed to meet human needs. In order to achieve both goals, the ALF has sought to drive companies and individuals profiting from abuse of animals out of business (Monaghan 1997: 110). The ALF, like many animal rights groups, very early on was willing to attack property as a means of achieving its goals. What has been somewhat different about the ALF and the animal rights movement in general is that the targets have not usually included the government or any of its agencies. These groups target individuals and firms that are in the private sector for the most part. Governments are usually on the wrong side of this policy debate since they attempt to protect the targets that are attacked or to prosecute the perpetrators when they are caught, but the government and its policies and personnel have not been seen as the main enemy (yet).

ALF members have broken into labs to free test animals and destroy the results of previous research, raising the cost of animal research to such levels that it could become prohibitive. They have also vandalized cars and buildings, set fires, poured glue into locks, and used similar tactics available to groups that seek to intimidate individuals and businesses. The disruptions to business from the attacks have resulted in costs that have run into hundreds of millions of dollars. Fur sales in particular have suffered a dramatic decline because of the peaceful and violent actions of such animal rights groups (Knickerbocker 1997: 5). The vandalism has extended to the homes of persons working in research institutions as a means of heightening the cost of continuing such research and frightening employees (Dodge 1997: 201). Many operations using animals or supplying animals for research have shut down as a consequence of the attacks (Loder 2000: 3). The animal rights groups have often been effective in using the media to publicize their cause and to send a message to all similar kinds of businesses operating elsewhere in the country and even abroad. It is very likely that at least some business decisions were altered by the violent actions undertaken by the ALF.

Notwithstanding the successes that were achieved with the property attacks, violence escalated to actions directed against people. A group called the Animal Rights Militia (ARM) has appeared, and it has been willing to use violence against people to prevent the abuse of animals. The attacks against people have included car bombs, letter bombs, and personal assaults that have led to severe beatings (Dodge 1997: 201). There have been physical attacks on hunters as well (B. Taylor 1998: 27). Letter bombs were sent to the leaders of the four major political parties in 1982 to publicize the cause (Monaghan 2000: 161). The ARM and its members have clearly progressed to the point where they feel that their political objectives are important enough to justify violence against human beings. The threatening nature of the animals rights groups has extended to hoaxes involving products coming from companies that continue to utilize animals in what the animal rights groups see as inappropriate ways. The hoaxes have indicated that certain products have been contaminated, and the perpetrators have introduced foreign substances of a non-harmful nature or written notes to indicate what they could do. There have, however, been some instances of actual product tampering and the inclusion of harmful substances (Dodge 1997: 201). Such product scares have expanded the target audience to include the public at large as the militants sought to generate additional adverse public reactions to the continued use of animals for experiments. The trend in recent years has been for an escalation of the violence or threatened violence. These more violent kinds of activities suggest that in the future there might be a significantly greater danger for persons who are considered to be abusing the rights of animals. Once individuals accept that it is moral to break the law in pursuit of a higher principle, violence becomes more likely (Monaghan 1997: 114). While injuries to date cannot compare with the casualties involved in many other terrorist groups, the potential for such violence could increase in the future.

It is not clear whether the ARM is a group that is really different from the ALF. Leftist dissidents in other countries that have engaged in violence have often credited fictitious organizations with violence in order to confuse the authorities and avoid recriminations for actions that have not been popular with the public. The ALF could have copied this tactic. The statements of the ARM make it clear that it seeks the same goals as the ALF, and this organizational separation permits the ALF to deflect negative opinion from itself while the ARM generates greater fear and pressure upon those who would continue to violate the rights of animals. It is very possible that there is some crossover between the personnel in the two groups, and there have even been some suggestions that the ARM is simply representative of the more violent wing of the ALF. If such is the case, the ALF may simply have invented the ARM to provide cover for the more violent activities (Monaghan 2000: 165).

The ALF has demonstrated another very modern characteristic of terrorist organizations. The way in which the group operates corresponds very closely to the idea of a loose network or leaderless resistance. The ALF lacks firm membership rolls, since maintaining them could make it easier for the government to track down members who might be responsible for property attacks or violence against individuals. It has extended notational or honorary membership to any individual who agrees with its goals. The ALF has also published newsletters and maintained web sites identifying possible targets, opponents of the movement, or members or former members who have provided information to the authorities. While the ALF has disseminated the information, it cannot be held responsible for the actions of isolated groups of individuals who act on their own to protect the rights of animals, even though provoking such attacks is the intent of the published lists (Monaghan 2000: 165). This organizational method has been very effective in permitting the ALF to present a non-violent image to the general public while still facilitating actions that are effective in shutting down the activities that the group opposes. Government prosecutions are also hindered as well since there is no hierarchical organization involved.

Animal rights groups have been successful in achieving policy changes by governments in power, but the limit of such policy changes may have been reached. It is unlikely that any new major changes are on the horizon for countries that have already enacted basic legislation. Protests and demonstrations and other pressures on lawmakers have achieved most of what they can. Violence against property has been successful as well. The activists have forced changes in practices by raising costs for the individuals or businesses involved. Many companies now forgo the use of animal experimentation (or one might suspect that they contract it out to braver souls in some cases) because of the costs involved from vandalism and other attacks. As a consequence, such attacks are likely to continue against groups that persist in using animals in ways that are unacceptable to the ALF and ARM. Some businesses, however, are not likely to give up their current practices, meaning that more personal violence may appear to be justified in the future for animal rights activists.

Summary

Except for the campaigns of assassinations of the anarchists in the late 1800s and early 1900s, Marxist-Leninist groups have usually avoided terrorism as a weapon before World War II. Major terrorist activities by leftists have been concentrated in the years after the war. Leftist dissidents engaged in other kinds of political violence prior to World War II. Revolution and uprising were the preferred courses of action. The communists under Mao Tse-tung's leadership in China opted for guerrilla insurgency based in the countryside. Even though uprisings and insurgencies as the preferred tactics of the left usually failed in this era, the emphasis on these particular techniques does explain the relative scarcity of examples of terrorism from the left in these decades.

After World War II, and especially in the latter part of the 1960s, terrorist groups from the left did appear with regularity. Students in many Western countries were attracted to such groups such as the Weathermen, the Red Brigades, the Red Army Faction, the Montoneros, the Tupamaros, and others. Most of these organizations had great attractions for the young, particularly in the 1960s when demonstrations and youthful protests appeared to have weakened the capitalist democracies and set the stage for even more progressive groups from the left to dominate in their countries. Opposition to the war in Vietnam, both as a specific event and as a representative event of Western domination and control of the developing world, furthered the mobilization of students to question the status quo. Since these movements were disproportionately movements of the young, however, they were at least initially also going to be movements of the weak. Mass membership was usually not possible. The terrorist movements in Italy, Germany, Greece, and Argentina started out small, and in Germany and Greece they remained small. In addition, dissident movements had to use violence to acquire financing for their activities unless they could enlist the support of a millionaire or foreign funds. Unless an organization had already proven itself, however, it was unlikely to receive such infusions of outside money. Revolutionary expropriation will work up to a point, but robbing banks to finance a revolution means that scarce resources actually have to be utilized in efforts to acquire more resources, and any robbery, even if successful, exposes the organizations to additional risks. Given the weaknesses of most leftist groups, at least initially, terrorism was one of the few methods of violence that was available to them. Popular uprisings, guerrilla warfare, insurrections, and even civil war might be the ultimate goals, but the radicals had to depend upon propaganda of the deed as a means of attempting to mobilize the populations of their countries.

These efforts by the left had mixed results. Some attempts to generate popular dissatisfaction with the governments in power were relatively successful. The Montoneros, partially because of their alliance with the Peronists, accomplished the most in this regard. Once Perón turned against the leftists, their influence waned and they were unable to recreate their early success. The military intervention then doomed the dissidents and their organizations. The changes in government structures wrought by the leftist in Argentina, and Uruguay as well, were significant ones, but they did not result in the improvements that the leftists had expected. The Red Army Faction in Germany was troublesome for the government, but it was never able to generate any kind of meaningful threat to the government. The 17 November

Movement in Greece had similarly limited results in its attacks upon various governments and the Greek political system. As noted, their small size was important for a long time in preventing the government from penetrating the organization, but their size also limited the extent of the damage that they could do. Since the Greek political system was fairly strong, the attacks mounted by the dissidents were insufficient to actually challenge the government's ability to survive. The Red Brigades presented a greater threat to the stability of the Italian political system, but they eventually failed as well. In Iran the leftist and secular groups were able to mount a significant challenge to the clerical government. These dissidents struck when the government was in a transitional phase and probably at its most vulnerable, but the popular support for the campaign was overshadowed by the popular support the Ayatollah Khomeini and other clerics were able to rally. The secular groups ultimately lost their struggle even though the possibility of success had been present. Finally, animal rights groups, as well as some environmentalist organizations, that have been willing to use violence have been less concerned with mobilizing the public to change the form of the governments in the countries where they operate. Of all the dissident groups described in this chapter, they have been most interested in influencing policies of governments or the policies of some businesses rather than changing governments.

While these various leftist movements failed to generate the major changes that they sought in their societies, it is more difficult to measure the long-term effects that they might have had. The struggle in Iran probably made it more difficult for moderate religious elements to be heard in the Islamic Republic. Thus, the eighteen-month terrorist campaign probably did make a difference in the development of the Islamic Republic. Similarly, the activities of the Montoneros did help Perón to return to power. His return, the resurgence of terrorism, the military coup against Isabel Perón, and the deadly suppression for dissidents were all linked. In Germany and Italy the leftist attacks eventually led to increased competency in the security forces, but few other ongoing changes occurred. No leftist group would consider improvement in the quality of the security services to be a worthwhile result. In neither of these cases did massive violations of civil rights of the populations result from the campaigns as was hoped. In the case of Greece, it is difficult to see any change that has occurred. There does not even appear to have been any improvement in the security forces. The efforts of the more violent animal rights groups in the long term are difficult to predict. The environmental groups using milder forms of violence have declined in importance and activity in recent years (Laqueur 1999: 204). It is possible that the animal rights groups will follow the same path. A major ecological disaster, however, could stimulate both the animal rights groups and the environmentalists to greater activity, and perhaps more violent activity.

None of the case studies involved movements that had major external support. The animal rights groups have cross-national contacts, but there is no indication of external government support. The Mujahedin in Iran gained some support from Iraq after they were defeated, but during the time that they posed the greatest threat to the religious government in power they lacked external backers. Their alliance with Iraq was in fact an admission of weakness, especially since many other Iranians, including those from the left and the secular middle class, rallied to support the Islamic Republic when the Iraqi invasion occurred. The Montoneros had some outside contacts, but there was no major foreign state backer for their efforts. Cuba was a sanctuary and an ideological beacon for many Latin American leftists, but it was too far away to offer practical support to dissidents in Argentina. The Greek dissidents have avoided any apparent foreign support. Western governments would have become aware of former Soviet support had it existed, since KGB files are no longer well protected state secrets. Had 17 November de-

pended on foreign support, its membership would have been exposed sooner. The Red Brigades and Red Army Faction did receive some external support, especially from Czechoslovakia and East Germany respectively. This support was helpful to the groups, but it was never essential for their survival when they were at the height of their activities. The various leftist groups in Europe did attempt to form some international linkages. The RAF was generally in the center of these efforts, and the German dissidents were able to coordinate actions with Spanish, Belgian, and French dissident groups. While contacts with the Red Brigades were frequent, attempts to coordinate the activities of the Italians and Germans were not successful due to theoretical differences. The Italians focused on their domestic enemies in Italy while the RAF was more concerned with the exploitation created by the international capitalist system (Merkl 1995b: 166–8). Cooperation between the RAF and the PFLP was more effective as demonstrated by the joint airline hijackings.

For the moment, the dissident terrorist organizations from the left have largely faded from the scene. The collapse of communism in East Europe and the Soviet Union with publicity about mistakes, torture, false arrests, and other deviations from ideological purity further undercut the appeal of leftist ideologies. The loss of models of future utopias was more devastating than the loss of the limited external support that came from these sources. Dissident movements based in Marxist ideologies, however, could reappear in the future. With time, the extremes of communism in power will fade as opponents of capitalism look for answers to the problems that come with that system. Marxism in one of its many forms could once again appeal to idealists seeking to deal with the inequities of world. The passage of time has unfortunately weakened memories of Nazi atrocities to the extent that some give credence to denials of the Holocaust, and a similar pattern could appear with Marxism. At some point there will be those who will deny the failures of communism and think that the negative images that have been publicized will have been the result of capitalist propaganda campaigns. Leftist ideologies will remain strong in some areas of the developing world where populations still face repressive regimes that continue to deny basic rights. In these situations, the left can encompass many different groups that are opposed to conservative and authoritarian governments. Today, Nepal is facing a serious insurgency from violent Maoist dissidents who have been using both guerrilla and terrorist tactics. Some leftist dissident groups remain active in India as well. Marxism in many of its varieties can still provide a critique of the evils that can come with globalization and modernization, which today are inevitably accompanied by capitalism. It would be premature, and even dangerous, to assume that the terrorist threat from the left has disappeared (Wilkinson 2003: 119). Thus, do not be surprised if leftist ideologies resurface and again become the basis for dissident groups, ones that could choose violence.

Further reading

Drake, R. (1989) *The Revolutionary Mystique and Terrorism in Contemporary Italy*, Bloomington, IN: Indiana University Press.

Eagan, S. P. (1996) "From Spikes to Bombs: The Rise of Eco-Terrorism," *Studies in Conflict and Terrorism*, 19, 1: 1–18.

Gillespie, R. (1982) *Soldiers of Peron: Argentina's Montoneros*, Oxford: Clarendon Press.

Kassimeris, G. (2001) *Europe's Last Red Terrorists: The Revolutionary Organization 17 November*, New York: New York University Press.

Monaghan, R. (2000) "Terrorism in the Name of Animal Rights," in M. Taylor and J. Horgan (eds) *The Future of Terrorism*, London: Frank Cass, 159–69.

Pluchinsky, D. A. (1992) "An Organizational and Operational Analysis of Germany's Red Army Faction Terrorist Group (1972–91)," in Y. Alexander and D. A. Pluchinsky (eds) *European Terrorism: Today and Tomorrow*, Washington, DC: Brassey's, 43–92.

Film

State of Siege (1973)

Terms

anarchism	Marx, Karl	Red Army Faction (RAF)
Animal Liberation Front (ALF)	Montoneros	Red Brigades
Animal Rights Militia (ARM)	Moro, Aldo	Red Cells
Baader-Meinhof Gang	Mujahedin-e-Khalq	Reign of Terror
"disappeared ones"	Mussolini, Benito	Rejectionist Front
Engels, Frederich	People's Revolutionary Army	17 November Organization
Feltrinelli, Franco	(ERP)	Students for a Democratic
Japanese Red Army	Perón, Isabel	Society (SDS)
June 2nd Movement	Perón, Juan	Symbionese Liberation
Khomeini, Ayatollah	Popular Front for the	Army
kneecapping	Liberation of Palestine	Trotsky, Leon
left-wing ideologies	(PFLP)	Tupamaros
Lenin, Vladimir	propaganda of the deed	Weathermen
Mao Tse-tung (Mao Zedong)	propaganda of the word	Will of the People

Chapter 8

Terrorism and ideologies of the right

Right-wing dissatisfaction: Marxism and minorities	144
Case studies	148
8.1 Stormtroopers in Weimar Germany 148	
8.2 Neo-fascism in postwar Italy 151	
8.3 The American militia/patriot movement 153	
8.4 Neo-Nazis and skinheads in Europe 157	
Summary	162
Terms	164
Further reading	164

Ideologies of the right, just like left-wing ideologies, have served as a basis or justification for terrorist acts. Right-wing groups usually seek to conserve what exists or seek to return to some recent or distant past situation that they feel should have been conserved. If the golden era is far enough in the past or different enough (Hitler's Germany), the changes being sought can be revolutionary rather than simply conservative. These groups will often seek to support the existing institutions in society and the ruling elites or to return these elites to power and re-establish institutions. These ideologies have gained strength as a result of some of the changes that appeared with modernization and globalization that threatened existing institutions and patterns of governance. Initially the ideologies of the right were reactive since they opposed changes sought by the left. As long as no group was threatening to bring about change, there was little need for groups supporting the status quo to become active. Groups seeking the restoration of monarchies could not appear until monarchies had been overthrown or were under threat. Similarly, right-wing ideologies frequently had to wait for left-wing ideologies to appear. Without the threat to government and other institutions that left-wing ideologies represented for some groups, there was no need for a defense against the left or for a reversal of changes already accomplished by the left. The use of terrorism by the right lagged behind that of left-wing groups because prior to World War I the ideologies of the right were in power as the political establishment (Laqueur 1999: 12).

Right-wing ideologies and associated violence go back to the days of the Roman Republic. The forces supporting the status quo were involved in the turbulent policies of the Republican era. The lesser nobles that opted to lead the commoners (or more precisely the upper middle classes and lower nobility) were particular targets for the aristocracy. The Gracchi brothers were both assassinated at different times for advocating changes that would have provided increased power to some of the middle-class groups in Rome. Tiberius Gracchus challenged the powers of the Senate and his supporters were threatening opponents when a group of Senators and their followers attacked. They killed Tiberius and many of his followers. Thirteen years later his brother Gaius was killed for again challenging the privileged position of the Senate and ruling groups (Ford 1985: 55–8). Such threats to the status quo were obviously taken quite seriously by the nobles, especially the great Senatorial families. The deaths of Tiberius and Gaius Gracchus and some of their followers as well indicated that costs could come with opposition. Challenges to the system were obviously not going to be tolerated. The message that challenges to the system would be met with violence by the opposition forces was clear.

In the centuries after the fall of the Roman Empire, there were relatively few recorded examples of terrorism by right-wing dissident groups. Peasant rebellions inevitably failed, and the retribution that followed in the wake of such rebellions was at the hands of the state, not dissident groups. Violent reactions to the Revolution in France generally came in the form of rebellion or insurrections rather than through campaigns of terror. The Vendée was a classic conservative rural uprising directed against the revolutionary regime with peasant groups fighting for God and the king. There was no effort to use terror to undercut the republican forces in France. In addition, the returns of monarchs to power in the seventeenth and eighteenth centuries did not involve terror. The Bourbons and other royal families were returned to power in France after the defeat of Napoleon and his armies by the allied powers of Europe. No resort to domestic violence to support the restoration was necessary.

Right-wing dissatisfaction: Marxism and minorities

In large measure it was the appearance of Marxist doctrines that stimulated the appearance of rightist groups that advocated violence. These groups from the right were committed to preventing the

Marxists from seizing power. Karl Marx thus unwittingly was the source for two types of ideologies that were willing to use violence and terror, even though Marx himself felt that terror was counterproductive. Dissidents from the right have been willing to use violence to keep leftist groups from obtaining power in a number of ways. They have targeted adherents of the left directly. Perhaps the first such group to appear in the defense of the status quo was the Black Hundred in Russia at the beginning of the twentieth century. This group targeted Jews and liberals who sought to challenge the monarchy and traditional society in Tsarist Russia (Laqueur 1999: 21). Supporters of right-wing groups and parties were mobilized to attack party rallies, buildings, or newspapers of the Marxists and other leftists. These assaults were designed to weaken the parties of the left in their competition for power. If supporters of the left were intimidated, then the parties would be weakened as a consequence. Benito Mussolini's fascists in Italy took to the streets to do battle with the socialists and the communists. The intent of the fascists was to fight fire with fire and defeat the relatively mild violence, demonstrations, and agitation from the left with counter-violence from the right. As it turned out, the street battles helped to promote the fascists as the best alternative available to conservative groups that wanted to prevent the socialists from disrupting the Italian political and economic systems or even of seizing power. It was the socialist agitation that permitted the fascists to organize and gain support from the middle classes and other groups in Italy. The fascists' violence and intimidation in Italy did weaken the left. Mussolini needed the socialist threat to give him the chance to gain political power for himself and his fascist party.

Another way in which forces of the right sought to battle the left followed a more indirect approach to achieving the desired goals. Marxist dissidents were considered to be much more likely to be able to seize power if the state was weak; consequently, fascists and other conservatives in the 1920s and 1930s considered weak states to be an open invitation to Marxist plots, disruptions, and take-overs. They felt that parliamentary democracies were vulnerable because they gave too many rights to potential traitors. Further, democracies invited dissent and disagreement, weakening the state, perhaps fatally. They had before them to heighten their concerns the examples of the Bolshevik takeover in Russia, as well as the short lived communist regimes in Bavaria and Hungary, and attempted seizures of governments elsewhere. They thought the best way to avoid dangerous attacks and the threats of takeovers from the left would be to take over the state and create a strong, authoritarian government that could and would deal with any plot from the left quickly and severely. Mussolini's assumption of power in Italy followed this path. Similar street fighting and violence was present in Austria and Romania where attacks on political opponents by right-wing activists occurred with great regularity in the 1930s (Berend 1998: 303, 337). The Romanian Iron Guard adopted the practices of the anarchists by emphasizing propaganda of the deed in their struggles to support conservative causes in that country (Laqueur 2001: 73). A direct takeover by a right-wing dissident group, like the fascists in Italy, would not always be possible. A number of right-wing groups therefore used violence to further other objectives. The violence was used to create a need for a conservative system to replace a democratic one. The violence was designed to expose the weaknesses of the democratic systems and lead to their replacement by a government that emphasized law and order. The violence from the right was introduced to force the government to be stronger, making it much more difficult for the leftists to use democracy against itself. The political objective of the right, therefore, was to create a crisis situation that would force the government to become stronger in self-defense, enacting sufficient measures to protect the country, doing away with weak democratic practices, and transforming the country into an authoritarian government that would be able to defeat any threats coming from the left. While this stronger government would also be able to deal better with threats from the right as well, dissident groups have been willing to accept this possibility since a stronger state is one of the principal goals that is being sought. Interestingly enough, there are thus circumstances where both left and right dissidents might seek to force a government to become more repressive. These two diametrically opposed groups, however, have drawn different conclusions from the prospect of a more authoritarian government. For the left the repressive regime would become an obvious defender of privilege and would lead to some kind of popular revolt against the ruling classes. For the right, the new government would also be more repressive, but it would be better able to deal with dissent. While both groups of dissidents have foreseen a similar process, they have anticipated dissimilar results.

For groups drawing upon right-wing ideologies policy changes by the government may be sufficient to meet their demands. If the government can be pushed to deal with leftist groups in an appropriate (i.e. repressive) fashion, the right-wing group may be satisfied. Such changes in policy, however, are likely to bring about basic structural changes in the government. More repression will mean a less democratic system or a harsher authoritarian government, so the sought-after policy changes are likely to breed structural changes. Similarly, the change in policies is likely to influence the type of leaders who will be governing. If the left is repressed, it is unlikely that leftists will be included in the government. The elimination of leftist groups will then shift the balance in the political system to the right, making it more likely that political groups of the right will be more influential. In these situations simple policy changes can have more far-reaching consequences.

Dissident groups depending upon ideologies of the right may have ethnic overtones, but these frequently are different from separatist movements or national liberation struggles. Right-wing ideologies may seek to force a government to

BOX 8.1 The Nivelles Group

There was an outbreak of leftist violence in Belgium in the 1970s involving the Communist Combat Cells (CCC). It was similar to the Red Army Faction in Germany in its ideology, but it was never very effective. Another organization, the Nivelles Group, gave every appearance of being a leftist group by its pronouncements, but its tactics and targets were very unlike the normal choices of Marxist-Leninist dissident groups. The attacks of the group resulted in the unnecessary deaths of bystanders and seemed especially geared towards alienating potential supporters of the left. As a consequence, it is thought that the group was more likely to have been composed of right-wing extremists established by police or intelligence officials who were attempting to provoke a crisis situation that would lead the government to adopt more repressive policies in order to defend itself from these attacks from the left (P. Jenkins 1990: 300). The attacks were very likely false flag attacks that were designed to force the government to crack down on leftist groups. This campaign failed to achieve this goal since the Belgian government did not adopt more repressive laws for dealing with terrorism. The relatively high casualties that occurred with these attacks in Belgium also suggest a source that was from the right. In this period of time right-wing dissident groups were generally weaker than leftist groups except in countries where the government was cooperating with and providing covert support to paramilitary groups. As a consequence, the rightist groups could mount fewer attacks. In order to have the impact of generating terror and publicizing a cause, the attacks that were undertaken by the right had to produce more casualties in order to have the desired effects on the population at large.

attempt to acquire territory with related peoples or to intervene to protect the rights of an "oppressed" minority in a neighboring country. The Nazi party in Germany, both before it was in power and obviously afterwards, sought to incorporate the Germans in Czechoslovakia into a Greater Germany as well as seeking a union of Germany with Austria. Junior officers in Japan in the 1920s and 1930s were responsible for a number of attacks on civilian leaders. The assassination of prominent opposing leaders have been part of Japanese politics for 60 years, beginning with its use by those seeking greater democracy (Angel 1990: 33). They either assassinated or attempted to assassinate prime ministers and other high-ranking officials when these leaders failed to follow policies that were nationalistic enough for the armed forces (Ford 1985: 256, 266–7). These assassinations destroyed the developing system of parliamentary democracy in Japan (Havens *et al.* 1975: 31). These actions also sent clear messages to politicians about the dangers that would be present for those opposing the nationalistic goals of the military, and Japan increasingly sought military solutions to its problems with reduced opposition from politicians. Right-wing extremists also assassinated key figures in Germany. Foreign minister Rathenau was killed in 1922 for signing a treaty establishing diplomatic relations between Germany and the Soviet Union (Otte 1997a: 76).

While there are some more modern right-wing groups that do not have racist overtones, most actually do (Bjorgo 1997: 21). Minority groups are despised, and they are targeted for attacks that are designed to inspire terror. The ethnic base of the terrorist group in these cases lies with the majority and does not reflect efforts of a minority to obtain equality or other goals. Such groups have become common. They have appeared in Eastern Europe and Russia. Vladimir Zhirinovsky, the leader of the Liberal Democrats in Russia, has advocated extreme Russian nationalistic views, the reclamation of lost lands, and hostility to the ethnic minorities in Russia. Parties with very clear fascist trappings have appeared in Romania and have

openly expressed their disdain for the ethnic minorities that reside in the country (Kurti 1998: 182). There have been attacks on Gypsies in Hungary and the Czech Republic and attempts to discriminate against Turks and Gypsies in Bulgaria (Wilkinson 1995). Attacks against the Gypsies began as soon as the restraining hand of communism was removed in many countries (Cooper 2001/2: 71). Violence against migrant communities has even appeared in Australia, albeit only rarely (Bessant 1995). The antipathy toward outsiders represents one facet of the need of the extreme right to create a stronger state. The outsiders and other minorities are seen as weakening the state because they create divisions in society (Hoffman 1998: 165). The ethnic exclusiveness of these dissidents frequently goes beyond migrants from other areas. It can include opposition to foreign ideas and influences of all kinds. All such potentially dangerous ideas must be kept out. The dissident groups are responding with violence to the challenges of globalization just as some religious groups have responded. The increase of the radical right can be seen as one response to the problems that come with globalization (Betz 1994: 184). Religion can play a supportive role in reinforcing attitudes opposed to outside influences if there is a dominant religion associated with the national population.

The Ku Klux Klan (KKK) in its second manifestation in the United States in the 1920s (the first manifestation being in the late 1860s) represented a right-wing movement that had many objectives that were related to the ethnicity and religion of the majority of the citizens of the country. The KKK was opposed to many things. It fought against anything approximating to equal rights for black Americans, but it also was opposed to increased immigration, particularly when the migrants were Oriental, Jewish, or Catholic. These groups were seen as carriers of foreign ideas that had to be opposed. The KKK utilized terror as part of its tactics, targeting members of the minorities. Lynchings of black Americans sent a clear message to other black Americans of what could happen if they persevered in seeking greater equality. Attacks on Jews, Catholics, and others with dangerous ideas were also frequent. Black Americans or immigrants in businesses that threatened the economic interests of white Protestants were also targeted (Gough 1997: 527). It became very clear that it was dangerous to oppose the ideas of the KKK. The KKK also involved itself in the political process in terms of supporting candidates and seeking to influence policies, most frequently at the state level. The violence against opponents at times had the extremely useful fringe benefit of cowing potential supporters of political opponents into apathy or even convincing the political opponents themselves not to run or to modify their opposition.

Since right-wing dissidents appeared as a reaction to Marxism in its many variations, it would be logical to expect ideologies of the right that favor violence to decline as well, but such has not happened. These ideologies have continued, and dissident groups subscribing to them have continued to use violence to achieve their aims. After the demise of communist states in Europe terrorism from the left declined, and the initiative in the use of terror and violence passed to groups on the extreme right (Laqueur 2003: 151). The increasing attention paid to issues of race, ethnicity, and religion might reflect a shift in the focus towards "new" enemies that was necessary with the disappearance of the Marxist enemies. Of course, to the extent that opposition to Marxism and its global ideology generated an earlier antipathy in the right towards change and globalization, other changes in society can play the same role today. There are indeed some indications that the conditions similar to the ones that led to the rise of fascism in Europe may now exist in at least some parts of the developing world (Jha 1994). The enemies are different, but they are still present, and democratic governments are seen as being just as weak and incapable of dealing with these threats as they were in the past. The underlying continuity in the justification for violence may not be these specific targets but the fear of change that exists for those attracted to the ideologies of the extreme right.

Case studies

There are only four case studies presented below, reflecting the fact that right-wing terrorism appeared later in time than its left-wing counterparts. There is an additional reason for the limited number of cases. In part, the violent groups from the right have often practiced leaderless resistance and have been involved in informal networks. As a consequence, it is difficult to discuss specific groups, so collections of related groups that are willing to use violence are considered together. The discussions of the neo-Nazi groups in Germany and the patriot/militia movement in the United States that appear below discuss a number of related groups. A second reason for the limited cases is that many paramilitary groups associated with the right wing and practicing terrorism have appeared in societies where they have received at least the covert support of the government in power in dealing with other political groups in the country. As such they provide examples of a type of governmental practice of violence and terror, and these groups will be discussed in Chapter 10. The four cases presented below deal with the use of violence by the stormtroopers (SA) associated with the Nazi party in Weimar Germany before Hitler came to power, the efforts of neo-fascist groups in Italy to provoke the Italian government into adopting authoritarianism in the decades after World War II, the violent tendencies of the American militias and patriot groups in the United States that culminated in the bombing of the federal office building in Oklahoma City in April 1995, and the rise of the neo-Nazis in Germany and elsewhere in Europe.

CASE STUDY 8.1

Stormtroopers in Weimar Germany

After the German Empire collapsed in the final days of World War I the Kaiser abdicated and a temporary government was put in place. The political leaders of the major parties created a new constitution, which was written in the town of Weimar. The new democratic system under this constitution has usually been referred to as the Weimar Republic. This initial attempt at democracy in Germany had a brief and troubled existence. The Republic finally ended when Hitler began to dismantle the democratic elements of the constitution after being appointed Chancellor (Prime Minister) in 1933. The end of the Weimar Republic set Hitler and the Nazi party firmly on the path that culminated in the Holocaust and the death and destruction of World War II. Violence and terrorism became an integral part of the history of the Weimar Republic. In its first years the new democracy faced an attempted coup by the radical elements of the Communist Party, an attempted takeover by forces of the right, and Hitler's abortive attempt in 1923 (the Beer Hall Putsch) to seize power in Bavaria—a seizure that was designed to signal a takeover by right-wing groups elsewhere in Germany. Hitler's failure to seize power in Munich and the lack of effort by other nationalist forces led him to rethink his options for assuming power. Hitler then chose an electoral approach, building the National Socialist Democratic Workers Party (NSDAP or Nazis) to the point where by the early 1930s it was the single largest party in terms of votes received. Hitler, however, did not give up on the use of violence to achieve his ends; the violence simply took new forms and became adjuncts to the election activities.

The violent arm of the Nazi party included two groups. The minor portion in the period before the Nazis came to power was the Schutzstaffel (SS). The SS was Hitler's bodyguard that served with him at party meetings. In these years it was relatively small and played only a subordinate part in the violence associated with the party. The more important group was the Sturmabteilungen (SA), literally meaning storm sections but usually translated as stormtroopers. To confuse matters, the SS in later years were also sometimes referred to as stormtroopers, and the term has sometimes been used to include both groups when mention is being made of violence in conjunction with party and election activities. The SA was a distinct organization that used street violence when the Nazi party engaged in parliamentary politics (Bjorgo 1993: 32). The SS was actually part of the Nazi party while

the SA was technically an independent organization that was associated with the party. Only Nazi party members could belong to the SS, while party membership was not a prerequisite for joining the SA (Bucheim 1972). Hitler, however, made it very clear that the SA as an organization was to be subordinate to the leadership of the party (Pridham 1973: 39). Hitler was able to ensure this subordination because he simultaneously served as head of the party and the head of the SA. This joint leadership also ensured that potential challengers to his leadership of the movement would find it more difficult to succeed.

The SA was initially formed to provide protection for Nazi party gatherings and campaign speeches against disruptions and assaults from members of other parties. Its activities quickly spread to include assaults on the activities of other parties. SA men would attempt to disrupt the gatherings and campaign speeches for other political parties, particularly those on the left. They would also attack leftist marchers when they were demonstrating or generate confrontations with leftist groups whenever possible (Shirer 1959: 43, 120). Newspaper offices and party reading rooms would be attacked, and eventually the violence extended to identifiable supporters of the opposition parties. Leftist groups in turn would sometimes provoke confrontations with the SA and the Nazi party as well.

The SA was not an unusual political organization in Weimar Germany in the 1920s. There were many organizations that were nationalist in their orientations and that sought to influence the government and its policies. Many of them ultimately sought to create a stronger Germany to recover territory lost in World War I and to establish a strong central government capable of generating a return to national glory. These groups also engaged in street violence, as did supporters of left-wing parties. All of these groups placed pressure on the government in a variety of ways, including violence, and some of them even openly discussed the need to overthrow the democratic government of Germany. The organizations attracted younger Germans who had difficulties in finding employment, especially after the onset of the Great Depression, and younger Germans who had accepted the basic ideas inherent in the right-wing nationalism that was central to these paramilitary organizations

(Merkl 1987: 202). The SA was also very effective in attracting both young rebels against authority (of all types) and young persons seeking action on the streets (Merkl 1986: 357–8). Many of the stormtroopers joined the SA for the marching and action (Merkl 1975: 592). The SA was to become the strongest of these paramilitary organizations, and eventually, after Hitler took power, all the others were disbanded. Many of their members were incorporated into various Nazi organizations.

Both left and right became very adept at provocation against the other, and these street battles were not one-sided affairs. The left organized its own groups and initiated some of the battles. Left and right attacked each other and street brawls between the two sides became the order of the day (Bessel 1986: 138). The groups that probably suffered the most from these confrontations were supporters of the more middle class parties in Germany whose supporters were less likely to take to the streets. The extremes progressively gained ground at the expense of the center groups, and many of the middle class and conservative groups in Germany came to prefer the Nazis to the socialists and communists. The street battles created an atmosphere of tension that attracted people to the Nazi movement since it was frequently seen as a defense against dangers from the left (Merkl 1987: 171). Ultimately, the street battles probably proved more useful to the Nazis than to the communists in this regard. The Nazi party became very adept at utilizing violence to create publicity; thus, "a small and uninfluential group soon became nationally known" (Laqueur 2001: 72). While the use of violence by the Nazis and SA frightened off some potential supporters, there were many others that came to accept the Nazis as a viable political alternative for Germany because of their activities (Bessel 1986: 137).

The street brawls, the attacks on meetings of other parties, and the attacks on individuals (selected because of their political beliefs) were designed to accomplish two basic purposes. On the one hand they were intended to terrorize and demoralize supporters of opposing political parties and the politicians themselves. It increasingly became more dangerous in at least some locales to openly support other parties at election where the Nazis or their sympathizers were dominant. This lack of outward support would progressively sap the strength of other parties as more and more individuals saw these parties as being less effective in terms of achieving policy goals or changes in government personnel. The second purpose of the street fighting and other violent activities was to serve as propaganda for the party, even if it was violent propaganda. The street actions provided demonstrations of the capabilities of the party and its level of support. The organized marches and military displays were designed to reinforce this propaganda by further demonstrating the strength of the Nazi Party (Merkl 1987: 105, 166). It was not even important for the SA to win the street battles or to control a certain section of a town or city; the propaganda purposes were served when the confrontation with the "enemy" occurred and the party and SA demonstrated their willingness to do battle (Merkl 1987: 164). Eventually, the Nazis came to be seen as the party most willing to defend Germany against the communists and the socialists, and the party most likely to be able to do so. The SA did not target the police or the authorities. The violence of the SA in the streets was largely focused on members of the opposition. The Nazi party almost always avoided any direct assaults on state power (Bessel 1986: 135).

The SA, with its use of violence to terrorize and as a propaganda device, was effective in helping Hitler and the Nazi party gain votes. By 1933, the NSDAP was seen as the one party most able to prevent the left from taking over the government. The violence and terrorism and street propaganda had weakened the parties in the center and even some on the right, leaving the Nazis as the clear alternative. Other options had fallen by the wayside. The SA and its tactics of street violence had been essential to creating these perceptions. Once Hitler was in power, however, the SA became something of a liability. Street violence became dysfunctional when the Nazis were the government. The leaders of the SA also had radical demands that Hitler as party leader was less interested in. He was also unwilling to alienate the regular army by integrating the SA into the armed forces (Merkl 1987: 181). As a consequence, in June of 1934 when Hitler moved to eliminate threats to his leadership, many prominent leaders of the SA were among the 400 to 1,000 persons who were assassinated (Shirer 1959: 221–5). The SA was gradually demobilized, and its members were transferred to the SS or other Nazi organizations that served Hitler's regime. Radical street fighters were valuable only in opposition, not as paramilitary extensions of the national government, especially once Hitler began to expand the regular armed forces.

CASE STUDY 8.2
Neo-fascism in postwar Italy

Fascist ideologies of the right did not die with the defeat of Italy and Germany in World War II or with the deaths of Benito Mussolini and Adolf Hitler. Because the fascists in Italy had never adopted the same extreme measures towards Jews and others as had the Nazis in Germany, the idea of fascism did not fall to the same level of disrepute in Italy, and fascist ideas survived defeat in World War II and have continued to be present in the political system. Arguments that violence and terrorism are a necessary means of saving the state from the wrong political forces that were heard in 1920 continue to be present today. Before 1960 there had been minor bombings, street violence that targeted groups on the left, and political intimidation of the left in Italy, but it was only in the later 1960s that more serious terrorism originating in right-wing groups appeared (Rimanelli 1989: 262). At this time there began a campaign of right-wing terrorism that has been considered the most severe that had been faced by any regime in Europe since World War II (Bale 1996: 132).

These right-wing efforts relied on many of the same themes that were important in the days before World War II and ideas current with other right-wing groups. The Italian neo-Fascists were, however, much more concerned with the communist threat and less concerned with immigrant communities and minorities (Weinberg 1995: 222). These Italian dissidents were afraid that communism would prevail in Italy, especially since a weak Italian state presented opportunities for the communists to seize power. The strength

of the Italian Communist Party (PCI), the largest communist party operating in democratic Western Europe, added to these concerns. The PCI did well enough in local elections, particularly in the areas around Bologna and other parts of central Italy, that it was able to dominate municipal governments and gain a reputation for honest and efficient local government—a relative rarity in Italy. The PCI was gaining increasing acceptance by Italian voters and other members of the political establishment. The extreme right regarded the PCI, despite its professed commitment to the democratic system, as a Trojan Horse that would permit a communist coup in the country. The weak democratic system contributed to these opportunities for the left; thus, the right attacked not only the communists as such but also the system of parliamentary democracy. Their goal was the creation of a strong government that would be able to deal with this threat from the left (Gurr and Cole 2000: 115). Some groups among the dissidents on the right that engaged in terrorist attacks feared, in addition, that if Italy was not dominated by communists it would be dominated by the United States. Thus, they sought a stronger state so that Italy could avoid being in a subordinate position vis-à-vis either the United States or the Soviet Union (Bale 1996: 132).

The dissidents hoped to achieve a number of different objectives by their actions. These groups sometimes used "false flag" attacks so that leftists would be blamed for the violence. They hoped to create a situation where the public would be willing to accept a coup d'état by the military to deal with the threat (Weinberg 1995: 232). An attack against a police station in Milan in 1973, for example, had the appearance of a left-wing terrorist action, but there is a wealth of information to suggest that the person responsible for the attack was at least manipulated by elements of the Italian intelligence agencies into making the assault in hopes of mobilizing support against the left (Bale 1996: 154). A somewhat different goal was the idea that outbreaks of violence would lead the general public to support the creation of a stronger government that would be able to deal with the increasing violence in the street. The population could be terrorized into demanding or accepting more repressive security measures. The left, including the PCI, might be provoked into overreacting to the violence. Finally, the armed forces might feel obligated to intervene in the government in order to deal with the violence and to establish a stronger state (Bale 1996: 132). The strategies of tension and attempting to have leftist groups blamed for violent actions were not mutually incompatible, so in a sense the dissidents did not have to make a conscious choice between the two strategies in any irrevocable fashion. Either outcome might work to their advantage, and from their political perspective either outcome was also an improvement over the current situation.

The dissident groups initially relied on the methods utilized in Mussolini's rise to power. There were thousands of street actions involving attacks by the right against leftist targets, and battles where the rightists were defending against attacks from youthful leftist groups (Weinberg 1995: 231). These kinds of activities were designed to place greater pressure on the government to deal with the violence in the streets. In addition, the extreme right escalated the violence by mounting a number of significant attacks against the Italian state. There were urban guerrilla attacks in 1970 and 1971 in southern Italy. The attacks included bombings in crowded squares, derailing of trains, and the detonation of a bomb in the crowded Bologna train station in 1980, as well as the assassination of particular individual officials (Rimanelli 1989: 264–7). There has been evidence of connections between the intelligence agencies and the right-wing groups. One judge was assassinated by terrorists on the right apparently for getting too close to the truth about these connections (R. Drake 1989: 22). While the public often blamed the left for many of these attacks, these incidents did not create the necessary tension to justify a takeover by the forces of the right. False flag attacks became unnecessary later when the real attacks from the left began in earnest.

There were indeed movements inside the Italian government, especially the intelligence agencies and parts of the military, that were considering strengthening the repressive capabilities of the state in order to be able to deal with any threat from the left. As it turned out, these efforts were stillborn when the maneuvering and plotting were exposed to the general public. The Red Brigades benefited when the security services were reorganized in the aftermath of publicity about plotting within government agencies that threatened the democratic system. In the final analysis, the terror from the right never matched that of the Red Brigades, even though it began earlier. The attacks from the right in some ways even weakened the security forces, so that they were less prepared to deal with the onset of the leftist violence that the right feared so much. Ultimately, not even these serious attacks from the left led to the harsh repressive measures that the right so greatly desired.

The evidence suggests that the various rightist dissident groups had at least some support within government agencies. There is no indication that any of the Italian parliamentary regimes actually supported the extreme right, but individuals in the security services most certainly appear to have done so. The shakeups within agencies and the discoveries of individuals linked to plots about government takeovers provide the best indication that the violence from the right was seen to be useful by these individuals and their political allies. The Italian rightists also had some external support for their activities. They had ties with other right-wing groups elsewhere in the world, the so-called Black International. Further, they received support, aid, and various other kinds of assistance from the security and intelligence services of conservative regimes in Spain, Portugal, Greece, and various Latin American countries were noticeably helpful (Bale 1996: 134). Members of various organizations on the right also received foreign training abroad in camps in Lebanon. Both Christian Phalangist (a right-wing militia group) and the Palestinians provided training at various times (Rimanelli 1989: 266).

Ultimately, the attacks from the right were not effective in bringing down the Italian system or in forcing it to become more repressive. One weakness of the extreme right was its division into many groups. The lack of unity, of course, in part represented competing ideological ideas and concepts, indicating that the right can be as badly divided in this regard as the left. The right-wing groups also lacked widespread popular support and apparently the ability to mount an extensive and continuing campaign against the democratic state. Notwithstanding the presence of domestic allies and foreign support, the Italian groups on the extreme right were tracked down and defeated by the Italian security forces, and most of the key leaders were killed or captured. During this same time period the political plotting was discovered and the potential internal threats to Italian democracy came to light and were dealt with. The plotters inside the government agencies were dismissed or retired and the system went on to deal with other threats and problems.

These terrorist attacks by the extreme right in Italy were significantly different from some of the other terrorist attacks carried out in Europe by nationalist groups and others opposed to foreign migrants. These attacks were not a short-term reaction to increasing immigration, an economic downturn or the sudden appearance of members of a racial or religious minority (Weinberg 1995: 223). The efforts of the Italian terrorists of the right to destabilize the government continued for a significant period of time and had support from important groups in society, yet they did fail. While the extreme right seems to have lapsed into inaction at the present time, there is no guarantee that similar dissident groups will not appear in the future. Economic difficulties, perhaps ones that might be linked to negative consequences from increasing unification within the European Union and an influx of refugees from elsewhere in the world, might provide a stimulus for the reappearance of this kind of violence.

CASE STUDY 8.3
The American militia/patriot movement

The extreme right wing in the United States has become more important in recent years as a political influence in the country. There have always been groups on the extreme right that have attacked the system or some groups within the country. There have been a variety of groups that have been willing to use terrorism to achieve political objectives, although they are divided and lack any formal unity. Terroristic violence in the United States has increasingly been from groups on the right (Smith and Damphousse 1998). Even at the height of violence from the left,

racist groups were responsible for more terrorist activities. The New Left groups, however, received more media attention (Clawson 1990: 4). The attack on the Murrah Federal Office Building in Oklahoma City focused attention on this increased use of violence. Extreme right groups include a variety of racist organizations, including the surviving elements of the Ku Klux Klan and the Aryan Nations among others, dissident groups that have a more obvious religious orientation, tax resistors, those who fear a takeover of the United States by traitors who favor one-world government, and some elements of the American militia movement and associated patriot groups. The extreme right in the United States is a rather disparate group. The Posse Comitatus believes that the highest official with constitutional authority is the county sheriff, and that a posse of citizens is the appropriate military authority. Of course, if the sheriff refuses to act in an appropriate fashion, he must be removed from office and replaced by someone who better represents the popular will. Alternatively, if he fails to lead the local citizens in the defense of their rights, the local posse can act on its own (Barkun 2000: 195–7). The members of this group believe that the federal courts, the Federal Reserve Bank, the income tax, and civil rights for minorities are not covered in the constitution (Levin 1998: 108). Other groups that fall under the tax resistor category agree that the income tax is not constitutional and even argue that the Internal Revenue Service (IRS) is not a true governmental agency. Many groups go even further and argue that gold is the only legal and official currency.

Some of these groups see the growth of government activity and increasing regulation as circumstances that will lead to an inevitable revolution. The militia movement itself is a diverse collection of organizations with varying ideologies and approaches to government, includes many individuals who are very suspicious of the national government and its agencies. This revolution in turn will give militia groups the opportunity to provide the framework for the new government (Mariani 1998: 131). Militia groups became more prevalent in the early 1990s. They generally attracted poorly educated men in jobs with limited opportunities and future potential. These militia members also frequently take the view that government programs only aid minorities rather than more appropriate groups of Americans like themselves (Snow 1999: 28). While there are many different groups with different ideas, the more extreme members of different groups move back and forth between different organizations, providing some connection and continuity to go with the shared ideas (Kaplan 1993: 34). Other organizations have in fact infiltrated the militia movement in search of recruits and wider support.

Most of the followers of extreme right groups subscribe to a variety of conspiracy theories to justify their existence and opposition to the government. These groups think that they must exist and remain armed to protect the true American people and their values against an insidious, clandestine takeover of the country by outsiders. They think that these outside conspirators are unwilling to challenge the white American majority openly since they are essentially cowards; thus, they have to sneak around in the shadows to accomplish their purposes. The various extremist groups generally agree on the elements of a generic conspiracy theory. There is an elite that operates through secret organizations. Its goal is world domination, and it will use the United Nations as one of its methods for taking over the United States. Special military forces (some think they are training in Canada with black helicopters) will strike when the time is right. In some versions of this conspiracy the Federal Emergency Management Agency (FEMA) has been building detention camps where the potential opponents to the takeover will be kept once they are rounded up (Barkun 1996: 51). While this conspiracy theory may not be logical, it is believed, and like all conspiracy theories, it can never be disproved. If there is no evidence that can be found to support it, the absence of evidence demonstrates that the conspirators are skillful.

The various right-wing movements share some other basic views of the threat that faces the United States. They see the traditional values of the country being threatened by outsiders. The threats come from non-white immigrants, who are disparaged, and the extreme right sees itself as defending the purity of the country, which usually also means the purity of the white race. These racist views are most obvious in groups like the KKK and the Aryan Nations, but it is also implicit in most of the other groups as well. Even the general militia movement is noteworthy for the fact that its members are almost all white. While hard-core racists are only a minority in the militia movement, they have been over-represented in positions of leadership (Lee 1997: 346). Anti-Semitism almost inevitably complements this racism. Most of the organizations of the extreme right regard the government of the United States as being dominated by international Jewry, and their usual term for the national government is Zionist Occupation Government (ZOG). The various components of the extreme right thus usually include Jews among the minority groups that are seen as threats to the United States and enemies of the white race.

Members of virtually all of the extreme right-wing groups and the militias around the country are committed to what they see as their Second Amendment rights to have weapons. They are among those who believe that the Second Amendment refers to individuals rather than the rights of states to run militias, and they do not accept Supreme Court rulings over the centuries that have limited the right to form militias to state authorities. The dissidents simply consider these rulings to be part of the plot to disarm citizens of the United States. The members of these organizations are also unwilling to accept regulation and control by state governments. These groups, as a consequence, have stockpiled arms and ammunition, including sophisticated weapons in many cases, for the coming conflict with foreign invaders, and they are often better equipped than local police forces.

Various extremists draw upon the ideas present in William Pierce's The Turner Diaries, which proposes a strategy for undermining the government and advocates the leaderless resistance approach. His book is often seen as a blueprint for actions that will overthrow the government and preserve the true America from the negative outside influences. Pierce, who died in 2002, was seen by many as a leading ideologist, and his writings continue to serve to spread the ideology of the extreme right. Web sites on the internet have facilitated the disseminating of information while avoiding direct contact. The leaders of extremist groups have used such mechanisms to advocate leaderless resistance and to indicate who the real enemies are, thus providing direction for members who are willing to actually undertake terrorist violence. The leaders have been careful to avoid any organizational links with potential activists; they have not issued precise directions or orders, and they have avoided hierarchical organizations to prevent them from being convicted as conspirators in criminal actions or any of the violence that results from their suggestions (Smith 2000: 59). The leaders continue to provide information on the legal means of obtaining weapons, on finding directions for preparing bombs, and praising actions undertaken by individuals. This style of leadership may be especially useful for the extreme right-wing groups in the United States since there is no centralized direction among the many groups. Lone wolf terrorists, who operate as individuals and who identify with the goals of one or the other of these organizations, can also be directed by the availability of literature and ideas (Kaplan 1993: 39). These individuals who belong to or identify with the extreme right know who the general targets are and can operate accordingly. It is difficult for law enforcement agencies to infiltrate such amorphous groups since they are so fluid and unorganized (Kushner 1998a: 15). The groups also often appeal to persons who are socially isolated and lack education (Whitsel 2001: 98). They can belong by self-enlistment as soldiers in the crusade against evil in the United States—and the world. These freelance terrorists operating within this kind of loose organizational structure may be the greatest continuing threat to the security of the United States in the future (Kushner 1998b: 92).

A number of right-wing groups incorporate elements of Christianity or at least their version of Christianity into their political beliefs. The various KKK groups operating in the United States often justify their actions by religious values. Other groups are part of what has been called the Christian Identity movement, which sees the attack from the outside as being an attack on a white, Christian nation. Their defense of the United States against non-Christian values has both religious and ethnic themes (Wilkinson 2000b: 57). Most of the people identified with the Christian Identity movement favor withdrawal and quietism

BOX 8.2 The Silent Brotherhood (the Order)

The Order, which operated in the Pacific Northwest, was formed by Robert Mathews in 1983. It was one of the few radical right-wing groups in the United States to actually launch a campaign of terrorism against the government and the groups supporting it. Mathews found inspiration in the writings of William Pierce for this campaign, and he copied the terrorist tactics used by the left in the 1960s in his efforts to change the political system (Kaplan 1997: 61). The group was overtly racist, anti-Semitic, and anti-government. In 1983 it launched a series of attacks on Jewish and minority individuals and businesses. The group relied on bank robberies to finance its operations. A year and a half later local police officials effectively destroyed the group. Mathews was killed in a gun battle with police, and many other members of the group were convicted of various crimes and sent to prison (Dees with Corcoran 1996: 139–45). More than $4 million was stolen by the Order in its bank robberies, yet most of the money was never recovered. It is believed that the unrecovered proceeds from the bank robberies had been channeled to other groups on the far right, including the one headed by William Pierce. Mathews' efforts were designed not only to attack the Zionist Occupation Government, as he and his followers saw it, but to inspire right-wing groups all over the United States to join in that attack against the government. His efforts in this regard obviously failed since similar groups did not join the offensive against the government. Even though he failed to inspire an uprising, he became a hero and a martyr to the extreme right, both in the United States and in Europe (Kaplan 1997: 66).

rather than violence, but a small portion of the persons affiliated with these groups does engage in violence (Kaplan 1993). Some extreme versions of Christian Identity have gone so far as to maintain the idea that the real people of Israel, and hence Jesus Christ, were actually white Aryans. The Jews have been falsely claiming to be the Chosen People, further justifying the anti-Semitic posture of the group (Kaplan 1995: 51). Such a religious belief increases the potential for anti-Semitism and reinforces the need to struggle against the ZOG. Not every group on the extreme right has this Christian element, although religious views can be mixed with political dreams, even utopian ones (Mayer 2001: 363). While some extreme right groups are basically non-religious, even these groups frequently have millenarian views in which they seek a perfect world (Whitsel 2001: 91). These groups can co-exist with the more religious portions of the extreme right and regard foreign religions such as Islam or Bhuddism—or Judaism—to be threatening to their vision of America as well.

Negative visions of the national government were increased by an incident at Ruby Ridge in Idaho in 1992 and the events at Waco, Texas, on April 19, 1993, involving the Branch Davidians (Lee 1997: 347). Randy Weaver had been charged with a minor gun offense, but had missed a court date. Federal agents attempted to arrest him at his rural home on Ruby Ridge, but he refused to go voluntarily. Before the standoff was resolved, Weaver's wife, his son, and a federal marshal had been killed. The extreme right saw this episode as an attempt by the government to begin the process of taking away the rights of Americans to own guns and proof that the government would attack citizens seeking to defend their rights. The events at Waco resulted in the deaths of many of the followers of David Koresh and some federal agents. They provided further fuel to the belief that the government was willing to attack its own citizens. Groups on the right have normally ignored the unusual religious beliefs of the Branch Davidians and focused on the fact that issues of illegal weapon possession were involved. Thus the Waco situation was also seen as proof that the government feared weapons in the hands of groups that would defend the country against invasion by foreign elements. Both

incidents provided important propaganda for the extreme right. At best, the officials on the scene mishandled the situation at Ruby Ridge, and there will always be a debate about Waco, even though it seems that the deaths of the members of the group resulted from a desire for martyrdom on the part of Koresh since the fires that killed so many were started internally. The extreme right, supported by some more mainstream conservative groups, has always claimed that government forces were directly responsible for the deaths. While the hard core of the extreme right was already opposed to the ZOG and to government in general, these incidents provided right-wing groups with opportunities to gain additional recruits and built their strength.

Members of the extreme right have been willing to resort to violence. Members from a variety of different groups have killed police officers in confrontations over speeding stops and subpoenas for relatively minor offenses. The paranoia of the extreme right wing, of course, could lead individuals to assume that any arrest is the excuse to send them to the detention camps that are held ready for them. These groups have often demonstrated an attraction for chemical and biological weapons. Four members of the Minnesota Patriots Council, a tax resistors group, processed and accumulated ricin, a deadly poison. (This was the same poison used by the Bulgarian secret police against East European dissidents in London.) While ricin is deadly, it is not useful for inflicting mass casualties. It has to be administered individually to the targets unless the terrorist could place the poison in food at a restaurant or similar location. It cannot be used as an airborne poison or spread by casual contact. The group intended to use against local and federal law enforcement and judicial officials, but they were caught before they had a chance to implement their plans (Tucker and Pate 2000: 159). Another group, the Covenant, the Sword, and the Arm of the Lord, had plans to poison municipal water supplies. It wanted to inflict mass casualties that would start the conflagration that would hasten the second coming of the Messiah (Stern 2000a). This fascination with such weapons indicates that at least some elements in the extreme American right would be willing to cause mass casualties and would also use the weapons against government targets. Concentrations of federal workers, including those in Washington DC, would seem to be prime targets for these groups (Post 2000: 288). The presence of a large minority population in Washington DC would also seem to make it a very inviting target for these groups.

There have been examples of militia movements becoming involved in the violence and intimidation that characterize the extreme right. The White Patriot Party, a citizens' militia group in Virginia and the Carolinas, sought to intimidate black Americans and promote a White Republic in the southern United States. In Texas, the Texas Emergency Reserve mounted a campaign against local Vietnamese fishermen and their supporters among the resident community. There were bombings of their boats and other threats. In both cases civil action was required to end the threats to minorities from these particular militia groups (Dees with Corcoran 1996: 35–8, 96–7). The militia movement also had links with Timothy McVeigh and Terry Nichols, both of whom were involved with the Michigan Militia, one of the larger such groups in the country. McVeigh and Nichols, of course, gained support for their views of the oppressive government that led them to become involved in the bombing of the Murrah Federal Office Building in Oklahoma City. The choice of April 19, the anniversary of the FBI assault on the Branch Davidian compound in Waco, was not a coincidence; it was apparently chosen to represent a counterattack against the government by those on the extreme right. While no other domestic terrorist attack in the United States so far has matched the death toll from Oklahoma City of 168 fatalities, members of various militias and patriot groups, racist organizations, and other elements of the extreme right continue to support the idea of attacks on the government and minorities and other outsiders. The attack in Oklahoma City demonstrated what the extreme right was capable of undertaking. Some members of militia movements have refused to believe to this day that a white American from their groups would undertake the attack. They prefer to believe that the federal government undertook the attacks as a means of discrediting the militia movement and other American patriots and setting the stage for government repression.

Efforts to unify the various elements of the extreme right have so far failed since the different groups have differences in doctrines. Ideological differences of opinion have separated the extreme right in the United States just as such differences have often divided the left in Europe, the Middle East, and Latin America. It is also apparent that the leaders of various individual groups are not willing to submerge their identities in some umbrella organizations, even when they are willing to cooperate. The extremes represented by the militia movement and other groups still remain in the United States. They have not disappeared, nor have they changed their views on the presence of a ZOG and the negative influences represented by outsiders and non-white elements. Extremist actions in the United States tend to come in waves, and it is quite possible for there to be a resurgence of militia and right-wing violence in the future (Whitsel 1995: 134). Attacks against blacks, homosexuals, Asians, and other minorities have continued in the years after Oklahoma City. In at least some cases the attackers have been motivated by links with the extreme right or propaganda emanating from those groups. The militia movement lost a lot of its members in the wake of the Oklahoma City bombing, but the hard core, dedicated members of the right-wing ideological groups remain committed to their cause. The attacks on the World Trade Center in New York on September 11, have also provided a cover for continuing attacks against at least some outsiders and may have produced an important recruiting tool for various groups on the extreme right and militias that purport to be prepared to defend the United States.

CASE STUDY 8.4
Neo-Nazis and skinheads in Europe

Right-wing neo-Nazi violence has been on the increase since the 1990s. This violence has often been directed against migrants and anyone or anything that is considered foreign. Groups linked with neo-Nazi or other racist organizations have appeared in most European countries. Attacks against immigrants and minorities in a number of countries came to total more than 1,000 per year in some European countries in the 1990s (Merkl 1995a: 103–6). Many European extreme right movements focus on preserving their national cultures. They fear that their countries will become like the United States with its great ethnic and cultural diversity, a fate they are fanatically seeking to avoid (Weinberg 1996: 85). This suggests that violence will continue even in good economic times, and that programs by the government to compensate those who cannot benefit from the good times may not be the answer to the problems. Domestic organizations and the government agencies that are seen as aiding foreign intrusion or contamination have also become targets. Germany has been one of the countries most affected by the appearance of these groups and the violence that has been associated with them.

After World War II, there were always some individuals that maintained emotional and political ties to the Nazi past. These individuals formed groups, some clandestine and some more open, that provided support for the members and even hoped that the Nazi form of government could be resurrected. Parties that directly linked themselves to the Nazi past, of course, were limited. Such groups were either outlawed outright in West Germany and some other countries or generated so much opposition that they had little hope of success. As a consequence, the more open groups that clearly aligned themselves with some portions of Nazi doctrine made it a point to proclaim their support of democracy. It might have been expected that as former Nazis and others associated with the old system died these types of organizations would disappear. In point of fact, while time removed most of the diehard Nazis from the scene, the passing of the Nazi generation did not mean the end of the threat to governments and citizens from groups on the extreme right willing to use violence to achieve their political goals. Europe has seen the appearance of neo-Nazi movements ("neo" since they lack the direct link to the old Nazi party) and other groups, such as skinheads, which identify with these extreme right organizations.

There are a variety of neo-Nazi groups that have appeared in Germany and elsewhere in Europe. These groups have been different from their American counterparts in one respect. They do not fear a strong

centralized government, and, in fact, they seek to strengthen it (Weinberg 1996: 82). The right sees strong governments as essential to provide protection to the state and its people. The state only becomes a target when it seeks to aid the victims of neo-Nazi violence (Gurr and Cole 2000: 144). In Germany such groups have become even more active since the unification of the two parts of Germany, even though they existed in West Germany before the collapse of communism in the east. In the mid-1990s it was estimated that there were over 80 extreme right groups in Germany with 42,000 members, 6,200 of which were involved in violent activities (Wilkinson 2003: 119). These neo-Nazi groups share certain common ideological themes. They oppose the idea of democratic government that they see as corrupt, they are opposed to any form of ethnic pluralism, and they seek the creation of a strong national state in which the leader will determine the course of action to be taken by the state. Neo-Nazi groups have also been active in the Holocaust denial industry, being among the most active in claiming that the death camps did not exist. The various groups also maintain the anti-Semitism that was so much a part of the original Nazi party.

The violence and appeal of the neo-Nazi groups increased after German unification for a number of reasons. Right-wing terrorism in Germany as elsewhere has often attracted those who have not benefited from changes in society. The young and unemployed have often viewed the state as part of the problem for their lack of status and opportunity. Their educational attainments have been insufficient to arrange for decent jobs, and government services and programs have been geared towards other groups. The conservative, free-market-type parties have supported policies that have provided few benefits for the young and unemployed since they could not aspire to good jobs, and the parties of the left have provided services that have benefited other groups; consequently, neither major ideological wing of the German party system offered any advantage or hope for improvement. Unemployed youths have, therefore, been attracted to neo-Nazi groups and become the activists who participate in actions against those the groups consider to be undesirable (Laqueur 1999:

124). Unification increased tensions within parts of Germany and provided a recruiting ground for the extreme right. Citizens of the former German Democratic Republic (East Germany) found themselves at obvious disadvantages compared with citizens from the western parts of the unified country. Their education, including the required dosages of Marxist-Leninist theory, was often less useful and less relevant than the education received in West Germany. The factories in the east were not as competitive as those in the west, and many of them ended up closing, leaving persons in the east unemployed. Reunification also meant a reduction in government services, programs, and agencies, resulting in additional unemployment and fewer benefits. The end result was an increase in dissatisfaction for many of the people in the east.

The collapse of communism in Eastern Europe and the Soviet Union led to increases in the number of persons seeking to emigrate to Germany in hopes of a better life. The newcomers increased pressures on public services and were potential competitors for jobs. In addition, Germany had also received refugees from elsewhere in the world who were seeking safety and asylum—persons fleeing conflicts in the Middle East, Bosnia, Sri Lanka, and Indonesia—as well as persons from all over the world seeking employment had entered the country. These outside groups were added to an existing population of guest workers, many of them Turkish, who had been brought to West Germany. These guest workers provided labor in areas where there was a labor shortage as well as being willing to do work that because of its menial nature, most Germans (or other Europeans) would not do. As a consequence, unemployed youth saw not only a scarcity of jobs and an absence of government programs but a whole group of outsiders who were using resources that should have been devoted to "real" Germans. The mix was a rather explosive one, and provided extreme right groups with many new recruits. It is important to note, however, that only a portion of the persons engaged in right-wing violence in Germany were unemployed. Many, in fact, did have jobs. Most, whether employed or unemployed, were of working class backgrounds and had lower levels of education (Willems 1995). The fear of unemployment and of resources being diverted to foreign

groups were two of the reasons why individuals with jobs participated.

Given the greater pressure on resources in the eastern part of Germany, it is probably not surprising that many of the attacks by the extreme right against the outsiders have occurred in this area of the country (Husbands 1995: 331, 334). To some extent, local factors contributed to the problems. Local political leaders were opportunistic and tried to gain advantage from their opposition to migrants and asylum seekers (Karapin 2002). It is important to note, however, that it has not just been persons from the east who have participated in the attacks, and many of the leaders of the neo-Nazi groups are from the west. In 1992 and 1993 there were over 4,000 acts of right-wing violence recorded in Germany, providing an indication of the extent of the problem (J. Anderson 1995: 39). Much of this violence has been directed against foreigners, including attacks on housing for migrants, guest workers, and those seeking asylum. Perhaps more disturbing than the attacks themselves has been the obvious support from local populations that the right-wing activists have received. The current public support has encouraged the activists and given hope to the leaders of the groups that there could even be an increase in public support in the future. One other disturbing aspect about the violence is the fact that at least one analysis of the outbreaks of violence in Germany found that unemployment had little effect on the violence directed against foreigners. The number of foreigners present in an area predicted the number of attacks. In difficult economic times just the presence of foreigners is sufficient for attacks to occur (McLaren 1999).

While the violence in Germany to date has included many violent actions, the number of deaths has so far been limited. Of course, as groups see little change in their circumstances or in the problems that they perceive to be present, the violence could escalate as it has for so many other groups willing to resort to terror. The target for many of the attacks are the "foreign" elements that the right-wing groups would like to see leave the country. If one injury can persuade some to leave, then increased violence is likely to persuade other members of foreign communities to flee as well. Many of the activists engaging in street violence may not share the ultimate right-wing goals of the leaders, but there is no indication that all the stormtroopers in the SA in the 1920s and 1930s shared the political ideas of the Nazi party leadership. In this regard, the extreme right groups have also been recruiting skinheads for violent activity. While the skinheads are difficult to organize, extremist groups have made the effort to use them for their own purposes, being successful often enough to indicate that this youthful and discontented segment of society is available for participation in violent activities (Sprinzak 1995: 36–7). The ideological commitment of these groups is probably not great, but it is violence from the right that provides them with an outlet for aggression, and members of the right have consciously sought to utilize these rebellious elements of German society to further their own extreme political agendas.

Germany has not been very effective in dealing with violence from the extreme right in many cases (Pedahzur 2001a: 352). The leadership of the groups retains a certain amount of separation from the street actions of the activitists. However, the leadership can provide funding and other support for the street activists, which can be quite important. Various extreme right political parties and political associations have been banned under the German law and the German constitution, which permit banning political groups seeking to undermine a democratic government. These efforts have been largely fruitless since the groups reappear under new names with the same leaders in relatively short order. Even when activists have been arrested, the sentences handed down have been relatively light, especially when compared to jail terms for leftists of the Red Army Faction. Part of the reason for the leniency has been the young age of the right-wing activists (J. Anderson 1995: 44). Also, since the right-wing violence has not usually resulted in fatalities, the offenses in question do not lead to jail sentences that are as severe as if there had been. In the short term, the absence of long prison terms has probably made the costs of action bearable by the activists in the street.

The appearance of extreme right groups has not been restricted by any means to Germany. Such groups have appeared in most other European countries. They all share virtually the same ideology,

including anti-Semitism, fear of that which is foreign, and a willingness to use violence. Some Swedish groups on the extreme right have even adopted the concept of a Zionist Occupation Government as being responsible for the problems of their society (Bjorgo 1993: 36). In some other countries the targeted outsiders have been Muslim migrants, and the right-wing groups see themselves as fighting "the Muslim invasion" (Bjorgo 1997: 314). In the Netherlands there have been attacks on Turks and other foreigners as well as bombings of mosques, coffee houses that are frequented by Muslims, and the living quarters of the migrants (Merkl 1995a: 102). A wide variety of small groups that exist in the Scandinavian countries have launched many attacks on foreigners and refugees living in their countries. As is the case in Germany, the activists are young while the organizers and supporters are older and more ideologically committed (Bjorgo 1997: 102). In some cases the attacks and violence have been broader. Not only have foreigners been attacked, but targets have included "national traitors"—such as politicians, journalists, political officials, and supporters of the migrants. These traitors have facilitated the migrant invasion and must be dealt with as well (Bjorgo 1995a: 202). In Sweden in some years as many as half the non-European migrants have been threatened or assaulted (Bjorgo 1997: 42).

While many of the groups have been very nationalistic and focused on their own countries, many of them have also developed international ties. The extreme right in Europe has availed itself of modern technology to coordinate activity. Internet access and networks have been established among various groups. International gatherings are fairly common, especially on important dates. Hitler's birthday often serves as a day for such meetings. Group meetings such as these probably serve to reinforce the commitments of the groups. The ideologically committed core of many of the groups is quite small. In their own countries they may feel like isolated elements. The international gatherings provide them with positive reinforcement for their ideas by permitting them to meet with fellow extremists from other countries. Electronic bulletin boards have increasingly been used to provide information on rallies and demonstrations

(Lee 1997: 273). While international gatherings facilitate feelings of solidarity, the focus on individual national glories and the personal rivalries of individual supreme leaders guarantees divisions and conflict (Wilkinson 1995: 91). The international contacts also provide the groups with some ways around national laws and restrictions. For example, Nazi material and some neo-Nazi material is banned in Germany, but such restrictions are not in place in other countries. Thus, such items can be ordered by Germans and other Europeans from web sites in European countries with fewer restrictions on political paraphernalia or unpopular ideas, such as Denmark (Bjorgo 1997: 84).

In Germany and elsewhere, while the actual violence may wane at particular points in time, the breeding ground for right-wing terrorism continues to exist (Laqueur 1999: 124). Should massive influxes of foreign elements or severe economic dislocations occur in Europe in the future, the possibility for increased violence is obviously present. As is true in the United States, such attacks tend to come in waves, but after each wave the level of violence is at higher levels than before the wave (Bjorgo 1997: 312). The potential for violence obviously remains. Just as religious fundamentalism may be a reaction to changes in the international system and the intrusion of foreign ideas, right-wing groups seem to gain strength in times of societal difficulties. Globalization and external influences will continue to create problems for European societies. These kinds of influences may have made at

---

BOX 8.3 The Danish Green Jackets

In the 1980s Denmark saw the emergence of a number of violent youth groups in Copenhagen. These youth groups adopted racist and anti-immigrant attitudes. One such group wore pilot jackets and became known as the Green Jackets. The term quickly came to be collectively applied to a variety of such groups, and many youth gangs accepted this collective designation. The members of the groups were often unemployed and from broken homes, and they lived in high-rise state housing projects. Members of the gangs saw migrants receiving apartments and other benefits at their expense. They proceeded to harass and attack immigrants, and they adopted symbols related to the Ku Klux Klan or neo-Nazi groups as well. The Green Jackets were actually successful to a degree in their use of violence. Immigrant families moved out of the neighborhoods, and local officials were careful to assign migrants to housing in other areas of the city, so one result of the violence was the successful "cleansing" of foreign migrants from the area (Bjorgo 1997: 127–32). The Green Jackets faded from the scene by the late 1980s. As the members aged, they moved on to other interests and had less time for street activities. The concessions made by government officials had removed the impetus for their activities and probably also limited their ability to recruit new younger members into the organizations by removing the source of local tension. One interesting aspect of the Green Jacket activity is that it occurred in areas of Copenhagen where immigrants were a smaller percentage of the population than in the capital as a whole. Both the total number of migrants and the number of migrants who could readily be recognized as foreign were smaller than in many other areas (Bjorgo 1997: 92). The violence, therefore, was not directly triggered by a large concentration of foreigners locally, although there may have been a threshold effect in terms of the presence of migrants citywide recieving benefits from the state. It is also possible that members of the youth groups as a consequence of their movements around the city saw the local immigrant residents as a part of an increased foreign presence in Copenhagen in general and reacted accordingly. While the Green Jackets turned out to be a temporary phenomenon in Denmark, they demonstrate how quickly violent youth groups could appear and how they can become connected to other elements of the neo-Nazi dissident culture in Europe.

least some young people susceptible to extremist ideologies, such as the ones presented by the far right (Bessant 1995: 113–14). The passage of the original generation of Nazis has not led to a decline in the racist and anti-democratic ideas that were so much a part of that generation. Such ideas keep reappearing, and the disappearance of communism in Europe does not seem to have had much of an impact. Fascism and the Nazis may have originally appeared as a counter to communism, but the neo-Nazis and related groups no longer require a left-wing enemy to continue to operate. While the old enemy is dead, the right wing has been able to find other enemies to fight and groups to hate. The danger may lie dormant in the best of times and be much more active in the less than ideal times.

Summary

Terrorism arising from right-wing ideologies has been most prevalent in the twentieth century. Conservative and authoritarian governments have often used violence to control their populations, and the Nazi regime was one of the most ruthless governments ever established in modern times. In the period before World War II, fascist parties and other movements subscribing to a variety of right-wing ideologies involving anti-socialist and anti-democratic themes utilized violence in their efforts to gain power. In some cases violence and intimidation played important roles in facilitating their increased prominence and even facilitated their eventual control of the government. Violence in the streets was essential for the assumption of power by the Fascist party in Italy and the Nazis in Germany. The street battles also attracted the support of other political groups and sectors of society opposed to the leftists. These successes encouraged similar right-wing parties elsewhere, and a number of fascist parties in other countries attempted to emulate these achievements, albeit ultimately with only limited success in most cases (Alapuro and Allardt 1978: 132; Edmonson 1978: Chapter 6).

Neither the Nazis nor the Italian fascists had any external support in their struggles against other domestic parties and the democratic governments of their countries. Both movements grew out of the domestic discontents of populations within their own countries. Their finances and other support were provided by domestic groups that were fearful of the communists and socialists or from domestic groups that favored the strongly nationalist agenda put forward by both Mussolini and Hitler. When Hitler was the leader of the Nazis as an opposition party he did have contacts with Mussolini (Hitler came to power eleven years later), but the fascist regime in Italy provided no assistance to the Nazis at this time (Flood 1989: 292–7). Once they were in power the two dictators eventually extended aid to other fascist parties and right-wing groups elsewhere in Europe. Thus, while neither the fascists nor the Nazis received outside aid, they were to become key sources of support for right-wing dissident groups in other countries.

After World War II, right-wing ideologies became a basis for dissident terrorism in Europe and North America. The neo-fascists efforts in Italy after World War II were clearly a continuation of the fascist experiences from the years between the wars, and some of the techniques that were used were the same as well. In the case of right-wing groups elsewhere, terrorism against minorities in the United States had been present since the end of the Civil War in the case of the first appearance of the Ku Klux Klan. In the latter part of the twentieth century, however, officials and governments agencies have increasingly been targeted in the United States as agents of the ZOG. The bombing in Oklahoma City was simply a culmination of such assaults. In Europe as well, attacks by right-wing dissidents have begun to include political figures and government officials who are seen as helping immigrants and other outsiders (Bjorgo 1997: 313–14). Right-wing violence has become more threatening in Europe than leftist terrorism, but it is in the United States that right-wing groups have displayed the greatest potential for violent actions (Wilkinson 2000b: 56–7).

The attacks by the extreme right in Europe have actually had some successes for the dissidents. A number of establishment parties have increasingly supported and argued for greater limitations on immigration and the granting of asylum (C. Anderson 1996; Van der Brug *et al.* 2000). In general the ability to secure the status of asylum or to be allowed to enter many European countries has become much more difficult. As a consequence, it is now harder to migrate to many European countries, meaning that the violence and attacks by neo-Nazis, racists, and skinheads have been successful at least in part. Governments have limited migration in an effort to reduce the violence and the appeal of the parties of the far right by these policy modifications, indicating their desire to limit the extreme right. Even so, the violence and terror has been successful, and these modifications of immigration policies run the risk of encouraging future violence since past violence has been rewarded. Of course, at least some of the dissidents on the far right have had more far-reaching objectives than simply the limitation of foreign migrants. Anti-migrant actions have been a step towards grander political plans, and the immigration restrictions may lessen these groups' appeal and support in the future since they will be less able to attract sympathizers from the population in general.

With the exception of the neo-fascists in Italy, there has been little evidence of outside support by governments for extreme right groups in Europe or North America. The extreme right groups in Europe and the United States have maintained links among themselves with modern technology, including the internet. Radical nationalism and intolerance have taken on a transnational character (Bjorgo 1997: 317). The international contacts also permit various dissident groups to maintain a presence even though a particular movement may be weak in a particular nation. To date, the various groups provide ideological support to each other but very little other assistance. At this point, the members of the extreme right groups do not appear to have developed any important cross-national linkages in planning

terrorist attacks, but such cooperation could occur in the future. Al Qaeda has demonstrated the possibilities for such cooperation with modern technology, and right-wing groups could adapt to these technological possibilities as well. The presence of this technology would also explain why leaderless resistance and individual activities have become more common, not only in the United States, but also in Europe (Bjorgo 1997: 56–7).

There are some indications that right-wing dissidents have been more intent on causing casualties than their counterparts on the left (Hoffman 1998: 164). A comparison of deaths from left- and right-wing violence in Germany and Italy provides evidence to support this conclusion. In Germany from 1968 to 1987 the number of terrorist actions by right-wing dissidents was a small fraction of the number of left-wing attacks, but the total number of fatalities was considerably higher (see Table 8.1). In the case of Italy, there is no breakdown on the number of attacks by the left and the right. The Red Brigades were obviously much more active than the neo-fascist dissident groups, yet more people died in attacks by the extreme right. The single incident of the bombing of the Bologna train station inflated the death toll by the violent right, but even if this event is excluded, right-wing attacks were more likely to result in deaths than actions by the left. Increased fatalities have been more likely with right-wing violence because some of the more racist groups have clear genocidal goals that require the infliction of mass casualties on a portion of the population (Gurr and Cole 2000: 113). When the targets are members of the minority groups that the dissidents dislike or hate, casualties are not a cause for concern and can even serve a purpose in terrorizing other members of the group. If minorities begin to feel uncomfortable and seek to leave, the terrorists have achieved their objective. Dissidents, however, have also been responsible for attacks that have resulted in large numbers of casualties among the general population. Oklahoma City and the Bologna train station attacks are prime examples. Since the objective of the right is to

TABLE 8.1 Number of deaths in left-wing and right-wing attacks in West Germany and Italy, 1968–87

Country and terrorist group	Number of incidents	Number of deaths
West Germany		
Left-wing groups	11,660	7
Right-wing groups	550	26
Italy		
Left-wing groups	n.a.	148
Right-wing groups	n.a.	193
External groups or		
unknown	n.a	78

Source: Jongman 1992
Note: n.a. = not available.

destabilize the government, high casualty figures can better serve their purpose. The strategy of tension advocated by the right requires dead and wounded. Attacks on empty buildings are less likely to be effective. Since the left has often sought to convert the general population, indiscriminate attacks on bystanders are counterproductive to the ultimate goal. Dissidents on the right may also have been more disposed towards more deadly attacks since in many countries they have had weaker popular support than the left has had. Since right-wing dissidents could mount fewer attacks, those attacks have had to be more spectacular. Should right-wing terrorism continue to occur in industrialized countries or even increase, high casualty figures are likely to continue to be present.

Further reading

Bale, J. M. (1996) "The May 1973 Terrorist Attack at Milan Police HQ: Anarchist 'Propaganda of the Deed' or 'False-Flag' Provocation," *Terrorism and Political Violence*, 18, 1: 132–66.

Bessel, R. (1986) "Violence as Propaganda: The Role of the Storm Troopers in the Rise of National Socialism," in T. Childers (ed.) *The Formation of the Nazi Constituency, 1919–1933*, Totowa, NJ: Barnes & Noble, 131–46.

Bjorgo, T. (1997) *Racist and Right-Wing Violence in Scandinavia: Patterns, Perpetrators, and Responses*, Oslo: Tano Aschehoug.

Merkl, P. H. (1987) *The Making of a Stormtrooper*, Boulder, CO: Westview Press.

Weinberg, L. (1995) "Italian Neo-Fascist Terrorism: A Comparative Perspective," in T. Bjorgo (ed.) *Terror from the Extreme Right*, London: Frank Cass, 221–38.

Terms

Aryan Nations	Ku Klux Klan (KKK)	Pierce, William
Beer Hall Putsch	leaderless resistance	Posse Comitatus
Black International	McVeigh, Timothy	ricin
Bologna train station bombing	Minnesota Patriots Council	Ruby Ridge
Branch Davidians	Murrah Federal Office	Schutzstaffel (SS)
Christian Identity	Building	skinheads
Communist Combat Cells	Mussolini, Benito	Sturmabteilungen (SA)
(CCC)	National Socialist Democratic	Turner Diaries, The
false flag attacks	Workers Party (NSDAP)	Vendée
fascist	Nichols, Terry	Zhirinovsky, Vladimir
Gracchi brothers	Nivelles Group	Zionist Occupation
Hitler, Adolf	Order, the	Government (ZOG)

Chapter 9

Terrorism and multiple motivations

Terrorist campaigns with complex causes   166

Case studies   170

    9.1 Insurgency and terror in Malaya   170

    9.2 Leftists and indigenous populations in Peru   172

    9.3 Irish republicanism   175

    9.4 Colombia—regionalism, ideology, and narcotics   179

Summary   182

Terms   184

Further reading   185

The preceding four chapters have focused on dissident groups and terrorist organizations that could be primarily categorized as being religious, ethnic/nationalist, or ideological. The examples and case studies in these four chapters were all discussed within the context of the dominant motivation for the dissidents and the political objectives that they were seeking. In a number of cases the dominant motivation for dissident groups was reinforced by other factors. National liberation movements occurred with populations that were often based in a different religious tradition than that of the colonial power. Elements of Marxist-Leninist ideology often appeared in the efforts of colonial populations to free themselves from capitalist colonial powers. Basic concepts present in various leftist theories were easily applied to the situations of subject populations in colonial empires. Notwithstanding the addition of these ideological elements, the movements in question were still essentially ethnic and nationalist efforts directed at creating a new independent state where a colony had been before.

Terrorist campaigns with complex causes

There remain, however, examples of dissident violence that have proven to be extremely difficult to categorize as involving one dominant type of objective or only one basic motivation. Many different factors become involved in the motivations of terrorists (Fox 1998: 56). Any of the case studies included in this chapter could have been placed in one of the preceding four chapters, but they could also have been placed in more than one, which illustrates the complexity of causation and objectives. If they had been placed in any of the preceding chapters, they would have provided very unclear examples. As a consequence, it made more sense to deal with these complex cases separately. Further, the fact that these examples of terrorist activities include some of the most important and longest enduring campaigns of violence made it essential to include these cases

in any discussion of terrorism in the world. Long campaigns may permit multiple objectives to develop within the dissident groups. Almost any movement that has been in existence for decades will necessarily have had to recruit new members to refresh the organization (although the 17 November group in Greece was for a long time an exception in this regard). Further, generational differences can appear and younger members of an organization may be more sensitive to different issues (such as discrimination in higher education) than older members who experienced different problems (attempts to extinguish cultural symbols, impose linguistic unity, or government repression). With the passage of time, dissident organizations may well have time to add ideological issues to nationalist or religious ones or to develop a regional base that in turn influences ideology. With time it is also possible for groups to splinter on ideological, ethnic, or religious grounds and, as a consequence, the battle between dissidents and governments will get more complex. The analysis of dissident groups that have been active for long periods of time may also suggest the future path that at least some ethnic, ideological, or religious groups that already exist may ultimately take.

Lebanon, especially during the civil war that began in the 1970s, supplies a clear example of complex causes underlying widespread violence, including various types of terrorism, including the taking of Western hostages. In this case, much of the complexity resulted from the fact that so many different groups relied on violence and terrorism in their efforts to achieve their political objectives. Christian–Muslim differences among the Arab population explained some of the violence, but there was also conflict among the Christians, within both the Sunni and Shia communities, and between Sunni, Shia, and Druze Muslims. At different times, groups of Christians or Muslims were in conflict with the PLO. Different groups of Palestinians also attacked each other at various times, and there were also Marxist-Leninist groups operating that sought to create a secular state that would be aligned with other radical states in the Middle East. Syria and Israel regularly intervened in Lebanon, in pursuit of their own goals, creating even more complex sets of conflicts, which in turn generated a different set of cleavages that reinforced the existing differences in the country. Groups could be anti-Christian, anti-Israeli, and anti-Syrian in their orientation or pro-PLO, pro-Syrian, and opposed to the traditional leadership patterns present in Lebanon (both Christian and Muslim). Hizballah, a Shiite group in Lebanon allied with Iran, was anti-Israel, but it was also very involved in attempting to improve the position of the Shiite community, and these efforts placed it at odds with Christian, Sunni, and the Druze political leaders at least part of the time.

Another factor that has frequently complicated an understanding of terrorism in some countries or in some circumstances has been attacks by criminal groups. As noted in Chapter 2, criminal activity for financial gain, such as kidnappings or extortions, are not acts of terrorism even though they are extremely frightening for the victims. Some attacks by criminal organizations, however, have only indirect relationships to motives of financial gain. The Mafia in Italy has assassinated judges, prosecutors, and other officials when they have been too efficient or too zealous in their investigative activities. While such deaths have the important goal of eliminating particular individuals who have constituted threats to the organization, there has been a broader target audience. Other officials have been warned of the dangers that can come from a too aggressive pursuit of certain criminals. These attacks were designed to force a modification of policy by the appropriate bureaucratic or police agencies (Wilkinson 2000b: 71). If other officials back off from their investigations because of fear, the terrorism has been successful. The violence and assassinations in many of the successor states of the Soviet Union have been difficult to fit into particular categories of violence. The background to individual deaths or attempted assassinations can be unclear to outsiders and the specific audiences that are being targeted may be difficult to specify (although

members of the target audience will often surely know who they are). The individual victims might have been chosen because of their political beliefs, but they could also have been attacked because they were interfering with criminal activities or even because they were demanding too much in the way of bribes or protection money. They could even have reneged on an arrangement they had already made with a criminal group (Pluchinsky 1998: 122). Some individuals in government or the police agencies in these states could have angered both criminal and dissident groups at the same time. If the victim is killed for personal reasons, as in the case of a criminal deal that has gone badly or disagreements about shares of the profits from criminal activities, then the death is not an example of terrorism. Similarly, if the target audience consists of government officials taking bribes, the action does not have the requisite political goals to qualify as terrorism. The objective in this case is financial gain rather than political changes. If the goal of the attacks is the reduction of active enforcement of existing laws, however, then the attack is intended to bring about changes in government policies, or at least changes in the level of enforcement of the government policies. Journalists have become a special target in Russia, especially if they have been investigating corruption. More than half the journalists killed in the world in 1995 died in Russia (Stern 1999: 104). The message to other crusading journalists interested in investigating Russian criminal activity is obvious.

The drug trade and the use of narcotics have further muddied the waters for some dissident organizations and led to the idea of narcoterrrosim where dissident groups involve themselves directly or indirectly in the drug trade. Terrorist groups often have developed clandestine channels of communications and supply routes that are appealing to criminal organizations involved in smuggling drugs. Drug organizations in turn can provide financial support to the political dissidents in return for assistance in moving drugs into or out of a country. The dissidents and drug organizations have a shared goal in avoiding detection

BOX 9.1 Russia's Chechnya quagmire

Russia has faced major problems with an insurrection, complete with terrorist actions, in the province of Chechnya in the Caucasus Mountains region of the country. The Chechens had been one of the most difficult groups in the region for Tsarist Russia to subdue, and their loyalty to Russia and then the Soviet Union had been in doubt. Among the millions deported by Stalin during and after World War II for actual or suspected disloyalty were approximately 400,000 Chechens (Bell-Fialkoff 1999: 32). The present underlying hostility of the Muslim Chechens towards the Russians involves both ethnic and religious elements. The drive for independence has been fueled by the ethnic identification of the Chechens or their adherence to Islam. Many of the dissident Chechens have had contacts with Islamic groups in other countries and have adopted a basically Islamic orientation towards the struggle. They have been involved with al Qaeda and have served in the Afghan campaigns on the side of the Taliban and al Qaeda. Chechens have been an important element in the Islamic Movement of Uzbekistan (Rashid 2002: 9, 174). Many Chechens have returned to do battle against Russian troops, and Muslims from other countries have supported them. There are many ethnic Chechens who have supported the rebellion for nationalist reasons without adopting the Islamic values of the Muslim fundamentalist. Should an independent Chechnya appear, there could well be a struggle between the religious and nationalist elements for control of the new country. A third element in the Chechen struggle involves a criminal element that works with the religious and ethnic elements. Chechen gangs have been among the best-organized criminal groups in the successor states of the old Soviet Union. These gangs have been involved in all kinds of criminal activities, including drug trafficking (Schmid 2000: 114). For these Chechens, the establishment of strong central rule by Russia in the province could limit profits from criminal activity, whereas a weak government in an independent state would be more amenable to bribery and coercion.

The Chechen separatist groups have been involved in a variety of violent activities. They have engaged in actions abroad to support the independence struggle (Barkey 1996: 44). They have fought pitched battles with Russian armed forces. By 2002 they had been forced out of the main cities and into the mountains, but Russian troops have been unable to control this difficult terrain, and the Chechen dissidents have continued to make guerrilla attacks. They have used a variety of techniques throughout Russia, including property attacks, kidnappings, and car bombs (Chalk 1999: 153). Chechen dissidents have also been involved in a number of mass hostage situations, culminating in the seizure of a large portion of the audience in a Moscow theater in 2002. There is some evidence that this bold attack, which resulted in the capture of so many hostages in the capital city of their adversary, was an effort to emulate the attacks of September 11 (Nacos 2003: 14). These hostage situations have resulted in many casualties, including those resulting from the flawed rescue attempt of the Moscow theater hostages. The deadly nature of these terrorist attacks has been more disturbing since there have been indications that the Chechens have sought to obtain weapons of mass destruction (Cronin 2002/3: 48). Regardless of the weapons used, Russia has been unable to defeat or control the dissidents and the violence and terror is likely to continue. Even if Russia were to grant Chechnya independence, terrorist violence from this source would be likely to continue given the international religious connections of some Chechens and the important role played by criminal organizations.

by security forces or the military. Opium producers in Afghanistan have supported one group or another in the various conflicts in that country. The Afghan rebels used drug profits to help finance their war against the Soviet Union (Miller and Damask 1996: 117). Drug producers have a common cause with many dissident groups since they want to avoid having an overly strong central government in power regardless of the religious, ethnic, or ideological complexion of that government. The Mafia in Italy has supplied arms to right-wing political groups in exchange for assistance in smuggling drugs (Schmid 1992b: 21). Al Qaeda has generated additional income for its activities by involvement in the drug trade (Foxell 2001: 125). Islamic dissidents in Uzbekistan have been involved in the drug trade (Rashid 2001: 52). Drug money has become the financial mainstay of the dissidents in this region (Rashid 2002: 229). Kurdish dissident groups have also partially funded many of their activities with proceeds from drug smuggling (Brown 1997: 592), and the

---

BOX 9.2 Kurdish Workers' Party (PKK)

The Kurdish Workers' Party (PKK), which has mounted terrorist operations in Turkey and against Turkish targets abroad, would appear at first glance to be an ethnic party that is seeking autonomy or independence for the Kurds. Somewhat surprisingly, however, the party, under the leadership of Abdullah Ocalan, has had strong Marxist-Leninist components that have influenced its activities. The party has clearly been striving not just for gains for Kurds in a Turkish state but to create a socialist community as well. The party, for example, has emphasized workers' rights and the need to eliminate colonialism and feudalism in Turkish society (Jongman 1992: 71–2). This ideological emphasis on the part of the PKK may reflect the fact that the Kurds are not as geographically concentrated in Turkey as they are in Iran or Iraq. While there is an area in southeastern Turkey that is overwhelmingly Kurdish, in nearby areas Kurds and Turks are intermingled. There are also large numbers of Kurds working in the major urban areas (Barkey 1996). Their location and occupations would make them obvious choices for a working class appeal by a party instead of a solely ethnic one. Despite very real discrimination in the past, the Kurds are better integrated into the Turkish state than has been the case for Kurds in Iraq. In addition to ideology and ethnicity, there have been times when the PKK has emphasized Islamic themes in its propaganda, but these efforts appear to have been attempts to increase support among religious Kurds (and Turks) and have not represented a commitment to furthering a more religious political system (Criss 1995: 22–3).

The PKK has also been one of the groups with an element of fanaticism since it has utilized suicide attacks to achieve its goals. It was responsible for the second-highest number of suicide attacks of any organization noted in Table 5.1. This fanaticism is related to the ideological beliefs of the attackers, not religion or ethnicity (Radu 2002: 280–1). The suicide attacks were designed to strengthen the morale of the group members after a series of defeats by Turkish forces (Dolnik 2003: 24). The Marxist-Leninist credentials of the PKK have made it possible for the party to cooperate with other leftist dissident groups in Europe. Its Kurdish base, on the other hand, has been a handicap since it has limited its ability to collaborate with other Turkish leftists. It has been even more difficult to cooperate with Armenian dissidents since the Kurds shared responsibility for the massacres that occurred in World War I. The PKK lost some of its willingness to persist in the struggle against the Turkish government when Ocalan was captured by Turkish commandos at the Greek embassy in Kenya. Kurdish nationalism with or without Marxism-Leninism could regain strength and again threaten the central government.

KLA in Kosovo developed links with drug smugglers (Macgregor 2001: 97, 103). Obviously many different groups with various causes have availed themselves of this source of funding. ETA in Spain, on the other hand, is an exception. It has interfered with drug smugglers because some of the drugs have stayed in the Basque country (Khatami 1997: 399–401). Narcoterrorism involving drug producers and processors with dissident movements has also appeared in Latin America in a variety of contexts as will be demonstrated in some of the following case studies. Conspiracy theorists put forward the argument that the Soviet Union was behind a global drug trafficking system that was designed to undermine Western democracies. There has been virtually no evidence that such a connection has ever existed (Miller and Damask 1996: 115). While narcoterrorism cannot be realistically used to describe one aspect of Cold War confrontation, it still can be used to describe alliances between dissident groups and drug operators, and clearly profits from the drug traffic have complicated contests between governments and dissident groups, including ones that have resorted to terrorism in efforts to achieve their objectives.

Case studies

Examples of dissident groups that have used terrorism within a complex set of circumstances or objectives include the insurgency in British Malaya after World War II, the Shining Path movement in Peru, the IRA and other groups in Northern Ireland, and the activities of dissidents in Colombia. The guerrilla insurgency and associated terrorism in British Malaya and Singapore after World War II combined ideology and ethnicity. The rebellion was very much a communist insurgency, but it was also clearly rooted in the Chinese community in the British colony. The well-known struggles in Northern Ireland are normally seen as involving Catholic Irish on one side against the British and Protestants in power in the province. In reality, this struggle has been more complex, including ethnonationalist differences that have pitted Irish against the British, and ideological factors that have appeared over time as some dissident terrorist groups increasingly incorporated elements of Marxist-Leninist concepts and justifications. In the case of Peru and the Shining Path movement and the other dissident groups, leftist ideology has combined with a solid base in the Indian population. The Peruvian insurgents also had some links with drug producers and distributors. In neighboring Colombia, violence and terrorism has included leftist revolutionaries that have frequently operated in league with drug cartels. There was even an independent terrorist campaign against the government undertaken by one of the drug organizations.

CASE STUDY 9.1
Insurgency and terror in Malaya

Japanese conquests in Asia and the Pacific during World War II upset the system of colonial control that was maintained by European powers. In British Malaya (which included Singapore) the Malayan Communist Party (MCP) organized resistance to the Japanese. After the war the party attempted to organize in order to overthrow the British colonial administration through strikes, demonstrations, and riots (Marshall 1997: 171). These efforts ultimately failed, leading the MCP to return to violence as the mechanism for establishing itself. The insurrection, which included both guerrilla warfare and terrorism, represented a mixture of ideological concerns and ethnicity. The dissidents were clearly inspired by leftist ideology, but what is equally important is the fact that the dissidents found virtually all of their popular support among the Chinese minority in the country. The British, once they re-established themselves in Malaya, also gave precedence to the native Malays. Citizenship requirements meant that many relatively recent Chinese migrants or the offspring of Chinese migrants were not automatically eligible, whereas Malays and members of their families were (Robinson 1956: 198). Many

Chinese in the rural areas had moved to the country-side during the Japanese occupation to engage in subsistence agriculture but they did not own the land. They were squatters on state land, and their insecurity provided a source of recruits for the MCP in its struggle with the government (R. Thompson 1966: 24). Communism in this era also had a particular appeal to many young Chinese in Malaya because the Chinese communists fought the Japanese so vigorously during World War II, both in China and in Malaya. The victory of the Chinese communists in China added to the appeal that the ideology had. It is not surprising that 95 percent of the communists in British Malaya were ethnic Chinese (Robinson 1956: 100). Thus, there were a variety of factors that tended to link the ideological background of the rebellion with the Chinese community in Malaya and Singapore, and the dissidents took advantage of this linkage to gain new recruits and to gain additional strength. The disadvantage of this approach, however, was that the dissident movement had relatively little appeal to other groups within Malaya. In fact, the ethnic conflict between Malays and Chinese was one of the greatest weaknesses of the rebellion (Desai and Eckstein 1990: 463). The linkage between ideology and ethnicity gave the dissidents an important element of strength since ethnicity reinforced ideology, but it also was a major limitation on the spread of support throughout the society.

The initial attempt of the MCP to challenge British rule was concentrated on developing an urban base in Singapore and other cities in accord with Marxist theory. This early focus on the cities weakened the rural organization that had been established during the struggle against the Japanese. When this strategy failed, the MCP decided to resort to guerrilla warfare in the Malayan countryside. By 1948, however, the colonial administration had been able to re-establish itself and become a presence in the countryside (Clutterbuck 1973: 265). Between 1948 and 1951 the guerrilla insurgency caused difficulties for the British, especially early on when the security and military forces available were clearly insufficient (R. Thompson 1966: 29). The Chinese guerrillas were able to draw support from Chinese villages in the countryside, and the guerrillas were frequently able to blend in with the population (Jackson 1991: 14). Eventually the dis-

sidents were forced to change their strategy to one of greater reliance on terrorism in their efforts to disrupt the administration and seek to undermine the colonial administration (Marshall 1997: 171–2). Abductions and kidnappings became frequent, as were attacks on the civilian population. British nationals in Malaya also became frequent targets for the terrorists. Civilian casualties during the time of the insurrection and the terrorist activities were almost double the casualties suffered by the security forces (Thompson 1966: 27). Terrorist attacks were also made against supporters of the British administration in an effort to frighten other members of the community away from active support. Anyone who cooperated with the administration could be executed (Purcell 1967: 113).

The British finally defeated the insurrection and the terrorist campaign. The government reinforced the troops in the colony and developed local units to battle with the insurgents. The major threat from the guerrillas was relatively quickly defeated, although some continued to fight on for many years. The rural Chinese population that supported the MCP was regrouped into villages that could be better controlled by the security forces, thus cutting the guerrillas off from their sources of supply. With the defeat of the guerrillas, the chances of a successful attack on the government were gone. The use of terrorism as an adjunct of the guerrilla insurgency had contributed to the successes that were achieved, but these kinds of attacks were clearly insufficient by themselves to bring down the government or to force changes. The final defeat of the surviving guerrillas took longer since they were able to retreat to relatively remote areas of the country-side while other dissidents continued to undertake more clandestine activities in the urban areas. There was still activity in 1957 when Malaya gained its independence, and British troops remained in the country for another three years, dealing with the remnants of the dissident campaign (Marshall 1997: 173). Despite the violence Malaya achieved independence pretty much on schedule. In fact, the British probably kept troops in newly independent Malaysia for a longer period of time because of the continuing campaigns by the dissidents. The connection of ideology with ethnic nationalism ultimately was not a successful merger of motivations in this case.

The dissidents in Malaya had some external support via supply networks and links with the Soviet Union. This external support, however, was never very extensive. Malaya was simply too far away and too inaccessible to be supplied in the late 1940s or the early 1950s by existing arrangements, and the dissidents could never rely upon a neighboring state to supply them or provide a refuge in case of defeat (Jackson 1991: 117–18). As a consequence, little external support was offered to the dissidents, and even the perceived link to the new communist regime in China may ultimately have been harmful to the local dissidents.

CASE STUDY 9.2
Leftists and indigenous populations in Peru

One of the most active terrorist and guerrilla organizations in Latin America in the 1980s and 1990s was the Shining Path group (Sendero Luminoso) in Peru. A university professor in the town of Ayacucho in the highlands of Peru formed this organization in 1980. It had a clear leftist ideology and drew heavily upon Marxist-Leninist doctrines. Even though its ideology was leftist, it established itself in the rural areas by appealing to the discontents among the Indian population, which had traditionally been neglected by the central government. The movement thus came to represent not only objectives that were related to the ideology of the founders but the ethnic grievances of a particular portion of the population as well. A similar movement, the Tupac Amaru Revolutionary Movement (MRTA), appeared nearby in highland Peru. It was also leftist, and it drew upon Indian grievances over the dominance of Peruvian society by European and Europeanized elements. The general failure of the government to provide much in the way of services or modernization to the rural areas inhabited by Indians speaking local languages was an issue for supporters of the MRTA as it was for the Shining Path. Further, both dissident organizations drew upon the resources available from local coca growers to help finance their campaigns against the government.

Shining Path could appeal for support in the local Indian communities in its campaigns against the government since the rural areas had been neglected. The combination of leftist doctrine and ethnicity worked in the Peruvian context. The Indian population joined because of their traditional distaste with the government and the lack of programs rather than as a result of any political commitment to a leftist ideology. Shining Path was able to build up strength in the rural areas near Ayacucho. Ayacucho, while not distant from Lima, is on the Amazon side of the Andes, and the region had been largely ignored by the central government. The government was weakly represented and not very alert to this developing challenge (Barnhurst 1991: 82). The movement quickly began to build strength. Shining Path combined guerrilla tactics, especially when battling with security forces, and terror. It first attacked local and government officials and the large landowners, who were hated by the peasants (Long 1990: 85). Local officials and clergy were assassinated as a warning against cooperating with the government. Shining Path was so effective in the late 1980s that many candidates refused to run for government positions and officials resigned their offices in fear. Voters either avoided the voting booths or spoiled their ballots (B. Roberts 1997b: 449). Removing officials from their positions or threatening others who might take their places not only demonstrated the power of the movement but also limited the ability of the government to initiate programs that might have dealt with local grievances. Without local administrators, the ability to push through reforms was much more difficult.

The local peasant communities were also ruthlessly punished for not supporting the organization. Any local political, social, or economic groups that showed any possibility of providing alternative leadership for the peasants were very quickly suppressed (Mason and Campany 1995: 161). The government security forces found it very difficult to control the areas for a long period of time, further reinforcing the need of local populations to cooperate with the dissidents if they wanted to survive. Further, the military and police in responding to the increasing attacks often resorted to repressive measures that drove more of the local population to support the dissidents (Palmer 1995:

301). The dissidents in Shining Path ultimately hoped to replicate the successes of the Chinese communists by first controlling the countryside and eventually encircling the cities and capturing them by isolating them from the rural population (Rosenau 1994: 312). In pursuit of this goal Shining Path eventually began bombing campaigns in the cities. Specific individuals were targeted for assassination, including police and politicians. The group also sought to cause casualties among the general population to demonstrate that the government was impotent to deal with the threat that the dissidents represented. It also wanted to increase insecurity among the social, economic, and political elite of Peru (Palmer 1992: 78). The shift to an urban campaign was an indication that the rural strategy had not been successful enough to destroy the system. The movement hoped that the urban attacks would force a military coup that would further polarize Peruvian society and increase the following of the dissidents (Hazleton and Woy-Hazleton 1988: 482). This dissident organization was clearly following the more or less classic left-wing strategy of attempting to force a more repressive government to appear in order to permit the rebels to mobilize the population against the government. The only difference from the strategy of left-wing groups such as the Red Brigades or the Montoneros was the addition of a clearly ethnic element to the revolt against government authority in the rural areas. The movement was partially successful in that the guerrilla violence and terrorist assaults were factors that led President Alberto Fujimoro to impose martial law and limit protections available to citizens in Peru. These harsher measures probably aided the government in dealing with the dissident groups in the country. The leftist goal of forcing government repression to alienate the population was not successful.

The Shining Path and local drug groups were initially at odds with each other, and there was actually fighting between the traffickers and the dissidents in 1987 (Miller and Damask 1996: 125). The dissidents and drug groups, however, eventually began to cooperate. The Upper Huallaga Valley became a center of their strength. It had ideal climate and soils for growing coca (Palmer 1992: 68). Shining Path was willing to work with the local producers in Peru who were supplying cocaine to markets abroad (especially in the United States). The dissidents, growers, and the shippers had a common aversion to government interference in their activities. Coca production has been quite important to the peasant cultivators since it is by far the most profitable crop they can grow. In fact, coca has provided the first opportunity for many farmers to increase their standard of living (Mason and Campany 1995: 143). Shining Path collected taxes from growers and charged fees for the small planes that carried coca paste to Colombia (Barnhurst 1991: 85). This alliance of convenience permitted Shining Path to finance arms purchases with the money received from the drug cartels. With these funds Shining Path militia units were quite well armed, and the Peruvian police and military forces were by comparison relatively underequipped for a long time (Combs 2000: 100). While the Shining Path supplied protection to the drug traffickers, it also protected the peasants from abuse from the local drug cartels and forced higher payments to the peasants for the coca production (Mason and Campany 1995: 146).

The Shining Path lost some of its momentum when its creator and leader, Abimael Guzman, was arrested in 1992. At about the same time, most of the central leadership was captured as well. Since the dissidents were organized in cells and groups in the field and were largely self-sufficient, however, the organization was able to continue. The existence of funding from the drug groups also meant the units in the areas of greatest strength could continue to finance themselves and to operate (Mason and Campany 1995: 166). Even so, the movement lost strength. Government forces eventually became more effective in gaining control of rural territory. Many of the dissidents accepted amnesties and peace offers, and their financial base disappeared when a fungus damaged the coca crop in one of their core areas of strength (Laqueur 1999: 187). While Shining Path no longer seems to be a threat to the government and the political system, the situation in the countryside in Peru has not changed enough to prevent some other dissident group that appeals to Indian grievances from appearing. Potential dissidents are all too aware of continuing corruption, discrimination, and a clack of commitment to real democracy in Peru (Zirakzadeh

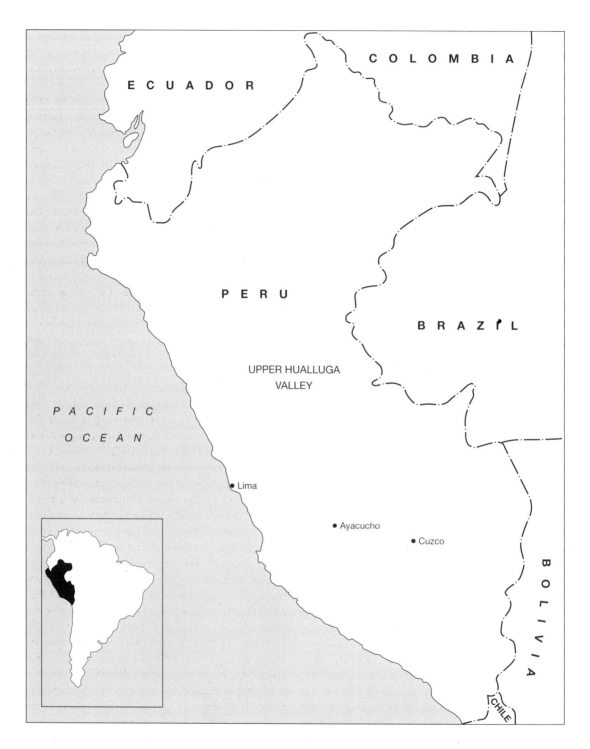

MAP 4 Peru

2002: 89). The motivating cause could again be ideological, given the previous experience, but it could also be even more directly rooted in the opposition of Indian groups to the government after decades of neglect and poor treatment.

MRTA was a more conventional Marxist group that drew upon Indian discontent. MRTA and Shining Path often operated in different regions, but they did not cooperate with each other. They even fought for control of the Upper Huallaga Valley. Like Shining Path this group formed a local alliance with drug producers and utilized financial support from the drug trade to aid in funding its activities. In 1993 many members of the group either were captured by the government or surrendered, apparently ending the threat from this group of dissidents. The announcement of the group's demise, however, was rather premature since it was members of this organization (and not survivors of the Shining Path) that seized the Japanese embassy in Lima in December of 1996 and held some of the guests hostages for many months. This was one of the most spectacular actions undertaken by any Peruvian dissident group, but it was in the nature of a last gasp gamble by a group that was in decline. The seizure ultimately failed to arouse public support or opposition to the government. When security forces attacked in a carefully controlled operation and recaptured the embassy, the crisis for the government was over.

The demise of the dissident violence in Peru has represented a victory for the government. The combination of terrorism and guerrilla insurgency, even when financed by drug money, had failed to bring down the government or even to force it into a permanent situation of authoritarian repression. The violence did result in the deaths of tens of thousands of Peruvians, many killed by Shining Path, but others were killed by government forces in their efforts to deal with the violence. The death toll was significant since the two largest opposition groups lasted a little more than a decade. Other than the financing that came from cooperation with the drug producers, there was no indication of any external support for the Shining Path movement. It was both anti-Soviet and anti-Chinese, and the group intentionally isolated itself from other movements, refusing to cooperate with the other local

Marxist-Leninist and leftist groups that operated in Peru (Hazleton and Woy-Hazleton 1988: 481). MRTA did not have the same aversion to outside connections as Shining Path, but there are no real indications that it received any external support beyond profits from the drug trade. The presence of some radical regime in the future in a neighboring country that favored the interests of the Indian population could stimulate dissidents inside Peru. Such a radical regime might provide a source of support for some future outbreak of violence. Even without a neighboring radical regime, however, violent opposition to the government remains possible. The needs of the Indian population are still largely unmet, and there have been some recent indications that remnants of the Shining Path have again been linking up with drug traffickers and that the movement is becoming active once again in the more remote areas of rural Peru.

CASE STUDY 9.3
Irish republicanism

The battle of Irish dissidents seeking to unite the province of Northern Ireland or Ulster with the Republic of Ireland to the south has been an extremely long one. While the most recent round of violence began in 1969 Irish dissidents have a long history of opposing the British presence in the island. In the years after World War I, the Irish Republican Army (IRA) successfully used guerrilla attacks and terrorism to convince the British to negotiate the peaceful separation of most of Ireland from the United Kingdom. The six counties of Northern Ireland were separated from the twenty-six counties in the south that became the Irish Free State and a dominion in the British Commonwealth. Many members of the IRA refused to accept the treaty and the loss of Ulster in the north. In fact, a civil war raged in the Irish Free State over this treaty. It was years before the violence in the south stopped. In the following years there were occasional efforts to launch attacks against the British position in the north, but they accomplished very little. They did, however, keep the spark of opposition alive (O'Day 1979: 125–6). The Irish Republican Army remained organized and present in both the south and the north even though it eventually became relatively dormant.

In Northern Ireland, the Protestants were in a majority but felt that their position was insecure since there was a substantial Irish Catholic minority in Ulster and the overwhelmingly Catholic Republic just across the border. Any form of unification of the two parts of the island would result in the Protestants becoming a clear minority. One line of division between the two groups became the one identified with religion— Protestants divided from Catholics even if many of the Catholics and Protestants in question were not active churchgoers. The differences went beyond religion to include national identifications. Many of the Protestants were also descendants of Scottish settlers who had migrated to Ireland, and they clearly saw themselves as British. Catholics were more likely to consider themselves as Irish and less likely to think of themselves as British citizens. An economic element reinforced the differences between the two groups since the Protestants were in the dominant economic position in the province. While many Protestants were poor and prone to unemployment, a larger percentage of the Catholic population was in poor economic circumstances. The Protestants actively discriminated against the Catholics in many ways. They dominated the political system so that government services disproportionately benefited the Protestant citizens in terms of employment opportunities and housing (Clutterbuck 1974: 51–2). The Catholics, as a consequence, adopted a civil rights strategy to protest about this treatment. The local government in Northern Ireland refused to grant the demands for greater equality and resorted to repression to deal with these demands. The failure of the government to respond to the civil rights effort gave opposition groups a chance to consider violence as an option in an effort either to support the Catholic community or to end British rule in the province. Repression led to confrontations, and the confrontations led to violence. In 1969 inter-communal violence broke out with Protestant groups attacking Catholic neighborhoods and isolated Protestant neighborhoods being attacked by Catholics. The political force and reserve police were overwhelmingly Protestant and offered relatively little real protection to the Catholic neighborhoods. The violence escalated to

the point where units of the British army were sent to Ulster. Initially the Irish and Catholic population accepted the British troops sent to Northern Ireland since they offered protection against repression and discrimination by the majority.

The Official IRA had decided that violence was unlikely to work and thus chose to avoid a confrontation with the British. The unofficial IRA or Provisional IRA (hence the term Provos) was willing to continue to attempt to free Northern Ireland through the use of violence. The Provos were able to rally those who were ready for military action and attacks against the British (Wilkinson 2000a: 31). Most active members of the IRA sided with the Provos. The Provos felt that it was necessary to protect the Catholics from oppression by the local Protestants and then from the British troops. They undertook actions to increase confrontations with the British. IRA members would fire on police or military patrols, so that the troops entered Catholic areas in efforts to capture the IRA members. An essential part of the dissident program was to force the British to come into Catholic neighborhoods and undertake searches that alienated the local population. Usually the IRA members involved were able to escape, but the occasional IRA member who was caught or killed was a bearable price if the community rallied behind them. This increasing antagonism served the purposes of the Provos very well as more and more members of the minority were driven to support the IRA in its struggles against the majority and the British, and the British became more distrustful of the minority. The terrorist attacks by the Provos also helped to raise the morale of the Catholic community, since they could see that the IRA was fighting back (O'Day 1979: 131). With time it became very difficult for members of the minority community to consider siding with the British against local heroes, and indeed it eventually became dangerous to do so.

As the violence continued, individuals in the Protestant community were targeted for assassination as warnings to broader groups in the majority community. Over time car bombs increasingly became a favorite weapon. Sometimes the bombs were used against buildings or symbolic targets. In other cases they were left in areas where people would be in danger but warnings were given. The police were then forced to clear areas and search for bombs, and if they failed to find them, the explosions caused significant property damage. In other cases, however, cars loaded with explosives were left in shopping areas with no warning or insufficient warning being given. Some bombs were intended to produce fatalities. When they went off, there were many dead or wounded. The car bombs were usually left in Protestant neighborhoods or in shopping areas dominated by Protestant businesses. Most of the casualties were Protestants, and Protestants largely suffered the property damage. There was an associated campaign of economic disruption that at times involved the killing of businessmen and industrialists. This economic warfare was designed to weaken the economy, which was seen as catering to British rather than Irish interests (C. Drake 1998: 57).

The dissidents have also targeted the security forces whenever possible. They killed members of the police while they were on duty or off duty in their homes. They have launched attacks against police stations, often using car bombs to destroy the buildings and inflict casualties. The British army became targets as well. Snipers fired on patrols in urban areas. The IRA proved to be quite capable of creating intricate ambushes for British patrols. The IRA has mined roads and set off the explosives when military vehicles have approached. Off-duty soldiers were considered fair game. All of these IRA actions have obviously been designed to put the police and the soldiers on edge, but they also served to drive a wedge between the security personnel and the minority population. The death of any off-duty soldier increased the anger and anxiety of other soldiers and led them to treat the Catholic population in a fashion that would further distance the security forces from the people. Creating even higher levels of distrust between the minority population and the security forces clearly worked to increase the support for the dissidents (Coogan 1993: 260–1). In addition to security personnel, informers and collaborators were targeted for death. While eliminating a particular informer removed a potential threat, the most obvious target audience was anyone else who might be tempted to inform. The dissidents have gone to great lengths to eliminate former informers, even when they have fled abroad, in order to demonstrate the dangers of cooperating with state authorities. Attacks on individuals seen to be collaborating with the authorities also occurred. The IRA punishment for collaboration with the British or local authorities had a progressive scale of penalties. Punishments included shaving women's hair for going out with British soldiers or other offenses, tarring and feathering, and kneecapping (Coogan 1993: 285). Punishment attacks against those suspected of collaborating with the officials have been a constant presence in Northern Ireland, and they even seem to have increased in periods when cease-fires have limited other forms of activities (Silke 1999).

The intimidation of members of the public has gone further. Anyone testifying in a court against the IRA or other dissident groups has been subject to the threat of assassination, and the intimidation has been carried over even to members of juries in court proceedings. Jurors who voted to convict members of the IRA were subjected to retaliation after the trial. Needless to say, it became very difficult for the authorities to attain convictions of any IRA suspects that were arrested and charged since the defendants would be acquitted or face a new trial because the jury could not reach a verdict. Without any real possibility of convictions it proved difficult to combat and restrain the IRA. The British had to resort to the Diplock Courts where IRA defendants were tried before a judge without a jury. These courts violated the basic rights of the British judicial system, but they did at least permit the British to try the defendants in a court of law. If the IRA had been using terror and violence with the intention of weakening the democratic principles of the British state, these measures by the authorities would have been rated a success. This goal, however, was not one that was sought by the IRA and other dissidents, although it had propaganda value as an example of British repression.

The IRA also carried its campaign of violence and bombings outside the territory of Northern Ireland. There were attacks or planned attacks on British military installations or soldiers in England, Germany, and Gibraltar. Three IRA members were actually killed by the Special Air Services (SAS) Regiment while planning an attack against a British military barracks in Gibraltar (Bell 1997a: 598–9). In 1979 a bomb on the boat of Lord Mountbatten (cousin of the Queen) killed him, his grandson, his daughter-in-law's mother, and a teenage Irish boat pilot (Bell 1997a: 450–2). The IRA also periodically undertook bombing attacks against sites in England. The IRA planted bombs in English cities as early as 1938 and 1939 (Bell 1975: 30). There were pub bombings in the mid-1970s in the London area and Birmingham as well as attacks on British military facilities in England, which were generally less well guarded than similar facilities in Northern Ireland. A Conservative member of the British parliament was killed, and the hotel where the Conservative party was holding its annual meeting was bombed. The IRA also mounted a remote control mortar attack against the Prime Minister's residence when John Major was the leader of government (Roberts, 1997a). Obviously, the reach of the IRA was quite extensive in terms of launching attacks against the British government in a wide variety of circumstances.

The violence from the IRA and other groups in the minority community generated counter-violence from Protestant paramilitary groups in return. A number of different organizations formed and sought to strike back with counterterrorist violence in an effort to intimidate the Catholic community or to force an end to the violence. The Protestants could also rely upon the state for protection and action against the IRA and similar groups; thus their terrorism was basically defensive (O'Day 1979: 128). While the violence from this source has not been as extensive, it has contributed to insecurity in the province and made agreement on political solutions to the problems in the province much more difficult. There were also earlier examples of Ulster Protestants using terror attacks against Catholics to disrupt truces and negotiations (R. White 1993: 579). The increase in animosity between the two groups has served the interests of the dissidents and the minority community.

While the Provisional IRA has been the key dissident group behind the violence in Northern Ireland, it has not been the only group involved, a fact that has complicated efforts directed at achieving peace. The Official IRA had taken on more of a Marxist perspective and this leftist orientation was part of the reason for the split between the Official IRA and the

Provos. The efforts of the Officials to unite the working classes against the British capitalists, therefore, ran counter to the Provisional effort to mobilize the minority community. The Officials eventually focused on political work and on becoming a labor party (Dingley 2001: 453). Another group with a distinctive leftist orientation that operated at the same time as the Provos was the Irish National Liberation Army (INLA). This group was smaller but it conducted similar kinds of campaigns as the Provisional IRA, and the two groups cooperated at times. In addition to these long-standing groups, the various peace efforts between the Provisionals and the British resulted in breakaway groups of Provos that refused to accept the idea that Northern Ireland would remain part of the United Kingdom even if this outcome was in accord with the will of a majority of the Catholics. The Continuity IRA and the Real IRA were two such groups that sought to prevent any accommodation with the British. The Continuity IRA continued attacks when the Provos were beginning serious negotiations with the British to end the violence. There was hope that the attacks would derail the peace process (Gurr and Cole 2000: 154). This splinter group has remained committed to using violence to force the British out of Northern Ireland completely and to reunite the north with the south (Holland 1999: 212). The Real IRA has similar aims and was responsible for the bombing in Omagh in 1998 that killed 29 people and injured over 200 more. Apparently the car bomb was designed to destroy the courthouse as the symbol of British authority only after a warning was given, but confusion in the dissident ranks resulted in a late warning and the death and wounding of so many (Dingley 2001). The attack was intended to demonstrate the continuing intention of portions of the dissidents to battle against the British until Ulster was reunited with the south. The IRA and the INLA both denounced this attack. The INLA even went so far as to support a cease-fire. The Real IRA eventually accepted the idea of a cease-fire in the aftermath of its miscalculation and the unexpected deaths at Omagh (Holland 1999: 222). The Real IRA, as well as the Continuity IRA, has continued its stance of opposition to negotiations that result in a solution short of reunification (Wilkinson 2000a: 77). Thus it would appear that the danger of attacks from the hardliners will continue to be a threat in the future.

The IRA has had some important external support, although not often from other governments. Probably the most important source of support for the dissidents has been from Irish-Americans abroad. They have operated a number of organizations that channel funds to the dissidents, providing them with the financial resources to buy arms and to pay for the expenses of the groups. Noraid in the United States is one group that has collected funds for charitable purposes in Ulster that appear to have helped to finance the IRA (Roberts 1997a: 584). Unlike some other groups supporting dissidents or terrorists in other regions or countries, the United States has failed to crack down on organizations with links to the IRA. The political clout of Irish-Americans sympathetic to the dissidents has been important in preventing the government from seeking to limit fund-raising activities or to ban the organizations as is possible under US law. Government responses elsewhere in the world have also been relatively weak in terms of limiting fund-raising amongst the Irish abroad. There has been some support for the IRA among the population in the Republic to the south, of course, but no Irish government has been supportive during the violence. Public opinion has gradually shifted towards a position of non-support for the IRA and even greater cooperation between the north and the south in dealing with the terrorist violence. The IRA has had occasional state support in the form of arms. Libya has at times aided the IRA in an effort to create as many difficulties for the British government as possible. While this aid predated the American bombing of Libya in 1986, Qadaffi in Libya increased the shipments of arms to the IRA after the attacks as a form of retaliation for British support for the American attacks (Holland 1999: 141). Irish dissidents have also received training in PLO camps and elsewhere. This support has actually had its drawbacks. One consequence of links with the PLO and other Palestinian groups has been the enmity of Israel, which has worked against the IRA whenever possible. Other dissident and insurgent groups have also sabotaged IRA efforts to purchase weapons since IRA efforts to acquire arms have threatened to compromise the

weapons market for their own causes (Bell 1997a: 567). On the whole, it would seem that the foreign support received has been most important in the case of the descendants of the Irish living abroad.

The struggle in Northern Ireland has been going on for over thirty years in its latest manifestation. While there are prospects for peace, the presence of extreme groups that have not given up on the idea of severing the tie between Ulster and the Great Britain does not bode well for future peace (Dingley 2001: 463). The north may even come to repeat the history of the south where disagreements about the degree of accommodation with the British generated violence within the ranks of the Republicans. The violence may continue because many in the IRA and other groups can argue that the violence has worked. The terrorism campaign was effective in bringing the British to the negotiating table (Alonso 2001: 142). It is unlikely that the British and moderate leaders in Northern Ireland would have been willing to negotiate with the dissidents if the decades of violence had not occurred. The hardliners in the majority community have been weakened, and much of the population of Northern Ireland is obviously weary of the violence. The attempts to disrupt the negotiations may yet succeed, and new problems could always appear, but there is at least some hope for the end to over three decades of violence.

CASE STUDY 9.4
Colombia—regionalism, ideology, and narcotics

Colombia has been a country long beset by violence, including civil wars, strikes with violence, and seizures of political power. Between 1948 and 1957 Colombia was wracked with violence—*La Violencia*—that was an outgrowth of the long competition between the two major political parties in the country. Internal wars in the nineteenth century had resulted in regions where villages in Colombia were either entirely supporters of the Conservative party or entirely supporters of the Liberal party. These villages, especially when they were neighboring villages, developed bitter antagonisms that were transmitted from generation to generation (Wilde 1978: 37). Broader political conflicts have since incorporated these localized power struggles and existing rivalries between villages. In 1948, however, a leading Liberal leader was assassinated, sparking a round of violence between Liberals and Conservatives that continued for approximately a decade. Although the initial violence was in the cities, it spread to the countryside as security forces and Conservative paramilitary forces attacked rural areas that were Liberal party strongholds. While figures on casualties are very imprecise, as least 200,000 people died in the ensuing violence (Walton 1984: 74, 91). The Colombian parties eventually ended the violence with an agreement that in effect led to power sharing and the alternation of their candidates in the presidency. The conflict from this period of violence, however, provided a source of discontent that the current dissidents have been able to draw upon. The violence destroyed governmental structures in many areas, giving alternative groups at least an opportunity to become more influential when they did appear (Ortiz 2002: 131). The power vacuum in the countryside was very helpful to the dissidents. Further, the period of La Violencia helped to prepare at least some communities to support more recent anti-government dissident groups.

In 1964 a new group of dissidences appeared. The Revolutionary Armed Forces of Colombia (FARC) was formed and began a guerrilla campaign against the government, drawing upon peasant discontent in some areas of the country and mobilizing at least some of those who had been involved in La Violencia. FARC has used guerrilla tactics and insurgency more than other types of violence. FARC as well as other leftist movements such as the National Liberation Army (ELN), the Popular Liberation Army (EPL), and the April 19 Movement (M-19) have utilized terrorism to further their cause. Bank robberies, kidnappings, and assaults on rich landowners and ranchers, as well as employees of large companies became common. These groups also attacked the security forces and have sought to undermine the capitalist economy through their attacks on economic targets (Ramirez 1997b: 430). Such assaults have largely been successful in undercutting the government and helping the

leftists to maintain their opposition to the government. Today there are significant areas of Colombia that are under effective control of FARC or to a lesser degree the ELN. Government forces can only go into these areas at great risk. In areas that they control, the dissidents have supplied their own brand of law and order and have provided protection for peasants (and others) that had never been present when government forces were supposedly in control. On the other hand, FARC has also been known to kill and terrorize opponents in areas under its control (Ramirez 1997b: 432). FARC has also continued its systematic campaign of assassinations of politicians (Laqueur 1999: 214). More recently, FARC has dramatized its position in the country by kidnapping high-ranking political figures, including a presidential candidate of one of the smaller parties. Such incidents clearly illustrate the use of terrorism to demonstrate the power of the dissidents and the weaknesses of the government.

The other leftist movements have been weaker than FARC. They have never controlled rural areas to the same extent as FARC, and they have had to rely more on terrorist attacks and less on any sustained guerrilla activities. These movements have been more urban in their activities. M-19 was able to mount some spectacular operations, including the occupation of the embassy of the Dominican Republic in 1980 and the holding of 57 hostages, including a number of ambassadors. In 1985 the group seized the Palace of Justice and captured hundreds of hostages, including most members of the Supreme Court. When the confrontation escalated to violence over 100 people were killed, including eleven judges of the Supreme Court (Ramirez 1997b: 430–1). After this confrontation with the security forces, support for M-19 weakened considerably. The media and propaganda advantages won by a daring action were dissipated when so many people died as a direct result of the attack.

The various leftist movements that have operated in Colombia have derived some external state support. Castro's Cuba provided a positive example for the leftists and the hope that they could eventually triumph. Castro's regime supplied what support when it could to leftist guerrillas and dissidents in Venezuela and Colombia. Cuban support, however, ended long ago (Laqueur 1999: 212). It is perhaps not surprising that when the M-19 members took over the Dominican embassy in 1980 and were granted safe passage out of the country, it was Cuba that was the chosen destination (Ramirez 1997b: 430). Even so, the Cuban aid has been relatively minor over the years, and FARC as well as the other groups have mobilized support internally and been able to continue to operate primarily as a consequence of domestic factors.

If FARC has simply continued to be a leftist dissident movement practicing guerrilla warfare and terrorism against the government, it would have been less successful and might not have become as powerful as it is today. FARC, however, has formed a working alliance with various drug producers, who themselves have a history of practicing terrorism. In the late 1980s the drug cartel based in Medellin began a terrorist campaign against the government. Car bombs went off in the streets of Bogotá, the capital, and other cities. Political leaders, judges, and journalists were assassinated for their efforts to attack the drug cartels. Three presidential candidates were murdered in this period ("Colombia" 2001: 9). Further, a Colombian airliner was blown up, killing 130 people, so that informants on the plane would be eliminated (Ramirez 1997b: 433). The intent of this campaign of terror was to dissuade the government from active investigation and prosecution of the members of the drug cartels. Judges who were too aggressive in their investigations, for example, were murdered. More than 350 members of the judiciary were killed, including 50 judges. Not only were judicial officials or police threatened, but their families were threatened as well (Lassen 1990: 113, 116). Car bombs were designed to display to the population at large that the government was unable to protect them, and to suggest that it was the people who were suffering from the government attempts to challenge and destroy the drug cartels. The battle between the cartel and the police was a bloody one. Police officers were killed or wounded, and the police themselves frequently provided summary justice for captured members of the cartel or suspected members of the drug organizations (D. Thompson 1996: 63). The immediate and primary objective of the campaign was political, although of course if the Medellin cartel had been successful the end result would have been an increase in profits. This round of

violence was effectively ended when Pablo Escobar, the leader of the largest drug group in Medellin, was arrested in 1991. He escaped from prison in 1992, but was killed by police in 1993 (D. Thompson 1996: 55). While drug production and trafficking has continued in Colombia, there has been no other attempt by other drug cartels to actively attack the government.

With the at least partial defeat of their terrorist campaign, the cocaine producers shifted to cooperating with FARC and the ELN in certain areas. Their alliance with the leftists has proven to be more durable and profitable. The leftist areas of power were concentrated in the poorer areas of Colombia where cocoa could also be grown and where there were relatively few meaningful economic alternatives. The poverty also provided the social and economic background to permit the leftists to more successfully recruit support since previous governments had done little to ameliorate the problems of these areas (Laqueur 1999: 213). The dissidents and the producers also had a shared goal in terms of keeping government forces out of certain areas. The government and its security forces constituted a major threat to the economic goals of the producers and cartels as well as to the political objectives of the leftists.

Although collaboration has become the norm between producers and leftists, there are examples of confrontation in the past. In areas that it controls, FARC has been able to force the drug producers to increase the money they pay to peasants for cocaine. More seriously for the alliance, fighting between guerrilla forces and members of the drug cartels has occurred (Laqueur 1999: 213–14). The financing of the guerrillas by the drug cartels has been voluntary in some areas while in other areas it has constituted more of a form of protection money. The relative balance of power between the producers and the guerrillas has determined the level and type of support that has been present. In the areas that are dominated by FARC troops, the drug producers have relatively little choice in terms of paying "revolutionary taxes," even though they would probably support the guerrillas in any event. In areas where the FARC or ELN are weak, the payments are voluntary and, one would assume, lower. One of the strengths of FARC has been the financial base from drugs. The organization has been able to finance its activities from its own resources with payments from the drug cartels and revolutionary taxes in the areas it controls, providing a secure base of funding. The movement has also invested in the legal economy to provide itself with a continuing flow of funds (Ortiz 2002: 137).

In recent years paramilitaries supporting the government, or at least opposed to the leftists, have appeared. In 1981 a paramilitary group known as Death to Kidnappers attempted to protect the citizens of Colombia from extortion and ransoms (Ramirez 1997a: 636). This group and later ones quickly began to attack and kill persons suspected of terrorist and criminal activities. The most active current group has been the Self Defense Forces of Colombia (AUC), which has targeted suspected leftists and their supporters, both in rural areas and in the cities. They have depopulated some rural areas by terrorizing the peasants and forcing them to flee to the cities. The government initially supported the paramilitary forces (Santina 1998/9). The paramilitary groups, operating with at least tacit government support initially, have reduced areas under control of the leftists. More recently the government has attempted to distance itself from these paramilitary groups given the increasing number of casualties that they have inflicted. Once created, however, they have proven to be difficult to control ("Columbia" 2001: 12–13). The paramilitaries have not always been as harsh on the drug producers when they have entered a region since they seem to have been open to payments or bribes to look the other way. The money available to the drug producers has continued to permit them to buy protection from whichever groups happen to control a particular area.

It is highly unlikely that there will be any immediate solution to the political violence in Colombia. Recent bombings in Colombian cities have indicated that terrorist violence is still possible, even though it has not been clear which groups had actually set the bombs. FARC has obviously been interested in expanding its activities to the cities. In 2002 three suspected members of the IRA were arrested. They had apparently come to Colombia to train FARC members in the building of bombs (Radu 2002: 283). Members of the Japanese Red Army have also been detected in Colombia. They had provided training that would permit FARC to expand its operations into urban centers (Ortiz 2002: 139). The different participants in the violence in Colombia have clearly had different motives, but all that has been necessary in the short term is that the objectives of the drug producers and the leftists have not been directly contradictory. The sources of different types of terrorist violence are too diverse for easy solution and the pervasive influence of drug money in Colombia will remain. The wealth generated by the cocaine trade means that drug producers can buy protection from corrupt government officials, from the leftist guerrillas, and from the paramilitaries as needed. The availability of the profits from the drug trade has also permitted FARC and other dissidents to purchase arms and other supplies pretty much as needed. In the short term, any government of Colombia will be hard pressed to deal with the mixture of well-funded dissidents, private groups, and criminal elements.

Summary

The above four cases and others like them indicate that insurgency and terrorist movements with long histories can indeed have complex motivations that play a role in the activities of dissidents. Of the four cases analyzed above, three have elements of ethnic or nationalist feeling involved in the violence—Irish versus British, Peruvian Indian versus European or Europeanized citizens, and the Chinese in Malaya versus the British and the Malay population. The endemic violence in Colombia lacks any ethnic component, and the era of great violence in Lebanon did not involve any ethnic considerations since virtually all the combatants were Arab. Thus, ethnicity or nationalism is not necessarily a common overriding theme in long-standing campaigns of political violence such as the ones discussed in this chapter.

Religion also failed to be a common link in all the cases. There have been no religious issues involved in the cases of Colombia and Peru.

Admittedly the leftist guerrillas may have been atheistic and generally opposed to religion. They appear to have considered the Catholic Church to be one of the instruments of oppression for the elites in both of these countries, but they have not put forward another religion nor have they mobilized their supporters on any religious basis. While Catholicism is the dominant religion in these two countries, it can hardly be claimed that the government and the political elite provided a front for organized religion or that they were especially religious. Religion, as a consequence, does not appear to have been a major theme in the violence in these two countries although liberation theology in Latin America has meant that at least some Catholic clergy have been sympathetic to leftist dissidents or have supported them. Religion did not play a major role in the Malayan insurgency. The Islamic faith of many Malays may have persuaded them not to support the communists, but the insurgents were not presenting an alternate religion nor were they mobilizing supporters on the basis of religion. Religion, however, clearly was a contributing factor in the case of Northern Ireland. The family religion, at least in a cultural sense, was important in drawing the battle lines between Irish and British. Mobilization on the basis of religious ideas has been a major element in the violence that occurred in Lebanon.

Criminal activity has become important in some dissident movements, including links with drug trafficking and other kinds of illegal criminal ventures, but again such links were not consistently present. Money from the drug trade was important in Peru. Narcoterrorism was more obvious in Colombia with both the direct attacks of the drug cartels on government officials and their alliance with the leftist dissidents in the country. The involvement of criminal elements was absent in Malaya or Northern Ireland, and criminal activity was not especially relevant for the violence in Lebanon. Drug production and export and criminal organization can provide very important sources of funding for violent dissident groups that do exist, but the presence of criminal activity cannot generate popular opposition to

governments nor effectively seek broad political objectives on its own. The failure of the drug cartels in Colombia to achieve any political objectives when they operated alone is a good illustration of the limitations of criminal organizations as groups seeking political objectives. The government was ultimately able to defeat this more direct attack of narcoterrorism. Once the cartels joined with the FARC, an existing dissident group, they became more successful in pursuing their "business" activities unimpeded by the government.

Ideology would appear to be a more consistent confounding element in cases of violence with complex motivations for the dissident groups and their allies, and it has been ideologies from the left rather than those of the right that have been the most relevant. Communism combined with Chinese ethnicity in Malaya, leftist doctrines with Indian ethnicity in Peru, and leftist ideologies with narcoterrorism and residual effects of La Violencia in Colombia. The presence of Marxist-Leninist views has also become involved at times with the violence in Northern Ireland. It would seem that on the whole leftist ideologies appear to have been a contributing factor in the long-standing complex examples of dissident uses of violence. The leftist ideology may actually serve to provide one additional rationale for the use of violence by the dissidents and may be effective in helping to portray the targets for the violence less as innocent bystanders and more as individuals involved in supporting the system.

Assistance from foreign states was not a particularly important element in any of the four cases that were analyzed in depth. There was limited early assistance by Cuba for some of the leftist dissidents in Colombia, but FARC was never dependent on such aid. Elsewhere in Latin America, there was little indication that Shining Path or MRTA received any outside state support. The IRA and ILNA occasional received some aid from foreign governments, but it was not major, and as noted above, the foreign links were sometimes counterproductive. The communist insurrection in Malaya did have external ties to the Soviet Union and China, but this rebellion occurred at a time when it was difficult for either of these countries to send significant assistance to the dissidents and guerrillas. What was of much greater importance to the dissidents in Peru, Colombia, and Northern Ireland, and what permitted them to continue the struggles, was the external support from non-state actors. In the case of Peru and Colombia the key source of support was funding from drug cartels. For the dissidents in Northern Ireland, it was Irish migrants and descendants of Irish migrants abroad who were important in channeling funds to the IRA and other groups. In this respect, the Irish diaspora was similar to that of the Palestinian and the Sikh diasporas discussed in earlier chapters in terms of being a key source of external aid. The funds from these sources have helped to keep the IRA active in its campaigns in the north. It is obvious from the Irish, Sikh, and Palestinian examples that not all the critical foreign support needs to originate with the government of some foreign country. While the money contributed by or extracted from drug cartels may be greater than the amount that can be raised from sympathizers abroad, it is not as secure in the long run. The dissident sympathizers living abroad may be able to supply less money, but they are also likely to be more loyal supporters and contributors. Drug cartels

can always revert to bribing government officials to survive—a process that could be less expensive than paying taxes or making contributions to a dissident movement or guerrilla organization. It could also prove to be much more difficult for governments to interdict the flow of funds from such supporters than would be the case with funds coming from more organized actors such as drug cartels and foreign states. The routes for funds from the diaspora community to help their embattled compatriots will be multiple ones and highly varied.

It is possible that dissident organizations able to mobilize support based on more than one element or characteristics might be expected to be more successful than other groups, but the success of the groups analyzed above was not noticeably greater than other dissident groups considered in earlier chapters. The insurrection in Malaya failed, notwithstanding ideological and ethnic supports. The British government was able to concentrate sufficient resources to defeat the dissidents in this colony, especially since a portion of the population remained loyal. In Peru, the combination of leftist ideology, Indian discontent, and drug money was insufficient to maintain the active campaigns against the government, although the drug cartels may be re-associating themselves with the remnants of Shining Path

Terms

April 19 Movement (M-19)	Kurdish Workers' Party (PKK)	Real IRA
Chechnya	Medellin cartel	Revolutionary Armed Forces of Colombia (FARC)
Continuity IRA	narcoterrorism	Self Defense Forces of Colombia (AUC)
Diplock Courts	National Liberation Army (ELN)	Shining Path (Sendero Luminoso)
Escobar, Pablo	Noraid	Special Air Services Regiment (SAS)
Fujimoro, Alberto	Ocalan, Abdullah	Tupac Amaru Revolutionary Movement (MRTA)
Guzman, Abimael	Official IRA	La Violencia
Hizballah	Popular Liberation Army (EPL)	
Irish National Liberation Army (INLA)	Provisional IRA	
Irish Republican Army (IRA)		

in a new alliance against the government. In Colombia FARC has been able to survive and even prosper in the territory under its control, but it currently does not appear to have the resources to force the actual collapse of the government or to bring about major policy shifts. FARC may have accepted a role as a *de facto* regional government or alternative government in some areas, a situation not unusual in Colombia with its history of regionalist influence. In any event, FARC does not currently seem to possess the necessary resources to actually replace the government of Colombia with one more amenable to its purported ideological objectives. The case of Northern Ireland is one where the dissidents have had some clear political successes. There have been changes in the government structures in Northern Ireland, and the Catholic community is treated more fairly and has a greater political role to play than it did twenty-five years ago.

Further reading

Bell, J. B. (1997a) *The Secret Army: The IRA*, revised 3rd edn, New Brunswick, NJ: Transaction Books.

Jackson, R. (1991) *The Malayan Emergency: The Commonwealth's Wars, 1948–1966*, London: Routledge.

Mason, T. D. and Campany, C. (1995) "Guerrillas, Drugs and Peasants: The Rational Peasant and the War on Drugs in Peru," *Terrorism and Political Violence*, 7, 4: 140–70.

Ortiz, R. D. (2002) "Insurgent Strategies in the Post-Cold War: The Case of the Revolutionary Armed Forces of Colombia," *Studies in Conflict and Terrorism*, 25, 2: 127–43.

Chapter 10

State use of domestic terrorism and repression

Government-induced fear and compliance 188

Government complicity in terrorism by non-state groups 189

Genocide and ethnic cleansing 192

Case studies 194

10.1 Terror in the first years of the French Revolution 194

10.2 The Cherokee Nation versus the State of Georgia 196

10.3 Paramilitary militias in East Timor 198

10.4 Farm invasions in Zimbabwe 200

10.5 Ethnic cleansing in Bosnia and Herzegovina 202

10.6 Genocide in Rwanda 204

Summary 208

Terms 210

Further reading 210

One issue that is frequently raised with the analysis of terrorism concerns the need to deal with state activities that fit within the broad framework of such violence. The definition utilized in Chapter 2 and all the following chapters required that at least one of the actors involved in the terrorism either as a perpetrator or a target be a non-state group. Covert attacks by one state against another were thus excluded, as were actions undertaken by nations and intelligence agencies during wartime, although state support of existing terrorist groups was not excluded. Government activities that seek to generate terror against its own citizens, however, remain an important concern. The types of activities that might qualify include the intentional use of secret police and the apparatus of the state to induce fear and compliance in a population, government complicity in the activities of death squads and other vigilante groups, and government involvement in genocide and ethnic cleansing.

It has indeed been suggested that governments do practice internal terrorism against their own citizens, and that such uses of violence logically should be included in any discussion of the prevalence of terrorism in the world. The inclusion of state violence in terrorist definitions does involve political questions and reflects the political agendas and motives of those seeking to include state actions (Sproat 1991: 20). Even so, states can and do encourage violence against domestic groups in a variety of ways, and the internal terrorism has as one goal the intimidation of the population (Raymond 2003: 71). While state practices involving the use of violence for control purposes can be included within a discussion of terrorism, it is necessary to do so with clear definitions that will provide as much clarity as possible. If terrorism by definition is restricted to non-state groups, then countries by definition cannot be considered terrorists in terms of dealing with their own citizens. The state and non-state distinction is obviously an important one, especially when used by the general public or in government pronouncements. In point of fact, at least some types of government actions or govern-ment supported actions undertaken in a domestic context can fall within a working definition of terrorism. If the state has a target audience beyond the victims and a political objective, the action could qualify as terrorism. One key for distinguishing terrorism by the state from repres-sion is that with repression individuals in the society have a chance to know the law and thus to avoid violations that would lead to punishment (Sproat 1991: 24). The laws can be repressive but will not constitute terrorism if the citizen has an opportunity to modify his or her behavior, while with terrorism the danger of violence will be unavoidable.

Government-induced fear and compliance

One discussion of terrorism begins with the misleading statement that there has been virtually no discussion of governmental uses of terror in the social science literature (Slann 1987: 39). In point of fact, the social sciences have long been interested in the use of violence by governments. Authoritarian and totalitarian governments that rely on the use of repression and force in control-ling their populations have actually been widely studied. Definitions of totalitarianism have even included the use of secret police and terror as one of the necessary characteristics of this type of regime (Neumann 1968: 183). Authoritarian governments are also likely to use repressive measures for controlling their populations and extraordinary mechanisms for dealing with dissi-dents and other opponents. Unlike non-state actors, it has been governments that have been able to use terror on a mass scale (Wilkinson 2000b: 1). In any event, while government use of force may not have been discussed with direct reference to terrorist practices, such practices have been analyzed in great depth.

A government action can be considered terrorism when the target group is the general population and the government is attempting to influence or control the population. In order for this approach at control to be effective, the government actions will have to be relatively open in order to have the desired results with the target population. A covert termination of an opponent via poison or a traffic accident (i.e. death by natural causes) will not constitute terrorism since there is no attempt to influence an audience. Labeling the death of an opponent or dissident as being due to natural causes keeps alive the fiction that the rule of law is still in operation. In this case the death cannot cause the necessary terror since it is disguised. If the death is passed off as being due to criminal action or a personal grudge, then it cannot be considered terrorism. When the police or secret police openly come to arrest individuals for political crimes or when it is widely known that individuals have been arrested for expressing the "wrong" opinions, however, then a government is obviously attempting to cow others in the population into submission. The Gestapo in Nazi Germany was a gray presence everywhere, ready to detect any trace of treason or anti-government activity. The NKVD (predecessor to the KGB) in Stalin's Russia came in the middle of the night to arrest people, but coming at night with the dreaded knock on the door was not to hide what was happening but to make the whole event more terrifying (Fitzpatrick 1999: 209). "Manipulation of various forms of terror and the threat of terror became the dominant characteristic of the Soviet art of government" (Henze 1996: 390). Arrests in Iraq under the regime of the Ba'ath Party and Saddam Hussein were equally obvious so that other potential opponents would be intimidated (al-Khalil 1989: 1–21). The persons arrested in these cases and similar ones were usually specific individuals who had run afoul of the authorities, but the arrests and punishments were also designed to have a deterrent effect on opposition tendencies within the rest of the population. These examples do indicate that governments as a matter of conscious policy can intend to terrorize their populations, but it is clearly a special kind of terrorism since it has the weight of the state behind it and is undertaken within some kind of legal framework, however arbitrarily the laws may be applied.

Government complicity in terrorism by non-state groups

Governments have frequently acquiesced in violent activities that have targeted certain groups in their societies because of their unpopularity with the general population. The record of governments attempting to deal with domestic violence against women has been highly mixed, and in some countries such violence is virtually ignored. The fact that men often use violence as a means of control as part of an effort to terrorize their partners emphasizes government complicity when such activities are not punished (M. Johnson 1995: 291). Unpopular minorities—cultural, religious, racial or ethnic, or groups identified by sexual preference—may be targets for such violence, and for government indifference as well. Continuing attacks on women, minorities, and homosexuals are ongoing examples of terrorism that can be present in a country, especially when such attacks are largely ignored by the authorities and the public (Grosscup 2000: 83). The government may fail to prosecute the attackers even when they are caught. The end result may be that the victims are terrorized and persons in similar situations begin to fear as well, in part because they know the government will not do anything to protect them. In some cases there may be a lack of any political goal on the part of the government. The government could be ignoring the problem because the minorities are indeed unpopular and the attacks have been deflecting public attention from other problems in the society, but such inaction still constitutes complicity. While the government's failure to react to injustice clearly contributes to the problem and is manifestly unfair, it is at best a marginal example of terrorism, especially when the victims are selected as individuals rather than as members of a group.

Assailants, however, have clearly directed some attacks towards influencing a wider audience. In Germany shortly after World War I paramilitary groups often used force against the left while the government did little to stop the violence (Brenner 2000: 60). In Poland before World War II, the government tolerated attacks on Jewish property by members of the Polish Nationalist Party. These attacks were not intended to kill the Jews who owned the property but to encourage them to migrate to Palestine (Schuddekopf 1973: 169). Similarly, in Germany before Hitler came to power, the police frequently did not interfere with attacks by the stormtroopers against leftist political activities. The courts were more likely to punish communists for violence that occurred than the Nazis (Lepsius 1978: 68). More recently, anti-Gypsy activities in Romania after the fall of communism have not been undertaken by the state, but local authorities have done virtually nothing to protect this minority or to arrest attackers (Merkl 1995a: 101). In Sweden in 1990 the police and authorities often failed to respond when neo-Nazi groups were assaulted by the left-wing groups opposed to these racist views (Bjorgo 1995a: 202). The government signals to the groups using violence in a variety of contexts were quite clear, indicating approval and acquiescence in the attacks.

Governments may participate in terrorism when they permit and even support paramilitary groups, vigilante organizations, and semi-official groups that use violence in efforts to support government policies. The government may wish to have these private groups target dissident elements in the population when government persecution may be difficult or unwise. Shortly after Hitler came to power in Germany, members of the SA and the Nazi party were used to attack Jewish businesses in the country when a German diplomat in Paris had been killed by a German Jew, who was protesting about Nazi anti-Semitic policies. The government organized the attacks, although they were supposedly a spontaneous outburst of anger by the German people. Further,

police authorities did not intervene to prevent these attacks (Read and Fisher 1989). The use of the stormtroopers and the party members permitted the government to deny official responsibility and to avoid the adverse publicity that would have come with official persecution. The unofficial groups that are supported by governments have the additional advantage of being able to inflict more severe punishments, such as execution. After the attempted communist coup in Indonesia in 1965–6, attacks that killed tens of thousands of local Chinese and known communists were undertaken by local vigilantes, but they operated with the blessing and support of the state leaders (Cribb 2000: 184). If dissidents are brought to trial by official agencies, however, the dissidents can use the trial as a forum for propagating their views. As occurred at times with the Red Brigades in Italy, fair judicial proceedings can even become a test of strength between the government and the dissidents. Ultimately, many governments may find it useful to turn a blind eye to the activities of these groups while always being able to disavow their actions if necessary. When the private groups use the attacks to create fear in a target audience to obtain political objectives, it qualifies as terrorism, and when the state tolerates and even encourages such terrorism, it is an example of state terrorism.

One of the most deadly forms of state assisted terrorism has been the activities of death squads, especially those that have been formed by police and military personnel. These groups have operated with the knowledge of the state, and they have the advantages of targeting dissidents using information that can be gained from official files and records but without the restrictions that could be present in more open efforts to deal with government opponents. These death squads are covert, but they are not secret; they are designed not just to kill but to spread terror as well (Campbell 2000: 2, 4–5). Their activities have to be known in order to initmidate other opponents, but ultimate responsibility is not attributed to the government. The state, however, has been instrumental in the formation of death squads and complicit in their activities (Campbell and Brenner 2000: xiv).

Death squads have been active in a number of countries. The use of such groups by the government in Argentina was mentioned in the discussion of the destruction of the Montoneros and other leftist groups in that country. The violence by the death squads sowed widespread fear in society (Gillespie 1995: 242). The terror caused by these death squads was so effective that friends, neighbors, public officials, lawyers, and others were unwilling to press investigations into the fate of those who disappeared for fear that they too would become one of the victims (Calvert 1997a: 631). Many of the leaders in power in El Salvador that had to deal with a leftist insurgency in that country also employed unofficial death squads during the long conflict (Calvert 1997c). Such groups accounted for only one-tenth of the deaths in El Salvador, but their ability to operate with impunity from punishment by state investigations or prosecution increased the potential for their activities to instill terror in the population

(Arnson 2000: 89). As noted in the previous chapter, the Colombian government tolerated the paramilitary groups that battled FARC and other leftists. Elsewhere in Latin America the repression has often been undertaken by government forces, but sometimes the state has been assisted by less official groups. Death squads have not been just a Latin American phenomenon. They operated in South Africa when the apartheid system was in effect. Some of the groups existed within the security forces (unofficially, of course), while in other circumstances private vigilante groups operated as death squads in support of government policies. Over 1,000 deaths have been attributed to the activities of these groups between 1969 and 1993 when the transition to a system of majority rule occurred (Gottschalk 2000: 232–3). The South African security forces often used former guerrillas from the African National Congress (ANC). These former guerrillas also served in hit squads that eliminated opponents of white minority rule (Welsh 1995: 243).

BOX 10.1 Death squads in India

Unofficial death squads and paramilitary groups have operated in India in a number of conflicts. When the government has been unwilling to use too much direct government violence in dealing with these threats as part of an effort to preserve its image, it has resorted to using unofficial groups (Campbell and Brenner 2000: xiii). The government actively permitted the activities of unofficial groups in the struggle with the Sikhs in the Punjab and in dealing with guerrilla insurgents and terrorists in Kashmir. Not only were suspected terrorists and dissidents subjected to summary justice, but individuals who protested against the deaths of suspects or otherwise opposed the harsh government practices were killed or disappeared without a trace. In both the Sikh area and Kashmir, the target audience has been both potential rebels and also those who might otherwise challenge the tactics of the government in dealing with these threats from separatists and religious minorities (Gossman 2000: 272–5). In the continuing struggle in Kashmir, Indian authorities have referred to the unofficial elimination of opposition members as the "Punjab" solution in reference to the employment of techniques that were first utilized against the Sikhs. Perhaps a more disturbing sign for the society has been the occurrence of similar violence by state affiliated groups against radical leftist dissidents and human rights activists in Andhra Pradesh in central India (Gossman 2000: 262–3). The contagion of paramilitary violence and violation of individual civil rights may be spreading, and future Indian governments may be inclined to rely on this technique even more.

Genocide and ethnic cleansing

While death squads, vigilantes, and support for paramilitary groups have been relatively common as methods in which governments deal with dissidents, state violence has taken on more extreme forms. The most deadly type of violence directed against citizens of countries has been attempts at genocide intended to kill everyone in a particular group in the country. In the late nineteenth century and the early twentieth century there had been rare massacres of Armenians by local villages or by the Ottoman authorities. During World War I, however, the leaders of the Ottoman Empire decide to eliminate the Armenian population. The Christian Armenians were seen as potential sympathizers both with the Russian armies that were battling Ottoman forces on the mutual frontier in the Caucasus region and with Western nations in general. The efforts to eliminate the Armenians involved direct executions in some cases and the encouragement of local Turkish and Kurdish villagers to attack and kill the Armenians in other instances. Many of the deaths were a consequence of mass expulsions, deportations, and relocations of the Armenian population. The Armenians, including the elderly and children, were forced to march across arid terrain and deserts with inadequate food and water. As expected and desired by the government officials, hundreds of thousands died in the process. When the attacks and deportations were over, almost two million Armenians had died (Fein 1979: 12–17).

The attempt of the Nazis in Germany to exterminate the Jews in Europe during the Holocaust clearly constitutes the worst example of government violence and genocide. The intent of the "Final Solution" was the death of the entire Jewish population in Europe, and by the end of World War II, the Holocaust had claimed the lives of six million Jews. There were also indications that the Nazis had intended a similar fate for other groups, such as the Gypsies (Lutz and Lutz 1995). The death camps that contained the Jews and others were clearly intended for killing the inmates. The fact that so few survived the death camps is clear evidence of the obvious intent of the Nazi government in Germany. The fact that any of the Jews in Nazi-controlled Europe survived was due to the efforts of individuals to rescue and hide Jews, the efforts of at least some of the governments of countries allied with Germany to protect their populations against Nazi collection and deportation to the death camps, and the activities of agents of some neutral countries to aid and shelter Jews when they could.

The initial assaults and persecutions against Jews by the Nazis and against Armenians by the Turks would qualify as terrorism since they seem to have been intended to overawe other members of the minority groups. The actual efforts at extermination do not constitute examples of government terrorism. The intent of the Ottoman Turks and the German Nazis and their collaborators was not to influence a target audience but to commit mass murder. To some extent both the German and Ottoman governments sought to hide the real objectives of the deportations from the intended victims to make them more compliant. Officials attempted to prevent fear from breaking out in the populations in question. Eventually the intent of the governments became obvious and there were fewer pretenses involved in dealing with the persons who would be killed, but the creation of terror was not a goal of the efforts to concentrate and then to kill the Armenians and the Jews. While it is necessary to recognize the distinction between true genocide and other actions, it is even more important to recognize that the Holocaust did indeed occur, notwithstanding the Holocaust denial industry that seeks to downplay the number of Jewish victims in World War II or to claim that the Holocaust itself is a myth generated by Jewish populations in the world to gain political leverage in various countries.

Since the elimination of a group is not the goal, neither government-sponsored nor government-supported terrorism qualify as genocide. Ethnic cleansing is an example of such government terrorism to achieve political objectives. Members of particular ethnic groups or religious groups will be attacked. Assaults, rapes, murders, and executions become weapons used against members of the target group. These actions, however, involve a target audience beyond the immediate victims. The real goal of the violence is to drive out members of the offending group, and the specific victims of the violence are chosen as a means of sending a message to other persons in the group. The target audience is more important than the immediate victims. The perpetrators of this type of violence, or at least the political leaders who instigate the violence, do not necessarily seek to eliminate all members of the target community. If they flee the country or the region, the political objective will have been achieved. Thus, for ethnic cleansing to work, it is important for the deaths and outrages to be communicated to the target population. Hiding the attacks from the community members would be counterproductive. It can even be in the interest of the government authorities to give extensive publicity to the events that occur, even while deploring the attacks and disavowing responsibility for the violence that has occurred. The ultimate goal of ethnic cleansing is designed to homogenize a population and to create opportunities for additional members of the dominant group to enter an area. The communal violence in India at independence between Muslims and Hindus was an implicit form of ethnic cleansing as the Muslim or Hindu majorities sought to drive the minorities out. More recently, Muslim rebels in Kashmir have practiced ethnic cleansing against Hindus in districts with Muslim majorities (Kumar 2002: 16). The goal of ethnic cleansing may be similar to the conquest in war in that some geographical area becomes available for control by a particular government or group. Conquest is no longer tolerated in the world, but actions within a state that generate violence against minorities often results in a more ambiguous response from other countries in the world community (Simons 1999: 14).

There have been other examples of efforts at ethnic cleansing. The Inquisition was a form of state supported, or at least state tolerated, terrorism directed at religious minorities (Cooley 2000: 8). The draconian laws applied by Oliver Cromwell in Ireland were an early version of

BOX 10.2 The Utashe in independent Croatia (1941–5)

Ethnic cleansing and genocide have occurred in a variety of regions and time frames. In 1941 Germany and its allies invaded Yugoslavia and quickly defeated the armed forces of the country. The country was dismembered with Hungary, Germany, Italy, and Bulgaria directly acquiring territory. A German puppet state of Croatia was set up under the Croatian fascist and nationalist Utashe party. The Croatian nationalists had finally achieved their own state, and as an ally of Italy and Germany, one that included much of the territory that now constitutes most of Bosnia. There were Jewish and Gypsy minorities, and Serbs inhabited many of the areas in this new state. The government of Croatia under the leadership of Ante Pavelich practiced both genocide and ethnic cleansing. The Croatian state was a willing ally in the Nazi Holocaust, sending virtually the entire Jewish population of territory under its control to the death camps. Almost the entire pre-war population of Gypsies was exterminated as well (Lutz and Lutz 1995: 349, 353). The Utashe also killed tens of thousands of Serbs who were located in its territory. While the atrocities against the Serbs were significant, there seems to have been no attempt at total extermination. Hundreds of thousands of Serbs were murdered, but more fled from the violence and threats of violence (Walters 1993: 291–2). The Serbs who were killed would appear to have been intended as examples to force other Serbs to flee to other areas (Milazzo 1975: 10–11). These attacks were, in effect, an early version of ethnic cleansing.

ethnic cleansing. The Catholic Irish were to be expelled to the northwestern and western areas of the island. Relocation rather than extermination was the goal. Ethnic cleansing has also occurred in Tajikistan where some groups fled to neighboring countries to avoid persecution (Auten 1996: 203). As noted in Chapter 6 the government of Yugoslavia (i.e. Serbia and Montenegro) in the 1990s sought to practice its own version of ethnic cleansing in Kosovo by driving out the Albanian population. The activities of government police, troops, and party militia were intended to clear the province of non-Serbs. The departure of over a million refugees to neighboring countries was an acceptable alternative for the government and the official and non-official groups attacking the Albanians. The government of the Sudan has undertaken similar actions against the Nubian population in the country in efforts to assimilate the Nubians into the dominant Islamic culture. Many Nubians have been relocated from their homeland and government supported militias have attacked those that remained (O'Ballance 2000: 174). Such ethnic cleansing clearly has involved the use of terror by governments or governmental support of the use of terror by private groups, paramilitary militias, or death squads. State violence can be considered terrorism when the actions of the government or its allies engages in violence that is systematic, has political objectives, is committed by the state or state proxies, is intended to generate fear and send a message to a wider audience, and is utilized against victims who are not armed at the time of the attacks (Claridge 1996: 52–3).

Case studies

The case studies considered below deal with a variety of activities that have been at the very least encouraged by governments. In some cases governments have even directly supported the violence and terror. Governments have, by intention or by lack of activity, permitted, supported, and even organized terrorist actions, including

examples of ethnic cleansing and mass murder. The first case considered below deals with the use of violence and terror in the first years of the French Revolution, including the Reign of Terror, the event that ultimately supplied a name for the idea of inspiring fear to attain political goals. A second case involves the efforts of the state of Georgia in the United States to dispossess the Cherokee Indians of their land by pointedly refusing to interfere with the violence directed against them by settlers. A third case considers the use of paramilitary groups and vigilante organizations by the government of Indonesia in East Timor in a failed attempt to eliminate opposition to continued Indonesian rule in that island. A fourth case deals with the use of militia of the government party and other informal groups in Zimbabwe to dispossess white land-owners of their property as a means of solidifying support for the government. The last two cases involve ethnic cleansing activities by the Serbs in Bosnia and the massive loss of life in Rwanda as the Hutu population massacred members of the Tutsi group in that country.

CASE STUDY 10.1

Terror in the first years of the French Revolution

The French Revolution was a very violent epoch in the history of that country. Mob violence played a role in the overthrow of the monarchy and the aristocracy, and the term terror was born during the Reign of Terror when the government sought out actual, suspected, and presumed enemies to eliminate them before they could overthrow the state. The revolution even turned on its own as many of the initial leaders of the revolt were executed. First, the more moderate members of the various national assemblies and legislative bodies that successively governed the country were forced out, and eventually many of the radical members were eliminated as well when the reaction to the violence set in. While much of the violence during this period was undertaken directly by the government, there were also activities by private groups that supported various factions in the government and thus constituted state support of private groups operating in conjunction with the activities of state officials.

The Reign of Terror itself was undertaken by the government to eliminate potential dissidents. The term Reign of Terror referred to the government instilling terror in the population as a means of control. While persons who might be actively opposed to the government were eliminated, there was a target audience. Anyone thinking of conspiring against the revolution would have to deal with the threat of exposure and the likelihood of execution. The revolutionary leaders were obsessed with the danger of treason and plots, especially by the nobility (Furet 1989: 147). Over 90 percent of the executions ordered by courts between the spring of 1792 and summer of 1794 were directed against individuals accused of conspiring with enemies of the revolutionary state (Tackett 2000: 692). Even successful generals in the revolutionary armies were sometimes executed because their noble birth led to suspicions that they had been disloyal or could be disloyal (Griffith 1998: Chapter 4). It is not surprising that many of the nobles who disagreed with the revolution and the new government or simply had some reservations about the new system chose to flee abroad rather than stay in the country and take a chance on a charge of disloyalty and possible death. Members of the clergy were another group that became a target for suspicion and arrests. Priests who refused to swear obedience to the new state as supreme over the church were targets as were those who were caught concealing members of the disloyal clergy or otherwise aiding them (Greer 1935: 16–17). While initially the executions were used against the nobles and presumed supporters of the old system, especially when Paris and France were threatened by armies of other European states, many individuals who were not members of the privileged classes were also executed for the flimsiest of reasons.

Once the immediate military threat ended, however, the guillotine and the executions became a method for political combat between different factions in the revolutionary government (Furet 1989: 148).

Eventually, the more radical elements were able to triumph, at least temporarily. They were seeking to purify society of corrupting influences (Boroumand and Boroumand 2002: 13). The Jacobin Clubs were among the strongest supporters of the radicals and they were generally associated with the more radical Montagnards who displaced the Girondins in the national legislature. The Clubs rallied public opinion against the moderates and at times organized demonstrations—including ones that led to violence—in their efforts to ensure that the new Republic was appropriately radical in its views. The Jacobins and other radicals also used the local Paris assemblies to achieve their goals. Riots were one mechanism used to pressure the various legislative bodies or their committees to undertake the appropriate actions (Griffith 1998: 62–3). The radicals eventually used the Parisian mobs to help them expel the more moderate Girondins from the legislature in 1793 (Rude 1959: 113). They proved to be especially adept at successfully branding all those that opposed them as being traitors and anti-revolutionary (Sydenham 1966: 166–7). Once the moderates had been expelled, the official executions increased tremendously as the radicals used the guillotine to intimidate groups that did not agree with them, including many former moderate members of the National Assembly (the Girondins). It is perhaps appropriate that when the radicals were finally displaced from their positions of power in the government, they were sent to the guillotine to share the fate that they had imposed on so many others.

While terror by the government was present in the first years of the revolution, there was also popular use of violence against individuals presumed to be enemies. The assembly utilized the presence of threats of popular violence, as well as actual violence, as one means of forcing concessions from the king and his supporters in the early days of the revolution (Rude 1959: 70–5). The general populace, and especially the militant members of the lower-middle classes, the sans-culottes, who undertook violent actions on their own in many cases. The march on the Tuileries Palace to arrest the king that resulted in the massacre of most of the Swiss Guards was undertaken by the Parisians with the support of some of the representatives in the government, but not the government as such (Rude

1959: 104–5). Soon thereafter mobs murdered over a thousand persons being held in the prisons (Lucas 1994: 62). The mob arrested some members of the Ministry of War in 1792 when they occupied the ministry building. There was a fear that the members were aligned with the aristocracy and therefore disloyal. There were even calls for their execution, but they were more fortunate than many since they were just dismissed from their jobs (Griffith 1998: 67). Efforts to control the mob violence often failed, and the use of official executions that occurred later was another way to channel and control these popular passions (Furet 1989: 147). At one point the National Assembly even dissolved the local government in Paris, but it was forced to rescind the order due to massive popular pressure (Sydenham 1961: 117). Late in 1792 the lower middle classes began to purge local popular governing bodies of suspect individuals and began to round up suspects on their own. These actions were not part of any state repression designed to intimidate opponents or to prevent treasonous activities. They were more the type of popular collective violence and executions "that enjoyed the tacit consent and support of the ruling power" (Baczko 1994: 25). These actions prompted the government to pass its own laws providing for the arrests of suspects, who came to eventually number some 300,000 persons (Sydenham 1966: 177).

The various factions also used the anger of the population and their willingness to use violence to advance themselves in the government. These attempts to gain advantages for one faction probably sped up the adoption of the official terror as opposed to street justice for suspects (Sydenham 1966: 174–8). The French Revolution was an event that was surrounded by violence in various forms. Much of the violent protest against the monarchy at the beginning of the Revolution was left-wing since the goals of the public and the leaders were definitely not conservative. The popular violence was also vaguely leftist in its targets. The whole revolutionary atmosphere led to a situation in which disagreements among different groups bore the threat of eventual violence or elimination. The Montagnards did eliminate their enemies, and at least some of their enemies took up arms, especially in the outlying provinces, in protest against the radical poli-

cies in Paris. The radicals in one sense were correct in assuming that if they lost the political debate their lives would be forfeited, and indeed they were eventually executed.

CASE STUDY 10.2
The Cherokee Nation versus the State of Georgia

The gradual dispossession of members of the Cherokee Nation of their lands in Georgia as a consequence of the actions of the state government and the inaction of the national government in the first quarter of the eighteenth century provides an example of government complicity in terrorizing a minority group that was unpopular with the majority. In this case a state government undertook the action within a federal system in a time period when the state governments had considerable power. It was indeed the state government that determined that local white settlers would be successful in acquiring the land and property of the Cherokees. Georgia not only failed to defend the Cherokees from the depravations of the local white settlers, it actually encouraged these assaults in a variety of ways. The national government eventually had a role in the dispute, but ultimately it too acquiesced in the dispossession of the Indians.

The essence of the conflict was the effort of Georgia to dispossess various Indian tribes—who still had title to approximately one-third of the state in 1820—of their land so that white settlement could occur (van Every 1966: 96). The state of Georgia had sought for many years to drive out the original indigenous inhabitants of the area. Georgia had made this goal very clear early on. In 1802 Georgia ceded all its western land claims in what were to become the states of Alabama and Mississippi in exchange for the removal of all Indians from Georgia proper (Tracey 2000: 50). The state government first was able to use state law and selected bribery to gain title to the lands of the Creek Indians within the state. The state then sent in the Georgia militia to enforce the claim. The Creeks, who were neither as numerous or so well organized as the Cherokees, recognized the inevitable and submitted to the loss of their lands (van Every 1966: 99–102). Soon thereafter they began the trek westward to the Indian Territory set aside for them in what is now Oklahoma.

Encouraged by the success achieved with the Creeks, the Georgians now began seeking to gain control of the Cherokees, who occupied a large amount of land in northwestern Georgia. The desire to acquire title to these lands was increased by the discovery of gold within the Indian lands in 1829. Thousands of whites rushed into the area to prospect for gold. The white miners then found themselves in competition with the Cherokees (Tracey 2000: 51). The gold fields were not themselves the principle explanation for Georgia's efforts to expel the Indians since the desire predated the discovery of gold. If the Cherokees were permitted to exploit these resources, however, their ability to resist the state efforts at eviction would be increased (Carter 1976: 88–9). The Cherokees, in contradiction to the normal view of Indian resistance to the encroachment of whites, generally did not opt for violence during this confrontation with Georgia and greedy settlers. Further, the Cherokees could not hope to compete militarily with Georgia and the United States since they were so badly outnumbered. The strategy adopted in the 1820s and 1830s was to appeal to public opinion and to use legal means to attempt to combat the efforts of the government of Georgia to drive them out.

The Cherokees had developed their own government structure, passed a series of laws, and had become self-governing in their own lands. The state of Georgia in response imposed laws that were designed to undermine the political structure of the Indians and to increase the vulnerability of the Cherokees to pressure. These laws gave a relatively free hand to white Georgians who were inclined to use violence to drive out the Indians. One law confiscated Cherokee land in order to form new counties that would be part of the state governmental structure. Cherokee laws were nullified, and all Cherokees were now subjected to state law. It even became illegal for any Cherokee to advise fellow Cherokees against migration to the west. Indian contracts with whites were not valid unless witnessed by two whites, and no Cherokee could testify in court against any white.

Cherokees were also denied the right to dig for gold on their lands (van Every 1966: 132). They became legally non-persons in court proceedings, and their contract rights were limited. They had no recourse against manipulation and fraud by whites. All of these state activities left the Cherokees incredibly vulnerable to pressure, intimidation, and violence by whites. Georgia sent the state militia into areas where the Cherokees still lived "to preserve order." The actual purpose of the militia was to crush any resistance by the Cherokees, and the militia activities appear to have been designed to provoke a violent response that would then give the state an excuse to forcibly remove them in the interest of public safety. Georgia eventually created a special police force, the Georgia Guard, to maintain order in the Cherokee lands. The state claimed no responsibility for the activities of this group, which clearly understood that its job was to harass the Indians and to side with white settlers (McLoughlin 1986: 432–3). The Georgia Guard was essentially a group of vigilantes that had the normal vigilantes' sense of "self-importance and disdain for civil rights" (Carter 1976: 100).

The Cherokees invoked their treaty rights and attempted to use the US courts to provide the necessary protection for themselves and their property. Since their case involved a treaty that had been signed with the United States, it was heard before the US Supreme Court. The court under Chief Justice John Marshall then rendered a judgment favoring the Cherokees. Andrew Jackson, the President at the time, supposedly responded to the court ruling with the famous, or infamous, phrase, "John Marshall has made his decision; now let him enforce it" (Filler and Guttman 1962: vii). While this quote may not be historically accurate, it clearly reflected President Jackson's opinions on dealing with the Indians. He was an old Indian fighter; consequently, he was not pro-Indian and was in favor of relocating Indians to lands west of the Mississippi. Even though the Cherokees had won their case in the courts, the failure of the government of the United States to support the implementation of the decision meant that they could not triumph. Eventually the Cherokees migrated to Oklahoma as did the Creeks before them, and Georgia was able to claim all of their land.

The activities of the government, both at the state level and with the national government, supported the efforts of local groups of whites to dispossess the Indians of their land and property. The Indians were subjected to a variety of insults, persecution, attacks, and even death (Finkelstein 1995: 38). Destruction of Indian property was widespread, particularly by white miners when the gold rush occurred (Tracey 2000: 51). While the number of Indians who were killed directly does not seem to have been large, it was very difficult for them to protect themselves in violent confrontations. The Georgia laws that were passed meant that they had no legal safeguards. Not all whites were anti-Indian, and missionaries were particularly supportive of the Cherokees but they could not be everywhere (Coulter 1962: 108). The Georgia Guard that had been created even arrested missionaries who were getting in the way of the efforts to force the Cherokees out (McLoughlin 1986: 433). The state policies were clearly designed to permit the local groups to use violence freely without any fear of prosecution by the state. Eventually the state government held lotteries giving out parcels of land in Cherokee country, even if the Indians were still living on the land. Prominent Cherokee leaders would return to find their property and homes in the possession of white settlers (Ehle 1988: 260–2).

The national government, especially under President Jackson, demonstrated the importance that a lack of activity can have. The failure to enforce the court decisions sent a signal to Georgia that it was free to continue with its efforts to evict the Cherokees. Earlier, when federal troops had been sent to the gold fields to control the violence, thus providing a measure of protection to the Indians, President Jackson removed them when he received protests about their presence from the state government (van Every 1966: 132–3). Bills supporting the position of the Cherokees and other Indians were proposed in Congress by its more fair-minded members, but the legislation was never passed. A majority of the legislative branch was unwilling to do anything to protect Indian property in Georgia. The courts were the one branch that sided with the Cherokees, but the weaknesses of this branch of government at this time meant that the judicial pronouncements were of little avail in the efforts of the

Cherokees to preserve what remained of their land and birthright. While many groups of American Indians were forced off their lands in the history of the United States, the case of the Cherokees involved a consistent and concerted effort by the Georgia government for more than twenty years to support violence by private groups in order to achieve its desired goals.

CASE STUDY 10.3
Paramilitary militias in East Timor

In 1975 the Portuguese pulled out of their remaining colonies around the world, conceding independence to the local inhabitants. East Timor was the surviving remnant of Portuguese journeys of exploration and conquest to the Spice Islands. Parts of the island had remained Portuguese while the remainder of the island came to be governed by the Dutch and then part of the state of Indonesia when the Dutch East Indies became independent. While there had been little in the way of active opposition to Portuguese rule in East Timor, it was granted its freedom with the rest of the colonies in 1975, and the Timorese proclaimed an independent republic. The Indonesian government claimed the territory was part of Indonesia. A week later Indonesian troops occupied the territory, and East Timor was formally annexed. The proponents of independence did not disappear. The national feeling of the East Timorese was buttressed in part by the fact that a large majority of the East Timorese was Roman Catholic, as opposed to largely Muslim Indonesian (Pateman 1998: 123). For over twenty years the Indonesians remained in control, notwithstanding efforts of the East Timorese to assert their independence. Initially the new government always utilized regular security forces in their efforts to control the area, but eventually the Indonesian regime came to utilize paramilitary groups and unofficial militias in its efforts to repress and intimidate the population.

After the initial East Timorese proponents of independence for the territory were repressed, a national liberation movement appeared to militarily contest control of the territory with the Indonesian forces that were present. The occupation and battle with the dissidents was often brutal, and the security forces and Indonesian military committed numerous atrocities in their battles with the guerrillas (Gerlovin 1995/6: 58). The guerrillas were unable to defeat the Indonesian army, but the Indonesian army was unable to totally eliminate the independence group. Over time, the Indonesian military forces became an army of occupation. The security forces were none too gentle with suspected dissidents, and torture and beatings by the security forces were not unusual. While some suspects were released after questioning, even questioning with torture, some of those who were detained simply disappeared (J. Taylor 1997: 660). The government also utilized other methods of disciplining potential dissidents or independence advocates, including dismissal from jobs, deportation to other provinces in the country, and loss of scholarships at universities (Salla 1994: 45). The Indonesian military and the militias also denied nationalists or suspected nationalists access to medical facilities as a weapon in their struggle to impose control and weaken support for independence (Stein and Ayotte 1999). In addition to their regular security duties, members of the military forces assaulted and attempted to intimidate the population at night with summary executions and beatings (Ramos-Horta 1997: 33).

Indonesian rule was anything but beneficial for the original population of the area. Given the opposition of the native population, most of the government and professional posts went to Indonesians from elsewhere in the country, further antagonizing the local population. The province also suffered from poor health care and very high poverty rates. More than 100,000 migrants came to the area as part of a plan to change the relative population balance. Towards the end of the Indonesian occupation there were attacks by the East Timorese against these migrants from other parts of Indonesia. Most of these attacks were attacks on the property of the migrants, but they were clearly designed to suggest to the migrants that they should depart (Pateman 1998: 130).

The regular military forces conducted operations in East Timor against the rebel forces and even used force against peaceful demonstrations by dissidents. Paramilitary groups (ninjas) and militias were created

to operate in the territory against those favoring independence. The use of these groups, frequently trained and supported by military units, reflected the efforts of at least some within governing circles to maintain Indonesian control of the territory (Schulze 2001: 79). The paramilitary groups targeted the local political leadership and the Catholic clergy, who often favored independence. Human rights activists were also targets for attacks by death squads or pro-Indonesian vigilantes (Zunes 2000: 329). These groups, in conjunction with Indonesian soldiers and police in civilian clothes, participated in attacks and murders of citizens in the province. Whatever was not looted was destroyed, leaving the inhabitants to attempt to survive without shelter or a means of livelihood (Traub 2000: 77–80). Many of the inhabitants of the province fled to West Timor for safety. The flight of a portion of the population to the Indonesian part of the island served the government's purpose. Support for the dissidents was weakened and the numerical advantage of the original inhabitants vis-à-vis the Indonesian migrants was decreased. The government acknowledged the presence of at least some of the violence perpetrated by the ninjas, but it claimed that the violence was either a result of conflicts between the pro-integration forces and independence groups or between different factions of the independence movement. An alternative explanation advanced by the Indonesian government was that groups in the independence movement undertook the violence in an effort to discredit the government and to gain foreign support for the idea of independence for East Timor (Claridge 1996: 60). The struggle in East Timor has been a bloody one. More than 200,000 people died, approximately one-third of the pre-annexation population of the country (Jardine 1998: 195). The violence has often been called genocide, but neither the Indonesian government nor the militias operating with government blessings intended to eliminate the population of East Timor. The goal was assimilation rather than destruction as evidenced by the favorable treatment for those East Timorese willing to work with the Indonesians.

The efforts of the East Timorese to form their own nation were finally rewarded. A relatively impartial referendum of the population indicated that there was overwhelming support for the idea of independence, and in 2002 East Timor became independent. The final efforts by the militias and other groups supported by Indonesia to disrupt the referendum and to attempt to intimidate the voters into supporting the continued association with Indonesia were unsuccessful. The decision to permit a referendum under international auspices in East Timor resulted from changing conditions within Indonesia itself when a more democratic regime replaced the military one in power. The new government chose to accept the separation of East Timor and use its resources to deal with problems elsewhere in the country. For a long period of time the international community had accepted the incorporation of East Timor into Indonesia. Eventually, as the struggle of the East Timorese continued and the media became more aware of what was happening in the country, there was more concern for investigations and then support for the idea of independence for East Timor. International pressure did eventually play a role in forcing the Indonesian government to consider a referendum and even the possibility of independence when the atrocities committed by government forces became known (Jardine 1998: 199). The involvement of outside states coupled with the dramatic political changes in Indonesia helped the East Timorese to achieve their goal of independence.

CASE STUDY 10.4
Farm invasions in Zimbabwe

In the early 1960s the colony of Southern Rhodesia had limited internal rule that favored the small white minority in the colony. When faced with the prospect that the British would create a political system for the black African majority in 1965, the local leadership in Southern Rhodesia issued a unilateral declaration of independence, establishing a political system where the white minority continued to rule the new country of Rhodesia. The British opposed the unilateral declaration of independence and refused to recognize the new government. Economic sanctions were eventually imposed on the country. The presence of Portuguese colonies in Mozambique to the east and Angola to the west, Southwest Africa (now Namibia) governed

by South Africa to the southwest, and the Republic of South Africa to the south, however, provided the minority Rhodesian government with important allies that supported the white government. Eventually in 1971 a guerrilla movement appeared to contest the control of the country with the minority government. After eight years of guerrilla warfare and the departure of the Portuguese from Angola and Mozambique the minority government conceded defeat and agreed to a transition to rule by the majority, resulting in the creation of a new political system. The new country then came to be known as Zimbabwe.

Initially politics in Zimbabwe was a contest between the Zimbabwean African National Union-Popular Front (ZANU-PF) of Robert Mugabe and the Zimbabwean African People's Union (ZAPU). ZANU and Mugabe had greater popular support and triumphed in the electoral arena. Slowly but surely, however, the government began to place greater and greater restrictions on the opposition until Zimbabwe became a one-party state and ZAPU was eliminated from the political scene and its leaders went into exile. Even when many more states were adopting democracy in the late 1980s and early 1990s, Mugabe maintained one-party rule under his leadership. Eventually toward the end of the 1990s opposition parties were permitted to form and present candidates for elections, but the government used both legal and illegal mechanisms to prevent the opposition parties from having any realistic opportunity of winning. Opposition party gatherings were attacked, and the police provided no protection. Members of opposing parties were arrested and otherwise harassed. In the legislative elections of 2000 supporters of the opposition were beaten and several dozen killed while veterans of the independence struggle intimidated voters likely to favor the opposition. The government also ordered hospitals and clinics to refuse treatment for supporters of the other parties (Rotberg 2000: 48). In 2002 there was a presidential election in which all of these types of tactics were again used. Other groups that favored Mugabe's re-election reinforced the activities of the veterans and militants (McGregor 2002: 36–7). The outcome of the election itself was predetermined, and Mugabe was guaranteed a victory. Intimidation was rampant; manipulation of voting records and harassment were present, and the final vote count was rigged.

While the above tactics are fairly typical for any authoritarian government that manages to ensure that they win elections, there was a related activity in Zimbabwe regarding white settler farms that provide an example of government support for non-state actors that have practiced terrorism. The key agricultural sector for Zimbabwe consisted of the farms owned by whites. These farms were among the most productive in the country and provided both food surpluses for the local population and crops for export. It is not surprising that these farms included much of the best agricultural land in the country (Griffiths 1984: 100–1). Given the output from these farms, the ZANU government initially made no attempt to seize all the farms of the settler population since such seizures could have resulted in productivity declines. Great Britain funded farm acquisitions for a period, but such support ended because of corruption in the program (I. Taylor and Williams 2002: 550). There was some agitation by ZANU supporters and others in Zimbabwe to redistribute the land from these farms, in part because of a general land shortage in the country and in part because the white farmers had usually supported the white minority government during the guerrilla struggle. The white farm owners also supported opposition parties instead of ZANU, providing the government with another grievance with them. While the government did not officially favor extensive land reform or expropriation, militants in ZANU did agitate for a policy of acquisition of the farms by native Africans. Eventually these militants, especially the former guerrilla fighters, began to occupy the farms of the white settlers as part of a campaign to drive them out.

The farm occupations involved physical force and violence. If the owners of the lands resisted, there was damage to their property and even assaults. Some of the owners were killed while attempting to defend their farms from the unauthorized takeovers. The use of force by the owners inevitably led to the use of force by the militants who were attempting to take over the property. While the state did not officially back the militants, Mugabe's government was very tolerant of the land occupiers, and there was no effective

protection offered to the farmers. Police were ordered not to enforce injunctions from the courts against the farm occupations (Rotberg 2000: 50). There were virtually no arrests of the persons who attempted to seize the farms, even in cases where violence was involved. At times the farmers would be arrested and charged for using violence against the militants. The government did not accept the use of violence by farmers in self-defense.

The inaction of the government has been vital for this campaign of land occupations. Despite the protests of the government, it is clear that there has been secret support for the ZANU militants. To some extent it is possible that Mugabe could not afford to alienate the militants in his own party given his declining popular support. While the governing party and the veterans shared many objectives, there were differences as well. Mugabe could not automatically count on their support (McGregor 2002: 10). It is doubtful that he would have won a fair presidential election in 2002, and the absence of support within his own party could even have meant his replacement by a leader more willing to cater to the desires of the militants. Mugabe's weak political position coupled with white farmer support for the opposition may indeed explain his willingness to overlook the illegal occupations and the attacks. Of course, these policies were popular in many parts of Zimbabwe, and relatively few Zimbabweans were likely to feel much sympathy for the white land-owners, even if they disapproved of the methods that were being used. The government, of course, could have accomplished the same goals by an official policy of land reform and redistribution, even outright expropriation of the land held by the white owners, but such an official policy would have raised difficulties abroad with foreign countries whose aid or support Mugabe needed or desired. The unofficial nature of the farm invasions permitted the government to separate itself from the actions of the people while still benefiting from the popularity that the actions generated in at least parts of the population of Zimbabwe. More recently the government of Mugabe has felt itself strong enough to use land reform programs to take some of the white farms for redistribution without compensation (Taylor and Williams 2002: 550). In the long run the change in ownership could reduce the resources available to the government in terms of lower tax revenues and foreign currency earnings, but in the short term the government gained at least politically. Most politicians, of course, have to worry about the next year, as well as the next five years, when making decisions, and staying in power is often the first priority, even if decisions made today make survival in the more distant future less likely.

CASE STUDY 10.5
Ethnic cleansing in Bosnia and Herzegovina

The breakup of Yugoslavia led to violence in many forms. The armed forces available to Croatia when it began its efforts to secede from Yugoslavia had to fight portions of the Yugoslav army. Later, when the Yugoslav army withdrew, parts of Croatia were held by separatist elements from among the local Serbian population for a significant period of time. The problems faced first by the Albanians in Kosovo and then the Serbs in that province have already been discussed in a previous case study in an earlier chapter. In addition, communal violence became the norm for many parts of Bosnia and Herzegovina as that new country sought to establish a government for itself and to gain control of its own territory (see Map 3). Many of the communal divisions that had undermined the unity of Yugoslavia were also present within Bosnia. Like Croatia, it faced intervention from what remained of the Yugoslav state (Serbia and Montenegro), and there was violence from Serbian separatist groups seeking to change their status within the state or to attach portions of Bosnia to what remained of Yugoslavia. Even democratization within Bosnia increased the level of confrontation since elections gave each communal group an opportunity to accurately gauge their share of support in the country. Further, the elections also provided an easy and relatively cost-free method for individuals to express their communal identification (Slack and Doyon 2001: 143). The murders and other violent actions undertaken by paramilitary groups to terrorize different portions of the population

of Bosnia came to be termed ethnic cleansing, especially in areas where Serbs were present in large numbers as they sought to drive out Muslim and Croat populations.

Bosnia is the most heterogeneous of the successor states to the old unified Yugoslavia. The three largest groups in the country have been the Serbs, the Muslim Bosnians, and the Croats. All three groups speak Serbo-Croatian as a language, but their community identification is still distinct. The Croats, the smallest of the three groups, generally have an affiliation with the Roman Catholic Church and have looked to the west. The Serbs were originally the largest identifiable group in the country, but by the 1990s had come to be the second largest community. Their identification has basically been with the Greek Orthodox Church, and they have identified with their fellow Serbs in Serbia (the historic kingdom, the core of the Yugoslav monarchy, the republic in communist Yugoslavia, and Serbia and Montenegro). The Bosnian Muslims have become a self-identified communal group that has come to be the single largest community in the country. The Bosnian Muslims are the descendants of Catholic and Orthodox Serbs, as well as members of more unorthodox Christian sects, who converted when the area became part of the Ottoman Empire centuries ago. Thus, at independence the country had three distinct groups, with Muslim Bosnians being the most numerous, the Orthodox Serbs nearly as large, and a much smaller Catholic Croat population. The differences among the groups were religious in large measure, but religious identity can spawn nationalist movements even when persons belong to the same ethnic group (Berend 1998: 189). The reaction of local Serbs to the Bosnian declaration of independence reflected their concern with their position as the second largest group in the country and one with a declining percentage of the population. As the second largest community the Serbs feared that they would face reduced employment opportunities and other disadvantages. The areas where the Serbian portion of the population had declined the most, thus endangering continued political control by the Serbs, were the areas where violence involving Serbian paramilitaries was to be the greatest (Slack and Doyon 2001). Both the Croats and Serbs in Bosnia could look to neighboring states (Croatia and the remainder of Yugoslavia respectively) where their community was a majority and which they might hope to join. The situation of the Muslims differed from the other two groups, however, in that there was no neighboring state with which the Bosnian Muslims could hope to affiliate.

The preferred choice of many of the Serbs was incorporation into what remained of Yugoslavia. Local Serb paramilitary groups also wanted to capture enough territory to create secure land links with Serbia and to link areas in Croatia occupied by local Serbian groups with Serbia as well (Pavkovic 2000: 162). The second choice was some form of greater autonomy within the Bosnian state for different areas organized on the basis of the predominant community in an area (Serb, Croat, or Muslim). Local governments would be dominated by the communal groups and would have a great deal of local power. The central government would be relatively weak and would have little opportunity to intervene in local affairs. Many plans were put forward incorporating this idea of local autonomy in one form or another. The dispersion of the population in Bosnia was such that the Serbs and the Croats tended to be concentrated in certain parts of the country, especially in the more rural locales. The Bosnian Muslims, on the other hand, were more concentrated in urban areas throughout the country. The fact that cities often had substantial Muslim populations made them special targets for Serbian military and paramilitary attacks (Simmons 2001). All of the decentralization plans put the largest communal group, the Muslims, at a disadvantage, but the presence of large numbers of Muslims in many areas of the country also meant that the Serbs (and the Croats) could not be absolutely sure of dominating their respective areas. The solution that was hit upon by the local Serbian political and military leaders was the policy of ethnic cleansing.

The ideas behind the policy of ethnic cleansing was to drive the Muslim populations, and in some cases Croats, out of particular areas and create relatively homogenous communities. The departure of the Muslims would increase the possibility that Serbs would then dominate these areas, and they might be able to detach the areas and incorporate them into Serbia. In these efforts what remained of Yugoslavia

provided important assistance to the Bosnian Serbs, including military aid and military personnel (Ron 2000: 286). In order to accomplish this goal, the Serbian militias in Bosnia supported by volunteers from rump Yugoslavia (who managed to volunteer with the equipment that was issued by the Yugoslav army) attacked areas where Bosnian Muslims were concentrated. Cities or the parts of cities with Muslim populations were shelled with tanks and heavy artillery and subjected to constant sniper fire. There has even been evidence that the shellings and sniper attacks intentionally targeted children as a means of increasing the terror value of the violence (M. Taylor and Horgan 2000: 87). Often escape routes were left open so that refugees could flee the places under attack, ultimately with many of them becoming concentrated in Sarajevo. Usually the Serb militias did not interfere with columns of Muslim refugees fleeing their homes for the presumed safety of Sarajevo or other cities where there was a United Nations presence, since the departure of the Muslims was indeed the desired goal. The military equipment available to the central government of Bosnia was clearly incapable of dealing with these kinds of attacks, and local armed Muslim groups could not begin to match the firepower available to the Serb paramilitary and militia units.

The fighting in many parts of the country created many refugees. Serbs, Croats, and Muslims all used force to expel members of the other groups from territories that they controlled. Sometimes the expulsions were accomplished through the use of military units, but on other occasions the authorities permitted local vigilantes or criminal groups to force out members of the other groups. The homes and property of the expelled populations were then used to house and support refugees from other parts of Bosnia (Pavkovic 2000: 167). Many of the refugees had no desire to return to their original homes, and for the others returning was not an option. Local majorities have only tolerated the return of refugees from the other communities when the returnees are older and have no children, thus constituting no demographic threat to local control (Macgregor 2001: 96).

While more conventional military attacks were successful in some areas, the ethnic cleansing took on a more frightening form in other areas. Especially in rural areas, Serb militiamen would appear. Young men and boys of fighting age were collected and marched off, usually never to be seen again. Other Muslims would be concentrated in makeshift camps and subjected to a variety of indignities. In some areas the Serb militias used mass rape as a method of achieving their political objectives. The violation of Muslim women was designed to humiliate them and their families and attach a stigma to the offspring. The threat of rape was intended to terrorize any Muslim groups that were considering remaining in areas dominated by the Serbs (Gavin 2001: 41). The vicious attacks of this type were designed not only to affect the immediate victims but a much wider target audience as well. The goal was to drive the Muslims from the area, and terror in different forms was the chosen weapon. It was not essential to kill all the Muslim men or rape all the Muslim women. Selected but widespread atrocities would cause most of the Muslim population to flee on their own.

This example of ethnic cleansing is included in this chapter as government supported terrorization of a population because the Serb areas of Bosnia were in effect governed by local politicians supported by a foreign state in the form of what remained of Yugoslavia. While at some level the Serbian militias could be considered dissidents seeking freedom from the central government in Sarajevo, the conflict with the central government also had aspects of a civil war, and in this civil war the politicians associated with the militias were governing portions of the country. The Serbian paramilitary groups clearly saw themselves as members of a broader Serbian nation and regarded their actions as efforts to eliminate internal enemies (Ron 2000: 308). The Serbian political leaders in Bosnia and Yugoslavia never publicly called for ethnic cleansing as such, but they managed to indicate their support for the activities of the militias. The murders, shellings, and assaults—including the rapes—were tolerated and supported by the local Serbian politicians in Bosnia and the Yugoslavian government in Belgrade. Thus, the experience of the Bosnian Muslims does clearly fall into the area of governmentally supported vigilante and paramilitary operations.

The ethnic cleansing activities by the Serbs directed against the Muslims finally ended when external military forces by the United States and other NATO countries were brought into play, but not before hundreds of thousands had died in the violence and much of the rest of the population had been terrorized in some fashion. Eventually a relatively decentralized form of government was created with some areas controlled by the Croat–Muslim groups and other areas under Serb domination. The Serbs eventually came to control 49 percent of Bosnian territory compared to the Croats and Muslims who controlled the other 51 percent (Pavkovic 2000: 169). The extent of the territorial control was disproportionate to the Serbian share of the population but it reflected the territory that the Serb groups had come to control this territory by the time of the fighting ended. In effect the ethnic cleansing activities of the local Serbs and their external supporters had been successful in permitting political domination of more territory.

CASE STUDY 10.6
Genocide in Rwanda

The slaughter of members of the Tutsi (Watutsi) group in Rwanda by some portions of the majority Hutu (Bahutu) population constitutes the case of government supported or tolerated violence in recent times that most clearly could be considered genocide. The loss of life among the targeted group was quite significant, and the goal of the attackers was to rid the society of the minority that for centuries had formed a ruling class in the region. In this case the extremists were relatively successful in their goal. The relative isolation of Rwanda from the rest of the world meant that the situation in the country was ignored in much of the rest of the world, much as was the case for the situation in East Timor, until it was too late for hundreds of thousands of victims. Both Rwanda and East Timor are small territories that are not in the public eye, in part because the Western media is normally not well represented in countries and places such as these.

Rwanda and neighboring Burundi are among the most densely populated areas in East Africa. The

MAP 5 East Africa

present territory generally corresponds to two indigenous kingdoms that were present when European explorers arrived in the area. When the European colonial powers were busy dividing up the continent, these two kingdoms became part of German East Africa. After World War I, Germany lost her colonies in Africa, with German East Africa being divided among the victorious allies. Portugal got a small boundary rectification to the advantage of its colony of Mozambique. Great Britain received the bulk of German East Africa, which then became the British Mandate of Tanganyika. Belgium received the territories of Ruanda-Urundi as a Mandate. The Belgian spoils of war (or spoils of victory) were actually quite valuable since they provided an important manpower source that could be utilized, not only locally but in the much larger Belgian Congo that bordered on Ruanda-Urundi as well. By the time independence came to this part of Africa in the early 1960s, the populations had grown considerably due to Western medicine and better health care. What had been an initial advantage for the Belgians had now become a liability since the new states of Rwanda and Burundi were among the most densely populated in Africa and there was great pressure for access to farmland.

The Hutu had been the original inhabitants of the region, and they were basically farmers. The Tutsi arrived in the region later as invaders. Their weapons and organization permitted them to assume the role of a ruling aristocracy in the area, and eventually two kingdoms under Tutsi royal families developed. In the two kingdoms that developed the Tutsi, who comprised approximately one-sixth of the population, became the ruling elite (Khan 2000: 3). The Hutu were co-opted to serve the Tutsi as herders and in other menial positions. Thus, the original society in the two kingdoms was stratified along ethnic lines, and the Germans and the Belgians did little to change the situation, preferring to work within the existing hierarchy when they governed the area. The reliance on traditional hierarchies meant that the Tutsi were relatively privileged. When the territories became independent as Rwanda and Burundi, the colonial administration considered establishing a hereditary monarchy for both states. Hutu politicians in Rwanda quickly eliminated any possibility of a monarchy in Rwanda, but Burundi actually did become a kingdom for a few years after independence.

Although both Burundi and Rwanda suffered from various kinds of violence between Hutu and Tutsi, they went in opposite directions with independence. The Tutsi continued to politically dominate Burundi, and a failed coup attempt in 1972, largely by Hutu officers, led to retaliation against the Hutu by the government. As many as 80,000 to 100,000 Hutu were killed in the massacres that followed, including virtually all the educated members of the Hutu majority (Shalom 2001: 45). Periodic outbursts of violence directed against the Hutu in Burundi by government security forces or Tutsi paramilitary groups have continued to

occur (Rieff 2001: 61). In Rwanda, on the other hand, the Hutu ruling groups discriminated against the Tutsi and limited their role in the political system. Many Tutsi fled the country, becoming refugees. Some of them eventually mounted raids into Rwanda seeking to overthrow the government. For almost thirty years the Rwandan government was able to deal with the incursions without too much difficulty, but each raid would then usually lead to violence against the remaining Tutsi (Khan 2000: 4). More Tutsi then left Rwanda, becoming refugees or residents in neighboring countries, but substantial numbers of Tutsi still remained in Rwanda. The departure of the refugees had a positive benefit for the government and many landless Hutu since scarce land was now available for redistribution in this densely populated country (Mamdani 2001: 201). Thus in 1990 the Tutsi were a minority governing in Burundi and a minority in Rwanda that was governed by the Hutu majority, who were not a monolithic group by any means.

In 1990 yet another invasion force of Tutsi entered the area and by 1993 had achieved some significant successes against the Rwandan armed forces. In the resulting civil war, tensions between the Hutu and the Tutsi increased. As troops of the regular army suffered losses in the civil war with the rebels, political parties and other groups formed militias and self-defense units. These militias took on paramilitary functions and proliferated in Rwanda, providing troops that could be used in a variety of ways when the political system was in turmoil (Mamdani 2001: 206–7). The government utilized death squads, and massacres of Tutsi by militia groups such as Interahamwe and the Impuza Mugambi that were supported by at least some extreme members of the government (Shalom 2001: 47). The numbers of Tutsi deaths in these cases were relatively few, but they were a symptom of what was to come. In addition, these groups and others had already provoked confrontations with members of other parties and they had murdered members of opposition parties (Scherrer 2002: 107). The government of Rwanda, with pressure from outside mediators, agreed to a negotiated power-sharing arrangement with the rebels. When it appeared that the government was giving in to the rebels, the President's plane was mysteriously shot down in 1994 with a surface-to-air missile, and extremist groups that had been preparing for action struck and gained control of the government. The extremists among the Hutu groups gained since their policies of Hutu nationalism attracted supporters as the rebels advanced. In addition, many Hutu feared the loss of their farms or other possessions if the Tutsi were permitted to regain power (Mamdani 2001: 190–1).

The new interim government under control of the extremists began attacks against the Tutsi and others. The extremists defined the Tutsi as a race that was alien to Rwanda; they were no longer a minority ethnic group that was still considered to be Rwandan but a foreign minority group (Mamdani 2001: 190). Demonizing a minority group is often the first step towards genocide, and it clearly played a role in Rwanda. The attackers included some elements of the armed forces and police, but the militias were dominant. The initial targets included the Tutsi political elite and leaders as well as any Hutu who were members of the opposition parties or seen as being too moderate. The prime minister was considered a moderate Hutu, and she was among the first to be killed (Khan 2000: 17). The militias then began to kill Tutsi wherever they could find them. As the genocide got underway, individuals caught alone had virtually no chance. Groups of Tutsi who banded together to defend themselves fared better until soldiers or police used their weapons to give the Hutu mobs the edge when attacking buildings sheltering Tutsi. The attacks involved great savagery, and neither the elderly, women, nor children were spared. Many of the victims were tortured before they were killed or allowed to die. Within the span of less than four months the majority of the Tutsi population of Rwanda had been slaughtered. Once the violence had started, there were indications of local initiatives by groups favoring pillage or robbery, but the impetus for this action came from the larger scale massacres encouraged and supported by the interim government (Mamdani 2001: 194). Individual Hutu who refused to join in the violence also became targets for the extremists. Officials who refused to go along with the genocidal attacks were killed in order to intimidate other government personnel into cooperating (Scherrer 2002: 110). Anyone who did not participate in the killing

faced the real possibility that he or she (and their families) would be killed. While some members of the clergy supported the genocidal attacks, other clergy were opposed, and many clergy were among the casualties (Mamdani 2001: 219, 226). Other Hutu were killed for attempting to protect Tutsi neighbors or refugees. Not all Hutu, of course, participated in the massacres. The deaths of Hutu moderates and those who attempted to rescue their Tutsi neighbors is a testimony to the bravery of individuals (Mueller 2000: 60), but they lacked the means to prevent the massacres that occurred.

The killing eventually stopped when the rebel forces representing the Tutsi refugees were able to advance on the capital and defeat the troops that remained loyal to the Hutu extremists. While the government could organize massacres of civilians, it proved incapable of directing the organized military forces that it had available to defeat the rebels. The massacres and violence in the areas that the government controlled and the participation of members of the Rwandan armed forces in the attacks on the Tutsi probably weakened the ability of the government to fight the rebels. Had the rebels not been victorious in driving the government from power, it is unlikely that any of the perpetrators would ever had been subjected to trial for their crimes (Snyder 2001: 446). Foreign peacekeeping forces also arrived on the scene, but by the time the rebels and foreign troops had arrived, the damage had been done and the extremists had achieved their goal of annihilation. Leaders of the slaughter of the Tutsi and many militia members fled from Rwanda to refugee camps in neighboring countries.

The death toll in Rwanda was indeed great in absolute and relative terms. The extremists among the Hutu were able to kill an estimated 500,000 Tutsi in the country by one estimate as well as perhaps as many as 100,000 Hutu (Kuperman 2000: 101). Others have put the number of Tutsi deaths as high as 800,000 (Shalom 2001: 56). Well over half of the Tutsi population of Rwanda was slaughtered during the massacres. It is not just the magnitude of the loss of life that makes the events in Rwanda genocide. The fact that the government and other Rwandan groups attempted to hide the fact of the massacres from other

Tutsi (and the outside world) while the killing was underway is an indication that the real goal was the elimination of the minority. When many Tutsi were killed early on in the attacks, the government hid the information so that outside intervention was less likely and so that Tutsi who were still alive were unaware of their probable fate (Kuperman 2000: 98).

The control of the state government was essential for the massacres to inflict such casualties on the Tutsi and to inflict them so quickly. State power not only facilitated the mass murder, but it even put a stamp of approval upon the proceedings (Mamdani 2001: 217–18). The Rwandan military units were invariably commanded by extremists, meaning that the units either participated in the massacres or they were neutralized and unable to intervene to protect Tutsis. The moderate officers and politicians simply had no troops at their disposal, and to attempt to prevent the massacres without troops would simply have exposed themselves to reprisals (Kuperman 2000: 111). As a consequence, the Hutu opposition was simply too weak to prevent the deaths that occurred. While the massacres clearly provide an example of genocide, earlier events are examples of the Rwandan governmental support for terrorism. The government ignored the activities of paramilitary groups, militias, and vigilantes that agreed with government policies. Assaults on opposition politicians and moderates before the death of the president were designed to intimidate those against the government. The use of death squads by the government and official toleration of the activities of the militias in the earlier periods were a prelude to genocide.

Summary

Government repression and the use of terror by state agents against citizens have been fairly common throughout the world and throughout time. In some cases governments have tolerated the use of violence by security forces against dissidents and their supporters. The rights of dissidents and opponents of the government have been violated and transgressions overlooked by superiors with a wink and nod to subordinates, who have thus been encouraged to continue the activities. In other cases private groups such as vigilantes, paramilitary groups, and militias that have engaged in violence have not been prosecuted, and if offenders have actually been brought to trial, they have been let off with a slap on the wrist. In the case of death squads, the governments concerned have been more actively involved in the use of terror against their own citizens while preserving the possibility of denying official participation. In the case of ethnic cleansing it is often the government's objectives that are being met and active government support is often present. Finally, with the occurrence of genocide, government organization is essential to the elimination of the target population.

The various case studies in this chapter represent a range of terroristic activities directed against groups of citizens. The activities of the state of Georgia and the ZANU militants in Zimbabwe were very similar in intent. The attacks of the private groups were designed to dispossess a portion of the population of valuable property. In both cases the government acquiesced in the dispossession of an unpopular group of citizens and made it clear that sanctions and legal remedies would not be applied against the offenders. The Cherokees and the white farmers did not receive the protection of the state authorities or the police. Interestingly enough, in both cases the political leaders made it very clear that judicial remedies and restraining orders providing protection would not be enforced. In both Georgia and Zimbabwe governments were catering to the needs of particular groups that were important politically. In the case of the French Revolution and the Reign of Terror, the role of the government in violence was less consistent. In some cases the use of terror originated with the groups that were in power, which led to government by intimidation and fear. In other cases factions in the government supported violence against suspect groups or their political opponents to further their political goals and used terror to advance their political agendas. Finally, there were examples of popular outbreaks that did not originate with the government in Paris or local authorities and which basically took place beyond the control of the political leadership.

The cases of East Timor, Bosnia, and Rwanda provide recent examples of the use or the increased use of ethnic cleansing tactics and even genocide. East Timor and Bosnia do not qualify as genocide, despite the death tolls, since the intent of the perpetrators was not physical elimination. The goal of the Indonesian government was the assimilation of East Timor and the suppression of the liberation movement. Thus, in both Bosnia and East Timor the target populations could survive by adopting the appropriate pattern of behavior (departure or assimilation). In Rwanda neither options of assimilation or departure was available, and a large portion of the Hutu population sought physical elimination of the Tutsi. The Holocaust required the active mobilization of millions of Germans and an even larger number of supporters in the German allies and occupied territories (Scherrer 2002: 124–5). Similarly, in Rwanda the massive death count could only have been achieved with the active participation of many members of the Hutu population, including the militias and paramilitary groups.

It has been suggested that ethnic warfare and ethnic cleansing are just cover terms for actions by thugs and marginal elements in society (Mueller 2000). Such a suggestion, however, overlooks the element of political direction supplied by governments or political leaders who encourage it. The key is the political objective, not the personnel who carry out the terror. Security force members and paramilitary groups often attract those prone to violence or who enjoy it, but it is the organization that makes the groups more deadly and effective and more of a threat to a political system or a target group. The active involvement or support of governments contributes to the possibility of increased death tolls since the administrative apparatus of the state is available. The casualty figures for Rwanda, Bosnia and Herzegovina, and East Timor were quite large, both in an absolute sense and in terms of percentage losses among the targeted group.

Government violence led to high tolls in Argentina as well under the post-Perón military regime, and if there had not been outside intervention the deaths in Kosovo might have been very high. The loss of life in France during the Reign of Terror reached high levels as well. The expulsion of the Cherokees from Georgia, as well as other eastern tribes, to what was to become Oklahoma was achieved with relatively few direct casualties. The forced migration to the Indian Territory, however, resulted in many deaths among the migrants. State terrorism and repression does not always result in high body counts. So far the totals from the violence in Zimbabwe have not been especially high, and the Tupamaros were suppressed in Uruguay with relatively few deaths.

State supported or tolerated terrorism is one area where the presence of external support has largely been a non-issue. The vigilantes, paramilitary groups, and death squads generally have had sufficient domestic political support so that they have not had to look to external backers. Often in the case of government supported terrorism, the outside involvement that does occur has been on behalf of the victims. In East Timor external pressures, domestic opposition and the fall of the military regime in Indonesia all combined to lead to the independence referendum. In Bosnia and Kosovo the ethnic cleansing operations were eventually terminated when force was applied against the groups using terror and violence. The ambivalent response of outside groups in areas where ethnic cleansing has been practiced has encouraged such activities since punishment equal to the crime has been unlikely (Simons 1999:15). Less than vigorous responses and prosecutions in effect will mean that ethnic cleansing has been allowed to be successful. In the case of large-scale attacks against targeted civilian population, intervention has to occur quickly if massive casualties are going to be prevented (Kuperman 2000: 117). In Rwanda, foreign involvement in the internal fighting in the country came far too late to do much good for the Tutsi victims. In the case of the French Revolution the support from foreign countries for the old system was never very effective. The presence of outside observers in the case of Zimbabwe has probably limited the violence directed against the white farmers and other opponents of the regime. International public opinion was probably one factor that led to the use of party militants and veterans in the land occupations and prevented much more direct expropriation by the government. Finally, in the case of the Cherokees in Georgia, the Cherokees never received any effective support from any source.

One final, and unfortunate, point needs to be made in regard to the direct use or support of terror by governments against their own citizens. Since the persons applying the violence have had the government behind them and external interference is belated or non-existent, it is not surprising that this type of terrorism has often been successful in terms of achieving the goals of the perpetrators. State support of terror in whatever form is more likely to succeed than dissident terror. Violence and terror in France led to the destruction of the pillars of the old system before the Revolution, and the political system was indeed transformed both in the short term and in the long term. The Cherokees were forced out of Georgia and lost their lands. Robert Mugabe continues to govern as President in Zimbabwe, and at least some of the Zimbabweans continue to support him and his policies while the position of the remaining white farm owners is not enviable. Serbs in Bosnia now control much more territory than they did before the violence and the political solution that has led to a federated political system in which they have been rewarded for the use of violence. Only in East Timor did the efforts to apply terror to intimidate the population fail to achieve any long-term results for those using the terror. East Timor has gained its independence notwithstanding the use of terror, but this failure has been more the exception than the rule. Elsewhere, government violence helped to destroy the Tupamaros in Uruguay, the Sikh dissidents, and the leftists in Argentina.

Further reading

Claridge, D. (1996) "State Terrorism? Applying a Definitional Model," *Terrorism and Political Violence*, 8, 3: 47–63.

Furet, F. (1989) "Terror," in F. Furet and M. Ozouf (eds) *A Critical Dictionary of the French Revolution*, trans. A. Goldhammer, Cambridge, MA: Belknap Press, 137–50.

Kuperman, A. J. (2000) "Rwanda in Perspective," *Foreign Affairs*, 79, 1: 94–118.

Mamdani, M. (2001) *When Victims become Killers: Colonialism, Nativism, and the Genocide in Rwanda*, Princeton, NJ: Princeton University Press.

Pateman, R. (1998) "East Timor, Twenty Years After: *Resistir e Vencer* (To Resist Is to Win)," *Terrorism and Political Violence*, 10, 1: 119–32.

Rotberg, R. I. (2000) "Africa's Mess, Mugabe's Mayhem," *Foreign Affairs*, 79, 5: 47–61.

Sydenham, M. J. (1966) *The French Revolution*, New York: Capricorn Books.

van Every, D. (1966) *Disinherited: The Lost Birthright of the American Indian*, New York: William Morrow, 1966.

Terms

African National Congress (ANC)	Impuza Mugambi	Reign of Terror
ethnic cleansing	Interahamwe	Tutsi (Watutsi)
genocide	Jacobin Clubs	Utashe
Georgia Guard	Montagnards	Zimbabwean African National Union (ZANU)
Gestapo	Mugabe, Robert	Zimbabwean African People's Union (ZAPU)
Girondins	NKVD	
Hutu (Bahutu)	Pavelich, Ante	
	"Punjab" solution	

Chapter 11

Countries with multiple crises of terrorism

The prevalence of multiple crises   212

Waves of violence and terrorism in Sri Lanka   214

Summary   221

Terms   222

Further reading   222

Terrorism has been a recurring theme in some areas of the world, even when it has occurred in different contexts. While some countries have experienced a particular type of terrorist violence over the course of many years such as the activities of ETA in Spain, other countries seem to have been prone to terrorist activities by different groups seeking different objectives. In fact, there would appear to have been a trend towards greater complexity where the governments and populations in some regions are increasingly facing violent dissidents belonging to groups with entirely different motives (Wilkinson 2000b: 4). A number of countries have faced such waves of terrorist activity. Sri Lanka is one country that has suffered from terrorism used in efforts to achieve a variety of political objectives. It has faced crises in political terrorism—plural occurrences that go beyond the well-publicized violence and civil war between the two largest ethnic groups on the island.

The prevalence of multiple crises

The area that now constitutes Israel and the Occupied Territories (the old Palestinian Mandate) has also had waves of dissident terrorism. The Arab and Jewish communities attacked each other, and both sides utilized terrorist tactics in the conflict. Both sides at various times attempted to convince broader target audiences of Palestinian villagers or Jewish settlers to relocate. Terrorism also became an important weapon used by extremists among the Jewish nationalists (Zionists) in their efforts to convince the British to leave the mandated territory. Leaders of the battles against the British and the Arabs in the period of the Mandate became heroes, especially to extreme right groups in Israel (Sprinzak 2000: 213). There have been the attacks by Palestinian groups, struggles between the secular PLO and Hamas, and attacks by Jewish extremist groups. The assassination of Prime Minister Yitzak Rabin did derail the peace process precisely as was hoped by the assassin and those who agreed with him. Palestinians have attempted to prevent negotiations as well. In 1951 a Palestinian assassinated King Abdullah of Jordan, destroying the chances of a permanent peace between Israel and Jordan, just as the assassin intended (Cooley 1997a: 288). In the violence that began in 2001 (the second intifada), extremists on both sides have been able to weaken the peace process by resorting to violence. The attacks by Palestinian suicide bombers have consistently led to the postponement of peace talks and heightened tensions and suspicion. These bombings are a repetition of earlier suicide attacks when Hamas and Islamic Jihad tried to use suicide attacks to prevent the implementation of the Oslo agreements between Israel and the PLO (Rathmell 1997d). The continuing violent campaigns by various groups, the failure of any successful negotiations for a future Palestinian state, and the limited prospects for such a state have created increased Palestinian support for the use of violence (Shikaki 2002: 92–3). The most recent round of violence in the area is simply another attempt to derail efforts at peace by extremists on both sides.

What used to be Yugoslavia has suffered from a number of outbreaks of terrorist violence. After World War I, there were difficulties with the Croatian nationalists and Bulgarians in the Macedonian region, and the external meddling of Italy, Hungary, and Bulgaria. In the 1990s nationalist feelings resurfaced with the conflict in Kosovo and independent Macedonia where the Albanians used violence very effectively to mobilize the popular support for the cause of autonomy or independence. State terrorism and government supported violence also appeared with the Utashe regime in Croatia, the efforts to terrorize the Albanians in Kosovo by the regime of Slobodan Milosevic, the particularly vicious ethnic cleansing activities that occurred in Bosnia and Herzegovina, and the activities of Albanian dissident groups in Macedonia. The potential for continued violence is still present since the situations in Kosovo, Bosnia, and Macedonia remain unstable. In the case of this region the severity of the violence and its recurrence has often been increased by the fact that nationalist differences were rein-forced by religious differences. Nationalism and religion have combined to strengthen communal antagonisms.

Indonesia is another country that has fre-quently been mentioned in the preceding pages. The demise of the Suharto regime and the move-ment towards establishing a functioning democ-racy under trying circumstances has meant that the political system has been in transition and is more vulnerable as a consequence. Indonesia as a multi-ethnic country has faced a variety of nationalist dissident groups. In Aceh in northern Sumatra violence has occurred not only between the dissidents and security forces; the dissidents have attacked Javanese migrants brought in by the government to solidify support for the nation (Chalk 1998a: 123). The failed attempt to incorp-orate East Timor encouraged opposition groups in Irian Jaya, the Indonesian portion of New Guinea that was joined to Indonesia in 1963 (Jones and Smith 2001: 281). Ethnic conflict lay behind the violence on Borneo between Dayaks and Madurese. The cohesion of the Indonesian state has also been threatened by religious differences. The communal violence between Christians and Muslims in Sulawesi and Ambion in the Moluccas has involved religiously inspired terrorism. Laskar Jihad, a militant Islamic group with some ties to bin Laden, has sent members to the Moluccas to fight against the local Christians (Desker 2002: 385). Members of the armed forces and govern-ment civil servants facilitated the movement of these militant Muslims to the area (Hefner 2002: 760). Al Qaeda operatives have increasingly been active in this region of the world. In addition to Indonesia, they have been active in Singapore, Malaysia, and the Philippines (Chalk 1998a: 127–28). The attack on tourists in Bali is one recent example. The presence of violent dissident groups in Indonesia has also affected the security forces. The use of terror by police and military personnel has been documented, and the govern-ment has tolerated attacks by paramilitary groups supporting the government, including the violence directed against the Chinese and communists

when the Suharto regime first came to power. Vigilantes trained and supported by the military were responsible for many of the deaths that occurred at this time (Cribb 2000: 184). In the waning days of the weakened military regime, Chinese and Christians served as convenient scapegoats for the economic problems in 1997–8. Violence against the Chinese led to more than 100,000 fleeing the country (Hefner 2002: 759). The multiple tensions inherent in Indonesia, the limited size of the armed forces to deal with unrest in multiple—and often widely separated—loca-tions, and the fragility of the new democratic system currently make the country especially vulnerable. The inability of the government to control the violence in Sulawesi, Ambion, and Borneo has dramatically demonstrated the vulner-ability of the system, and the potential for a variety of domestic dissident groups to resort to violence and terrorism in the future would appear to be relatively high.

India is another country facing a variety of dis-sident groups and the use of violence to achieve political objectives. A large portion of the unrest is related to the multi-ethnic nature of the state and religious differences among the population, but ideological concerns have also played a role. India has also been notable in that civilians have been the targets so often. In terms of total casualties, India has been one of the "most terrorism battered countries in the world" (Chalk 1996: 15). The reli-gious unrest manifested itself in the revolt of the Sikhs in the Punjab and unrest among the largely Muslim population of Kashmir. There have also been attacks against Christians, especially West-ern missionaries, as well as communal violence between Muslims and Hindus. The confrontation over the grounds at Ayoda where Hindu militants have sought to reclaim the land and replace the mosque with a temple for their religion is a recent example. The Hindus have been at least partially successful in that the Ayoda site is no longer used as a mosque. Recent attacks on Hindus returning from the temple site (and the resulting retaliation by Hindus against Muslims elsewhere in India) have resurrected tensions between the two communities (just as some elements within each religious community hoped). Ethnic unrest has been present in India as well. Violence and terrorism have surfaced in Assam and other territories in the northeast where the indigenous peoples fear the encroachment of outsiders, especially Bengalis (Wilson 1992). There have been signs of some unrest in Tamil Nadu in the southwest, related in part to the problems in Sri Lanka that will be discussed in detail below. Earlier there had been ideological terrorism. There was an outbreak of terrorism by the Naxalites, a Marxist-Leninist group in West Bengal. The group targeted capitalists and landlords for death (Qureshi 1976: 185). Ideological groups on the left have occasionally resorted to violence especially in southern India, and the presence of a Marxist-Leninist insurgency complete with terror in neighboring Nepal could bode ill for India. Further, the fact that the government has tolerated the activities of death squads, vigilantes, and zealousness by security forces in dealing with many of these conflicts is another indication of the potential for terrorist violence in the future.

In Weimar Germany in the late 1920s and early 1930s both the communists and the Nazis used violence and terror to bring down the democratic government. Once the Nazis were in power, they continued the use of violence by directing state terrorism against opponents, finally resorting to genocide in the case of the Holocaust and attacks on Gypsies. Later in the 1960s in West Germany the period of left-wing violence occurred that continued until reunification. With reunification there then was a clear increase in the level of violence by neo-Nazis, skinheads, and associated groups. In effect, Germany has seen waves of dissident terrorism, and state terror in the case of Nazi Germany as well. Similarly, in Italy attacks from the left and right overlapped as both ideological groups sought to change government policies and leadership and to undermine the democratic system in that country. This violence after World War II was preceded by the use of street violence by the fascists to obtain power under Mussolini early in the 1920s.

The United States is a country that has also had a history of domestic terrorist violence, although not necessarily as organized or extensive as the political violence that has occurred in some other countries. The Boston Tea Party was a prelude to a rebellion. The conflict between Georgia and the Cherokees was an example of state support for terrorism conducted by private groups. The KKK in its first incarnation in the period after the Civil War practiced terrorism, and eventually this group came to have the support of the state governments in the south when Reconstruction was over. There was anarchist violence at the end of the nineteenth century, culminating in the assassination of President McKinley. The war in Vietnam generated left-wing dissent, which in turn generated the usually low-level terrorism of the Weathermen and other groups of dissidents. In the 1980s and later years anti-abortion violence and other uses of terror increased. Assaults on unpopular minorities occurred more frequently. Right-wing extremist groups also used violence in efforts to achieve their political objectives. The bombing in Oklahoma City was an example of just how deadly such actions could become. Actions by right-wing groups have been less obvious in the years since Oklahoma City, but they have not disappeared from the scene. Domestic terrorism in the United States has usually been sporadic and many dissident groups have never reached the position of threatening the system, but there would still appear to be an undercurrent of strong political feelings and the presence of many dissident groups willing to use violence to intimidate or terrorize in efforts to bring about policy changes in the political system.

Waves of violence and terrorism in Sri Lanka

Current analyses of terrorism in Sri Lanka today focus on the activities of the Tamil Tigers and their efforts to create an independent Tamil state in the northern and eastern parts of the island. Sri Lanka in its half century of independence, however, has experienced a series of violent dissident activities, many of which have included the use of terrorism. Sri Lanka is a diverse society in many respects. The largest identifiable group in the country is composed of the Sinhalese, who comprise a majority of the population. They speak Sinhala and are largely Buddhist. They also have been located in those portions of the island less influenced by the presence of European colonialism (first the Portuguese, then the Dutch, and finally the British). As a consequence, they have had the least exposure and access to European education and were relatively underrepresented in positions of authority and influence, first in the colony and then in the independent nation. The Tamils are the second largest group in Sri Lanka, comprising about a sixth of the population. There are actually many more Tamils just across the narrow straits from Sri Lanka in the Indian state of Tamil Nadu, but it is the proportion of Tamils in the Sri Lankan population that makes them important for the political stability of that country. These inhabitants of the island speak Tamil and are largely Hindu or Christian. The Tamils interacted more with the colonial government, and they were more likely to know English. They eventually moved into positions in the British administration and professions in numbers greater than their proportion of the island's population. In addition, there is a small Muslim population, often Tamil, that was converted by Arab and Persian traders and merchants in the past. There is also a small Eurasian group, referred to as Burghers, a term derived from the Dutch colonial era. This group was the most overrepresented in positions of authority given the early linkages of its members with colonial administrations. As the violence in Sri Lanka increased, however, most of the Burghers left the country for safer locales (Crossette 2002: 27).

In the colonial period the major conflicts were religious, pitting Buddhists against the Christians and Muslims (Bell-Fialkoff 1999: 190). After independence, conflicts based in religion, ethnicity, and ideology appeared. The earliest symptom of problems in Sri Lanka occurred with an attempted coup d'état by military officers and police officials, as well as a few civilians, in 1962. The plotters were arrested before they could move against the government. The coup itself reflected concern among many officers about increasing ethnic tensions in the country and the policies of the government for dealing with them. Sinhalese political leaders were seeking to increase the number of Sinhalese in the officer corps and command positions and to do the same in the bureaucracy and civilian sectors at the expense of the other groups. Tamils and the other minorities were overrepresented in the officer corps at independence, and this government policy obviously limited their career options in the future (Horowitz 1980: 21–30). There were also efforts to make Sinhala the national language, placing Tamils at a disadvantage. Both Sinhalese and Tamil officers were included in the coup attempt since they saw the government policies as weakening the professional norms of merit in the military system of promotion and assignment (Horowitz 1980: 80–1).

The next crises that the political system faced came from the left. Sri Lanka had a strong and active leftist tradition, and at independence there was both a sizeable traditional Communist Party and a Trotskyite party committed to its own version of Marxism (Laqueur 1999: 191). This strength led to young students creating another party, the Janatha Vimukthi Peramuna (JVP), to represent their Marxist-Leninist ideological views of the political system and its future. In order to free the country from these negative influences of global and local capitalism, the JVP organized an uprising to overthrow the government in 1971. They were sure that a one-day uprising in the cities would be sufficient to bring down the whole political system (Samaranayake 1999: 114). The attempt at a quick seizure of power in the country failed as the government and the political system were not nearly as fragile as the students had predicted. The JVP continued a guerrilla insurgency in the countryside for a few months, but the government security forces proved to be able to contain the threat without too much difficulty, and in less than a year the insurgency was over. There were only a few terrorist actions involved with this attempted insurgency, since the dissidents expected a quick takeover.

Continuation of policies favoring the Sinhalese, including the proclamation of Sinhala as the national language and the adoption of Buddhism as the national religion, threatened the Tamils and other minorities (Austin and Gupta 1990: 16). The two major Sinhalese parties competed for votes within the majority community by increasingly stressing their commitments to providing the native Sinhalese with their fair share of positions in government and additional educational opportunities. Although extreme views had been apparent as early as 1959 when two Sinhalese Bhuddist monks assassinated the prime minister because in their view he was not sufficiently nationalist in furthering the interests of the Sinhalese majority (Laqueur 1999: 191), extremism was now on the increase. At the same time, Tamil political parties found that they had to demand greater guarantees and more protection for the rights of the minorities in order to collect votes. Tamil demands thus increasingly included calls for greater local autonomy in areas where there were Tamil majorities. Eventually, some extreme groups even began to argue that an independent Tamil state on the island was the only way to prevent the Sinhalese from submerging the Tamils and their culture. This tension eventually led to the outbreak of violence between the communities, and this violence quickly generated terrorist actions in a variety of situations. Both government forces and Tamil dissidents became perpetrators.

The simmering tensions between the Tamils and Sinhalese broke into the open with an incident in July of 1983. Tamil rebels ambushed a small military patrol and killed the soldiers. Sinhalese in various parts of the island proceeded to take part in anti-Tamil riots in retaliation for this attack. The resulting mob violence killed 2,000 to 3,000 Tamils. There were numerous indications that the government helped to organize and support the violence by Sinhalese mobs (Krishna

1992: 270). This mob violence did not dissuade the Tamils from continued opposition; instead, it increased the support within the Tamil community for the use of violence to protect the position of their community, the interests of its members, and even the lives of Tamils in the country. A large number of Tamil political organizations appeared, ranging from moderates who still advocated some form of negotiated settlement with the Sinhalese parties in the government to those advocating complete independence for the Tamil areas of the island. The Liberation Tigers of Tamil Eelam (LTTE) or the Tamil Tigers became the most important of these dissident groups and the most powerful in terms of military resources that it could command and the types of actions that it could undertake.

Violence against the government by the Tigers and by other Tamil dissident groups initially began at a low level and gradually increased until it reached a full-scale civil war. Early in the struggle there were divisions among the Tamil dissidents. While the moderates were able to gain some government concessions on autonomy, the LTTE continued to hold out for independence for the Tamil areas of Sri Lanka and has, at least to date, managed to effectively short-circuit any meaningful implementation of compromises. Initially the Tigers fought against the government and other Tamil groups. The Tigers won out in their battles with the other Tamil groups, using measures as harsh as necessary to eliminate the competing organizations within the minority community. Leaders of other groups have been assassinated, both in Sri Lanka and abroad, and soldiers and guerrilla units of the other groups have been attacked inside Sri Lanka. In 1983, for example, over 150 members of rival organizations were killed (Albin 1989: 215). The LTTE has eliminated approximately thirty other Tamil dissident groups. Interestingly enough, there is a separate front organization that takes credit for the attacks against the other Tamil organizations, sparing the Tigers from the disrepute of attacking their own (Gunaratna 1997: 474). There is little doubt, however, that the LTTE has been behind these attacks.

The Tigers have used many of the standard mechanisms of dissident groups to battle the central government. Their overall approach has been one of guerrilla insurgency supported by extensive terrorist actions. Initial tactics included hit and run attacks against security forces and isolated military targets. The Tigers also attempted, with some success, to provoke harsh responses from the military against the Tamil population in general, making it more likely that larger numbers of Tamils would rally to the dissident side. With the passage of time the Tigers grew stronger and were able to field larger units and even to place some areas of the countryside under their effective control. There have been times when they have been strong enough to effectively control the major cities in the Tamil areas. The Sri Lankan military has not been strong enough to control the entire countryside continuously, and any attempts to do so would simply open up government forces to the types of ambushes and hit and run tactics at which guerrilla forces excel. At one point, the Sri Lankan military forces in the north, especially in the Jaffna Peninsula, were restricted to their military bases and could only venture into the countryside or even the cities if they sent out large forces. In 1996 the Tigers overran and captured a military base, killing all 1,200 military personnel stationed there. The death of the entire garrison was designed to further inflame differences between the Sinhalese and Tamils since some of the troops on the base were undoubtedly captured or wounded during the attack. In a daring action underwater frogmen penetrated the main naval base in Sri Lanka and sank two of the larger ships in the Sri Lankan navy (Laqueur 1999: 193–4). In another action, the main airport and military base near the capital was attacked, damaging military aircraft and destroying half of the planes in the national airline (Crossette 2002: 31). By the 1980s, the battles between the LTTE and the government forces often reached the scale of civil war. The civil war has continued as the Tigers have not been able to defeat the government, and the government has been unable to eliminate the rebels.

In addition to the guerrilla strikes, the Tamil Tigers have utilized terrorism in their causes. There have been a few kidnappings of foreigners (Bray 1986: 141). The Tigers have practiced assassinations against key government officials with great regularity. Victims have included a president of Sri Lanka, a defense minister, a minister of national security, and the head of the naval forces (Joshi 1996: 19). The attacks, however, have extended beyond key individuals in positions of national authority or prominence. The Tigers have attacked government officials in general to frighten other government officials into leaving threatened areas. When these officials flee, government control is weakened. Tamils seen to be cooperating with the government have also become targets, with cooperation being defined as a willingness to accept government positions or the advocating of a compromise or some form of settlement that falls far short of the goals of the Tigers (Gunaratna 1997: 472). Ultimately, if these kinds of attacks intimidate large sections of the population of Sri Lanka, they may achieve their objective of establishing regional autonomy or independence for the Tamil areas.

The Tigers have also launched attacks on the general population, particularly in areas that are predominantly Sinhalese or where most of the casualties would be Sinhalese or pro-government Tamils. They have detonated bombs that have killed hundreds, and the bombs have obviously been placed to inflict significant casualties. They have destroyed an airliner and all the passengers on board (Long 1990: 55). The LTTE has also used suicide bombers who have driven explosive-laden trucks into targets or who have otherwise set off explosives once they have got close enough to their targets. In fact, the Tamil Tigers have the highest rates of the use of suicide missions of any dissident organization in the world. These attacks have been both deadly and sophisticated (Dolnik 2003: 24). Captured members of the organization have also frequently committed suicide while in custody to demonstrate their dedication and the strength of the dissidents. All of these attacks, like those on leading politicians, have been designed to indicate the extent of the weaknesses of the central government and the power of the dissidents.

The Tigers have also practiced their own version of ethnic cleansing, encouraging Sinhalese and Muslims to vacate areas claimed by the Tamil dissidents, leaving behind a homogenous Tamil population. In areas that the Tamils hoped to incorporate into either an autonomous region or an independent state, non-Tamil populations have been targeted. When insurgent forces were able to occupy villages, all the non-Tamils in the village would be killed. In other cases the insurgents would set up roadblocks, and any Sinhalese or Muslims who were caught would be killed. When buses were stopped, the Tamils would be released and the others would be killed. Muslims were often special targets because the Tigers feared that they might be a group that would cooperate with the government (Samaranayake 1997: 116–17). One consequence of this campaign, favorable to the other objectives of the dissidents, was that the government forces were now more likely to use indiscriminate artillery shelling and air attacks against areas that had been cleansed of all but the Tamil inhabitants, further alienating the Tamils in the area and driving them to side with the dissidents. The attacks against Sinhalese and Muslim civilians have also served to send another form of warning to potential and actual government supporters that the military and security forces of the state are not capable of protecting them on a daily basis.

The Tamil Tigers developed a sophisticated and extensive support network for their battles with the government. The LTTE maintained contacts with various Palestinian organizations and trained in their camps (Joshi 1996: 21). The Tigers also developed links with various criminal groups that operated in Sri Lanka. Smuggling, including drug smuggling, between Sri Lanka and nearby India has always been common and difficult to stop. While the Tigers may not have been directly involved in the smuggling of drugs, the organization has tolerated the activity and has

undoubtedly profited from it in the form of taxes, contributions, payments, and access to the smuggling routes in order to ship arms from India to Sri Lanka (Laqueur 1999: 194–5). The LTTE has also created its own companies, both to generate profits and to provide cover for various activities such as purchasing and transporting arms. The Tigers have received funds from Tamils living abroad. Since their struggle has been reasonably popular with many Tamils in foreign lands, some of the money has been voluntarily contributed to the liberation cause. There have also been indications that some of the contributions have been coerced by the LTTE (Laqueur 1999: 194). As a result of this foreign fund raising, business activities, criminal activities, and even some foreign government support, the Tamil Tigers have been able to purchase arms pretty much at will. The end of the Cold War has meant that there are major arms surpluses on the clandestine global market. The surpluses have meant that armaments are available at lower costs, a situation that clearly benefits well-to-do dissident groups such as the LTTE.

One surprising source of foreign support for the Tamil Tigers for a period of time was India. India has always been concerned that a successful Tamil rebellion in Sri Lanka could spill over to southern India where over 50 million Tamils live. Should the LTTE or other groups be successful in creating an independent Tamil state, it might set an example that would encourage the Tamils of India to seek independence and that could lead to the breakup of multi-ethnic India. As a consequence, support for the Tamil rebels would at first glance makes no sense. The options for the Indian government in dealing with the violence in Sri Lanka, however, were somewhat limited. When Indira Ghandi was prime minister, she had to provide at least some diplomatic support to the Tamils in their demands in order to pacify the Tamil voters in India. Openly siding with the Sri Lankan government could have triggered the unrest in India that the government was seeking to avoid (Crenshaw 2000: 139). The seats won by local Tamil state parties has also been important for providing for a legislative majority to control the national government, and various prime ministers have had no choice but to take into account the responses of voters in Tamil Nadu to actions in Sri Lanka. There is clear evidence that the Indian political leaders and the Indian intelligence services felt that they could manipulate the Sri Lankan rebellion to the advantage of India. In retrospect it is obvious that this was a major miscalculation, since the guerrillas proved to be uncontrollable and the LTTE was able to use the Indian support to further its own goals rather than the reverse (Joshi 1996: 21). As the independence of the organization became very obvious, Indian support declined.

In 1987 India made a major effort to help broker a peace settlement in Sri Lanka between the government and the Tamils. The arrangement called for the Indian army to monitor the disengagement of the LTTE guerrillas and the Sri Lankan armed forces and provide a setting wherein an autonomy arrangement between the government and the rebels could be implemented. The Sri Lankan military withdrew and India sent troops as a peacekeeping force. The Tamil Tigers turned in a few weapons in the early stages of the arrangement, but this cooperation soon ended. Ultimately, this peace effort failed. Most of the leaders of the LTTE still wanted an independent state rather than autonomy, and it appears that they had no intention of honoring the arrangement. Their short-term tactical objective in agreeing to the disengagement was to bring about the withdrawal of the Sri Lankan armed forces to give the Tigers an opportunity to regroup and consolidate their support among the Tamil population in Sri Lanka. Soon, Tamil guerrillas began to attack the Indian troops, and the attacks eventually provoked the peacekeepers into retaliation. The guerrillas managed to lead the Indian military forces into situations in which they retaliated indiscriminately and alienated the local Tamil civilian population, undercutting any chance of local support. The Indian armed forces then became involved in the fighting on the side of the government but proved to be no more effective in dealing with the rebels

than the Sri Lankan army had been. The military options for the Indian army were limited since the presence of so many Tamils in India made it difficult for the Indian military to follow any consistent strategy in trying to deal with the LTTE (Crenshaw 2000:156). The Indian forces never really had the option of employing sufficient force to defeat the LTTE. Eventually the Indian peacekeeping effort was ended and the troops were withdrawn.

The violence that India feared all along did spill over from the Sri Lankan conflict. There have been a few attacks against supporters of the central government in Tamil Nadu and indications that the success of the LTTE has inspired some Indian Tamils. The pattern of attacks is similar to those in Sri Lanka in that the targets have often been those individuals who have been pushing for the establishment of Hindi as the sole national language to the exclusion of other languages such as Tamil (Joshi 1996: 34). The most spectacular attack in India, however, had a different target— it was directed against former prime minister Rajiv Ghandi. He had been in power when the peacekeeping effort was undertaken, and he was held responsible for the fact that the Indian military had ended up fighting against the Tigers. While he was campaigning for his party in Tamil Nadu in 1991, a Tamil suicide bomber killed him. The key members of the team assigned to the assassination were Tamils from Sri Lanka with links to the LTTE, although it was obvious that they received support for their activities from local Indian Tamils (Joshi 1996). The assassination demonstrated the power of the LTTE, but it may have had some negative consequences for the LTTE. Adverse reactions in India gave the central government more freedom to deal with the Sri Lankan conflict. The Indian security and military forces became more effective in interrupting communications and supplies crossing the narrow strait between northern Sri Lanka and Tamil Nadu.

While the struggle with the Tamil dissidents was ongoing, the Sri Lankan government faced a renewed assault from the left. The JVP revitalized itself and launched a second violent effort in 1987 to install a socialist political system in the country. Unlike its earlier effort at seizing power, this attack was based on the idea of a long-term insurrection. This attack would rely on a strategy of both terrorism and guerrilla strikes. Attacks were launched against government officials of all types. Targets included politicians, members of the parties in the government and those in opposition, political supporters of these parties, and even members of their families. University personnel, journalists, and religious leaders became targets as well. The goal of the assassination campaigns was to paralyze the state leaving the JVP as the only alternative for governing the state (Samaranayake 1999:115; Samaranayake 1997: 114). There was, in fact, a period in which government officials and leaders were in danger of assassination by either the JVP or the LTTE. The JVP undertook bloody terrorist actions in the cities to demonstrate the general vulnerability of the governments and its supporters. The campaign against the JVP continued for two years before the government was able to bring it under control. The government did derive a benefit from the presence of the Indian military units during this period. Since Indian troops were dealing with the Tamils in the north, the government was able to mobilize larger forces to deal with the threat by the JVP (Crenshaw 2000: 143). Even so, tens of thousands of Sri Lankans died before the violence was contained. The JVP made no attempt to cooperate with the LTTE since the JVP unequivocally opposed the separation of the Tamil areas from the country. Unlike the Tamil insurgents, the JVP had no external support network. In fact, the JVP prided itself on having no external ties. The JVP also vehemently opposed the presence of the Indian peacekeepers on Sri Lankan soil as a matter of principle (Samaranayake 1997: 108). After this second defeat the JVP has transformed itself into a conventional political party, and it has denounced the use of terror and violence to achieve political objectives.

Yet another type of terror has appeared in Sri Lanka. There have been increasing examples of the use of violence and terror by government forces or groups supported by the government. The indirect government support for the Sinhalese mobs in the earlier anti-Tamil riots was one early example. The security forces at various times have been overzealous in dealing with the Tamil rebels and other dissidents as well as their supporters or suspected supporters. It would be amazing if such a long civil war did not result in atrocities by the security forces or the military, especially when the dissidents have done everything in their power to stimulate or to encourage such overreactions on the part of the government forces. The Sri Lankan government has also used death squads, torture, and counter-terror as a matter of policy, especially in the struggle against the JVP. Sympathizers with the leftists were targeted for government violence, not just the active dissidents (Samaranayke 1999: 117). Government personnel have also been involved in attacks against Tamil cultural activities and symbols of the Tamil culture (Krishna 1992: 270). In addition, Sinhalese Buddhist activists have on occasion attacked Christians in the country, and there has been a general increase in religious intolerance in the country (Crossette 2002: 34). Overall, polarization among the ethnic and religious communities in the country has increased.

The discussion of Sri Lanka in some detail has illustrated that different types of terrorist violence can afflict a country at virtually the same time. The political system has been sorely tested with the deadly civil war with the LTTE and the battles with the left. The second JVP campaign would qualify as one of the bloodier examples of internal violence except when it is compared to the battles between the government and the Tamils. The government itself has resorted to the use of terror as well. Further, there have even been a few examples of right-wing terrorism and the attempted military coup. The Sri Lankan violence clearly spilled over into neighboring India as well. What is surprising is that in the midst of this violence the Sinhalese majority has been able to maintain a reasonably democratic political system. While the government has not been overthrown by any of the dissident groups, the LTTE is still in effective control of a significant portion of the country, and threats from the left could reappear. Nor can the possibility of a terrorist campaign from the right be entirely excluded.

Summary

In some cases there is evidence that one type of terrorist violence does indeed lead to others. There are many countries, however, which have faced terrorist violence but have not experienced waves of terrorism. The Scandinavian countries have had to deal with right-wing radicalism but virtually no other form of terrorism. Greece has faced leftist violence for over twenty-five years, but no new waves of terrorism from other sources have appeared. Canada has had a brief flurry of ethnic violence in Quebec and Nepal is currently experiencing a leftist insurrection complete with terrorism, but no other forms of terrorist violence have taken place in either country. Clearly one form of terrorism need not lead to or inspire other dissidents in these nations to use the same methods. Even long campaigns such as those conducted by ETA in Spain or 17 November in Greece have not led other dissident groups to adopt the same approach. Terror does not always beget terror.

Sri Lanka has suffered so much violence because it is a divided society and because it has been a political system in transition, and systems in transition are most vulnerable to such violence. The movement from colonial status to independent democracy started out well, but the transition was complicated by the ethnic differences. The relative lack of repression gave the JVP what seemed like an excellent opportunity to seize control of the country, both in the case of the first attempt and even the second. Many of the other countries suffering waves of violence, such as Indonesia and Yugoslavia, have also had political systems in transition or political systems that qualify as democracies or weaker authoritarian systems. Another commonality among the countries facing waves of terrorism is their status as successor states to empires. India, Sri Lanka as Ceylon, and Indonesia were colonial creations that brought together diverse populations. Unity in India only occurred within the context of empires, the last of which was British India. The unity of India did not survive when Pakistan became independent. Disputes over borders and places like Kashmir continue to be important issues. The constant concerns about the boundaries of the country, which are present in Indian political discussions, are a symptom of anxieties related to the colonial period (Weiss 2001: 39). Indonesia is analogous to India in being a former colonial empire composed of disparate parts. Yugoslavia was also the product of the breakup of empires, and its own breakup in the 1990s provides a similar example of imperial decline. Yugoslavia was a small multi-ethnic empire, but the problems faced by Croatia, Bosnia, and Macedonia, as well as Serbia in Kosovo, are similar to the problems faced by the successor states of larger empires or former colonies. The diversity of the successor states to the USSR suggests that terrorism will be a continuing problem in that area of the world as well. The empire is gone, and the new governments clearly qualify as political systems in transition.

Even though political systems in transition, and perhaps especially successor states of empires, are most vulnerable, not every country that has faced waves of terror qualifies on these counts. The United States has not been a political system in transition for a long time nor is it a successor state to an empire. Germany in the 1970s would no longer qualify either—although the Weimar Republic was a very good example of a vulnerable system in transition in an earlier period. Some countries will suffer from multiple types of terrorism despite having had long established political systems and histories as independent countries within the same general boundaries. Terrorists do learn from each other, and it is possible for dissidents in the same country to borrow the tactics of others. National vulnerabilities are different, and no one type of country is doomed to face terrorist violence, although only those ruled by totalitarian and very strong authoritarian governments seem to be immune to serious terrorist threats. To some extent previous terrorist actions do not always indicate there will be future campaigns, and the absence of previous terrorism cannot guarantee a terrorism-free future.

Further reading

Crenshaw, M. (2000) "Democracy, Commitment Problems and Managing Ethnic Violence: The Case of India and Sri Lanka," *Terrorism and Political Violence*, 12, 3/4: 135–59.

Joshi, M. (1996) "On the Razor's Edge: The Liberation Tigers of Tamil Eelam," *Studies in Conflict and Terrorism*, 19, 1: 19–42.

Terms

Aceh
Assam
Ayoda
Burghers
Ghandi, Rajiv
Hamas
Irian Jaya (Western Papua)
Jammu and Kashmir
Janatha Vimukthi Peramuna (JVP)
Laskar Jihad
Liberation Tigers of Tamil Eelam (LTTE)
Tamil Nadu
Tamil Tigers
Zionist

Chapter 12

Counterterrorism

Techniques of counterterrorism   224

    Increased security   224

    Intelligence gathering—detection and prevention   225

    Finances   227

    Repression   228

    Retaliation or punishment   230

    Preemptive action   232

    Special counterterrorism units   234

    Concessions and reform   235

    Diplomatic approaches   237

Weapons of mass destruction and mass casualties   238

Summary   239

Terms   241

Further reading   241

The previous chapters said relatively little about what measures might be effective in dealing with terrorist movements, although the successful responses were fairly obvious in some of the case studies. Potential solutions to terrorism in the world will be discussed below. Programs to counter terrorism run the gamut from detection and prevention of violent dissident activities by police, security agencies, and military forces to more involved efforts to eliminate support within society for the dissident groups. The techniques are available to all kinds of governments, although in some cases different regimes will find some approaches more in keeping with their style of governance. How governments attempt to deal with terrorist threats will influence the future of the dissident organizations and their societies. Some actions may defeat dissidents, but failures could strengthen terrorist groups. Even short-term successes could have negative consequences if they sow the seeds of future problems.

Techniques of counterterrorism

It is important to recognize from the outset that no one solution exists for dealing with all types of dissident groups. What works in one place or time could fail in another. Terrorism is far too complex for one solution to be effective in dealing with all the possible threats. Among the more obvious possible responses to the threat of terrorism are the provision of greater security, better detection and prevention, repression, retaliation or punishment for foreign supporters of dissident groups, a firm stance of refusing to negotiate with terrorists as opposed to granting concessions, and international cooperation.

Increased security

Increased security, especially around critical targets or personnel is one solution to the terrorist threat. Remove the targets that provide dissident groups with so much publicity, and the incentive to launch attacks may be eliminated. Greater security can help, but there are far too many targets for security measures to be effective. If the potential targets include any government or party official or any member of the security forces as potential targets, no defense is completely effective.[4] If the entire population or a substantial portion of the population is the target, there will always be someone who is vulnerable. Car bombs are too easy to create and use, and there are far too many offices, monuments, buildings, schools, places of worship, and other structures to defend. In an environment that is rich with potential targets, terrorists can always avoid heavily defended targets and find easier alternatives (Raymond 2003: 76). For example, Hizballah operatives bombed the Israeli embassy in Buenos Aires in 1992 and a Jewish cultural center in 1994 in the same city in retaliation for Israeli actions in the Middle East. Buenos Aires was apparently chosen for the attacks because Hizballah had supporters in the area and because Argentina lacked a rigorous security apparatus (at this time); Argentina as a country had no special significance beyond convenience (Pillar 2001: 59). Even in countries with high levels of security, it is possible for terrorists to find targets. Israel is as security conscious as any country in the world and is as practiced in detecting terrorists as any nation, yet suicide bombers and other attackers have been able to almost routinely penetrate into many parts of the country and launch their attacks.

Of course, the fact that absolute security is impossible to achieve does not mean that improved security is not worthwhile. Improvements in airport security over the decades meant that many hijackings were avoided, although not those of the September 11 attacks. In the past total airport security has never been possible, and it would probably be foolish to expect it to be so in the immediate future. Metal detectors in buildings have deterred some assaults but have failed to detect weapons in other cases. Bombs still get through, as do armed terrorists; it is just much more difficult to accomplish. Key personnel can vary their routines or take suitable precautions to prevent kidnappings or assaults. Such actions are eminently wise, but they cannot grant immunity. Any measure "that would preclude every possible attack by every possible terrorist group for every possible motive is not even theoretically conceivable" (Hoffman 1997: 10). Enhanced security and prevention can limit the damage that attacks will generate, but they cannot currently eliminate all danger of such attacks. Further, it is possible that enhanced security will only have temporary effects in reducing attacks. Groups will be willing to lie low until security is relaxed (Gurr 2003: 212). Such increased security, however, can have a down side. The widespread use of metal detectors in airports led to more deadly attacks with bombs against airliners (Enders and Sandler 2002: 152).

Enhanced security measures will increase the costs to the government and private companies and groups. Resources will be diverted away from other purposes towards providing protection. While the security measures might pay for themselves in terms of the death and destruction that are prevented, there are still the opportunity costs that come from not being able to use the resources elsewhere. If security forces, police, or the military have to be expanded, then the money and resources have to be taken from other sectors of the economy. If one of the goals of the dissident group is to cause economic dislocation and hardships by launching attacks, they will have already succeeded when extra security measures go into effect. It is even possible in extreme cases that the resulting strains on the economy could eventually lead to the downfall of the government in power or even a change in the political system.

Intelligence gathering—detection and prevention

Prevention via intelligence gathering and infiltration of dissident groups is another possible solution in the battle against terrorism. In the wake of the 2001 attacks on the World Trade Center and the Pentagon, the CIA and other US intelligence agencies were faulted for not having discovered what was about to happen or for not having recognized the value of information that was available to them. Hindsight, of course, is almost always nearly perfect. The existence of a multitude of targets in any country makes effective detection of terrorist plans much more difficult and all the potential targets cannot be protected. Even if the intelligence agencies had known an attack was coming, they would not have known the method that was going to be used. Generals have often been accused of preparing to fight the last war, and intelligence agencies are likely to focus on preventing reprises of successful attacks like car bombs, not new methods. Since even the old methods can succeed, barring very precise information of tactics and targets, prevention via intelligence gathering is difficult. Without someone inside the planning group itself or the chance to interrogate someone involved in the planning, information is not likely to be precise enough to provide the details necessary for effective prevention from normal intelligence sources. The great multitude of potential targets that terrorists have makes prevention very difficult. US intelligence services are also handicapped by the devotion of its intelligence resources to Cold War enemies for fifty years. Resources were directed toward gaining information on the Soviet Union, China, and their allies, not to countries and regions where many terrorist organizations now have their headquarters and recruit members (L. Johnson, 2003). As a consequence, it could be necessary for the CIA to undergo a complete reorientation from its Cold War days if it is to become effective in combating terrorism (Berkowitz 2002). Intelligence agencies in other countries face the same kinds of difficulties in detecting threats.

Effective intelligence requires allies whose national police forces can gather the essential raw data for analysis. US intelligence agencies, for example, cannot be as effective working alone, even with greater resources (Posen 2001/2: 46). Both US agencies and other intelligence services need to recruit and train local agents to supply them with information, but these kinds of efforts take time. While intelligence agencies *should* be able to predict which areas will become trouble spots, they cannot really do so with any certainty. It would have been very unlikely in September 1991 for the CIA to correctly perceive the danger that a Saudi billionaire headquartered in Afghanistan would constitute for the United States ten years later, and that it would be necessary to train or recruit Pathan-speaking operatives to be ready in the future. Had a CIA operative actually suggested such a scenario, in all likelihood he or she probably would have been in danger of losing his or her job.

Security services have some advantages when fighting domestic dissident groups as opposed to foreign ones. Potential operatives or agents will know the language and local culture and will not need advance training to attempt to penetrate groups or gather information. The Japanese were able to defeat domestic terrorist operations by leftists with surveillance and informers (Clawson 1990: 26). But even in the domestic area, security services may still have difficulties. The United States has not done particularly well over the years in dealing with local right-wing extremist groups, partially because law enforcement agencies lack the appropriate experience (Wilkinson 2003: 121). French domestic intelligence gathering improved over time after being relatively ineffective. The security agencies were ill prepared when they had to face terrorist attacks in the 1980s. The government and agencies did not predict the attacks, and they were unable to catch the perpetrators. By the 1990s French authorities proved to be much more capable in gathering information on terrorist groups associated with the rebels in Algeria and then al Qaeda in later years (Shapiro and Suzan 2003: 80, 86–7). They learned by experience, albeit experience of failure. Improved capabilities are thus possible, but they have to be learned over time, and new types of threats are likely to require new capabilities, meaning that learning curves for intelligence agencies will always be present since the initiative for attacks almost always lies with the dissident groups.

Intelligence operations are likely to be more effective against larger organizations that are more vulnerable to penetration and gathering of information (O'Neil 2003). Difficulties with detection, and therefore prevention, are increased when the dissident group is small. When all the members know each other on a face-to-face basis, the infiltration of informers is extremely unlikely. The 17 November Movement in Greece survived for as long as it did because of its small size. While the Greek authorities did not show any special competence in dealing with the dissidents, more vaunted security agencies did no better when assisting the Greeks. The first target for the group was a CIA section chief, yet the resources of the CIA did not provide any help for decades, nor was the assistance of British intelligence of immediate aid in identifying members of the group. Constant efforts to penetrate dissident groups or discover facts about them should eventually succeed, but it may take years or decades to do so as it did in Greece. Leaderless resistance types of operations further complicate the task of intelligence agencies in detecting planned assaults since the potential terrorists undertaking the attack have no direct organizational link with the planners or ideological leaders. Discovering the plans of these kinds of terrorists or other ad hoc groups formed for particular actions will be quite difficult. There are too many groups to monitor, especially since some groups may never get beyond the stage of talking about resistance or the use of violence. Yet some of these groups will actually launch attacks. Detecting and monitoring all such groups will be beyond the scope of any country facing any significant dissatisfaction. Keeping tabs on such groups when their headquarters are abroad raises additional complications. US security agencies cannot operate in every country at will, any more than British, Israeli, or Russian intelligence operatives are free to gather information in the United States.

It is only when a new terrorist group strikes that the real threat becomes obvious. Many potential terrorist groups never actually attempt an attack. It is important to note that others are caught before they can do any real damage. The Minnesota Patriots Council was caught stockpiling ricin poison before they had a chance to use it. In Iran under the Shah leftist groups were routinely infiltrated and destroyed. The Soviet KGB had little trouble dealing with Ukrainian dissidents supported by the West. Al Qaeda cells have been discovered in many parts of the world. Yet some groups will not be detected until they strike. One of the great difficulties for intelligence services is keeping track of all potentially violent dissident groups that a society may have to deal with. Some will inevitably escape notice. Others may attack in unexpected places and in unexpected ways. Ultimately, "no strategy for a war against terror can bank on prevention" (Betts 2002: 59). Determined dissidents, especially ones who are prepared to die in the attempt, cannot always be stopped (Cilluffo and Tomarchio 1998: 443). India's intelligence services have mounted a number of sophisticated clandestine operations that have detected and defeated terrorist groups (Raufer 2000: 49). Notwithstanding these successes, terrorist attacks have continued. The failure of the Israeli security forces to detect and prevent Palestinian bombings, including suicide attacks, is further testimony to the fact that prevention is not always possible. The Israeli intelligence agencies have proven their worth many times over, and they have a wealth of experience in dealing with Palestinian dissident groups, yet they cannot detect all the attacks that are coming or provide information on all aspects of the leadership and planning groups of all the varied Palestinian nationalist groups that are currently willing to use violence as well as information on groups that *may* be willing to use violence. The Israeli security services also seem to have been ineffective in detecting attacks by Jewish extremist groups, probably in part because they were focusing almost all their resources on Palestinian threats. In Israel and elsewhere, no matter how vigilant security forces are, the disastrous terrorist attacks are from groups that have gone undetected (Imai 2002: 99).

Finances

A special area where intelligence can be combined with other efforts involves attempts to limit or eliminate the flow of financial support to terrorist organizations. This financial support has been important for many terrorist groups. Some financial aid has been direct and in other cases it has been indirect. Money can come from foreign governments, but it can also come from private sources. The United States government encouraged individuals to provide funds for the Contras in Nicaragua when official funding was limited. Fertinelli eased financial problems for the Red Brigades. Osama bin Laden's wealth and the support from other Muslim contributors have helped to make al Qaeda as dangerous as it has become. The PLO set up various businesses and developed its own sources of income to complement support from Arab governments. Diaspora populations have provided funding for dissident groups such as the PLO, the IRA, and the Tamil Tigers. Profits from the drug trade have become very important for a number of other dissident groups. Whatever the source, money has been important for either maintaining the dissident groups or making them more dangerous. When the financial sources of these groups can be stopped, their ability to mount attacks is reduced, even if not eliminated, and the groups become less dangerous. Governments can attempt to disrupt the financial operations of dissident groups. Intelligence agencies can identify dummy corporations, charities, or other groups that are used to channel funds to the terrorists, as recently occurred with an Islamic association in Chicago, which was serving as a conduit for funding al Qaeda. There are national laws that prohibit contributions to terrorist groups or money laundering, and these financial flows can be tracked and stopped at least some of the time. Accountants and corporate auditors may also be able to discover connections between supporters of dissidents and attacks that are going to be launched by following the money trail.

Unfortunately, success in closing off financial support for violent dissident organizations has been limited. Overall, efforts to disrupt the financial resources and links of dissident group have proven to be quite difficult. Earlier efforts in the United States to seize assets that belonged to groups that were officially identified as terrorist organizations resulted in the identification and collection of only $104,000 in assets (Pillar 2001: 261). Contributions for Noraid (and the IRA) continued in the United States with little interruption for many years. The initial efforts of either accountants or intelligence operatives to find or track the funding sources for al Qaeda have not met with great success. Al Qaeda has apparently been able to move some of its financial resources into commodities like precious stones and gold that are more difficult to trace (Shultz and Vogt 2002: 379). Al Qaeda has been very flexible. It has used both the modern international banking systems and traditional mechanisms for transferring funds, including informal exchange methods (Cronin 2002/3: 50). The failure of governments around the world to find profits from the drug trade, whether the money is funding dissident groups or criminal organizations, is another indication of the difficulties involved. Most drug money gets laundered successfully. Drug cartels match the sophistication of large multinational corporations in their ability to use the international banking system with relative secrecy and impunity from indictment and conviction (Klare 2003: 28). A group like al Qaeda is organized like an international criminal group and is as effective (Schneider and Schneider 2002). Many dissident groups have become quite adept at using offshore banking systems, numbered accounts, dummy corporations, and other mechanisms to hide their transactions and to make purchases. The same banking systems that provide benefits to multinational corporations, wealthy individuals, and criminal organizations in terms of laundering and secrecy can also serve the more sophisticated dissident groups. The funds involved with terrorist groups are more difficult to detect since they are only a faction of the amounts that are moved by criminal organizations (Cronin 2002/3: 50).

While interdicting financial flows is not easy, many governments already have the resources in place to make the attempt. Such efforts need not start from scratch. In addition to looking for criminal profits or persons or companies dodging taxes, government tax agencies can now also look for money being channeled to dissident groups. While the success in blocking the flow of financial support has been small to date, any successes do contribute to a weakening of such groups. If they have to allocate resources (money, man-hours) to cover their financial tracks more carefully, the resources used in this fashion are not available for lethal attacks. These efforts to interrupt financial flows will also not require major expenditures on the part of the developed countries, and any successes that are attained will be beneficial.

Repression

One factor that has made a difference to the occurrence of non-state terrorism, or its absence, has been the presence of a totalitarian political system or a powerful authoritarian state. These types of states are likely to have very effective intelligence agencies as part of their control mechanisms (Heymann 2001/2: 34). Since totalitarian governments have a great deal of control over society, they have managed to avoid many terrorist threats because of their ability to eliminate dissidents or potential dissidents before they can organize[3]. Ruthlessness is often a hallmark of such governments, and they can strike at not only the dissidents themselves but at their family members or friends. Democratic states, on the other hand, pay a price in terms of vulnerability to attacks by domestic dissident groups or foreign ones that find it convenient to launch attacks on their soil. The benefit of a democratic system for the citizens is that they do not have to worry about arbitrary arrests, contrived prison sentences in concentration camps or gulags, or execution without cause. State imposed or state supported terrorism on national soil is not normally present in a democratic system, although democratic governments at times have looked the other way when unpopular groups have been the victims of vigilante violence or mob action. While democracy may have a price that must be paid in terms of the loss of life because of greater susceptibility to terrorist attacks, the loss is normally less than what could occur in a strong authoritarian system or a totalitarian one. Even in the case of efforts to deal with terrorist attacks, democracy as a system of government would appear to still have more advantages than disadvantages.

Of course, repression of violent groups is an option for all states, including democracies. In fact, virtually every state facing the threat of terrorist violence will choose repression if such a course of action seems likely to succeed. The regular police or security forces defeat most dissident groups that resort to terror before they actually constitute a real threat to a state by creating major disruptions. The successful defeat of these groups depends on luck, the use of intelligence sources, and normal police investigatory methods for discovering perpetrators of criminal or terrorist actions. The detection and arrest of members of violent dissident groups is fairly common in democracies, weak and strong authoritarian systems, totalitarian states, and even political systems in transition. Even terrorist groups that successfully launch more serious attacks on the political system can usually be contained with the usual police routines. Timothy McVeigh was caught. The Red Brigades in Italy and the Red Army Faction in Germany were eventually defeated by the state *without* any major reduction in democratic practices or the protection of civil liberties. Even the 17 November Movement in Greece would appear to have finally been broken by the use of normal police and intelligence methods, however belatedly. Various right-wing groups in the United States have been uncovered and their members arrested by the police without resorting to extraordinary laws. Europeans and Israelis, who have had to face terrorism for years, have accommodated themselves to the dangers with only occasional abridgements of civil liberties (Malkin and Elizur 2002: 67).

There is no guarantee that repression will be successful. In Colombia the government has failed to regain control of its territory by concessions to the FARC. It has been suggested that repression would work better than compromise or concessions (Radu 2000). To date the efforts at repression have been noticeably ineffective. Continued efforts at repression have failed in Sri Lanka with the Tamil Tigers (although not with the leftists), in the Basque region, and elsewhere. Israel has used great force and an extensive and sophisticated intelligence-gathering network in efforts to control the Palestinians in the Occupied Territories without defeating the nationalist and religious groups involved. Repression alone will not end the terrorism that Israel has been facing, and repression can even result in new recruits joining the dissident groups. IRA recruitment dramatically increased in some periods when the British were vigorous in dealing with suspects (Heymann 2001/2: 29). Regimes in transition may be less able to use repression if the regular police or security forces are in disarray. New groups can appear to threaten a state in these times as well. Even when repression does work, the elimination of the terrorist threat may be a long and costly battle. The struggle of the Italian government with the Red Brigades resulted in the deaths of thousands. In Algeria, over a hundred thousand have died in the battles between the secular government and the Muslim dissidents, and there is no guarantee that the Muslim rebels will not succeed in overthrowing or bringing about a major transformation of the state.

State terrorism is an extreme form of repression for dealing with violent dissidents. Not all state terrorism is designed to be a counterterrorist strategy. The expulsion of the Cherokees from Georgia, the ethnic cleansing in Bosnia, and attacks on white farmers in Zimbabwe were not responses to terrorist attacks. In the case of East Timor and Rwanda, the state support for terrorist militias and death squads was to some degree a consequence of guerrilla campaigns that did not involve significant terrorist actions. In other cases, however, governments have chosen to use extra-legal violence to search out and destroy the terrorist groups. Just as government repression and terror may trigger the formation of violent dissident groups, dissident terrorism may lead to governmental use of terror as a counterterrorist weapon (Wilkinson 2003: 108). These kinds of efforts have proven to be effective in the short run in many cases. The initial Algerian uprising for independence from France led to local authorities and the military using torture, indefinite deten-tion, and other techniques to acquire information. The French were able to destroy the National Liberation Front's organization in the cities and weaken it in the countryside as well. The military regimes in Uruguay and Argentina were able to defeat their domestic leftist groups by using state terror. Governments in many other parts of the world have resorted to these techniques as well. Giving free rein to vigilantes and death squads, however, does not always destroy the opposition. In El Salvador and South Africa the dissidents survived, East Timor became independent, and India does not control Kashmir.

Retaliation or punishment

Striking back is an obvious counterterrorism option, and one that is often popular, but it is a choice fraught with difficulties. Countries retaliate when there is evidence of support for domestic terrorists by another country. It has also been argued that security alone cannot prevent terrorist attacks; it is also necessary to go after nations that harbor terrorists (Chellaney 2001/2: 99). During the Cold War, direct military incursions by the superpowers were limited since the two antagonists were roughly equal in capabilities. Soviet support for dissidents in a Western ally often resulted in Western support for rebels in a pro-Soviet state. US aid for the Mujahedin in Afghanistan repaid the Soviet Union for its support for national liberation struggles in Latin America, Asia, and Africa. The aid did not really end the

Soviet support for terrorism by dissident groups, but it did make it potentially more costly. It is a response favored by many since it provides an immediate response to attacks. Many countries have felt free to bomb or attack guerrilla and terrorist camps in other states—the United States in the case of Libya and the attacks against al Qaeda camps in Afghanistan when President Clinton was in power, Israeli attacks into Lebanon and Jordan, and South African incursions into Angola during the struggle for control over Southwest Africa or Namibia. South Africa made sure that any state that offered sanctuary to the exiled African National Congress (ANC) knew it could expect either attacks against ANC bases or the pursuit of guerrilla forces into its territory (Welsh 1995: 243). Turkish forces have engaged Kurdish insurgents in northern Iraq. Indian artillery has regularly fired on presumed guerrilla camps and positions in that portion of Kashmir under the control of Pakistan. The recent attack by the United States and its allies on the Taliban regime in Afghanistan for supporting the al Qaeda network is simply a recent and massive example of military retaliation against a government supporting terrorist attacks. One explanation for the rarity of attacks on US soil by foreign terror-ists is that such attacks would have resulted in retaliation against the governments of the coun-tries (such as Iran, Iraq, or Syria) that supported the terrorist groups in question (Heymann 2001/2: 25). Of course, such self-imposed limita-tions are less relevant to loosely connected net-works of terrorist groups like al Qaeda. Retaliation is not even a realistic option when the local dissi-dents are supported by a stronger state. Nicaragua could not do much to retaliate against American support for the Contras, nor could Sri Lanka effec-tively threaten India when the Indian intelligence agencies were aiding the Tamils.

Retaliation can take forms other than military action. Economic sanctions can be applied against the country suspected of encouraging terrorism. Potential sanctions can include a virtual trade embargo, such as was imposed on Cuba by the United States. The economic sanctions can also be subtler or less obvious. The country harboring or supporting terrorists may not be able to get loans or only get them at higher interest rates. Foreign investors may not receive guarantees or aid from their home governments for doing business in a given country, reducing the incentives for them to invest. Arms sales to the country may be curtailed. The US unilateral sanctions against Iran ultimately limited the ability of the Islamic Republic to purchase arms and thus weakened that country's military capacity. The sanctions, however, had little effect on Iranian support for foreign terrorist groups since that support did not depend on a strong Iranian military establishment (Pillar 2001: 168). Iranian support for dissident organization in the Arab countries in the Persian Gulf region appears to have moderated in recent years. Iran paid a price for its previous support for such dissidents when it found itself virtually alone in the world when it faced the Iraqi invasion and the long war that followed. The apparent unconcern of many countries was the price Iran had to pay for previous support of terrorist groups. Membership of international economic organizations or other groups may be denied. Tourist visas for visits to the country that supports a terrorist group may not be issued. Libya faced many of these types of sanctions in the 1980s in response to its reported support of terrorists (Oakley 1987: 619). Sanctions like these supported by the United Nations and the United States were effective in eventually reducing Libyan support for terrorism (Crenshaw 2003b: 165). Syria has managed to have itself removed from the list of countries that have supported terrorism by taking appropriate actions. The Abu Nidal Organization was asked to move on, given that its presence could be taken to indicate support for groups that other countries considered terrorist. Even Iraq was relatively quiet in supporting dissident groups in other countries after the first Persian Gulf War with the United States and its allies. The military defeat and continuing military and economic sanctions had an impact on that country's actions or lack of actions.

Retaliation can also be attempted against terrorist organizations. Some groups, like Hizballah, are simply too large to be destroyed by a few well-conceived attacks, even if they can be weakened (Pillar 2001: 33–4). Israel has frequently retaliated against suspected Palestinian militants when faced with suicide bombings and other attacks. To date the retaliation seems to have kept a cycle of violence going where Palestinian groups feel bound to retaliate in turn. Indiscriminate retaliation against presumed supporters has largely failed to control increased support for terrorists. The events with the Israelis indicate that the deterrent effect of retaliatory strikes is more likely to be effective against state actors, not dissident groups (Chyba 2002: 129). The Albanians in Kosovo and Macedonia proved to be very effective in generating such retaliation and then taking advantage of the anger at the government to recruit additional support. There are additional problems when attempting to retaliate against groups. Some dissident groups are more difficult to target than others. If military action fails to damage an elusive terrorist group, the effort could be counterproductive. The launching of expensive missiles that miss their targets may increase the publicity for the groups responsible for attacks and even increase the prominence of its cause (Pillar 2001: 105). If splinter groups, instead of the main organization, are involved in the attacks, government retaliation against the main organization could lead these groups to restart campaigns of violence. Breakaway groups have been real enough, as demonstrated by the Real IRA and Continuity IRA, the departure of groups from the PLO for its conciliatory policies, splits within ETA, and the divisions among the Algerian dissidents battling the current government of that country. It has been argued that some splits within dissident organizations are basically tactical. The "militants" leave, vowing to continue to use terrorism while the "moderates" declare a truce and negotiate. Unfortunately for counterterrorist campaigns, it is often difficult to determine which splits represent real differences and which ones are fictitious divisions. Uncertainty, however, does make effective retaliation more difficult, and retaliating against the wrong group is likely to generate new attacks. There is even the possibility of some outside organization mounting false flag attacks as a means of forcing governments to crack down on a dissident organization rather than negotiating with it.

Failure to retaliate may hold costs for states suffering from terrorist attacks. The inability or unwillingness to strike back might encourage terrorists to continue attacks just as retaliation or the threat to retaliate *might* convince them to cease their operations in at least a specific locale. Japan, in dealing with terrorist incidents abroad, has encouraged further attacks by concessions and failing to retaliate (Angel 1990: 41). It has been suggested that terrorists see India as a soft target because the government imposes no costs on them or their foreign supporters for their activities (Chellaney 2001/2: 99). The lack of punishment or retaliation simply encourages renewed attacks. Of course, the Indian intelligence services have been willing to use death squads and other forms of repression against domestic groups that are within their reach. The United States could not use economic measures to retaliate against the Taliban in Afghanistan. The regime in power was almost entirely uninterested in tourists, foreign aid, foreign investment, or even trade.

Preemptive action

A country can attempt a preemptive strike; preemption may be a necessary strategy if the threat of retaliation has no deterrent effect (Richelson 2002: 246). Strikes can be against the training camps of the terrorist group or against state supporters. Such an attack could be designed to prevent terrorist actions or as retaliation. The 2002 attack against al Qaeda and the Taliban in Afghanistan was both retaliation and an attempt to preempt additional attacks. If such strikes work, preemption is an ideal strategy for threatened states since it will limit the number and intensity of future terrorist operations, at least in the short run. While preemptive action will work in some circumstances, it is highly unlikely that such attacks will be successful enough to eliminate the threat for terrorist organizations (Sederberg 2003: 274).

Preemptive action, of course, requires excellent intelligence gathering in order to be effective. Without detailed knowledge of the activities of the terrorist groups and the whereabouts of their personnel, it will not be possible to identify targets with enough precision. It is also necessary to detect those groups that have the potential to strike some time in the future. Not all groups in the process of forming are equally dangerous. Only a handful will pose a serious threat, and by the time they do act, the responses are likely to be one of retaliation rather than preemption. While strong authoritarian states might be able to eliminate most potential threats through an extensive security apparatus, at the present time it seems unlikely that a democratic state can consistently preempt dissidents who might use violence and still remain democratic.

Preemption against dissidents who become violent will be even more difficult when terrorist groups rely on organizational attributes such as leaderless resistance. Targeting members is difficult in the best of circumstances. Loosely connected networks like al Qaeda are difficult to attack in any preemptive fashion. Linkages among the groups often only become apparent *after* the attacks have occurred, such as those among the al Qaeda groups that were present in Southeast Asia. Once an attack has occurred, normally police and intelligence methods will be sufficient to track down the individuals involved and their support network. Preemptive attacks against state supporters of terrorist groups have similar limitations. True state support may be difficult to prove, and rallying support for preemptive actions can be difficult as evidenced by the situation of Saddam Hussein's regime in Iraq. Even successful preemption against a state might have negative diplomatic consequences elsewhere in the international system. The threat of preemption or the attack itself might stimulate the actions that the military

BOX 12.1 Assassination

Assassinations can be undertaken by governments as a form of retaliation or as an effort at preemption. The Assassins demonstrated the deterrent effect that could occur with this technique against government officials, and it could serve the same purpose with dissident leaders. Assassination could serve a preventative function if the death of a leader leads to the disruption of the organization. Like other forms of preemption, successful assassination requires high quality intelligence efforts to locate the targets. The death of leaders is unlikely to affect large organizations since they have the capacity to replace individuals who may be killed. Smaller organizations are more vulnerable to this type of action, but then these are the groups for which it is harder for authorities or security forces to gain information. There are at least some cases where the death of individuals is likely to disrupt an organization. The death of Hasan al-Banna, leader of the Muslim Brotherhood, at the hands of Egyptian operatives in 1949, disrupted the Muslim Brotherhood in that country for a significant period of time (Havens *et al.* 1975: Chapter 10). The death of Osama bin Laden would undoubtedly disrupt al Qaeda, at least for a period, given his organizational talents. Further, since face-to-face contact is important in the Middle East, the disruptions could probably not be totally repaired by any successor. But even in bin Laden's case, the organization would not disappear overnight (Pillar 2001: 56), and the threat from the component parts would continue since important linkages and contacts among various groups have already been established. Assassination would also make bin Laden a martyr in Arab and Muslim eyes, giving additional support to terrorist groups at least in the short term (Nacos 2003: 2).

There have been some efforts to assassinate leaders and key members of various groups, but the results have not suggested that this type of activity is likely to be very successful. Israel has frequently targeted specific members of Palestinian groups for death, either because of their leadership or their involvement in particular actions such as the attack on the athletes at the 1972 Munich Olympics. Such assassinations have also complicated Israeli relationships with other states (Wilkinson 2003: 130–1). Even when the assassins have been successful, the result has often been an upsurge of support for the PLO or the Palestinian cause. Assassinating Palestinian militants in the more recent confrontations has simply resulted in retaliation and more Israeli casualties (Luft 2003: 3). The PLO and Hamas are not dependent on any one individual to survive, and provocations by Israel may even strengthen their hand. The assassinations also seem to have had absolutely no deterrent effect. In 1984 when the United States bombed Libya in retaliation for supporting terrorist attacks on US soldiers in Germany, one of the targets was the palace where Qadaffi was presumed to be sleeping, clearly with the intent to remove him from political power as a casualty in a conventional attack. It is possible that there was a deterrent effect from this attempt since Libyan support for terrorism did eventually decline. In 1994 when cruise missiles were launched against al Qaeda bases in Afghanistan, it was thought that bin Laden and other key members of the organization were present. The obvious intent of the targeting in Libya and Afghanistan was to take out the key leaders of the group in a conventional retaliatory strike. In both cases, however, the missiles or bombs missed, indicating how difficult it can be to target individuals.

attack was designed to avoid (Posen 2001/2: 54). Even if there are no immediate negative political, military, or diplomatic consequences, the seeds may be sown for the formation of new groups willing to use violence in the future.

Special counterterrorism units

Many countries have trained special forces to deal with terrorist situations. These forces can play a role in rescues but can also serve for retaliation and for preemptive actions. The presence of special forces can change the contexts in which terrorism can occur and can modify the options available to governments in dealing with violent dissident groups. The creation of such forces is a tacit admission that terrorist incidents cannot always be prevented and that there could be situations where there is a need for such forces. These units can be used either in a domestic situation or as part of efforts to rescue hostages held abroad. If such units are frequently successful in rescuing hostages or retaking buildings, they will have a positive deterrent effect on terrorist organizations in at least some cases. Planned dissident operations will appear to be more costly since members of the organization are more likely to be killed or captured. Successes by the special forces also could make the dissident group appear to be more vulnerable and less able to achieve its objectives.

The record of special units has been a mixed one. When members of April 19 Movement captured the Ministry of Justice in the Colombian capital of Bogotá, the effort to retake the building resulted in over 100 dead among the hostages, terrorists, and troops involved in the assault. Colombia lacked any special units trained for such a situation. On the other hand, Peruvian troops were very successful in recapturing the Japanese embassy in Lima from MRTA dissidents. In this case, the lengthy period that the crisis lasted served the government and security agencies well since the assaulting troops had ample time to rehearse the assault and observers could discover patterns being used by the dissidents in control of the embassy. These two cases from neighboring countries demonstrate how successfully things can go as well as how badly they can go.

The 1972 Munich Olympics provides another example of a failed rescue attempt. West Germany at that time lacked a trained counterterrorism force, and the effort to rescue the hostages resulted in the deaths of all the Israeli athletes. The German governments learned from the experience and trained a special unit for possible use in the future. When a hijacked Lufthansa airliner was taken to Mogadishu, Somalia, West Germany received permission from the Somali government to attempt a rescue. The special unit successfully undertook an assault on the plane. An effort by Egyptian commandos to emulate this success with a hijacked plane in Malta resulted in the deaths of 60 of the 98 passengers and crew (Pillar 2001: 98). The Russian "rescue" of theatergoers held by Chechen rebels in 2002 was another costly failure when the immobilizing agent that was used resulted in the deaths of many of the hostages. In 1975, on the other hand, Dutch marines succeeded in rescuing hostages that were being held by South Moloccans, a dissident Indonesian group who wanted to create their own independent state. The loss of life in the rescue effort was quite small (Yaeger 1990). The United States has a variety of special operations units divided among the different branches of the armed forces. The closest they came to a hostage rescue attempt was the effort to release the hostages at the American embassy in Tehran in 1980, but the rescuers never reached the target area after mishaps in a staging area in the desert in Iran.

The British SAS is perhaps the special military unit with the greatest training for anti-terrorist operations, and probably the most experienced as well. The SAS was long involved in operations against the IRA units in Northern Ireland, often but not always successfully. It has also been called upon to deal with special situations, such as the occupation of the Iranian embassy in London by dissidents. Even with its training and its operations experience, it has not always been successful in its missions. Israeli special units also have had a great deal of experience with hostage cases and similar situations. Most people are aware of the spectacular successes, such as the raid on Entebbe in Uganda that freed virtually all of the hostages being held by German leftists and Palestinians. There have been other examples of successful rescues inside of Israel. On the negative side, however, many such situations have resulted in the deaths of many hostages. The record for Israel has been very mixed, indicating that even special units with extensive field experience will often fail to achieve their objectives.

Special units are desirable from the perspective of governments and their publics. They will not always be successful, but their existence will improve the chances of hostage rescues, recapture of facilities, and the capture or death of dissidents. Just as successful operations by such units may deter at least some terrorist attacks, the absence of such units could encourage hostage taking or other actions. Of course, special units may be useful in dissuading terrorists from attacking in a particular country, but the terrorists can simply choose to launch their attacks elsewhere. The absence of special forces might provide an additional inducement to undertake an action in a particular country. Special units in one country could simply lead to the relocation of terrorist activities without having any major effect on the likelihood of their occurrence. Further, they will normally serve as a mechanism to deal with the symptoms of terrorism (hostage situations, hijackings, etc.) rather than as a mechanism for eliminating the problem of terrorism.

Concessions and reform

Another potential approach to dealing with terrorism takes a dramatically different tack. A government may see the violent actions of a dissident group as the result of the fact that an ethnic minority, religious group, or ideological faction has been neglected or faced discrimination. Instead of using repression or security measures

to deal with the dissidents, it may therefore decide to change some of its policies in order to address the issues that led to the dissident violence. (Crenshaw 1995b: 23). These concessions may be made as part of an effort to reduce support for the dissidents among those likely to favor their cause or the government may make policy changes because there is a real problem that needs to be addressed. Reforms thus become a response to the presence of terrorism in the society. Realistically, reform efforts may dissuade new members from joining dissident organizations or supporting the violence, but such efforts are unlikely to get active members to leave the groups (Gurr 2003: 210). Efforts at concession could fail if the grievances that fueled terrorist actions are multicausal rather than deriving from just one factor (Ross 1993). It may also be true that it will be difficult to find changes in policies that will be acceptable to the dissidents. Elements of a society supporting dissidents, even if small, have objectives that extend well beyond acceptable reforms (Gurr 2003: 212). For example, in Sri Lanka by the time the government was willing to discuss autonomy for Tamil regions, many of the Tamil rebels were unwilling to accept anything less than independence.

Of course, concessions are not always a realistic option for a government, even if the dissidents are willing to listen. Democracies cannot banish racial minorities targeted by right-wing terrorist groups. Further, a democratic government may find it difficult to establish the majority religion as a state religion. It is possible that the proposed domestic policy changes required by the dissidents or even changes in the government structure could lead to violent opposition by other groups. Settler populations in Algeria in the 1960s and the West Bank resorted to violence when the governments in power were negotiating with the Algerian Muslims and the Palestinians (Sederberg 2003: 281). If the terrorism originates from a group located abroad, foreign policy changes may not be possible, or the changes in foreign policy could even be unwise. The original groups could even add new demands to their list once the initial concessions were gained. Negotiations and concessions might also encourage a terrorist group to escalate the violence to achieve additional objectives (Gurr 2003: 210). Countries can also be caught in the middle of foreign conflicts. Taking no action could be deemed offensive by the losing side, while any action favoring one side could lead to violence from the other. A country can be condemned for interfering where it has no interests or it can be condemned for indifference and abdication of responsibility, all in regard to the same conflict (Ajami 2001: 10). One of al Qaeda's criticisms of the US and Western foreign policy was that for years there was no intervention in Bosnia to protect the Muslim population from attack.

Concessions in some cases would appear to have worked as a response to violence by dissidents. The ultimate concession in colonial situations has been to grant independence to the territory where the violence is occurring. The British left Cyprus and Palestine, while the French gave Algeria its independence. In the Basque region, the activities of ETA led to concessions by the Spanish government in terms of regional autonomy. These concessions have limited the support for ETA. British negotiations with the IRA have offered the hope of peace after more than three decades of violence. In Algeria the government released the FIS leaders from prison and began negotiations for permitting fair elections, leading to a decline in the level of violence. A number of European governments have tightened up immigration policies in an effort to deprive their domestic extremists on the right of a focus for the agitation and violence. The Indonesian government did not choose to continue its policy of encouraging Madurese to settle in Borneo. Israel eventually agreed to negotiate with the PLO, and there is now a Palestinian National Authority that has some governmental power. The decision to grant concessions, however, can create a dilemma for governments. Reform efforts to deal with grievances after a terrorist attack run the danger of suggesting to the terrorists (and other dissidents)

that they have been successful, encouraging further attacks and the possibility of escalating violence (Heymann 2001/2: 28). Failure to undertake reform, however, could also lead to continued or escalating violence.

Another type of reform could include government programs to address the concerns of that portion of the population supporting the dissidents. Socioeconomic reform programs have been considered to be the best antidote against terrorism from the left or the right (Wilkinson 2000a: 82). Economic development, education, and political participation may be the long-term solutions to religious terrorism in the Middle East (Gurr 2003: 215). Of course, this type of remedy will mean that change must occur. Any groups that experience negative effects from such changes may resort to their own forms of violence to protect what they have or to protest what they have lost. The dispersion of ethnic and religious minorities means that resolving one grievance will simply create new ones (Laqueur 2001: 119). Concessions and government programs may also not be able to address all or even some of the underlying issues of dislocation due to modernization. Modernization has brought dramatic changes throughout the world, and resistance to modernization has led to violence and terrorism, whether it is by Islamic radicals, neo-Nazis in Europe and the United States, Dayaks in Borneo, the sans-culottes in the French Revolution, or the Animal Rights Militia in Great Britain. Addressing the underlying problems for a portion of the country and implementing solutions may be more difficult than it sometimes appears to be. Further, to the extent that the terrorism has weakened the economy and limited the resources available to the government, such corrective programs become more difficult. Efforts at reform can be quite costly. If attempts are going to be made to eliminate the root causes of terrorism, especially in poor countries, it will be expensive. If reforms are designed to deal with the problems that come with globalization and modernization that contribute to the rise of terrorist groups, it will require extensive sums. It would require significantly greater levels of foreign aid from the United States, for example, than that country has been willing to spend—in the neighborhood of $5 billion a year (McCaffrey and Basso 2002: 218). Changes in policies and concessions will work in some circumstances, but short of total surrender to dissidents this option is not always one that can be pursued.

Diplomatic approaches

International agreements achieved through diplomacy are an additional possibility to complement efforts at dealing with terrorism. Cooperation among nations in terms of dealing with terrorism has increased, providing some hope that this approach can help (B. Jenkins 2001: 323). Major problems, however, still remain for using diplomatic approaches for ending terrorism. Some countries will avoid signing such conventions since they currently do not face any terrorist threats and since signing and abiding by such conventions may lead to retaliation by terrorist groups (Wilkinson 2000b: 200). In other cases, the problem of definition once again becomes important (Richardson 2000: 203). Governments will need some form of legal definition of terrorism in order to agree to an international convention. Does a murder or assassination of a political figure by a dissident constitute terrorism or a political act? If it is terrorism, can the person be extradited? In the case of a murder without a political motive, extradition would be likely, but once politics becomes involved, issues become less clear cut. It would have been hard to imagine the United States extraditing an individual to Iraq for the assassination or attempted assassination of Saddam Hussein, yet a formal treaty might in theory require such an action. As a consequence, many states have been and will be unwilling to sign diplomatic agreements that will limit their discretion when dealing with individual cases. They prefer the flexibility of defining unacceptable

violence, and determining on a case by case basis whether or not to cooperate in dealing with cases involving persons accused of terrorism. Conventions and supposed international rules can still be ignored when states choose to do so (Crelinsten 2000: 174). Diplomatic conventions and resolutions, even vague statements and platitudes can be useful. They help to reinforce international norms against accepting and supporting terrorism (Pillar 2001: 77). As such they may help to set the stage for more meaningful agreements. Some governments are more concerned with the international aspects of terrorism and desire to leave domestic issues to national governments (Dartnell 2000: 199–200). Other countries have different definitions or concerns as well.

There is always the possibility of reaching some limited agreements. For example, persons suspected of detonating bombs on civilian airliners may not be allowed to claim the status of a political refugee. In the nineteenth century in Europe, most countries allowed asylum for individuals involved in political actions that were also normally criminal acts. An exception was made, however, for attacks against the heads of government (presidents and monarchs) and members of their families. Attempted assassinations of these targets were not considered acceptable, and the assassins would not be granted asylum because by definition this kind of assassination would not be considered a political crime (Schreiber 1978: 152). Ultimately, international conventions and diplomatic approaches will be limited by the failure of the international community to arrive at a definition of terrorism and the failure to guarantee that persons identified as terrorists will be brought to trial (Dartnell 2000: 203–4). It may be possible to develop less than global approaches to dealing with terrorism among nations. Countries with similar political systems—the United States and Great Britain as democracies or Argentina and Uruguay when they were both governed by military regimes—might reach formal or informal arrangements for returning suspected terrorists. European countries have cooperated more in this area in recent years, and in the aftermath of September 11, 2001, there has been improved coordination of efforts to arrest persons affiliated with al Qaeda or organizations working with bin Laden. While such cooperation is unlikely to continue indefinitely, it does demonstrate what can be accomplished through international cooperation even when conventions and treaties are absent. While such limitations may be less than ideal, they are still one step closer to controlling terrorism.

Weapons of mass destruction and mass casualties

Responses to the threat of weapons of mass destruction and other efforts to inflict large numbers of casualties, even by conventional means, deserve special attention. The same principles in terms of security, intelligence gathering, and diplomacy hold for these types of weapons, but repression and retaliation may have to be evaluated differently as options by government leaders and security agencies. In addition, there clearly has been a great deal of public and political concern about the possibility of biological, chemical, and nuclear terror attacks, leading governments to increase resources devoted to preventing such attacks or dealing with the aftermath of such attacks, such as providing medical attention to large numbers of people.

In terms of the provision of enhanced security, potential targets that would directly contribute to the prospect of mass casualties should get top priority for greater protection. Nuclear power plants, biological labs dealing with contagious substances, storage facilities for chemicals, and similar sites should be protected against the possibility that they could be sabotaged or otherwise used to inflict mass casualties. Security and monitoring of viruses and nerve gas obviously deserve high priority as well. It is also necessary to protect against conventional weapons of mass destruction designed to kill large numbers

of people. Shopping areas, schools, stadiums, bridges and tunnels, and entertainment facilities are far too numerous for it to be possible to provide sufficient and effective protection against car bombs and other attacks. Depriving dissidents of chemical, biological, and nuclear weapons is important, but it will not eliminate the threat of mass deaths by other means. There may be political reasons to focus on the unconventional weapons in the case of the United States, but conventional terrorism is still likely to cause the most damage in the immediate future (Pillar 2001: 23). Oddly enough, one factor that may lead to the use of unconventional weapons of mass destruction is greater physical security and the hardening of targets towards the use of conventional explosives. When bombs will no longer work, terrorists may expand their arsenals to include the unconventional weapons of mass destruction (Quillen 2002: 290).

Another issue for counterterrorist efforts relates to the allocation of resources in terms of intelligence gathering, security, and other activities for weapons of mass destruction versus conventional weapons. Concern about nuclear weapons in the past had led to expending funds at levels out of proportion to the danger involved (Stern 2002/3: 121–2). The recent emphasis on possible biological and chemical attacks has meant, in effect, that there were gaps in dealing with more conventional weapons (Hoffman 2002: 306). These expenditures have occurred even though the successful use of such weapons has been unlikely. While such successful use is unlikely, one such attack could kill thousands or tens of thousands. On the other hand, even discounting highly lethal conventional attacks such as September 11, the continued use of conventional weapons by terrorists will take their toll slowly but surely. The number of dead from conflicts involving terrorism in Algeria, Sri Lanka, Colombia, Peru, and the Punjab have all exceeded the death toll of September 11 or even the likely death toll from the sarin gas released by Aum Shinrikyo in the Tokyo subway if it had been more successful. If governments focus too many resources on the threat of weapons of mass destruction, they may permit the continuation of conventional attacks where death totals steadily mount. If they ignore the threat of weapons of mass destruction, they risk a major catastrophe. It is surely not an easy choice, and it is also one where the correct choice can only be known after the fact. One advantage for government security agencies is that it is only the largest groups that are likely to be able to acquire such weapons or to be able to successfully create their own weapons with sophisticated production facilities, and these groups are more susceptible to effective penetration or intelligence gathering by security agencies than smaller groups (O'Neil 2003).

Weapons of mass destruction create special concerns for efforts at countering terrorism. While the same mechanisms that work with other terrorist weapons apply to a certain extent, any groups with these weapons must be handled with more care, given the potential for mass casualties. Even the most hardline government might consider concessions or negotiations under these circumstances. Other governments might be more tempted to undertake preemptive actions in these cases if success seems likely. Repression could trigger the use of such weapons. A group facing detection and destruction might utilize such a weapon as a last ditch measure for protection or in a final effort to inflict as much destruction on the enemy as possible. Aum Shinrikyo used the sarin gas when it feared increasing scrutiny by Japanese authorities. Such a reaction might occur with other groups in the future. Fear of retaliation has been present with terrorist groups. Foreign countries are unlikely to risk retaliatory strikes if they are discovered to have been accomplices in attacks killing large numbers of people. Even terrorist groups have balked at the possibility of using such weapons. Hamas has indicated that chemical weapons have not been used because of a fear of reprisals (Dolnik and Bhattacharjee 2002: 121). Weapons of mass destruction clearly complicate the options for both governments and terrorist groups.

Summary

There is no one counterterrorist technique that surfaces as the solution to the challenges provided by violent dissident groups in the world. Effective intelligence (when such is possible), of course, is invariably useful, but once the information has been gained, decisions will have to be made on the appropriate course of action to be taken. Heightened security, while expensive in some cases, is likely to play a role, but not all attacks can be prevented. Governments will have to decide, often on a case by case basis, what mix of repression, retaliation, preemption, diplomacy, reforms, and concessions and negotiations to pursue when dealing with terrorist groups. Negotiations with a group that controls a weapon of mass destruction may be necessary even if the government would normally prefer some other tactic. If special commando teams are available, they may be effective in some hostage situations or building seizures but may be less advisable in others. Not only is there no one technique that works, there is no one equation that provides the exact amount of repression and reform that will eliminate a terrorist threat.

The counterterrorist techniques available are accessible to all types of governments just as terrorist techniques are available to all kinds of dissident groups. Democracies and authoritarian societies can use the same mechanisms, although the mix might vary among different kinds of political regimes. Strategies that work to defeat domestic extremists or foreign attackers in a democracy may work equally well in an authoritarian system by a government determined to repress local democratic dissidents or to keep an ethnic or religious minority suppressed. A minority government can even use control techniques to keep itself in power. Effective intelligence gathering may serve to destroy a dissident movement seeking democratic reforms just as much as it can undermine a religious cult seeking to trigger the apocalypse. On the other hand, the same techniques may not work equally well against different terrorist groups. Normal police

BOX 12.2 **The issue of civil liberties**

It is worth emphasizing that counterterrorist techniques may threaten the presence of civil liberties in a society. There is a constant tension between freedom and safety although the two are not mutually exclusive except at the extremes. A totally free society is very vulnerable. Europe has become more vulnerable, in fact, as the European agreements have removed many border controls (Chalk 1996: 3). Even if the country itself is not a target for domestic groups because of religious, ethnic or ideological reasons and not a target for foreign groups due to national foreign policy, the country will still be a convenient location for attacks on embassies or offices of foreign corporations by activities of terrorist groups in other countries. Strong authoritarian governments and totalitarian regimes, on the other hand, avoid the problem of civil liberties interfering with efforts to repress violent dissident groups. Democracies and even many mildly authoritarian states that have a concern for the rule of law and providing civil liberties (if not political liberties) will find balancing the tension difficult. A democracy that does not implement stringent enough safeguards faces the danger of attacks. A government that makes sure that terrorists are rooted out and dealt with faces the danger of transforming the political system from a democracy into something much less free.

The United Kingdom placed limits on civil liberties in Northern Ireland. The loss of civil liberties may be most severe for certain segments of the population. The Irish became a suspect community in England because of the IRA and its activities (Hillyard 1993). The government used the SAS and special courts and other limitations on civil liberties to control the activities of the IRA and to prevent a victory for the nationalists. France has recently been effective in limiting terrorism as a result of greater government ability to monitor and detect dissident groups. The increased counterterrorist ability did not result from a peculiarly French civic culture that tolerated the greater government intrusion into personal lives; it was "born of a necessity revealed by an inability to combat terrorism in other ways" (Shapiro and Suzan 2003: 92). Israel has used martial law and other mechanisms in efforts to eliminate the threat from Palestinian nationalists, but the government has avoided the extreme measures necessary to make prevention more effective. Suicide bombings in Israel have been as effective as they are because they can only be prevented with extreme suppression of the rights of the Israeli population as well as the Palestinian population (Dolnick and Bhattacharjee 2002: 116).

In the aftermath of the September 11 attacks, however, more extraordinary measures have been taken in the United States that have affected some citizens and residents, and there have been suggestions of the necessity of even greater latitude for government surveillance and detention of suspicious individuals. The reaction among European democracies led to changes in anti-terrorism laws and restrictions on civil liberties. Britain, France, and Germany joined the United States and Canada as the most restrictive of individual rights among democracies (Haubrich 2003: 7). Muslims and persons from the Middle East have increasingly become suspect communities in the United States and parts of Europe just as the Irish became one in the United Kingdom. In the United States Homeland Security Institutes at universities and in the private sector have rushed to provide better methods of increasing security, monitoring activities, and searching out the terrorists in the countries with more regard for the technical possibilities than for the rights of citizens. Bin Laden himself recognized that one outcome of his campaign would be a reduction of civil liberties and freedom in the United States (Nacos 2003: 6). It is even possible that increased security and limitations on civil liberties will not only weaken democracy but might even lead to an increase of internal dissidence that could increase the likelihood of terrorism in the future (Sederberg 2003: 273). Democracies, however, can win without drastic changes. Spanish democracy has been able to contain ETA, although the brief experimentation with a death squad was a significant aberration from normal democratic practice. Similarly, the Scandinavian countries have been able to control their right-wing extremists that have targeted minorities and immigrants without resorting to dictatorial methods. Even Sri Lanka's hard-pressed democratic government has managed to prevent a victory by the Tamil Tigers without imposing an authoritarian system of government. India, which has used extra-constitutional violence with some regularity, still remains largely democratic.

investigations in France have worked well against leftist terrorists but have failed to defeat separatist violence in Corsica (Wieviorka 1990: 77).

One final point that needs to be emphasized in any analysis of counterterrorist techniques is that there will be an ongoing need for such efforts. There are too many groups and too many causes for terrorist activity around the world for attacks and violence to disappear any time in the immediate future. Even if international terrorist activity is eliminated from the scene, there were still be eruptions of domestic terrorism, and sooner or later such domestic terrorism is likely to overflow into the international system and involve other countries. Fighting terrorism is more akin to fighting crime than it is to fighting a war. In wars one can hope to win and achieve final victory by defeating an enemy. When governments fight crime, they realize that the battle is an ongoing one—that crime can be dealt with but not eliminated. Unlike war, the "struggle against terrorism, however, is never-ending" (Hoffman 2002: 314). As a consequence, the concern about counterterrorist tactics and techniques is one that will remain important for the immediate future.

Terms

African National Congress (ANC)
CIA
KGB
suspect community
weapons of mass destruction

Further reading

Johnson, L. K. (2003) "Strategic Intelligence: The Weakest Link in the War Against World Terrorism," in C. W. Kegley, Jr (ed.) *The New Global Terrorism: Characteristics, Causes, Controls*, Upper Saddle River, NJ: Prentice Hall, 239–52.

Pillar, P. R. (2001) *Terrorism and U.S. Foreign Policy*, Washington, DC: Brookings Institution.

Chapter 13

Terrorism: a continuing phenomenon

Why terrorism continues   244

    Continuing causes of terrorism   245

    Terrorism works   246

What we know from the historical experience   249

The discussions in the previous chapter indicated that terrorism is not likely to disappear anytime soon. The United States announced the beginning of a war against terrorism, one that is being prosecuted as vigorously as possible. This war against terrorism is not the first one to be declared. In September 1901 President Theodore Roosevelt called for a campaign to exterminate terrorism in the aftermath of the assassination of President McKinley by an anarchist (Rapoport 2003: 36). Needless to say, terrorism was not eliminated in the century that followed the McKinley assassination. Notwithstanding the hopes of some in the West, it is also not likely to disappear anytime in the immediate future. Frustrations among those not in power, the effects of globalization, and the continuing effects from the breakup of empires and states will continue to fuel problems and violence. Trouble spots in various parts of the world will continue to be present and contribute to circumstances that are conducive to political violence.

The discussions in the previous chapters clearly demonstrate that violent attacks by dissident groups have not just been a recent phenomenon. Terrorism did not begin with the attacks of September 2001 in New York City and Washington DC, or in April 1995 with the bombing in Oklahoma City, or with the hostage taking at the Munich Olympics in 1972. Nor did terrorism begin with the Cold War or the establishment of the Soviet Union after World War I. Nor has terrorism been restricted to activities by groups from the Middle East or those parts of the world with large Muslim populations. Terrorism has been a nearly universal phenomenon. The Red Brigades were a threat to Italy. Violence and terror have continued for decades in Sri Lanka. The Boston Tea Party was a successful prelude to the American War of Independence. Rwanda was a late twentieth century example of genocide. Right-wing groups have resorted to violence in the United States and Europe. Ethnic cleansing has occurred all too widely, practiced by both governments and dissidents. Al Qaeda and Osama bin Laden have had no connection with most of this violence. Terrorism has been present in many locations and many different time periods; it has involved a great many types of organizations and groups. Some have been religious, some ethnic, and some ideological. Some dissident groups have been successful and some groups have failed to achieve their goals. We know more about the ones that became prominent, of course, than we do about the ones that failed and quickly disappeared. It would be extremely useful to know how many dissident groups have actually attempted terrorist violence, but the historical record is far too incomplete. As important as it would be, it is not possible to calculate the percentage of violent movements that actually survived long enough to have a major effect on a political system because it is impossible to document all the attempts that quickly failed. The overall ratio of successful terrorist operations to unsuccessful terrorist operations is probably a relatively small percentage. The previous chapters have contained a bias since they have focused on those movements that became important enough to have some effects in a particular society or the world. While the percentage of successful movements may be relatively low, there have been enough of them to justify this book. If the past is prologue to the future, then terrorism will continue and will have at least some major effects on individual countries and maybe even the world at large.

Why terrorism continues

There are three principal reasons why terrorism is likely to continue to be a problem for the immediate future. First, as was obvious from discussion in the previous chapter, there is no single counterterrorist technique that is likely to work. Nor is it likely that governments will be able to always find the correct mix of techniques to solve domestic terrorist problems. Cooperation across international boundaries among countries will remain difficult as well, even when governments seek to help each other. The correct response for dealing with dissident groups using terrorism is only obvious in hindsight in many cases. Secondly, the events, circumstances, and issues that have fueled terrorism have not disappeared, nor is it likely they will be resolved any time soon. Third, while some would deny the possibility of successful terrorist campaigns, there are indications that such violence has indeed been successful.

Continuing causes of terrorism

One major reason that terrorism is likely to continue is that the issues underlying this kind of political violence have persisted. The problems present with the breakup of empires and states still plague the successor states. Problems also remain in countries that are not the remnants of empires. The threat of majority violence against religious or ethnic minorities has not disappeared, while ethnonationalist groups and some religious dissident groups are still seeking autonomy or separate status. While it is possible that some new states may appear in the future, thus pacifying separatist groups, it is not possible for all the disaffected minorities to create the independent states that they desire. Further, establishing boundaries for independent states or autonomous provinces will always face the challenge of intermingled populations. Even if the British had done a better job of drawing boundaries for Northern Ireland to separate Protestants from Catholics, the intermingling of the two populations would have been unavoidable. There would have been members of each group on the wrong side of the border. The problem was particularly problematic in Belfast with its Catholic and Protestant neighborhoods. When members of different groups end up on the wrong side of the borders the danger of ethnic cleansing being chosen as an option is always present.

As noted in Chapter 12, no amount of reforms or concessions will be sufficient to meet the demands of some dissident groups. The state structure will not be changed to accommodate supporters of left-wing or right-wing ideologies, religious laws will not be revoked or created, districts with mixed populations will not be granted their independence, and ideally racial or religious minorities will not be persecuted or exiled to appease extremists in the society. When the demands of the dissidents conflict with the wishes of the majority, change will not occur, and the potential for violence by the dissatisfied dissidents will be present. The Baader-Meinhof Gang would only have been content with the end of capitalism in West Germany and the world. Most West Germans clearly did not desire such an outcome. As long as groups demand more than can possibly be achieved, terrorist violence can occur. While democracies are vulnerable to terrorism because they are democracies, there is little doubt that government repression and state use or support of terror against its own citizens can generate violence. In an ideal world, the use of death squads and vigilante groups by governments would cease, but as long as the crown rests uneasy on the heads of the ruling elite, governments will be tempted to repress opposition groups. Such repression may also lay the groundwork for terrorism and other violence in the future.

The appearance of terrorism has also been a reaction to globalization and modernization, processes that place great stress upon societies and political systems. Globalization will continue to generate instability in societies. There will be winners and losers because of the changes, and the losers will be tempted to resort to violence. The various types of terrorism discussed in earlier chapters involve many cases of reaction to globalization. Religious groups frequently seek to return to a purer past and to purge society of outside influences. This reaction was as true for the Jewish Zealots as it is for al Qaeda. Many nationalist or ethnic dissidents also see their societies threatened by the outside world and foreign cultures. ETA is afraid that Spain will absorb the Basque cultural area, and the Dayaks in Borneo were seeking to avoid becoming a minority in their own land. Right-wing groups frequently have fought against changes that have come with globalization, including immigration of peoples of different racial stock or religious communities. Left-wing dissidents have battled against the evils that they see as coming in the train of global capitalism, sharing some of the same fears as religious groups and some ethnic groups (Mousseau 2002/3: 19). Since greater global integration is not going to disappear in the world, the potential for violent reactions is going to remain.

Terrorism works

It has been argued that terrorism never works— that either in the short run or in the long run the resort to violence is counterproductive. Throughout history states relying on terror as a policy, both during war and in dealing with domestic opponents, and by dissident organizations using violence against governments always create enough negative consequences to suggest that it is an ineffective strategy (Carr 2002). Many early Marxists and other leftists opposed the use of terror in their campaigns to gain power, and it was groups such as these that practiced restraint that have been the ones that normally survived and even flourished. Similarly, Hizballah in Lebanon fared better once it abandoned terrorist tactics as well (Blackburn 2002: 28). In fact, however, the cases analyzed in this volume have demonstrated that terror can be a very effective technique for a group to use. As noted in Chapter 10, state sanctioned terror often accomplishes the immediate goals of the government or its agents because the power of the state is behind the action, but terrorism by non-state actors has been successful as well. The idea that terrorism is "a futile strategy" is one of the major erroneous images about this type of violence (Stohl 2003: 87).

There are a few obvious examples of successful terrorism that most analysts will accept. The urban terror campaign in Cyprus was important in convincing the British to give that colony its independence. The French gave up the battle for Algeria in the face of a guerrilla insurgency and continuing terrorist attacks. The French had

defeated the rebels in Algeria in military terms through the use of torture and extra-legal means with the resulting cost in terms of civil liberties in Algeria and France. The French did not lose the battle militarily—they decided that the prize was no longer worth the battle (Crenshaw 1995a: 499). The departure of the British from Palestine under violent pressure from the Jewish settlers in the Mandate would generally constitute a third example for the successful use of terrorism (Wilkinson 2000b: 12). All of these cases, however, were colonial situations in which the occupying power had a home that served as a place for relocation. Surrender to the terrorist demands for independence may be painful, but the cost of surrender is not overwhelming. The colonialists simply retire, retreat if you like, to their own homeland. Not all anti-colonial campaigns relying on terrorism or terrorism and guerrilla tactics have worked. The British defeated the Mau Mau in Kenya and the Communists in Malaya. The Spanish "colonialists" are still present in the Basque country, while Muslim dissidents in the southern Philippines have yet to establish the independent state that they seek. Still there have been enough successful national liberation campaigns to provide examples to other groups in other countries that see terrorism as a possible solution to their problems with governments or policies (Hoffman 1998: 65).

A more careful look at the track record of terrorism, moreover, suggests that such campaigns have been more successful than this focus on colonial struggles would suggest. The Jewish Zealots were very successful in eliminating opposition to the revolt that was being planned. Unifying the population behind the revolt was, in fact, the immediate objective of their attacks and violence. The Assassins were also very successful in protecting themselves against the Sunni majority and the leaders of nearby Muslim states and in preventing even more active persecution of the members of the sect for their beliefs. Their form of violence proved to be a very effective weapon of the weak in terms of achieving a very immediate goal for the sect—survival. The fact that the Assassins were ultimately defeated is less important than the fact that they survived as long as they did. Other cases in the preceding chapters also demonstrate relatively successful uses of terror by non-state actors. The Montoneros helped to bring down the military regime that was in power and to facilitate the return to power of Juan Perón. In the United States anti-abortion violence has been at least partially successful because it has indeed become more difficult to get an abortion. The Dayaks in Borneo persuaded the Madurese to leave and successfully negated the government policy on internal migration by terrorizing and killing the recent arrivals. Various Middle Eastern groups also perceive that violence has forced changes in US policies. It could even be argued that the September 11 attack and its aftermath effectively soured relations between the United States and Saudi Arabia and forced the Bush administration to place more pressure on Israel to compromise with the Palestinians (Nacos 2003: 11). Dissident groups feel that the attack against the US marines and French paratroopers in Beirut led to a withdrawal of these foreign forces as desired. Even fewer casualties led to the end of US involvement in peacekeeping and humanitarian efforts in Somalia (Crenshaw 2003b: 172). Osama bin Laden has used exactly these arguments of terrorist successes in his efforts to inspire continued attacks against the United States (Hoffman 2002: 310). Mounting US casualties from terrorist actions in the rebuilding of Iraq might lead to pressure for an early US departure from that country, and clearly those who are calling for such attacks have accepted the theory that such actions will work. Even though there have been many failures among violent dissidents for each of the successes, other dissidents are more interested in the successes from the past. An "*image* of success that recommends terrorism to groups who identify with the innovator" (Crenshaw 2003a: 98, emphasis added) may be more than sufficient to encourage other dissidents to resort to violence.

Evaluations of the success of terrorism can also be difficult because the criteria for success by the

dissidents may be different than the criteria of governments or academics. Total success may not be necessary. For guerrillas and terrorists everywhere "not losing is winning" (Hoffman 2002: 311). Survival holds forth the hope of future victory or concessions by the government. In other cases, dissident groups have achieved partial successes through the use of violence (Havens *et al.* 1975: 172). The PLO has yet to be successful in creating a Palestinian state, but it is now the recognized negotiating agent for the Palestinian people. The British have similarly accepted the IRA (Provisional), and the IRA's political wing, the Sinn Fein party, as organizations that should be involved in negotiations on the future of Northern Ireland. In the 1930s in Eastern and Central Europe, the fascist parties using violence were successful in preventing the leftist parties from coming to power and aided in destroying parliamentary democracies, even when they did not take power themselves. The governments adopted other authoritarian styles of government to help them deal with that violence originating with these parties (Berend 1998: 301). ETA in Spain has not won the battle for an independent Basque homeland, but the region has much greater autonomy and there have been concessions to Basque culture that otherwise would not have been granted. The Scandinavian governments have made their immigration policies more restrictive in an effort to keep support for the far right from increasing. Macedonia has offered new programs and greater opportunities for its Albanian minority. The Albanian dissidents in Macedonia concluded that more was won by a few months of violence in Kosovo than in a decade of peaceful politics, thus leading them to adopt the same tactics in Macedonia (Ash 2003: 63). While the conflict in Sri Lanka seems likely to continue, the Tamils have also been offered greater autonomy, and if any solution is reached in the near future, it is likely that the Tamils will have some guaranteed protections as a minority in a state with a Sinhalese majority. In all these cases, terror (combined with guerrilla activity as in Sri Lanka) has led to gains for the dissident groups that were unlikely to otherwise have been granted. Most of the above examples of reasonably complete or partial successes involve ethnic or religious communities, but ideological groups relying on violence and terror have had some successes as well. The violence in revolutionary France served the purposes of some of the political factions and permitted them to govern for at least a period of time. The fascists in Italy and the Nazis in Germany used street violence and intimidation as a successful adjunct to other political activities in their rise to power even if they could not maintain themselves in power.

Terrorist violence can be successful in the eyes of the practitioners for additional reasons. Some terrorist actions will be counted as successes if they attract attention to the cause of the dissidents (Pimlott 1997: 685). They may be able to publicize grievances that otherwise would have been overlooked (Hoffman 1998: 65). The availability of the modern media and mass communications has actually encouraged dissident groups to use terrorist attacks to publicize their cause (Chalk 1996: 36). The violence could also be used to enhance group solidarity, not only within the dissident organization but among a segment of the larger population. There could be an increase in communal identification as a consequence of the violence. Hindu nationalist groups have been relatively successful in this regard as noted earlier. In a different way, the KLA was able to increase solidarity among the Albanians in Kosovo. The same pattern can be observed in Bosnia among all the groups. Attacks by Kurdish dissidents against Turkish targets have undoubtedly been successful in slowing down the process of the assimilation of the Kurdish population into Turkish culture, an obvious acceptable intermediate goal for the dissident Kurdish organizations. The suicide attacks by the PKK (as well as the Tamil Tigers) have furthered group solidarity and improved morale within the group (Dolnik 2003: 21). In other cases terrorism may mobilize populations. The political direction of the mobilized populations may be unclear but the status quo may be threatened. The attacks of September 11 had major impacts around the world. Many Muslims in the Middle East and elsewhere may now perceive that it is possible to challenge the West (Ajami 2001: 9). Just as the United States will not be the same as a result of the attacks on the Pentagon and the World Trade Center towers, Muslim societies in many countries will be different as well. It is still too soon to see what the exact consequences will be, but there can be little doubt that there will be continuing effects.

Terrorist groups have also been successful in a negative sense. Attacks have been used to good effect (or to bad effect, depending on your point of view) to disrupt peace processes. In Israel/Palestine extremists on both sides have become adept at using violence to inflame public opinion and to make negotiations difficult or next to impossible. Splinter groups in the IRA have attempted to disrupt recent negotiations, and the IRA itself has used violence to undermine peace efforts that excluded it. The campaigns of the Contras in Nicaragua prevented the Sandinista government from consolidating its power and implementing many of its programs in the countryside. Violent attacks could also convince a government to continue to keep repressive legislation on the books and delay plans for democratization. If the dissidents are seeking the continuation of authoritarian measures as one policy objective, then the use of violence has prevented a course of action that the dissidents oppose. Another advantage with negative goals is that they can sometimes be easier to attain than more ambitious goals of changing current government policies, replacing the governing elite, or achieving an independent state. All of these examples indicate that terrorism can be an effective means for attaining goals, either completely or partially, either obtaining change or preventing change. The total successes and the partial successes all supply hope to other groups of dissidents that seek to redress power relationships by the use of terrorism. Ultimately, since it cannot be argued conclusively that terrorism never works, it cannot be expected that all groups will renounce terrorism as a potential weapon (Falk 2003: 550).

What we know from the historical experience

There are some obvious facts that have surfaced in regard to terrorism in the world. The most successful form of terrorism, and often the most deadly, is that involving the government. Direct state use of terrorism as occurred in Nazi Germany or Stalin's Soviet Union is more extreme but this form of terror needs to be acknowledged. When governments use terror against their own citizens or permit some groups to use violence, it is often effective in repressing those citizens. Terrorism is likely to continue to be used by non-state groups against the state not only because it has worked at least some of the time in the past but because it may bring major results for a small investment in time and resources at least in terms of publicity. If properly managed, there may even be relatively little risk to the perpetrators (Chalk 1998a: 119). Both of these characteristics were aptly demonstrated for decades by the 17 November Movement in Greece. Of course, in some cases legal or political channels fail the dissidents because a popular majority disagrees with their position, not because the state is repressive. The disenchanted and frustrated minority, however, can still choose to resort to violence, explaining away the majority opposition as being due to lack of information, manipulation by elites, capitalist coercion, or other types of pressures. Terrorism will, consequently, continue to be used as a weapon of the weak because it has been used in the past and because it is available to groups with limited resources.

There are very few final conclusions that can be reached with any certainty in a study of terrorism. It is a widely prevalent phenomenon. It is unlikely to disappear in the immediate future. Beyond these simple facts, conclusions become difficult because the whole topic is a very complex one. Real conclusions can only begin to be formulated when there is an understanding of the subject. Since terrorism and dissident violence cannot always be defeated, terrorism will continue. Even in defeat dissidents will be partially successful, encouraging others. Further, there have been just enough complete successes or major gains related to the violence to provide encouragement to other potential terrorists and to indicate that government responses may be inadequate. Most dissident groups never resort to the use of violence; instead they seek change through non-violent means. Many groups willing to use violence are detected before they can act and most are quickly suppressed by police or security forces. Enough dissident groups, however, survive the initial period of vulnerability and become strong enough to use violence to disrupt their societies. Some of these surviving movements are defeated without creating the changes they seek. Others, however, manage to win some gains. As long as this possible success by organized dissident groups continues, the world will face the continued threat of violent terrorist attacks by the weak against the strong.

Glossary

Abu Nidal Organization: This Palestinian group was formed by Abu Nidal and sought to perpetuate terrorist actions against the West. It has been responsible for some of the more spectacular actions undertaken. It has been headquartered in Iraq, Syria, and Libya at various times. He was found dead in Iraq in 2002.

Abu Sayyaf group: This group has appeared among the Muslim population of the southern Philippines. It is one of the more extreme dissident groups operating in that country, and it has links to al Qaeda.

Aceh: This region is in the northernmost portion of the island of Sumatra in Indonesia. It was one of the last areas brought under the control by the Dutch in their colony. The population has long sought greater autonomy or even independence from the rest of Indonesia, and there has been simmering conflict between the central authorities and local population for decades.

African National Congress (ANC): This dissident organization in South Africa was in the forefront of the struggle of the black majority to achieve equal rights. It was largely non-violent in its opposition to the former white minority government.

Akali Dal: This is the largest Sikh political party in the province of Punjab and in India.

Alexander of Yugoslavia, King: King Alexander attempted to unify the various ethnic groups in Yugoslavia after World War I. His assassination at the hands of Croat nationalists weakened the possibilities of creating a unified Yugoslav state.

al Qaeda: *see* al Qaeda under "Q".

anarchism: Practitioners of and adherents to this left-wing ideology believed that capitalism would be overthrown by a spontaneous uprising of the people. The anarchists could try to inspire the masses to begin this uprising through education or action.

Animal Liberation Front (ALF): This animal rights organization in the United Kingdom has been heavily involved in the fight to protect animals. It has resorted to acts of violence, principally against property, in these efforts.

Animal Rights Militia (ARM): The ARM is an animal rights organization in the United Kingdom that has demonstrated its willingness to use violence, including attacks on people, in the pursuit of its political objectives. The group is supposedly an independent organization, but there are indications that the members are simply the hard-core members of the Animal Liberation Front using a different name as a cover for their more violent activities.

anthrax: Anthrax is a biological weapon that is derived from cattle waste. It occurs naturally in nature and comes in many forms. In its most deadly forms it can kill very quickly, but it is not contagious.

Anti-Liberation Terrorist Group (GAL): This was the cover name for a government death squad in Spain that targeted members of ETA and other Basque dissident groups. A number of dissidents were killed before the public knew about the activities of the group. The public awareness was a major embarrassment to the government, and the group was disbanded as a consequence.

April 19 Movement (M-19): This Colombian leftist movement was not the most powerful ideological dissident group, but it did mount some spectacular attacks against the Colombian state. Members of the group took over the Ministry of Justice in 1985 holding over a hundred persons hostage. The group had links to the Castro regime in Cuba.

Armenian Secret Army for the Liberation of Armenia (ASALA): This group has sought to publicize the fact of the Armenian genocide at the hands of the Turks at the beginning of the twentieth century. When it was most active in the 1970s and 1980s, it undertook many attacks against Turkish officials around the world.

Army of God: This organization has been willing to use violence as part of efforts to end abortions in the United States. Little is known about the actual extent of the organization, and there are indications that this group relies on the idea of leaderless resistance.

Aryan Nations: This group is one of the racist organizations in the United States that have been opposed to the national government and programs for minorities. It has been linked with other right-wing organizations in the country that have been willing to use violence.

Asahara, Shoku: He was the founder of the apocalyptic Aum Shinrikyo sect.

Assam: This state in northeastern India has been the scene of communal violence and terrorism directed against recent migrants to the region.

Assassin sect (The Assassins): This unorthodox Shia Muslim group was present in the Middle East beginning in the eleventh century. The groups established bases in the Levant and Persia, and it used assassination as a weapon to prevent the more powerful Muslim states and empires from destroying the sect. It also targeted selected leaders in the Christian Crusader states.

Aum Shinrikyo: This Japanese sect believed that salvation for the world required the instigation of World War III. Its leader would then appear to rescue the world and create an ideal society.

Ayoda: This town in northern India has been the center of religious conflict. It was the site of a Muslim mosque, but religious Hindus have claimed that it was an even earlier sacred site of the Hindu religion. Hindu extremists desecrated and then destroyed the mosque and have begun building a temple there. The controversy has led to communal violence between Hindus and Muslims on various occasions.

Baader-Meinhof Gang: This leftist dissident group, also know as the Red Army Faction, mounted many attacks in the 1970s and into the 1980s in Germany. Members also cooperated with leftist groups elsewhere in Europe and with Palestinian groups.

Ba'ath Party (Arab Socialist Renaissance Party): The Ba'ath party has been a support for the ruling elite in both Syria and Iraq. The party has favored pan-Arabism and has been supportive of violent action against Israel.

Bakhtiar, Shahpur: He was the last prime minister of Iran under the regime of the Shah. He was later assassinated in Paris where he was living in exile.

Beer Hall Putsch: This name has been given to the initial attempt of Adolf Hitler to seize power in Germany via an armed uprising in 1923. Hitler and others started the attempt in Munich, but it never attracted support elsewhere, and the local authorities were able to contain it easily.

Bekaa Valley: This area in Lebanon is a stronghold for Hizballah and the Shi'ite population.

Bernadotte, Count Folke: Count Bernadotte was a Swedish diplomat working for the United Nations who was assassinated by Jewish extremists in Israel in 1948 for taking positions perceived to be favorable to the Palestinian refugees.

Bharatiya Janata Party: This large national party in India has supported the idea of recognizing the role of Hinduism in the state and perhaps even establishing it as the state religion.

Bhindranwale, Sant Jarnail Singh: He was a charismatic leader in the Sikh community who favored the use of political violence and whose followers were involved in some of the first terrorist actions designed to gain greater autonomy or independence for the Sikhs.

Biafra: Name for the eastern region of Nigeria when it tried to break away to form an independent state in 1966. In the ensuing civil war, the central government triumphed and reintegrated the area into the Nigerian state.

Black Hand: This organization of Serbs sought to unite all Southern Slavs in the Serbian state.

It included members of the Serbian military and planned the assassination of Archduke Ferdinand of Austria-Hungary at Sarajevo in August 1914.

Black International: The occasional cooperation between various fascist, neo-fascist, and rightwing groups after World War II has been termed the Black International (as opposed to the various Socialist—or Red—internationals that existed). Authoritarian governments or their security agencies and intelligence ministries that at times provided aid to such groups were included in this cooperative network.

Black September: Black September was one of the more radical Palestinian liberation groups. It took is name from the battle with the Jordanian armed forces that led to the PLO being expelled from that country in 1970. Black September was responsible for some of the more spectacular terrorist actions undertaken against Israel and countries that supported Israel.

Bologna train station bombing: This attack on the train station in Bologna in 1980 was one of the single most deadly terrorist incidents in Italian history. The attack was undoubtedly undertaken by a neo-fascist organization, although there was an initial attempt to place the blame on leftist dissidents.

Branch Davidians: This group, under the dominance of David Koresh, established a compound near Waco, Texas, where members of the cult could live. An effort to arrest members for weapons charges led to a shootout and a months-long standoff between the authorities and the Davidians. An attempt by the FBI to gain control of the compound led the cult members to set fire to their compound resulting in the deaths of most of them.

Burghers: This term is applied to the small Eurasian population of Sri Lanka.

Chechens: The province of Chechnya in Russia has been the scene of guerrilla fighting and terrorist attacks as the Chechens have sought to obtain their independence. The Chechens are descendants of an Islamic culture and have gained support from other Islamic groups, including the al Qaeda network.

Chechnya: This province in federal Russia has attempted to win its independence. The population is primarily Muslim, and separatist dissidents have engaged in terrorism and guerrilla warfare in their efforts to win freedom.

Christian Identity: Many Christian Identity movements in the United States follow right-wing political prescriptions for solving the problems of the United States. Most of the groups do not support violent attacks against the government or other groups, but a few of them have been involved in right-wing terrorist actions that have occurred in the United States.

CIA: The Central Intelligence Agency (CIA) is that branch of the US government charged with intelligence activities outside the United States. These activities have included supporting dissident groups in other countries.

colons: This name was given to the Frenchmen in Algeria who had been long-term residents or descendants of settlers from earlier decades and even the nineteenth century.

Communist Combat Cells (CCC): The CCC was a left-wing dissident group that appeared in Belgium in the 1970s. It undertook a few attacks but never achieved the prominence of other left-wing dissident groups in Europe.

Continuity IRA: This group is one that left the Provisional IRA when it agreed to a cease-fire and negotiations over the future of Northern Ireland.

Contras: The US-supported opponents of the Sandinista were considered counterrevolutionaries by the new regime, hence the term Contras. Their battle against the Sandinista government involved both guerrilla insurgency and terrorism.

Dayaks: The local population in the Indonesian portion of Borneo (Kalimantan) consists largely of the Dayaks. They can be distinguished from other Indonesians, and the Dayaks are also frequently Christian, setting them apart from the vast majority of Indonesians who practice some version of Islam.

Diplock Courts: These courts in Northern Ireland had only a judge for trying IRA defendants. The courts were established because local jurors in IRA trials were at risk of retaliation when they voted to convict members of the IRA.

disappeared ones: This term was given to the individuals in Argentina who were abducted and killed by the death squads associated with the military and security forces in the country.

Duvalier, François: Duvalier was long-term president of Haiti. He organized a very effective security apparatus that terrorized the population of the country and kept him in power for decades.

Engels, Frederich: Engels was Karl Marx's closest companion and collaborator. He helped to write some of the key documents for what came to be Marxist theory and compiled much of Marx's writings.

Escobar, Pablo: He was one of the leaders of the Medellin Cartel when it launched its terror campaign against the government of Colombia.

ethnic cleansing: This term refers to the efforts of governments and other groups to drive a particular ethnic or religious group out of an area. The usual method is to use violence against some members in order to inspire terror in others.

Euzkadi ta Askatasuna (ETA): ETA has been the longest lasting and most determined proponent of independence for the Basque region in Spain that has been willing to use violence. There have been various splinter groups that have developed over the years, but ETA has consistently been considered the militant spokesman for Basque interests.

false flag attacks: This term is used when one type of dissident organization uses violence to discredit another group of dissidents. False flag attacks have generally been undertaken by right-wing groups with the intent of having left-wing dissidents blamed for the violence.

fascist: This generic political term (as well as being the name of Benito Mussolini's party in Italy) refers to political movements of the 1920s or later that were opposed to communists and socialists as well as the idea of parliamentary democracy. Fascist parties were often extremely nationalistic and often opposed to minority groups. Fascism as an ideology has not necessarily been anti-Semitic, although some parties following the ideology did develop such a posture.

Fatah: Fatah is the largest component group in the Palestinian Liberation Organization. Yassir Arafat was the head of Fatah at the time that he assumed the chairmanship of the PLO. Given Arafat's position in the PLO, the identity of the two groups has tended to merge even though Fatah is still technically separate.

Feltrinelli, Franco: Feltrinelli was the very rich son of an Italian capitalist. He used his money to finance the Red Brigades in the early years of the organization.

Franco, Francisco: General Franco was the leader of the nationalist side in the Spanish Civil War. With the victory of the nationalists he became the ruler of Spain, serving as the Regent for the Bourbon monarchy until his death in 1975.

Fujimoro, Alberto: He was the elected president of Peru who authorized martial law and other harsh measures for dealing with Shining Path and MRTA dissidents. His harsh stance was successful, although Peruvian principles of democracy were weakened as a consequence of the policies.

furores: These documents were ancient grants to villages in the Basque country from Spanish monarchs, giving the local inhabitants a measure of autonomy in tax policy and local governance. The nationalist government of Francisco Franco revoked them. The Basque separatists have always held them up as the ideal for the Basque region and as an historical indication of the distinct character of the region.

Gaza Strip: The city of Gaza and the nearby shoreline on the Mediterranean was to be part of the Arab state of Palestine created after the Mandate. The population of the area has been overwhelmingly Arab. In 1948, the Egyptian Army maintained control of the area, and it was under Egyptian administration until the Six Day War in 1967 when it was captured by Israel. Most of the Gaza Strip, if not all of it, is expected to become part of the area governed by the Palestinian Authority.

genocide: Genocide is an effort, inevitably by a government, to totally wipe out particular ethnic or religious groups.

Georgia Guard: The Guard was the police or militia unit used by the state of Georgia to ensure order in the Cherokee lands in the first part of the nineteenth century. This paramilitary group was one mechanism that was used to help drive the Indians out of the state.

Gestapo: The Gestapo was the German secret police during the period of Nazi rule. The Gestapo was responsible for internal security in Germany and areas of Europe occupied by German forces.

Ghandi, Indira: She was prime minister of India and was assassinated by Sikh bodyguards after an assault on the Sikh Golden Temple of Amritsar in 1984 killed many innocent religious Sikh pilgrims as well as dissidents.

Ghandi, Rajiv: A suicide squad of Tamil nationalists from Sri Lanka assassinated Ghandi in 1991. He was targeted for death because of the assistance that India gave to the Sri Lankan government in its fight with Tamil dissidents.

Girondins: This term was applied to members of the national legislature in revolutionary France who were relatively moderate. More radical groups in the political infighting displaced them in the early years of the French Revolution.

Gracchi brothers: These brothers attempted to introduce reforms favoring the lower nobility in the Roman Republic. They were both assassinated on separate occasions by the supporters of the status quo (and the upper classes).

Gush Emunim: This group represents many of the settlers living in the West Bank territories of Judea and Samaria. It has demanded the incorporation of a maximum amount of territory on the West Bank or all of it into the state of Israel. Gush Emunim has been involved in a variety of violent activities and has supported extreme views for the future of the Occupied Territories and the Palestinians.

Guzman, Abimael: Guzman was the founder and leader of the Shining Path guerrilla movement until his capture by the Peruvian security forces.

Hamas (Islamic Resistance Movement): This organization is based in the Occupied Territories of Israel, and opposes the existence of the state of Israel. It seeks instead to create an Islamic state in the area of Israel/Palestine. It has been responsible for many of the suicide attacks in Israel.

Hinduvata: This term refers to the idea that basic tenets of Hinduism should become enshrined in the legal system of India.

Hitler, Adolf: Hitler was the leader of Germany from 1933 to 1945. His Nazi party and allied organizations used violence and terror to help win elections. The Nazi party under Hitler's leadership was also responsible for the Holocaust.

Hizballah: This Lebanese organization represents the Shia population of the country. It has received significant support from Iran and Syria and has engaged in at least some terrorist actions.

Hussein, Saddam: Hussein is the former dictator of Iraq who was in power at the time of both the Iraqi invasion of Iran and the subsequent invasion of Kuwait. He was displaced from power in the US invasion of Iraq in 2003.

Hutu (Bahutu): The Hutu comprises the majority of the population of both Rwanda and Burundi. The political elite before independence in both countries was overwhelmingly comprised of members of the Tutsi community. Communal violence between the two groups was particularly pronounced in the 1990s in Rwanda.

Ibos: The Ibos was the dominant ethnic group in eastern Nigeria that attempted to set up the independent state of Biafra.

Impuza Mugambi: This Hutu paramilitary militia was one of the groups heavily involved in the genocide in Rwanda in the 1990s.

Interahamwe: This Hutu paramilitary group was associated with the radical wing of the ruling party in Rwanda. It was the largest paramilitary group and very active in the genocide against the Tutsi minority.

intifada: This is the Arabic term for the uprising in the West Bank and the Gaza Strip to protest against continuing Israeli military administration. It literally means "shaking off," including the idea of shaking off Israeli rule. The activities of the Palestinians in this uprising were locally directed, even though the Palestinian population in the two areas still looked to the PLO for leadership.

Irian Jaya (Western Papua): This Indonesian province occupies the western half of the island of New Guinea. Its population is ethnically quite distinct from the other groups in Indonesia.

Irish National Liberation Army (INLA): The INLA was a dissident group in Northern Ireland, seeking to end British rule by the use of violence. It was much smaller and had a much stronger Marxist-Leninist orientation than the Provisional IRA.

Irish Republican Army (IRA): The IRA was formed in the early 1900s to contest British rule of Ireland. After the Irish Free State was formed, the IRA eventually went into decline. It resurfaced in the 1960s in Northern Ireland. It has since split a number of times. Currently, the term is normally used interchangeably with the Provisional wing of the IRA.

Islamic Army Group (GIA): The GIA is one of the larger and most violent of the dissident organizations in Algeria that draws upon more fundamentalist Muslims for support.

Islamic Jihad (Palestine): This dissident group is opposed to the Israeli state and occupation of Palestine on both nationalist and religious grounds. It has sought to undercut various peace agreements between Israel and the PLO.

Islamic Movement Army (MIA): The MIA is one of the larger organizations composed of Muslim dissidents in Algeria. It has more connections with the Islamic Salvation Front than some of the other rebel groups.

Islamic Salvation Front (FIS): The Front was an electoral organization of Muslim groups that sought to bring about political reform in Algeria. The group also supported more reliance on Islamic tenets in the national law. Its initial success in the electoral process in Algeria resulted in the canceling of further elections and the eventual banning of the FIS.

Jacobin Clubs: These clubs attracted some of the more radical elements involved in the French Revolution. The Jacobins supported more radical policies, including the death of the king and other potential counter-revolutionaries.

Jammu and Kashmir: This Indian state has a Muslim majority but became part of India in 1948. It has been the scene of guerrilla fighting and terrorism at high or low levels of intensity for over half a century.

Janatha Vimukthi Peramuna (JVP): This leftist party in Sri Lanka launched attempts to take over the government in 1971 and 1987. It was defeated both times.

Japanese Red Army: Young Japanese leftists formed this group. It never became very effective within Japan itself, but it engaged in a number of actions outside of Japan, often in collaboration with other leftist or nationalist groups.

jihad: This Arabic word translates with a number of meanings. Its most literal meaning is "striving", but it also has had the connotation of "holy war." Extreme Muslim groups tend to use it in the sense of holy war as an indication of their willingness to use violence, including acts of terror, to achieve their goals.

Judea and Samaria: Some Israelis refer to the West Bank occupied after the Israeli victory in the Six Day War in 1967 as Judea and Samaria to indicate the historical and biblical significance of the area.

June 2nd Movement: This group was one of the successors to the Baader-Meinhof Gang.

Justice Commandos of the Armenian Genocide (JCAG): This Armenian dissident groups used terrorist attacks in an effort to get the Turkish government to acknowledge the genocide committed by the Turks against the Armenians in the waning years of the Ottoman Empire.

Kahane, Meir: This American Rabbi espoused an extreme version of Jewish nationalism, arguing that all Arab inhabitants of Israel and the Occupied Territories should be expelled. He also argued that virtually any violent actions against Palestinians were justified.

KGB: The KGB was the intelligence agency for the Soviet Union. It engaged in a variety of foreign espionage activities, including support for various kinds of dissident groups in the West.

Khalistan: This name is used for the independent Sikh homeland sought by terrorist groups in the Punjab.

Khomeini, Ayatollah: Khomeini was the religious leader who came to head the opposition to the Shah of Iran. His activities were instrumental in leading to the overthrow of the Shah, and he became the effective leader of the Islamic Republic of Iran until his death in 1989.

Kikuyu: The Kikuyu is the dominant ethnic group that resides near the Kenyan capital of Nairobi. It was also the major source of the recruits for the Mau Mau rebellion in that British colony in the 1950s.

kneecapping: This term applies to the practice utilized by the Red Brigades in Italy of approaching targets and shooting them in the knees or legs as punishment for their participation in the capitalist system or government. Wounding the victims demonstrated their vulnerability and the inability of the state to protect them more clearly than assassination.

Kosovo: Kosovo is a province in Serbia largely populated by Albanians. It has been a scene of tension between Serbs and Albanians.

Kosovo Liberation Army (KLA): The KLA was formed to fight against Serbian oppression in the province of Kosovo. It proved especially effective in generating violent responses from the Serbian police and military.

Ku Klux Klan (KKK): The KKK was first formed just after the Civil War in the United States to further the rights of former Confederate soldiers and officials who were disenfranchised. The KKK attempted (successfully) to intimidate former slaves in the south. With the advent of reconstruction and the dominance of white southerners, the KKK became less prominent. It reappeared in the 1920s in the south and elsewhere in the United States. It was anti-black, anti-Jewish, anti-Catholic, and anti-immigrant. The KKK was responsible for attacks against black Americans and occasionally members of other groups in this period. It has continued to be involved in violence against groups it opposes.

Kurdish Workers' Party (PKK): This group has carried a long campaign against Turkish chauvinism in the Kurdish areas of Turkey. It has combined Marxist-Leninist ideology with Kurdish nationalism in its appeals to ethnic Kurds.

Kurds: The Kurds are a non-Arabic people residing in areas of Turkey, Iraq, Syria, and Iran. They have sought an independent homeland since the end of World War I. Kurdish groups in Iraq, Iran, and Turkey have fought against their respective governments at various times, and independence movements or groups seeking greater autonomy have engaged in terrorist activities at times in all three of these countries.

bin Laden, Osama: This Saudi Arabian millionaire has led and financed a group of Muslims dedicated to expelling Western influence from the areas where Islam is the dominant religion. Bin Laden's supporters were responsible for the devastating attacks on New York and Washington DC on September 11, 2001.

Laskar Jihad: This Muslim group formed in Indonesia to support Muslims in their disputes and battles in those areas of the country where there are significant Christian populations.

leaderless resistance: Dissident groups that use violence, especially many groups in the extreme right in the United States, have adopted this organizational approach. The activists undertaking the violence do not have hierarchical links with the leaders. The leadership provides general guidelines and directions, but the persons involved in the violence choose the time and targets on their own.

left-wing ideologies: Ideologies of the left stress greater equality among different classes and less reliance on the free market to distribute resources.

Lenin, Vladimir: Lenin was the organizer of the successful Bolshevik takeover in Russia in 1917. His writings formed a key component of the Marxist-Leninist theory that forms the background of communist theories.

Liberation Tigers of Tamil Eelam (LTTE): This dissident group has conducted a guerrilla and terrorist campaign to create an independent Tamil state on Sri Lanka for over twenty years. Its members are more commonly known as Tamil Tigers.

Macedonia: This region was the southernmost part of the unified Yugoslavia, and is now the independent country of Macedonia. The traditional region of Macedonia included territory in present day Bulgaria and Greece.

McVeigh, Timothy: McVeigh was arrested, convicted, and executed for setting off the bomb in Oklahoma City that destroyed the Murrah Office Building in 1995.

Mao Tse-tung (Mao Zedong): Mao was the leader of the Communist Party in China before, during, and after World War II. He successfully organized the party in the countryside and used peasant support to eventually overthrow the government. Maoist theories of communism, as a consequence, frequently stress victory in the countryside as the means of acquiring power.

Marx, Karl: Marx is clearly the father of most strands of modern leftist theories. His writings from the nineteenth century have been modified and interpreted in many different ways to explain the diversity of latter-day left-wing ideologies.

Mau Mau: This term is applied to the Africans in Kenya who engaged in a rebellion against continued British rule and domination by white settlers in the 1950s.

Medellin cartel: This Colombian drug organization attempted to force the Colombian government to stop interfering with the drug trade by launching a terrorist campaign against the government in the 1980s. The cartel was defeated in this effort, but other drug producers have remained important in the country.

Milosevic, Slobodan: Milosevic was the ruler of Serbia when Yugoslavia fell apart. He adopted an extremely nationalistic posture for his government. He is currently on trial for his support of ethnic cleansing and genocide in other parts of the formerly unified country.

Minnesota Patriots Council: This right-wing group has opposed a strong central government and any restrictions on the right to own guns. The group was stockpiling ricin to poison national and state officials. It was exposed in 1995 before it could take action and most of its members were convicted and sent to prison.

Montagnards: This term, meaning the mountains, was applied to the most radical elements present in Revolutionary France. Leaders from this faction were responsible for much of the violence associated with the Reign of Terror.

Montoneros: The Montoneros was the largest leftist group that appeared in Argentina in the 1970s. It helped restore Juan Perón to power, but were destroyed by the military regime that eventually took power after Perón's death.

Moro, Aldo: Moro was a former Italian prime minister and leader of the Christian Democratic Party. He was kidnapped by the Red Brigades in a spectacular terrorist action and was later executed by members of the group.

Mountbatten, Lord: Mountbatten rose to high rank in the British military during World War II and was a member of the royal family. His assassination by the IRA while on vacation in the Republic of Ireland was one of the spectacular actions undertaken by this dissident organization.

Mugabe, Robert: Mugabe has been the President of Zimbabwe since the country gained its independence in 1980. He has rigged elections, most recently in 2002, and refuses to give up power. His supporters have used a variety of violent techniques to intimidate the opposition.

Mujahedin-e-Khalq (MKO): This group was composed of secular and leftist opponents of the Shah of Iran who were eased out of any share of political power by the clerics supporting Ayatollah Khomeini. They launched a number of successful terrorist actions against the regime before being decimated by countermeasures.

Munich Olympics (1972): Black September group seized Israeli athletes and coaches at the Olympic village in Munich to publicize the Palestinian cause. The terrorists and their hostages were all killed in a failed rescue attempted by West German police.

Murrah Federal Office Building: This building in Oklahoma City was the target for Timothy McVeigh in 1995. The blast killed 168 people and wounded hundreds.

Mussolini, Benito: Mussolini was the fascist dictator of Italy from 1922 to 1943. The fascists used street violence against leftists to position themselves for support from conservative groups in Italy and to eventually take power.

narcoterrorism: This term has been applied to the idea that a Soviet-led group of drug organizations was part of an effort to weaken the West. It has also been used to refer to cooperation among drug producers and dissident organizations.

National Liberation Army (ELN): This dissident group was formed in Colombia by leftist groups. It operated in the urban areas rather than rural locales.

National Liberation Army (NLA): The NLA was the term for the military units formed by Iranians opposed to the Islamic Republic. These units fought alongside the Iraqis in the war with Iran.

National Socialist Democratic Workers Party (NSDAP): This party, usually referred to as the Nazi Party, was led by Adolf Hitler both before he came to power and when he ruled in Germany.

Nichols, Terry: Nichols was Timothy McVeigh's accomplice in the bombing of the Murrah Federal Office Building in Oklahoma City.

Nivelles Group: This name was given to the terrorist group in Belgium in the 1980s that robbed banks and stores and was prone to inflicting casualties on the general public. The group gave the appearance of being a left-wing dissident group using terror, but it was generally thought to be a group on the extreme right seeking to make the left look bad.

NKVD: The NKVD was the official designation of the Soviet secret police when Stalin was in power. Its name was changed to the KGB, but the agency was not changed under the new title.

Noraid: This charity organization in the United States has collected funds for aid to persons in Northern Ireland. Much of the funding has apparently been used to support the IRA.

Ocalan, Abdullah: Ocalan was the long-time leader of the Kurdish Workers Party battling against the government of Turkey.

Occupied Territories: This term refers to the Gaza Strip and those areas of the West Bank that have not been incorporated within the boundaries of Israel. These territories have often been administered by the military with frequent reliance on martial law.

Official IRA: With the outbreak of violence in Northern Ireland in 1969, the leadership of the IRA followed a Marxist-Leninist line that argued against the use of terrorism. The Officials became relatively insignificant when the Provos began the campaign of violence against continued British rule.

Operation Black Thunder: This military action against Sikh dissidents in the Golden Temple of Amritsar in 1988 was undertaken with great care to limit casualties among innocent civilians and to minimize damage to the temple grounds.

Operation Blue Star: This code name was used for the attack on the Golden Temple of Amritsar in 1984. Hundreds of innocent pilgrims were killed in the attack, and the temple itself was damaged.

Order, the: This far right group operated for eighteen months in the Pacific Northwest. It began to rob banks in 1983 and even robbed an armored truck. Local police broke the organization, but most of the money taken in the robberies has never been recovered.

Palestinian Authority: This is the name given to the administrative agency headed by Yassir Arafat in the West Bank and Gaza Strip. The authority has had limited autonomy over those areas of the Occupied Territories where Israel has relinquished its responsibility for direct administration.

Palestinian Liberation Organization (PLO): This organization has long represented the interests of the Palestinians in territories administered by Israel and in other countries. The PLO itself is an umbrella organization that is made of many different Palestinian groups. The PLO served as the basic unit for creating the Palestinian Authority in portions of the West Bank and Gaza Strip.

Pavelich, Ante: Pavelich was the leader of the Utashe, the Croatian fascist party that cooperated with Italy and Germany during World War II.

People's Revolutionary Army (ERP): The ERP was one of the leftist groups in Argentina that was opposed to the various military governments in power. There were under attack by the government of Juan Perón and then Isabel Perón and then destroyed by the military government that came into power in 1976.

Perón, Isabel: Isabel was the wife of Juan Perón when he returned to power in Argentina in the 1970s. She served as his vice-president and assumed office when he died. She proved to be an ineffective political leader.

Perón, Juan: Juan Perón was the ruler of Argentina in the 1940s and 1950s until overthrown. He became the focus of much of the opposition to governments in Argentina in ensuing years. Perón returned in triumph in 1973 and became president, but he died in 1974.

Pierce, William: Pierce wrote *The Turner Diaries* (1980), which he regarded as a blueprint for overthrowing the government of the United States. Many members of right-wing groups regarded Pierce, who died in 2002, as the leading ideologue for their groups.

Popular Front for the Liberation of Palestine (PFLP): This Palestinian nationalist group was formed by George Habash, a Greek Orthodox Arab. The organization's views incorporated a clearly leftist ideology and have long favored greater efforts to link the struggle of the Palestinians to class conflict.

Popular Front for the Liberation of Palestine-General Command (PFLP-GC): This Palestinian organization was an splinter group from the Popular Front for the Liberation of Palestine, and it has continued to espouse terrorism after the PLO modified its stance towards global attacks.

Popular Liberation Army (EPL): This organization was one of the smaller leftist dissident groups that have operated in Colombia.

Posse Comitatus: This right-wing tax resister group in the United States believes that almost all government as currently set up is unconstitutional. They regard the county sheriff as the highest official to obey, and only if he or she is making the right decisions.

propaganda of the deed: Anarchists originated this term to describe violent attacks that were designed to educate the general public to the repressive nature of the governments in power. The demonstration of opposition by individuals was intended to inspire popular insurrections.

propaganda of the word: Anarchists considered educational activities to be propaganda of the word. Some anarchists believed that educational efforts would be sufficient to mobilize the public to oppose governments in power.

Provisional IRA: The Provisionals (Provos) have been synonymous with the use of the term IRA since the 1970s. They have formed the core of those opposed to continued British control of Northern Ireland.

"Punjab" solution: This term has been used to refer to the activities of death squads and extra-legal executions of dissidents and guerrillas in a variety of areas of India. The term derives from the use of such squads in the Punjab during the fighting with the Sikh dissidents.

Qaeda, al: This network is comprised of loosely organized extremist Muslim groups from various countries. It was created by Osama bin Laden.

Quebec Liberation Front (FLQ): This separatist group wanted to create an independent Quebec nation and drew support from French-speaking inhabitants of the province. It was active in the 1960s and early 1970s.

Rabin, Yitzak: Rabin was the prime minister of Israel assassinated by an Israeli Jew in 1995 for compromising with the Palestinians.

Rashtriya Swayamsevak Sangh (National Patriotism Organization): This group was formed in the 1920s in India to protect Hindu culture against outside influences. In more recent times the group has practiced violence against non-Hindu groups in India.

Real IRA: This name has been adopted by a group of IRA members opposed to the peace initiatives between the IRA and the British government.

Red Army Faction (RAF): The official name of the Baader-Meinhof Gang was the Red Army Faction, representing the leftist ideology of the members.

Red Brigades: The Red Brigades was the most important left-wing dissident group using terrorism in Italy in the 1960s, 1970s, and 1980s. The death toll attributed to the Red Brigades totaled thousands. The group was eventually defeated only after the Italian police upgraded their capabilities and after captured members were offered reduced sentences for informing on their fellow members.

Red Cells: This organization was one of the successor groups to the Baader-Meinhof Gang in Germany.

Reign of Terror: This term refers to a period of the early years of the French Revolution when radicals gained control of the revolutionary government and used terror to control the population. Tens of thousands went to their deaths in Paris and elsewhere in the country, often by facing the guillotine.

Rejectionist Front: This term was used for a group of Palestinian nationalist organizations that were opposed to PLO negotiations with Israel. They choose to continue the struggle against Israel and to continue to use terrorism.

Revolutionary Armed Forces of Colombia (FARC): This leftist group has provided long-lasting opposition to the government in Colombia. Its alliance with drug producers has given it the financial resources to arm itself and to battle with the government for control of rural areas.

Revolutionary Guards: This group of supporters of the Islamic Republic in Iran were formed to defend the regime and to deal with dissidents. The Guards have also provided personnel to staff terrorist training camps in Iran, Lebanon, and the Sudan.

ricin: This poison is made without too much difficulty from castor beans. Extreme right-wing groups in the United States have shown a great deal of interest in this particular poison.

Ruby Ridge: Ruby Ridge was the home of Randy Weaver, who failed to appear in federal court to face a weapons charge. Mishandling by the local federal officials resulted in the death of Weaver's wife and a federal officer in 1992. The mishandling of the whole situation provided right-wing groups with proof that the federal government was out to disarm individuals and was serving as a front for foreign interests.

Sandinistas: The opponents of the Somoza regime in Nicaragua took this name from an opponent of an earlier government in Nicaragua. They were successful in ousting Somoza and his supporters from power.

sarin: Aum Shinrikyo used this nerve gas in its efforts to cause mass casualties in the Japanese subway system in 1994.

Schutzstaffel (SS): The SS was originally formed to provide a personal bodyguard to Hitler as the leader of the Nazi party. The SS provided the core of the personnel who operated the death camps during World War II.

Self Defense Forces of Colombia (AUC): This paramilitary group appeared to battle with leftist forces in Colombia. It has generally supported the government, but its tactics have included efforts to terrorize presumed supporters of the leftist dissidents.

17 November Organization: This left-wing Greek dissident organization has been one of the most successful in avoiding any infiltration or exposure by official agencies. After almost 30 years of activity the Greek authorities finally captured members of the group.

Shariat: The guidelines and the directives of the Qur'an and the early life of the Prophet Muhammad form the Shariat and provide the basis for an Islamic legal system.

Shia (or Shi'a): This is a breakaway branch of Islam. Clerical leaders have somewhat greater weight in this version of Islam, which is practiced by most of the inhabitants of Iran. There are also significant Shia populations in Lebanon and Iraq.

Shining Path (Sendero Luminoso): This leftist group in Peru mounted a major challenge to the government, in large measure because it could draw upon Indian dissatisfaction with inadequate government policies that had failed to do much for them.

Sicarri: These Jewish daggermen attacked supporters of Rome in Judea or those who were opposed to the idea of revolt in order to force consensus within the Jewish community in favor of the upcoming revolt.

Sikhs: Sikhs are followers of this Indian religion, which has some similarities to Hinduism, but it generally is considered to be a separate religion.

skinheads: These groups of undereducated youths with limited job prospects have often joined in attacks against immigrant and foreign communities in Europe. Although they do not usually belong to right-wing organizations, they frequently provide personnel for attacks undertaken by these right-wing groups.

Somoza, Anastacio: Somoza was the former dictator of Nicaragua who was overthrown by a popular uprising led by the Sandinistas. He was assassinated in exile in Paraguay—apparently by Argentine leftists.

Special Air Services Regiment (SAS): This elite British military has been used in special operations to combat terrorists. Its rigorous training has meant that it has often been very successful in these efforts.

Stern Gang: This organization was composed of Jewish inhabitants of British Palestine. They used terrorism against both the British and the Arab inhabitants as part of their campaign to force the British to withdraw so that an independent Jewish state could be created.

Students for a Democratic Society (SDS): This student group formed in the 1960s in the United States to oppose the US involvement in the war in Vietnam. The students also used leftist ideology to attack capitalism and government practices. Members of the movement in small numbers did go on to engage in terrorist actions, but mostly limited themselves to symbolic property attacks.

Sturmabteilungen (SA): The SA, or stormtroopers, provided the Nazi Party in Germany with street fighters to attempt to intimidate the opposition and to protect Nazi Party rallies. The group was organizationally independent of the party, but Adolf Hitler was leader of the SA as well as the party. When the Nazis came to power, the SA was disbanded.

Suharto, General: General Suharto was the long-time ruler of Indonesia who came to power through a coup in the 1960s. His resignation of the presidency and the return of at least partially democratic rule to Indonesia have been accompanied by communal violence between Muslims and Christians, ethnic fighting, and separatist movements in various parts of the nation.

Sunni: This is the orthodox version of Islam. The vast majority of Muslims in the world consider themselves to be Sunni.

suspect community: A group in the population becomes a suspect community when government officials or the rest of the population fears that any member is involved in terrorist actions and needs to be watched carefully.

Symbionese Liberation Army (SLA): The SLA was one of the more violent leftist groups that appeared out of the anti-war movement in the United States. It operated for a few years in California and is probably best known for the kidnapping of Patty Hearst.

Taliban: This group of Islamic fundamentalists has provided the leadership for most of Afghanistan after the withdrawal of Soviet troops. The Taliban leadership also provided a safe haven for Osama bin Laden and many of his operatives and supporters.

Tamil Nadu: This Indian state is near Sri Lanka, and it is populated by India's Tamil minority.

Tamil Tigers: This name is the one normally used by the members of the Liberation Tigers of Tamil Eelam who support the idea of independent Tamil state in Sri Lanka.

terrorism: Terrorism involves political aims and motives. It is violent or threatens violence. It is designed to generate fear in a target audience that extends beyond the immediate victims of the violence. The violence is conducted by an identifiable organization. The violence involves a non-state actor or actors as either the perpetrator, the victim of the violence, or both. Finally, the acts of violence are designed to create power in situations in which power previously had been lacking (i.e. the violence attempts to enhance the power base of the organization undertaking the actions).

Trotsky, Leon: Trotsky was one of the leaders of the Bolshevik Revolution in Russia. He was a rival of Stalin and was eventually forced to leave the country. Trotskyite versions of communism place greater stress on participation by the rank and file of the party.

Tupac Amaru Revolutionary Movement (MRTA): This leftist movement in Peru was never as strong as Shining Path. It was largely eliminated as a threat to the government, but it was responsible for the takeover of the Japanese embassy during a Christmas celebration in 1996.

Tupamaros: The Tupamaros were a left-wing group in Uruguay opposed to the government in power. The Tupamaros attracted students from middle class and upper middle class families.

Turner Diaries, The: This book, written by William Pierce (and published in 1980), outlines a plan of action for its fictional hero to use in resisting a dictatorial government in the United States. The book also calls for returning the country to its basic, democratic roots by defeating the Jewish and foreign groups that have conspired to destroy the country.

Tutsi (Watutsi): The political elite before independence in Rwanda and Burundi was overwhelmingly comprised of members of the Tutsi, who had formed the ruling class before the arrival of the Europeans. The Hutu comprise the majority of the population of both Rwanda and Burundi. Communal violence between the two groups was particularly pronounced in the 1990s.

Unabomber: This name was given to the unknown individual who sent bombs to various individuals over ten years as part of a protest against modernization in the world. Theodore Kaczynski was finally identified as the Unabomber and caught.

USS Cole: This American destroyer was attacked in the harbor at Aden in Yemen. Two terrorists used a motorboat filled with explosives in a suicide attack that killed more than thirty crewmembers on the ship.

Utashe: This party contained the more extreme nationalist and fascist elements in the Croatian state created in 1941. Under the leadership of Ante Pavelich, the Croatian fascists attacked Jews, Gypsies, and Serbs. The victims numbered in the hundreds of thousands.

Vendée: The Vendée is a French region bordering on the Bay of Biscay north of Bordeaux. It is also the name given to a counterrevolutionary uprising that was opposed to the republic established by the French Revolution. The peasants in the uprising were fighting to restore the monarchy and the Catholic Church to their previous positions.

Violencia, La: This term is applied to the violence between political factions in the late 1940s in Colombia.

weapons of mass destruction: These weapons are ones that are designed to cause massive causalities among target populations. Some biological weapons, chemical weapons, and nuclear devices are considered weapons of mass destruction.

weapons of mass disruption: These weapons are designed to disrupt the target society when used by terrorists or a state. Such weapons might disable communications networks or disrupt important computer systems. Such weapons would not necessarily directly cause major casualties in the target society.

Weathermen: This group was a radical offshoot of the Students for a Democratic Society. Protests against the war in Vietnam and capitalism in general led the group to adopt violent methods. The violence was largely restricted to attacks on property in efforts to change government policies.

Will of the People: This Russian anarchist group sought to inspire a popular rebellion by a campaign of assassinations against key officials and leaders, especially the Tsar. The group did manage to assassinate key figures, including Tsar Alexander II.

Zealots: This group of Jewish patriots in the Roman Empire instigated a revolt in 66 CE that was temporarily successful in liberating Judea from Roman rule.

Zhirinovsky, Vladimir: Zhirinovsky was the leader of the Liberal Democrats in Russia after the dissolution of the Soviet Union. The Liberal Democrats have been an extremely nationalistic party that had similarities to the fascist parties that appeared in Europe prior to World War II.

Zimbabwean African National Union (ZANU): ZANU was one of the major groups involved in the guerrilla struggle in Rhodesia. It is the party of President Mugabe, and has been in power since Zimbabwe gained its independence.

Zimbabwean African People's Union (ZAPU): ZAPU was the second largest group involved in the independence struggle in Rhodesia. The ruling party eventually banned this party once Rhodesia became independent as Zimbabwe.

Zionist: This term is applied to Jewish nationalists who have desired the creation of a Jewish Homeland in Palestine (the land of Zion).

Zionist Occupation Government (ZOG): This term is used by extreme right-wing groups in the United States (and by some groups in Europe as well) to refer to the belief that Jewish financial interests control the government.

Bibliography

Abuza, Z. (2002) "Tentacles of Terror: Al Qaeda's Southeast Asian Network," *Contemporary Southeast Asia: A Journal of International and Strategic Affairs*, 24, 3: 427–65.

Ajami, F. (2001) "The Sentry's Solitude," *Foreign Affairs*, 80, 6: 2–16.

Alapuro, R. and Allardt, E. (1978) "The Lapua Movement: The Threat of Rightist Takeover in Finland," in J. J. Linz and Alfred Stephan (eds) *The Breakdown of Democratic Regimes: Europe*, Baltimore, MD: Johns Hopkins University Press, 122–41.

Albin, C. (1989) "The Politics of Terrorism: A Contemporary Survey," in B. Rubin (ed.) *The Politics of Terrorism: Terror as a State and Revolutionary Strategy*, Washington, DC: Foreign Policy Institute, 183–234.

Alexander, Y. and Swetnam, M. S. (2001) *Usama bin Laden's al-Qaida: Profile of a Terrorist Network*, Ardsley, NY: Transnational Publishers.

Alonso, R. (2001) "The Modernization in Irish Republican Thinking toward the Utility of Violence," *Studies in Conflict and Terrorism*, 24, 2: 131–44.

Anderson, C. J. (1996) "Economics, Politics, and Foreigners: Populist Party Support in Denmark and Norway," *Electoral Studies*, 15, 4: 497–511.

Anderson, J. H. (1995) "The Neo-Nazi Menace in Germany," *Studies in Conflict and Terrorism*, 18, 1: 39–46.

Anderson, R. P. (1997) "Terrorism and Revolution in Iran," in M. Crenshaw and J. Pimlott (eds) *Encyclopedia of World Terrorism*, Vol. 2, Armonk, NY: M. E. Sharpe, 385–91.

Andriolo, K. (2002) "Murder by Suicide: Episodes from Muslim History," *American Anthropologist*, 104, 3: 736–42.

Angel, R. C. (1990) "Japanese Terrorists and Japanese Countermeasures," in B. Rubin (ed.) *The Politics of Counterterrorism: The Ordeal of Democratic States*, Washington, DC: Foreign Policy Institute, 31–60.

Applebaum, S. (1971) "The Zealots: The Case for Revaluation," *Journal of Roman Studies*, 61: 155–70.

Arian, A. (1998) *The Second Republic: Politics in Israel*, Chatham, NJ: Chatham House.

Arnson, C. J. (2000) "Window on the Past: A Declassified History of Death Squads in El Salvador," in B. D. Campbell and A. D. Brenner (eds) *Death Squads in Global Perspective: Murder with Deniability*, New York: St. Martin's, 85–124.

Ash, T. G. (2003) "Is There a Good Terrorist?" in C. W. Kegley, Jr (ed.) *The New Global Terrorism: Characteristics, Causes, Controls*, Upper Saddle River, NJ: Prentice Hall, 60–70.

Austin, D. and Gupta, A. (1990) *The Politics of Violence in India and South Asia: Is Democracy an Endangered Species?* Conflict Studies 233, London: Research Institute for the Study of Conflict and Terrorism.

Auten, B. (1996) "Tajikistan Today," *Studies in Conflict and Terrorism*, 19, 2: 199–212.

Baczko, B. (1994) "The Terror before the Terror? Conditions of Possibility, Logic of Realization," in

K. M. Baker (ed.) *The French Revolution and the Creation of Modern Political Culture: Volume 4, The Terror*, Oxford: Pergamon, 19–38.

Badey, T. J. (1998) "Defining International Terrorism: A Pragmatic Approach," *Terrorism and Political Violence*, 10, 1: 90–107.

Bahgat, G. (1999) "Iran and Terrorism: The Transatlantic Response," *Studies in Conflict and Terrorism*, 22, 2: 141–52.

Bale, J. M. (1996) "The May 1973 Terrorist Attack at Milan Police HQ: Anarchist 'Propaganda of the Deed' or 'False-Flag' Provocation," *Terrorism and Political Violence*, 8, 1: 132–66.

Banac, I. (1984) *The National Question in Yugoslavia: Origins, History, Politics*, Ithaca, NY: Cornell University Press.

Barker, T. (1997) "Islamic Fundamentalism and Terrorism in Algeria," in M. Crenshaw and J. Pimlott (eds) *Encyclopedia of World Terrorism*, Vol. 2, Armonk, NY: M. E. Sharpe, 410–14.

Barkey, H. (1996) "Turkey, Islamic Politics, and the Kurdish Question," *World Policy*, 13, 1: 43–52.

Barkun, M. (2000) (1996) "Religion, Militias and Oklahoma City: The Mind of Conspiratorialists," *Terrorism and Political Violence*, 8, 1: 50–64.

—— "Violence in the Name of Democracy: Justifications for Separatism on the Radical Right," *Political Violence and Terrorism*, 12, 3/4: 193–208.

Barnhurst, K. G. (1991) "Contemporary Terrorism in Peru: Sendero Luminoso and the Media," *Journal of Communication*, 41, 4: 75–89.

Barry, D., Vergara, R., and Castro, J. R. (1988) "'Low Intensity Warfare': The Counterinsurgency Strategy for Central America," in N. Hamilton, J. A. Frieden, L. Fuller, and M. Pastor, Jr (eds) *Crisis in Central America: Regional Dynamics and U.S. Policy in the 1980s*, Boulder, CO: Westview, 77–96.

Behrooz, M. (2000) *Rebels with a Cause: The Failure of the Left in Iran*, London: I. B. Tauris.

Bell, J. B. (1975) *Transnational Terror*, Washington, DC: American Enterprise Institute.

—— (1997a) *The Secret Army: The IRA*, revised 3rd edn, New Brunswick, NJ: Transaction Books.

—— (1997b) "Terrorist Fundraising," in M. Crenshaw and J. Pimlott (eds) *Encyclopedia of World Terrorism*, Vol. 1, Armonk, NY: M. E. Sharpe, 239–40.

Bell-Fialkoff, A. (1999) *Ethnic Cleansing*, New York: St. Martin's Griffin.

Benard, C. and Khalilzad, Z. (1984) *"The Government of God": Iran's Islamic Republic*, New York: Columbia University Press.

Berend, I. T. (1998) *Decades of Crisis: Central and Eastern Europe before World War II*, Berkeley, CA: University of California Press.

Berkowitz, B. (2002) "Intelligence and the War on Terrorism," *Orbis*, 46, 2: 289–300.

Bessant, J. (1995) "Political Crime and the Case of Young Neo-Nazis: A Question of Methodology," *Terrorism and Political Violence*, 7, 4: 94–116.

Bessel, R. (1986) "Violence as Propaganda: The Role of the Storm Troopers in the Rise of National Socialism," in T. Childers (ed.) *The Formation of the Nazi Constituency, 1919–1933*, Totowa, NJ: Barnes & Noble, 131–46.

Betts, R. K. (2003) "Suicide from Fear of Death?" *Foreign Affairs*, 82, 1: 34–43.

—— (2002) "Fixing Intelligence," *Foreign Affairs*, 81, 1: 43–59.

Betz, H.-G. (1994) *Radical Right-Wing Populism in Western Europe*, New York: St. Martin's.

Bill, J. A. and Leiden, C. (1984) *Politics in the Middle East*, 2nd edn, Boston: Little Brown.

Bjorgo, T. (1993) "Militant Neo-Nazism in Sweden," *Terrorism and Political Violence*, 5, 3: 28–57.

—— (1995a) "Extreme Nationalism and Violent Discourses in Scandinavia: 'The Resistance', 'Traitors', and 'Foreign Invaders'," in T. Bjorgo (ed.) *Terror from the Extreme Right*, London: Frank Cass, 182–220.

—— (1995b) "Introduction," in T. Bjorgo (ed.) *Terror from the Extreme Right*, London: Frank Cass, 1–16.

—— (1997) *Racist and Right-Wing Violence in Scandinavia: Patterns, Perpetrators, and Responses*, Oslo: Tano Aschehoug.

Blackburn, R. (2002) "The Imperial Presidency, the War on Terrorism, and the Revolution of Modernity," *Constellations: An International Journal of Critical and Democratic Theory*, 9, 1: 3–33.

Bobrick, B. (1997) *Angel in the Whirlwind: The Triumph of the American Revolution*, New York: Simon and Schuster.

Boroumand, L. and Boroumand, R. (2002) "Terror, Islam, and Democracy," *Journal of Democracy*, 13, 2: 5–20.

Bouchat, C. J. (1996) "A Fundamentalist Islamic Threat to the West," *Studies in Conflict and Terrorism*, 19, 4: 339–52.

Bray, J. (1986) "Asia," in R. Clutterbuck (ed.) *The Future of Political Violence: Destabilization, Disorder and Terrorism*, New York: St. Martin's Press, 133–42.

Brenner, A. D. (2000) "*Feme* Murder: Paramilitary 'Self-Justice' in Weimar Germany," in B. D. Campbell and A. D. Brenner (eds) *Death Squads in Global Perspective: Murder with Deniability*, New York: St. Martin's, 57–83.

Brown, A. (1997) "Terrorism in Turkey," in M. Crenshaw and J. Pimlott (eds) *Encyclopedia of World Terrorism*, Vol. 3, Armonk, NY: M. E. Sharpe, 591–2.

Brownfield, A. C. (2000) "Jewish/Zionist Terrorism: A Continuing Threat to Peace," *Global Dialogue*, 2, 4: 107–17.

Bucheim, H. (1972) "The Position of the SS in the Third Reich," in H. Holborn (ed.) *Republic to Reich: The Making of the Nazi Revolution, Ten Essays*, New York: Pantheon Books, 251–97.

Bunker, R. J. (2000) "Weapons of Mass Disruption," *Terrorism and Political Violence*, 12, 1: 37–46.

Byman, D. (1998) "The Logic of Ethnic Terrorism," *Studies in Conflict and Terrorism*, 21, 2: 149–69.

Calvert, P. (1997a) "Argentine Government's Responses to Terrorism," in M. Crenshaw and J. Pimlott (eds) *Encyclopedia of World Terrorism*, Vol. 3, Armonk, NY: M. E. Sharpe, 629–31.

—— (1997b) "Terrorism in Argentina," in M. Crenshaw and J. Pimlott (eds) *Encyclopedia of World Terrorism*, Vol. 2, Armonk, NY: M. E. Sharpe, 417–21.

—— (1997c) "Terrorism in El Salvador," in M. Crenshaw and J. Pimlott (eds) *Encyclopedia of World Terrorism*, Vol. 2, Armonk, NY: M. E. Sharpe, 434–5.

—— (1997d) "Terrorism in Nicaragua," in M. Crenshaw and J. Pimlott (eds) *Encyclopedia of World Terrorism*, Vol. 2, Armonk, NY: M. E. Sharpe, 442–5.

—— (1997e) "Terrorism in Uruguay," in M. Crenshaw and J. Pimlott (eds) *Encyclopedia of World Terrorism*, Vol. 2, Armonk, NY: M. E. Sharpe, 450–4.

Cameron, G. (1999) "Multi-Track Microproliferation: Lessons from Aum Shinrikyo and Al Qaida," *Studies in Conflict and Terrorism*, 22, 4: 277–309.

Campbell, B. D. (2000) "Death Squads: Definition, Problems, and Historical Context," in B. D. Campbell and A. D. Brenner (eds) *Death Squads in Global Perspective: Murder with Deniability*, New York: St. Martin's, 1–26.

Campbell, B. D. and Brenner, A. D. (2000) "Preface," in B. D. Campbell and A. D. Brenner (eds) *Death Squads in Global Perspective: Murder with Deniability*, New York: St. Martin's, vii–xvii.

Carr, C. (2002) *The Lessons of Terror: A History of Warfare against Civilians, Why It Has Failed and Why It Will Fail Again*, New York: Random House.

Carter, S., III (1976) *Cherokee Sunset, A Nation Betrayed: A Narrative of Travail and Triumph, Persecution and Exile*, Garden City, NY: Doubleday.

Carus, W. S. (2000) "The Rajneeshees," in J. B. Tucker (ed.) *Toxic Terror: Assessing Terrorist Use of Chemical and Biological Weapons*, Cambridge, MA: MIT Press, 115–37.

Chalk, P. (1996) *West European Terrorism and Counter-Terrorism: The Evolving Dynamic*, Houndsmill, Basingstoke: Macmillan.

—— (1998a) "Political Terrorism in South-East Asia," *Terrorism and Political Violence*, 10, 2: 118–34.

—— (1998b) "The Response to Terrorism as a Threat to Liberal Democracy," *Australian Journal of Politics and History*, 44, 3: 373–88.

—— (1999) "The Evolving Dynamic of Terrorism in the 1990s," *Australian Journal of International Affairs*, 53, 2: 151–68.

Chamberlin, W. H. (1935) *The Russian Revolution, 1917–1921: Vol. 1, 1917–1918, From the Overthrow of the Czar to the Assumption of Power by the Bolsheviks*, New York: Grosset & Dunlap, reprint edition, 1965.

Chandra, K. (1999) "Post-Congress Politics in Uttar Pradesh: The Ethnification of the Party System and Its Consequences," in R. Roy and P. Wallace (eds) *Indian Politics and the 1998 Election*, New Delhi: Sage Publications, 55–104.

Chellaney, B. (2001/2) "Fighting Terrorism in Southern Asia: The Lessons of History," *International Security*, 26, 3: 94–116.

Chima, J. S. (2002) "Back to the Future in 2002? A Model of Sikh Separatism in Punjab," *Studies in Conflict and Terrorism*, 25, 1: 19–39.

Chyba, C. F. (2002) "Toward Biological Security," *Foreign Affairs*, 81, 3: 122–36.

Cilluffo, F. J. and Tomarchio, J. T. (1998) "Responding to New Terrorist Threats," *Orbis*, 42, 2: 439–51.

Claridge, D. (1996) "State Terrorism? Applying a Definitional Model," *Terrorism and Political Violence*, 8, 3: 47–63.

—— (2000a) "The Baader-Meinhof Gang (1975)," in J. B. Tucker (ed.) *Toxic Terror: Assessing Terrorist Use of Chemical and Biological Weapons*, Cambridge, MA: MIT Press, 95–106.

—— (2000b) "Exploding Myths of Superterrorism," in M. Taylor and J. Horgan (eds) *The Future of Terrorism*, London: Frank Cass, 133–48.

Clawson, P. (1990) "U.S. Options for Combating Terrorism," in B. Rubin (ed.) *The Politics of Counterterrorism: The Ordeal of Democratic States*, Washington, DC: Foreign Policy Institute, 3–29.

Clutterbuck, R. (1973) *Riot and Revolution in Singapore and Malaya, 1945–1963*, London: Faber and Faber.

—— (1974) *Protest and the Urban Guerrilla*, New York: Abelard-Schuman.

—— (1975) *Living with Terrorism*, London: Faber and Faber.

"Colombia" (April 21, 2001) *Economist*, 359, 8218, 1–16 (Survey Section).

Combs, C. C. (2000) *Terrorism in the Twenty-First Century*, Upper Saddle River, NJ: Prentice Hall.

Conroy, M. E. and Pastor, M. Jr (1988) "The Nicaraguan Experiment: Characteristics of a New Economic Model," in N. Hamilton, J. A. Frieden, L. Fuller, and M. Pastor, Jr (eds) *Crisis in Central America: Regional Dynamics and U.S. Policy in the 1980s*, Boulder, CO: Westview, 207–25.

Coogan, T. P. (1993) *The IRA: A History*, Niwot, CO: Roberts Rineheart.

Cooley, J. K. (1997a) "Arab Nationalism and the Rise of Fatah," in M. Crenshaw and J. Pimlott (eds) *Encyclopedia of World Terrorism*, Vol. 2, Armonk, NY: M. E. Sharpe, 288–91.

—— (1997b) "The Beginning of International Terrorism," in M. Crenshaw and J. Pimlott (eds) *Encyclopedia of World Terrorism*, Vol. 2, Armonk, NY: M. E. Sharpe, 298–300.

—— (1997c) "Terrorism in the 1948–1949 Arab-Israeli War," in M. Crenshaw and J. Pimlott (eds) *Encyclopedia of World Terrorism*, Vol. 2, Armonk, NY: M. E. Sharpe, 284–7.

—— (2000) "Terrorism: Continuity and Change in the New Century," *Global Dialogue*, 2, 4: 7–18.

Cooper, B. (2001/2) "'We Have No Martin Luther King': Eastern Europe's Roma Minority," *World Policy Journal*, 18, 4: 69–78.

Corrado, R. R. (1997) "Basque Nationalist Terror: ETA," in M. Crenshaw and J. Pimlott (eds) *Encyclopedia of World Terrorism*, Vol. 3, Armonk, NY: M. E. Sharpe, 572–6.

Corsun, A. (1992) "Group Profile: The Revolutionary Organization 17 November in Greece (1975–1991)," in Y. Alexander and D. A. Pluchinsky (eds) *European Terrorism: Today and Tomorrow*, Washington: Brassey's, 93–125.

Coulter, E. M. (1962) "Georgia's Destiny," in L. Filler and A. Guttmann (eds) *The Removal of the Cherokee Nation: Manifest Destiny or National Dishonor?* Boston: D. C. Heath, 106–10.

Crelinsten, R. D. (2000) "Terrorism and Counter-Terrorism in a Multi-Centric World: Challenges and Opportunities," in M. Taylor and J. Horgan (eds) *The Future of Terrorism*, London: Frank Cass, 170–96.

Crenshaw, M. (1994) "Political Violence in Algeria," *Terrorism and Political Violence*, 6, 3: 261–80.

—— (1995a) "The Effectiveness of Terrorism in the Algerian War," in M. Crenshaw (ed.) *Terrorism in Context*, University Park, PA: Pennsylvania State University Press, 473–513.

—— (1995b) "Thoughts on Relating Terrorism to Historical Contexts," in M. Crenshaw (ed.) *Terrorism in Context*, University Park, PA: Pennsylvania State University Press, 3–24.

—— (2000) "Democracy, Commitment Problems and Managing Ethnic Violence: The Case of India and Sri Lanka," *Terrorism and Political Violence*, 12, 3/4: 135–59.

—— (2003a) "The Causes of Terrorism," in C. W. Kegley, Jr (ed.) *The New Global Terrorism: Characteristics, Causes, Controls*, Upper Saddle River, NJ: Prentice Hall, 92–105.

—— (2003b) "Why is America the Primary Target? Terrorism as Globalized Civil War," in C. W. Kegley, Jr (ed.) *The New Global Terrorism: Characteristics, Causes, Controls*, Upper Saddle River, NJ: Prentice Hall, 160–72.

Crenshaw, M. and Pimlott, J. (eds) (2000) *Encyclopedia of World Terrorism*, Vols. 1–3, Armonk, NY: M. E. Sharpe.

Cribb, R. (2000) "From Petrus to Ninja: Death Squads in Indonesia," in B. D. Campbell and A. D. Brenner (eds) *Death Squads in Global Perspective: Murder with Deniability*, New York: St. Martin's, 181–202.

Criss, N. B. (1995) "The Nature of PKK Terrorism in Turkey," *Studies in Conflict and Terrorism*, 18, 1: 17–37.

Cronin, A. K. (2002/3) "Behind the Curve: Globalization and International Terrorism," *International Security*, 27, 3: 30–58.

Crossette, B. (2002) "Sri Lanka: In the Shadow of the Indian Elephant," *World Policy Journal*, 19, 1: 25–36.

Cuthbertson, I. (2001/2) "Whittling Liberties: Britain's Not-So-Temporary Antiterrorism Laws," *World Policy Journal*, 18, 4: 27–33.

Dale, S. F. (1988) "Religious Suicide in Islamic Asia: Anticolonial Terrorism in India, Indonesia, and the Philippines," *Journal of Conflict Resolution*, 32, 1: 37–59.

Dartnell, M. (2000) "A Legal Inter-Network for Terrorism: Issues of Globalization, Fragmentation and Legitimacy," in M. T. and J. Horgan (eds) *The Future of Terrorism*, London: Frank Cass, 197–208.

Dees, M. with Corcoran, J. (1996) *Gathering Storm: America's Militia Threat*, New York: Harper Collins.

della Porta, D. (1995) "Left-Wing Terrorism in Italy," in M. Crenshaw (ed.) *Terrorism in Context*, University Park, PA: Pennsylvania State University Press, 105–59.

Denning, D. E. (2000) "Cyberterrorism: The Logic Bomb versus the Truck Bomb," *Global Dialogue*, 2, 4, 29–37.

Desai, R. and Eckstein, H. (1990) "Insurgency: The Transformation of Peasant Rebellion," *World Politics*, 42, 4: 441–65.

Desker, Barry (2002) "Islam and Society in South-East Asia after 11 September," *Australian Journal of International Affairs*, 56, 3: 383–94.

Deutch, J. (1997) "Terrorism," *Foreign Policy*, No. 109: 10–22.

Dillon, S. (1991) *Comandos: The CIA and Nicaragua's Contra Rebels*, New York: Henry Holt.

Dingley, J. (2001) "The Bombing of Omagh, 15 August 1998: The Bombers, Their Tactics, Strategy, and Purpose behind the Incident," *Studies in Conflict and Terrorism*, 24, 6: 451–5.

Dishman, C. (2001) "Understanding Perspectives on WMD and Why They Are Important," *Studies in Conflict and Terrorism*, 24, 4: 303–14.

Division of Archives and History (State of New York) (1926) *The American Revolution in New York: Its Political, Social and Economic Significance*, Albany: The University of the State of New York.

Dodge, T. (1997) "Single-Issue Group Terrorism," in M. Crenshaw and J. Pimlott (eds) *Encyclopedia of World Terrorism*, Vol. 1, Armonk, NY: M. E. Sharpe, 200–1.

Dolnik, A. (2003) "Die and Let Die: Exploring Links between Suicide Terrorism and Terrorist Use of Chemical, Biological, Radiological, and Nuclear Weapons," *Studies in Conflict & Terrorism*, 26, 1: 17–35.

Dolnik, A. and Bhattacharjee, A. (2002) "Hamas: Suicide Bombings, Rockets, or WMD?" *Terrorism and Political Violence*, 14, 3: 109–28.

Doran, M. S. (2002) "Somebody Else's Civil War," *Foreign Affairs*, 81, 1: 22–42.

Dragnich, A. N. (1992) *Serbs and Croats: The Struggle in Yugoslavia*, New York: Harcourt Brace.

Drake, C. J. M. (1998) "The Role of Ideology in Terrorists' Target Selection," *Terrorism and Political Violence*, 10, 2: 53–85.

Drake, R. (1989) *The Revolutionary Mystique and Terrorism in Contemporary Italy*, Bloomington, IN: Indiana University Press.

—— (1997) "Red Brigades," in M. Crenshaw and J. Pimlott (eds) *Encyclopedia of World Terrorism*, Vol. 3, Armonk, NY: M. E. Sharpe, 561–5.

Eagan, S. P. (1996) "From Spikes to Bombs: The Rise of Eco-Terrorism," *Studies in Conflict and Terrorism*, 19, 1: 1–18.

Edmonson, C. E. (1978) *The Heimwehr and Austrian Politics, 1918–1936*, Athens, GA: University of Georgia Press.

Ehle, J. (1988) *Trail of Tears: The Rise and Fall of the Cherokee Nation*, New York: Anchor Books.

Enders, W. and Sandler, T. (1991) "Causality between Transnational Terrorism and Tourism: The Case of Spain," *Terrorism*, 14, 1: 49–58.

—— (1996) "Terrorism and Direct Foreign Investment in Spain and Greece," *Kyklos*, 49, 3: 331–52.

—— (1999) "Transnational Terrorism in the Post-Cold War Era," *International Studies Quarterly*, 43, 1: 145–67.

—— (2000) "Is Transnational Terrorism Becoming More Threatening?" *Journal of Conflict Resolution*, 44, 3: 307–32.

—— (2002) "Patterns of Transnational Terrorism, 1970–1999: Alternative Time-Series Estimates," *International Studies Quarterly*, 46, 1: 145–65.

Enders, W., Sandler, T., and Parise, G. F. (1992) "An Econometric Analysis of the Impact of Terrorism on Tourism," *Kyklos*, 45, 4: 531–54.

Esposito, J. L. (1995) *The Islamic Threat: Myth or Reality?* revised ed., New York: Oxford University Press.

—— (2002) *Unholy War: Terror in the Name of Islam*, Oxford: Oxford University Press.

Fagen, P. W. (1992) "Repression and State Security," in J. E. Corradi, P. W. Fagen, and M. A. Garreton (eds) *Fear at the Edge: State Terror and Resistance in Latin America*, Berkeley, CA: University of California Press, 39–71.

Falk, R. A. (2003) "A Dual Reality: Terrorism against the State and Terrorism by the State," in C. W. Kegley, Jr (ed.) *The New Global Terrorism: Characteristics, Causes, Controls*, Upper Saddle River, NJ: Prentice Hall, 53–9.

Fein, H. (1979) *Accounting for Genocide: National Responses and Jewish Victimization during the Holocaust*, Chicago: University of Chicago Press.

Filler, A. L. (2002) "The Abu Sayyaf Group: A Growing Menace to Civil Society," *Terrorism and Political Violence*, 14, 4: 131–62.

Filler, L. and Guttmann, A. (1962) "Introduction," in L. Filler and A. Guttmann (eds) *The Removal of the Cherokee Nation: Manifest Destiny or National Dishonor?*, Boston: D. C. Heath, v–vii.

Finkelstein, N. (1995) "History's Verdict: The Cherokee Case," *Journal of Palestine Studies*, 24, 4: 32–45.

Finlayson, J. (1997) "Terrorism in Kenya," in M. Crenshaw and J. Pimlott (eds) *Encyclopedia of World Terrorism*, Vol. 1, Armonk, NY: M. E. Sharpe, 174–5.

Fitzpatrick, S. (1999) *Everyday Stalinism: Ordinary Life in Extraordinary Times: Soviet Russia in the 1930s*, New York: Oxford University Press.

Flood, C. B. (1989) *Hitler: The Path to Power*, Boston: Houghton Mifflin.

Ford, F. L. (1985) *Political Murder: From Tyrannicide to Terrorism*, Cambridge, MA: Harvard University Press.

Fox, J. (1998) "The Effects of Religion on Domestic Conflicts," *Terrorism and Political Violence*, 10, 4: 43–63.

—— (1999) "Do Religious Institutions Support Violence or the Status Quo?" *Studies in Conflict and Terrorism*, 22, 2, 119–39.

Foxell, J. W., Jr (2001) "Current Trends in Agro-terrorism (Antilivestock, Anticrop, and Antisoil Bioagricultural Terrorism) and Their Potential Impact on Food Security," *Studies in Conflict and Terrorism*, 24, 2: 107–29.

Friedman, J. (2001) "Impaired Empire," *Anthropological Quarterly*, 75, 1: 95–104.

Fuller, G. E. (1996) *Algeria: The Next Fundamentalist State?*, RAND.

—— (2002) "The Future of Political Islam," *Foreign Affairs*, 81, 2: 48–60.

Furedi, F. (1989) *The Mau Mau War in Perspective*, East African Studies, London: James Currey.

Furet, F. (1989) "Terror," in F. Furet and M. Ozouf (eds) *A Critical Dictionary of the French Revolution*, trans. A. Goldhammer, Cambridge, MA: Belknap Press, 137–50.

Gavin, P. (2001) "Ethnic Cleansing in Bosnia-Herzegovina," in William Dudley (ed.) *Genocide*, San Diego: Greenhaven Press, 39–42.

Geiger, H. J. (2001) "Terrorism, Biological Weapons, and Bonanzas: Assessing the Real Threat to Public Health," *American Journal of Public Health*, 91, 5: 708–9.

Gerlovin, L. (1995/6) "The Forgotten War: Conflict and Coercion in East Timor," *Harvard International Review*, 18, 1: 58–9, 79–80.

Gillespie, R. (1982) *Soldiers of Peron: Argentina's Montoneros*, Oxford: Clarendon Press.

—— (1995) "Political Violence in Argentina: Guerillas, Terrorists, and Carapintadas," in M. Crenshaw (ed.) *Terrorism in Context*, University Park, PA: Pennsylvania State University Press, 211–48.

Goldberg, J. E. (1991) "Understanding the Dimensions of Terrorism," *Perspectives on Political Science*, 20, 2: 78–88.

Gorenberg, G. (2000) *The End of Days: Fundamentalism and the Struggle for the Temple Mount*, Oxford: Oxford University Press.

Gossman, P. (2000) "India's Secret Armies," in B. D. Campbell and A. D. Brenner (eds) *Death Squads in Global Perspective: Murder with Deniability*, New York: St. Martin's, 261–86.

Gottschalk, K. (2000) "The Rise and Fall of Apartheid's Death Squads," in B. D. Campbell and A. D. Brenner (eds) *Death Squads in Global Perspective: Murder with Deniability*, New York: St. Martin's, 229–59.

Gough, A. J. (1997) "Ku Klux Klan Terror," in M. Crenshaw and J. Pimlott (eds) *Encyclopedia of World Terrorism*, Vol. 3, Armonk, NY: M. E. Sharpe, 527–9.

Gourdoumbas, A. (1997) "Modern Greek Terrorism," in M. Crenshaw and J. Pimlott (eds) *Encyclopedia of World Terrorism*, Vol. 3, Armonk, NY: M. E. Sharpe, 566–7.

Grant, M. (1974) *The Army of the Caesars*, New York: M. Evans.

—— (1992) *Julius Caesar: A Biography*, New York: M. Evans, first published in 1969.

Green, J. D. (1995) "Terrorism and Politics in Iran," in M. Crenshaw (ed.) *Terrorism in Context*, University Park, PA: Pennsylvania State University Press, 553–94.

Greenway, H. D. S. (2001) "Hindu Nationalism Clouds the Face of India," *World Policy Journal*, 18, 1: 89–93.

Greer, D. (1935) *The Incidence of Terror during the French Revolution: A Statistical Interpretation*, Cambridge, MA: Harvard University Press.

Griffith, P. (1998) *The Art of War of Revolutionary France, 1789–1802*, London: Greenhill Books.

Griffiths, I. Ll. (1984) *An Atlas of African Affairs*, London: Methuen.

Griset, P. L. and Mahan, S. (2003) *Terrorism in Perspective*, Thousand Oaks, CA: Sage.

Grosscup, B. (2000) "Terrorism-at-a-Distance: The Imagery that Serves US Power," *Global Dialogue*, 2, 4: 74–87.

Gunaratna, R. (1997) "Tamil Tiger Terror in Sri Lanka," in M. Crenshaw and J. Pimlott (eds) *Encyclopedia of World Terrorism*, Vol. 2, Armonk, NY: M. E. Sharpe, 472–7.

Gurr, N. and Cole, B. (2000) *The New Face of Terrorism: Threats from Weapons of Mass Destruction*, London: I. B. Tauris.

Gurr, T. R. (2003) "Terrorism in Democracies: When It Occurs, Why It Fails," in C. W. Kegley, Jr (ed.) *The New Global Terrorism: Characteristics, Causes, Controls*, Upper Saddle River, NJ: Prentice Hall, 202–15.

Hacker, F. J. (1976) *Crusaders, Criminals, and Crazies*, New York: Norton.

Hanauer, L. S. (1995) "The Path to Redemption: Fundamentalist Judaism, Territory, and Jewish Settler Violence in the West Bank," *Studies in Conflict and Terrorism*, 18, 4: 245–70.

Harmon, C. C. (2000) *Terrorism Today*, London: Frank Cass.

Haubrich, D. (2003) "September 11, Anti-Terror Laws and Civil Liberties: Britain, France and Germany Compared," *Government and Opposition*, 38, 1: 3–28.

Havens, M. C., Leiden, C., and Schmitt, K. M. (1975) *Assassination and Terrorism: Their Modern Dimensions*, Manchaca, TX: Sterling Swift.

Hazleton, W. A. and Woy-Hazleton, S. (1988) "Terrorism and the Marxist Left: Peru's Struggle against Sendero Luminoso," *Terrorism*, 11, 6: 471–90.

Hefner, R. W. (2002) "Global Violence and Indonesian Muslim Politics," *American Anthropologist*, 104, 3: 766–75.

Henze, P. B. (1996) "Russia and the Caucasus," *Studies in Conflict and Terrorism*, 19, 4: 389–402.

Herman, E. S. (2000) "The Semantics of Terrorism," *Global Dialogue*, 2, 4: 1–6.

Heymann, P. B. (2001/2) "Dealing with Terrorism: An Overview," *International Security*, 26, 3: 24–38.

Hillyard, P. (1993) *Suspect Community: People's Experience of the Prevention of Terrorism Acts in Britain*, London: Pluto Press.

Hoffman, B. (1995) "'Holy Terror': The Implications of Terrorism Motivated by a Religious Imperative," *Studies in Conflict and Terrorism*, 18, 4: 271–84.

—— (1997) "The Confluence of International and Domestic Trends in Terrorism," *Terrorism and Political Violence*, 19, 2: 1–15.

—— (1998) *Inside Terrorism*, New York: Columbia University Press.

—— (2001) "Change and Continuity in Terrorism," *Studies in Conflict and Terrorism*, 24, 5: 417–28

—— (2002) "Rethinking Terrorism and Counter-Terrorism since 9/11," *Studies in Conflict and Terrorism*, 25, 5, 303–16.

Hoffmann, S. (2002) "Clash of Globalizations," *Foreign Affairs*, 84, 1: 104–15.

Holland, J. (1999) *Hope Against History: The Course of Conflict in Northern Ireland*, New York: Henry Holt.

Holoboff, E. M. (1997) "National and Ethnic Terror in the Former Soviet Union," in M. Crenshaw and J. Pimlott (eds) *Encyclopedia of World Terrorism*, Vol. 2, Armonk, NY: M. E. Sharpe, 486–90.

Hoptner, J. B. (1962) *Yugoslavia in Crisis: 1934–1941*, New York: Columbia University Press.

Horowitz, D. L. (1980) *Coup Theories and Officers' Motives: Sri Lanka in Comparative Perspective*, Princeton, NJ: Princeton University Press.

Howell, L. D. (2003), "Is the New Global Terrorism a Clash of Civilizations? Evaluating Terrorism's Multiple Sources," in C. W. Kegley, Jr (ed.) *The New Global Terrorism: Characteristics, Causes, Controls*, Upper Saddle River, NJ: Prentice Hall, 173–184.

Hughes, M. (1997) "The Birth of Jewish Terrorism," in M. Crenshaw and J. Pimlott (eds) *Encyclopedia of World Terrorism*, Vol. 2, Armonk, NY: M. E. Sharpe, 278–80.

Huntington, S. P. (1993) "The Clash of Civilizations?" *Foreign Affairs*, 72, 3: 22–49.

Husbands, C. T. (1995) "Militant Neo-Nazism in Germany," in L. Cheles, R. Ferguson, and M. Vaughan (eds) *The Far Right in Western and Eastern Europe*, 2nd edn, London: Longman, 327–53.

Imai, R. (2002) "Weapons of Mass Destruction: Major Wars, Regional Conflicts, and Terrorism," *Asia-Pacific Review*, 9, 1: 88–99.

Jackson, R. (1991) *The Malayan Emergency: The Commonwealth's Wars, 1948–1966*, London: Routledge.

Jacquard, R. (2002) *In the Name of Osama Bin Laden*, trans. G. Holoch, Durham, NC: Duke University Press.

Jardine, M. (1998) "Power and Principle in East Timor," *Peace Review*, 10, 2: 195–202.

Jenkins, B. M. (1990) "International Terrorism: The Other World War," in C. W. Kegley, Jr (ed.) *International Terrorism: Characteristics, Causes, Controls*, New York: St. Martin's, 27–38.

—— (1998) "Will Terrorists Go Nuclear?: A Reappraisal," in H. W. Kushner (ed.) *The Future of Terrorism: Violence in the New Millennium*, Thousand Oaks, CA: Sage, 225–49.

—— (2001) "Terrorism and Beyond: A 21st Century Perspective," *Studies in Conflict and Terrorism*, 24, 5: 321–7.

Jenkins, P. (1990) "Strategy of Tension: The Belgian Terrorist Crisis 1982–1986," *Terrorism*, 13, 4/5: 299–309.

Jha, P. S. (1994) "The Fascist Impulse in Developing Countries: Two Case Studies," *Studies in Conflict and Terrorism*, 17, 3: 229–74.

Jimenez, F. (1992) "Spain: The Terrorist Challenge and the Government's Response," *Terrorism and Political Violence*, 4, 4: 110–30.

Jones, D. M. and Smith, M. L. (2001) "The Changing Security Agenda in Southeast Asia: Globalization, New Terror, and the Delusions of Regionalism," *Studies in Conflict and Terrorism*, 24, 4: 271–88.

Johnson, L. K. (2003) "Strategic Intelligence: The Weakest Link in the War against World Terrorism," in C. W. Kegley, Jr (ed.) *The New Global Terrorism: Characteristics, Causes, Controls*, Upper Saddle River, NJ: Prentice Hall, 239–52.

Johnson, M. P. (1995) "Patriarchal Terrorism and Common Couple Violence: Two Forms of Violence against Women," *Journal of Marriage and the Family*, 57, 2: 283–94.

Jongman, A. J. (1992) "Trends in International and Domestic Terrorism in Western Europe, 1968–1988," *Terrorism and Political Violence*, 4, 4: 26–76.

Josephus (1971) *The Jewish War*, trans. G. A. Williamson, New York: Dorset Press.

Joshi, M. (1996) "On the Razor's Edge: The Liberation Tigers of Tamil Eelam," *Studies in Conflict and Terrorism*, 19, 1: 19–42.

Judah, T. (2000) *Kosovo: War and Revenge*, New Haven: Yale University Press.

Juergensmeyer, M. (1996) "The Worldwide Rise of Religious Nationalism," *Journal of International Affairs*, 50, 1: 1–20.

—— (1997) "Terror Mandated by God," *Terrorism and Political Violence*, 9, 2: 16–23.

—— (2000) *Terror in the Mind of God: The Global Rise of Religious Violence*, Berkeley: University of California Press.

Kaplan, D. E. (2000) "Aum Shinrikyo (1995)," in Jonathan B. Tucker (ed.) *Toxic Terror: Assessing Terrorist Use of Chemical and Biological Weapons*, Cambridge, MA: MIT Press, 207–26.

Kaplan, J. (1993) "The Context of American Millenarian Revolutionary Theology: The Case of the 'Identity Christian' Church of Israel," *Terrorism and Political Violence*, 5, 1: 30–82.

—— (1995) "Right Wing Violence in North America," in T. Bjorgo (ed.) *Terror from the Extreme Right*, London: Frank Cass, 1995, 44–95.

—— (1997) *Radical Religion in America: Millenarian Movements from the Far Right to the Children of Noah*, Syracuse, NY: Syracuse University Press.

Karapin, R. (2002) "Antiminority Riots in Unified Germany: Cultural Conflicts and Mischanneled Political Participation," *Comparative Politics*, 34, 2: 147–68.

Kassimeris, G. (1995) "Greece: Twenty Years of Political Terrorism," *Terrorism and Political Violence*, 7, 2: 74–92.

—— (2001) *Europe's Last Red Terrorists: The Revolutionary Organization 17 November*, New York: New York University Press.

Kegley, C. W., Jr (ed.) (2003) *The New Global Terrorism: Characteristics, Causes, Controls*, Upper Saddle River, NJ: Prentice Hall.

Kelly, R. J. (1998) "Armed Prophets and Extremists: Islamic Fundamentalism," in H. W. Kushner (ed.) *The Future of Terrorism: Violence in the New Millennium*, Thousand Oaks, CA: Sage Publications, 21–32.

Kennedy, R. (1999) "Is One Person's Terrorist Another's Freedom Fighter: Western and Islamic Approaches to 'Just War' Compared," *Terrorism and Political Violence*, 11, 1: 1–21.

al-Khalil, S. (1989) *Republic of Fear: The Inside Story of Saddam's Iraq*, New York: Pantheon Books.

Khan, S. M. (2000) *The Shallow Graves of Rwanda*, London: I. B. Tauris.

Khashan, H. (1997) "The New World Order and the Tempo of Militant Islam," *British Journal of Middle Eastern Studies*, 24, 1: 5–24.

Khatami, S. (1997) "Between Class and Nation: Ideology and Radical Basque Ethnonationalism," *Studies in Conflict and Terrorism*, 20, 4: 395–417.

Kibble, D. G. (1996) "The Threat of Militant Islam: A Fundamental Reappraisal," *Studies in Conflict and Terrorism*, 19, 4: 353–64.

Kim, J. T. (1988) "North Korean Terrorism: Trends, Characteristics, and Deterrence," *Terrorism*, 11, 4: 309–22.

Kim, S. H. (1987) "The Issues of International Law," in T. W. Walker (ed.) *Reagan versus the Sandinistas: The Undeclared War on Nicaragua*, Boulder, CO: Westview, 265–84.

Kimmerling, B. (1997) "The Power-Oriented Settlement: PLO-Israel—The Road to the Oslo Agreement and Back?" in A. Sela and M. Ma'oz (eds) *The PLO and Israel: From Armed Conflict to Political Solution, 1964–1994*, New York: St. Martin's, 223–51.

Kirkbride, W. A. (1994) *North Korea's Undeclared War: 1953–*, Seoul: Hollym.

Klare, M. T. (2003) "The New Face of Combat: Terrorism and Irregular Warfare in the 21st Century," in C. W. Kegley, Jr (ed.) *The New Global Terrorism: Characteristics, Causes, Controls*, Upper Saddle River, NJ: Prentice Hall, 27–35.

Knickerbocker, B. (1997) "Mink Wars: Animal Rights Activists Get Violent," *Christian Science Monitor*, 89,193: 5.

Kornbluh, P. (1987) "The Covert War," in T. W. Walker (ed.) *Reagan versus the Sandinistas: The Undeclared War on Nicaragua*, Boulder, CO: Westview, 21–38.

Kostiner, J. (1989) "War, Terror, Revolution: The Iran-Iraq Conflict," in B. Rubin (ed.) *The Politics of Terrorism: Terror as a State and Revolutionary Strategy*, Washington, DC: Foreign Policy Institute, 95–128.

Krishna, S. (1992) "India and Sri Lanka: A Fatal Convergence," *Studies in Conflict and Terrorism*, 15, 4: 267–81.

Kumar, R (2002) "Untying the Kashmir Knot," *World Policy Journal*, 19, 1: 11–24.

Kuperman, A. J. (2000) "Rwanda in Retrospect," *Foreign Affairs*, 79, 1: 94–118.

Kuramatsu, T. (1997) "Japanese Terrorism," in M. Crenshaw and J. Pimlott (eds) *Encyclopedia of*

World Terrorism, Vol. 3, Armonk, NY: M. E. Sharpe, 568–70.

Kurti, L. (1998) "The Emergence of Postcommunist Youth Identities in Eastern Europe: From Communist Youth to Skinheads, to National Socialists and Beyond," in J. Kaplan and T. Bjorgo (eds) *Nation and Race: The Developing Euro-American Racist Subculture*, Boston: Northeastern University Press, 175–201.

Kushner, H. W. (1996) "Suicide Bombers: Business as Usual," *Studies in Conflict and Terrorism*, 19, 4: 329–27.

—— (1998a) "The New Terrorism," in H. W. Kushner (ed.) *The Future of Terrorism: Violence in the New Millennium*, Thousand Oaks, CA: Sage, 3–20.

—— (1998b) *Terrorism in America: A Structured Approach to Understanding the Terrorist Threat*, Springfield, IL: Charles C. Thomas.

Landau, S. (1993) *The Guerrilla Wars of Central America: Nicaragua, El Salvador & Guatemala*, New York: St. Martin's.

Laqueur, W. (1987) *The Age of Terrorism*, Boston: Little, Brown.

—— (1998) "Terror's New Face: The Radicalization and Escalation of Modern Terrorism," *Harvard International Review*, 20, 4: 48–51.

—— (1999) *The New Terrorism: Fanaticism and the Arms of Mass Destruction*, New York: Oxford University Press.

—— (2001) *A History of Terrorism*, New Brunswick, NJ: Transaction Publishers.

—— (2003) "Postmodern Terrorism," in C. W. Kegley, Jr (ed.) *The New Global Terrorism: Characteristics, Causes, Controls*, Upper Saddle River, NJ: Prentice Hall, 151–9.

Lassen, S. B. D. (1990) "Drug Trafficking and Terrorism in Colombia," in B. Rubin (ed.) *The Politics of Counterterrorism: The Ordeal of Democratic States*, Washington, DC: Foreign Policy Institute, 107–36.

Leckie, R. (1992) *George Washington's War: The Saga of the American Revolution*, New York: Harper Collins.

Lee, M. A. (1997) *The Beast Reawakens*, Boston: Little, Brown.

Leitenberg, M. (2000) "Aum Shinrikyo's Efforts to Produce Biological Weapons: A Case Study in the Serial Propagation of Misinformation," in M. Taylor and J. Horgan (eds) *The Future of Terrorism*, London: Frank Cass, 149–58.

Lepsius, M. R. (1978) "From Fragmented Party Democracy to Government by Emergency Decree and National Socialist Takeover: Germany," in J. L. Linz and A. Stephan (eds) *The Breakdown of Democratic Regimes: Europe*, Baltimore: Johns Hopkins University Press, 34–79.

Levin, B. (1998) "The Patriot Movement: Past, Present, and Future," in H. W. Kushner (ed.) *The Future of Terrorism: Violence in the New Millennium*, Thousand Oaks, CA: Sage, 97–131.

LeVine, V. T. (1995) "The Logomachy of Terrorism: On the Political Uses and Abuses of Definition," *Terrorism and Political Violence*, 7, 4: 45–59.

Lifton, R. J. (2000) *Destroying the World To Save It: Aum Shinrikyo, Apocalyptic Violence, and the New Global Terrorism*, New York: Henry Holt.

Loder, N. (2000) "Britain May Boost Protection of Researchers from Intimidation," *Nature*, 407, 6800: 3.

Long, D. E. (1990) *The Anatomy of Terrorism*, New York: Free Press.

Lonsdale, J. (1986) "Explanations of the Mau Mau Revolt, Kenya, 1952–1956," in T. Lodge (ed.) *Resistance and Ideology in Settler Societies*, Southern African Studies, Vol. 4, Johannesburg: Ravan Press, 168–78.

Lucas, C. (1994) "Revolutionary Violence, the People and the Terror," in K. M. Baker (ed.) *The French Revolution and the Creation of Modern Political Culture: Volume 4, The Terror*, Oxford: Pergamon, 57–80.

Luft, G. (2003) "The Logic of Israel's Targeted Killing," *Middle East Quarterly*, 10, 1: 3–8.

Lutz, B. D. and Lutz, J. M. (1995) "Gypsies as Victims of the Holocaust," *Holocaust and Genocide Studies*, 9, 3: 346–59.

Lutz, B. J., Lutz, J. M., and Ulmschneider, G. W. (2002) "British Trials of Irish Nationalist Defendants: The Quality of Justice Strained," *Studies in Conflict and Terrorism*, 25, 4: 227–44.

McCaffrey, B. R., and Basso, J. A. (2002) "Narcotics, Terrorism, and International Crime: The Convergence Phenomenon," in R. D. Howard and R. L. Sawyer (eds) *Terrorism and Counterterrorism: Understanding the New Security Environment, Readings and Interpretations*, Guilford, CT: McGraw-Hill/Duskin, 206–21.

Macgregor, D. A. (2001) "The Balkan Limits to Power and Principle," *Orbis*, 45, 1: 93–110.

McGregor, J. (2002) "The Politics of Disruption: War Veterans and the Local State in Zimbabwe," *African Affairs*, 101, 402: 9–37.

McLaren, L. M. (1999) "Explaining Right-Wing Violence in Germany: A Time Series Analysis," *Social Science Quarterly*, 80, 1: 166–80.

McLoughlin, W. G. (1986) *Cherokee Renascence in the New Republic*, Princeton, NJ: Princeton University Press.

Maddy-Weitzman, B. (1997) "The Islamic Challenge in North Africa," in B. Maddy-Weitzman and E. Inbar (eds) *Religious Radicalism in the Greater Middle East*, London: Frank Cass, 171–88.

Malka, H. (2003) "Must Innocents Die? The Islamic Debate over Suicide Attacks," *Middle East Quarterly*, 10, 2: 19–28.

Malkin, L. and Elizur, Y. (2002) "Terrorism's Money Trail," *World Policy Journal*, 19, 1: 60–70.

Maloba, W. O. (1993) *Mau Mau in Kenya: An Analysis of a Peasant Revolt*, Bloomington, IN: Indiana University Press.

Mamdani, M. (2001) *When Victims Become Killers: Colonialism, Nativism, and the Genocide in Rwanda*, Princeton, NJ: Princeton University Press.

Mariani, M. (1998) "The Michigan Militia: Political Engagement or Political Alienation?" *Terrorism and Political Violence*, 10, 4: 122–48.

Marshall, C. (1997) "Terrorism in Malaya," in M. Crenshaw and J. Pimlott (eds) *Encyclopedia of World Terrorism*, Vol. 1, Armonk, NY: M. E. Sharpe, 171–73.

Mason, T. D. and Campany, C. (1995) "Guerrillas, Drugs and Peasants: The Rational Peasant and the War on Drugs in Peru," *Terrorism and Political Violence*, 7, 4: 140–70.

Mayer, J.-F. (2001) "Cults, Violence and Religious Terrorism: An International Perspective," *Studies in Conflict and Terrorism*, 24, 5: 361–76.

Merari, A. (2000) "Terrorism as a Strategy of Struggle: Past and Future," in M. Taylor and J. Horgan (eds) *The Future of Terrorism*, London: Frank Cass, 52–65.

Merkl, P. H. (1975) *Political Violence under the Swastika: 581 Early Nazis*, Princeton, NJ: Princeton University Press.

—— (1986) "Conclusion: Collective Purposes and Individual Motives," in P. H. Merkl (ed.) *Political Violence and Terror*, Berkeley, CA: University of California Press, 335–74.

—— (1987) *The Making of a Stormtrooper*, Boulder, CO: Westview Press.

—— (1995a) "Radical Right Parties in Europe and Anti-Foreign Violence: A Comparative Essay," in T. Bjorgo, *Terror from the Extreme Right*, London: Frank Cass, 96–118.

—— (1995b) "West German Left-Wing Terrorism," in M. Crenshaw (ed.) *Terrorism in Context*, University Park, PA: Pennsylvania State University Press, 160–210.

Milazzo, M. J. (1975) *The Chetnik Movement and the Yugoslav Resistance*, Baltimore: Johns Hopkins University Press.

Miller, A. and Damask, N. A. (1996) "The Dual Myths of 'Narco-Terrorism': How Myths Drive Policy," *Terrorism and Political Violence*, 8, 1: 114–31.

Mohan, A. (1992) "The Historical Roots of the Kashmir Conflict," *Studies in Conflict and Terrorism*, 15, 4: 283–308.

Monaghan, R. (1997) "Animal Rights and Violent Protest," *Terrorism and Political Violence*, 9, 4: 106–16.

—— (2000) "Terrorism in the Name of Animal Rights," in M. Taylor and J. Horgan (eds) *The Future of Terrorism*, London: Frank Cass, 159–69.

Mousseau, D. Y. (2001) "Democratization with Ethnic Divisions: A Source of Conflict?" *Journal of Peace Research*, 38, 5: 547–67.

Mousseau, M. (2002/3) "Market Civilization and Its Clash with Terror," *International Security*, 27, 3: 5–29.

Mueller, J. (2000) "The Banality of 'Ethnic War'," *International Security*, 25, 1: 42–70.

Mylroie, L. (2000) *Study of Revenge: Saddam Hussein's Unfinished War against America*, Washington, DC: AEI Press.

Nacos, B. L. (2003) "The Terrorist Calculus behind 9–11: A Model for Future Terrorism," *Studies in Conflict and Terrorism*, 26, 1: 1–16.

Nahm, A. C. (1988) *Korea, Tradition and Transformation: A History of the Korean People*, Elizabeth, NJ: Hollym.

Nandi, P. K. (1996) "Socio-Political Context of Sikh Militancy in India," *Journal of Asian and African Studies*, 31, 3/4: 178–90.

Nedoroscik, J. A. (2002) "Extremist Groups in Egypt," *Terrorism and Political Violence*, 14, 2: 47–76.

Neumann, F. L. (1968) "Notes on the Theory of Dictatorship," in R. Macridis and B. E. Brown (eds) *Comparative Politics: Notes and Readings*, 3rd edn, Homewood, IL: Dorsey Press, 178–88.

Newman, S. (2000) "Nationalism in Postindustrial Societies: Why States Still Matter," *Comparative Politics*, 33, 1: 21–42.

Oakley, R. (1987) "International Terrorism," *Foreign Affairs*, 65, 3: 611–29.

O'Ballance, E. (1967) *The Algerian Insurrection, 1954–62*, Hamden, CT: Archon Books.

—— (2000) *Sudan: Civil War and Terrorism, 1956–99*, New York: St. Martin's.

O'Brien, S. P. (1996) "Foreign Policy Crises and the Resort to Terrorism: A Time-Series Analysis of Conflict Linkages," *Journal of Conflict Resolution*, 40, 2: 320–55.

O'Day, A. (1979) "Northern Ireland, Terrorism, and the British State," in Y. Alexander, D. Carlton, and P. Wilkinson (eds) *Terrorism: Theory and Practice*, Boulder, CO: Westview, 121–35.

O'Neil, A. (2003) "Terrorist Use of Weapons of Mass Destruction: How Serious Is the Threat?" *Australian Journal of International Affairs*, 57, 1: 99–112.

Ortiz, R. D. (2002) "Insurgent Strategies in the Post-Cold War: The Case of the Revolutionary Armed Forces of Colombia," *Studies in Conflict and Terrorism*, 25, 2: 127–43.

Otte, T. G. (1997a) "The Murder of Rathenau," in M. Crenshaw and J. Pimlott (eds) *Encyclopedia of World Terrorism*, Vol. 1, Armonk, NY: M. E. Sharpe, 76.

—— (1997b) "Red Army Faction: The Baader-Meinhof Gang," in M. Crenshaw and J. Pimlott (eds) *Encyclopedia of World Terrorism*, Vol. 3, Armonk, NY: M. E. Sharpe, 552–6.

Palmer, D. S. (1992) "Peru, the Drug Business and Shining Path: Between Scylla and Charybdis?" *Journal of Interamerican Studies and World Affairs*, 34, 3: 65–88.

—— (1995) "The Revolutionary Terrorism of Peru's Shining Path," in M. Crenshaw (ed.) *Terrorism in Context*, University Park, PA: Pennsylvania State University Press, 249–308.

Parachini, J. V. (2001) "Comparing Motives and Outcomes of Mass Casualty Terrorism Involving Conventional and Unconventional Weapons," *Studies in Conflict and Terrorism*, 24, 5: 389–406.

Partrick, N. (1997a) "The Black September Organization," in M, Crenshaw and J. Pimlott (eds) *Encyclopedia of World Terrorism*, Vol. 2, Armonk, NY: M. E. Sharpe, 303–7.

—— (1997b) "Jewish Terror in the West Bank," in M. Crenshaw and J. Pimlott (eds), *Encyclopedia of World Terrorism*, Vol. 2, Armonk, NY: M. E. Sharpe, 326–7.

Pastor, R. (1987) *Condemned to Repetition: The United States and Nicaragua*, Princeton, NJ: Princeton University Press.

Pateman, R. (1998) "East Timor, Twenty Years After: *Resistir e Vencer* (To Resist Is to Win)," *Terrorism and Political Violence*, 10, 1: 119–32.

Pavkovic, A. (2000) *The Fragmentation of Yugoslavia: Nationalism and War in the Balkans*, 2nd edn, New York: Longman.

Pedahzur, A. (2001a) "Struggling with the Challenges of Right-Wing Extremism and Terrorism within Democratic Boundaries: A Comparative Analysis," *Studies in Conflict and Terrorism*, 24, 5: 339–59.

—— (2001b) "The Transformation of Israel's Extreme Right," *Studies in Conflict and Terrorism*, 24, 1: 25–42.

Perlstein, G. R. (1997) "Anti-Abortion Activists' Terror Campaign," in M. Crenshaw and J. Pimlott (eds) *Encyclopedia of World Terrorism*, Vol. 3, Armonk, NY: M. E. Sharpe, 542–4.

Pettigrew, J. J. M. (1995) *The Sikhs of the Punjab: Unheard Voices of State and Guerrilla Violence*, London: Zed Books.

Pillar, P. R. (2001) *Terrorism and U.S. Foreign Policy*, Washington, DC: Brookings Institution.

Pimlott, J. (1997) "The Changing Face of Terrorism," in M. Crenshaw and J. Pimlott (eds) *Encyclopedia of World Terrorism*, Vol. 3, Armonk, NY: M. E. Sharpe, 682–6.

Pizam, A. and Fleischer, A. (2002) "Severity versus Frequency of Acts of Terrorism: Which Has a Larger Impact on Tourism Demand," *Journal of Travel Research*, 40, 2: 337–9.

Pluchinsky, D. A. (1992) "An Organizational and Operational Analysis of Germany's Red Army Faction Terrorist Group (1972–91)," in Y. Alexander and D. A. Pluchinsky (eds) *European Terrorism: Today and Tomorrow*, Washington, DC: Brassey's, 3–92.

—— (1993) "Germany's Red Army Faction: An Obituary," *Studies in Conflict and Terrorism*, 16, 1: 135–57.

—— (1998) "Terrorism in the Former Soviet Union: A Primer, A Puzzle, A Prognosis," *Studies in Conflict and Terrorism*, 21, 2: 119–47.

Poneman, D. (1987) *Argentina: Democracy on Trial*, New York: Paragon House.

Posen, B. R. (2001/2) "The Struggle against Terrorism: Grand Strategy, Strategy, and Tactics," *International Security*, 26, 3: 39–55.

Post, J. M. (2000) "Psychological and Motivational Factors in Terrorist Decision-Making: Implications for CBW Terrorism," in J. B. Tucker (ed.) *Toxic Terror: Assessing Terrorist Use of Chemical and Biological Weapons*, Cambridge, MA: MIT Press, 271–89.

Pridham, G. (1973) *Hitler's Rise to Power: The Movement in Bavaria, 1923–1933*, New York: Harper and Row.

Purcell, V. (1967) *Malaysia*, New York: Walker.

Quillen, C. (2002) "A Historical Analysis of Mass Casualty Bombers," *Studies in Conflict and Terrorism*, 25, 5: 279–92.

Qureshi, S. (1976) "Political Violence in the South Asian Subcontinent," in Y. Alexander (ed.) *International Terrorism: National, Regional, and Global Perspectives*, New York: Praeger, 151–93.

Radu, M. (2000) "The Perilous Appeasement of Guerrillas," *Orbis*, 44, 3: 363–79.

—— (2002) "Terrorism after the Cold War," *Orbis*, 46, 2: 275–87.

Ramirez, J. (1997a) "Colombian Government's Responses to Terrorism," in M. Crenshaw and

J. Pimlott (eds) *Encyclopedia of World Terrorism*, Vol. 3, Armonk, NY: M. E. Sharpe, 636–7.

—— (1997b) "Terrorism in Colombia," in M. Crenshaw and J. Pimlott (eds) *Encyclopedia of World Terrorism*, Vol. 2, Armonk, NY: M. E. Sharpe, 430–3.

Ramos-Horta, J. (1997) "Casualties of Silence: East Timor's Struggle for Self-Determination," *Harvard International Review*, 19, 4: 32–6,

Ranstorp, M. (1996) "Terrorism in the Name of Religion," *Journal of International Affairs*, 50, 1: 42–62.

—— (1998) "Interpreting the Broader Context and Meaning of Bin-Laden's *Fatwa*," *Studies in Conflict and Terrorism*, 21, 4: 321–30.

Rapoport, D. C. (1984) "Fear and Trembling: Terrorism in Three Religious Traditions," *American Political Science Review*, 78, 3, pp. 658–77.

—— (1990) "Religion and Terror: Thugs, Assassins, and Zealots," in C. W. Kegley, Jr (ed.) *International Terrorism: Characteristics, Causes, Controls*, New York: St. Martin's, 146–57.

—— (2003) "The Four Waves of Rebel Terror and September 11," in C. W. Kegley, Jr (ed.) *The New Global Terrorism: Characteristics, Causes, Controls*, Upper Saddle River, NJ: Prentice Hall, 36–52.

Rashid, A. (2001) "The Fires of Faith in Central Asia," *World Policy Journal*, 18, 1: 45–55.

—— (2002) *Jihad: The Rise of Militant Islam in Central Asia*, New Haven, CT: Yale University Press.

Rathmell, A. (1997a) "Iranian Sponsorship of Terrorism," in M. Crenshaw and J. Pimlott (eds) *Encyclopedia of World Terrorism*, Vol. 2, Armonk, NY: M. E. Sharpe, 392–5.

—— (1997b) "Iraqi Sponsorship of Terrorism," in M. Crenshaw and J. Pimlott (eds) *Encyclopedia of World Terrorism*, Vol. 2, Armonk, NY: M. E. Sharpe, 375–8.

—— (1997c) "Jewish Terrorism in the 1990s," in M. Crenshaw and J. Pimlott (eds) *Encyclopedia of World Terrorism*, Vol. 2, Armonk, NY: M. E. Sharpe, 354–7.

—— (1997d) "Palestinian Islamic Fundamentalism," in M. Crenshaw and J. Pimlott (eds) *Encyclopedia of World Terrorism*, Vol. 2, Armonk, NY: M. E. Sharpe, 348–53.

—— (1997e) "State Sponsored Terrorism," in M. Crenshaw and J. Pimlott (eds) *Encyclopedia of World Terrorism*, Vol. 3, Armonk, NY: M. E. Sharpe, 652–6.

Raufer, X. (1993) "The Red Brigades: Farewell to Arms," *Studies in Conflict and Terrorism*, 16, 4: 315–25.

—— (2000) "New World Disorder, New Terrorisms: New Threats for Europe and the Western World," in M. Taylor and J. Horgan (eds) *The Future of Terrorism*, London: Frank Cass, 30–51.

Raymond, G. A. (2003) "The Evolving Strategies of Political Terrorism," in C. W. Kegley, Jr (ed.) *The New Global Terrorism: Characteristics, Causes, Controls*, Upper Saddle River, NJ: Prentice Hall, 71–83.

Read, A. and Fisher, D. (1989) *Kristallnacht: The Unleashing of the Holocaust*, New York: Peter Bedrick Books.

Reid, A. (1997) *Borderland: A Journey through the History of Ukraine*, Boulder, CO: Westview Press.

Reinares, F. (1998) "Democratic Regimes, Internal Security Policy and the Threat of Terrorism," *Australian Journal of Politics and History*, 44, 3: 351–71.

Richardson, L. (2000) "Terrorists as Transnational Actors," in M. Taylor and J. Horgan (eds) *The Future of Terrorism*, London: Frank Cass, 209–19.

Richelson, J. T. (2002) "When Kindness Fails: Assassination as a National Security Option," *International Journal of Intelligence and Counterintelligence*, 15, 2: 243–74.

Rieff, D. (2001) "Suffering and Cynicism in Burundi," *World Policy Journal*, 18, 3: 61–7.

Rimanelli, M. (1989) "Italian Terrorism and Society, 1940s-1980s: Roots, Ideologies, Evolution, and International Connections," *Terrorism*, 12, 4: 249–96.

—— (1992) "Foreign Comrades in Arms: Italian Terrorism and International Ties (1968–91)," in Y. Alexander and D. A. Pluchinsky (eds) *European Terrorism: Today and Tomorrow*, Washington, DC: Brassey's, 127–80.

Robbins, J. S. (2002) "Bin Laden's War," in R. D. Howard and R. L. Sawyer (eds) *Terrorism and Counterterrorism: Understanding the New Security Environment, Readings and Interpretations*, Guilford, CT: McGraw-Hill/Duskin, 354–66.

Roberts, B. (1997a) "Nationalist Terror in Northern Ireland, 1976–1996," in M. Crenshaw and J. Pimlott (eds) *Encyclopedia of World Terrorism*, Vol. 3, Armonk, NY: M. E. Sharpe, 581–5.

—— (1997b) "Terrorism in Peru," in M. Crenshaw and J. Pimlott (eds) *Encyclopedia of World Terrorism*, Vol. 3, Armonk, NY: M. E. Sharpe, 446–9.

Roberts, H. (1995) "The Islamists, the Democratic Opposition and the Search for a Political Solution in Algeria," *Review of African Political Economy*, 22, 64: 237–44.

Robinson, J. B. P. (1956) *Transformation in Malaya*, London: Secker & Warburg.

Rohde, D. (2001) "Indonesia Unravelling," *Foreign Affairs*, 80, 4: 110–24.

Rolef, S. H. (1997) "Israel's Policy Toward the PLO: From Rejection to Recognition," in A. Sela and M. Ma'oz (eds) *The PLO and Israel: From Armed Conflict to Political Solution, 1964–1994*, New York: St. Martin's, 253–72.

Ron, J. (2000) "Territoriality and Plausible Deniability: Serbian Paramilitaries in the Bosnian War," in B. D. Campbell and A. D. Brenner (eds) *Death Squads in Global Perspective: Murder with Deniability*, New York: St. Martin's, 286–312.

Rosberg, C. G., Jr and Nottingham, J. (1966) *The Myth of "Mau Mau": Nationalism in Kenya*, New York: Praeger Publishers for The Hoover Institution on War, Revolution, and Peace.

Rosenau, W. (1994) "Is the Shining Path the 'New Khmer Rouge'?" *Studies in Conflict and Terrorism*, 17, 4: 305–22.

—— (2001) "Aum Shinrikyo's Biological Weapons Program: Why Did It Fail?" *Studies in Conflict and Terrorism*, 24, 4: 289–301.

Ross, J. I. (1993) "Structural Causes of Oppositional Political Terrorism: Towards a Causal Model," *Journal of Peace Research*, 30, 3: 317–29.

—— (1995) "The Rise and Fall of Quebecois Separatist Terrorism: A Qualitative Application of Factors from Two Models," *Studies in Conflict and Terrorism*, 18, 4: 285–97.

Rotberg, R. I. (2000) "Africa's Mess, Mugabe's Mayhem," *Foreign Affairs*, 79, 5: 47–61.

Rubenstein, R. E. (1987) *Alchemists of Revolution: Terrorism in the Modern World*, New York: Basic Books.

Rubin, B. (1989) "The Political Uses of Terrorism in the Middle East," in B. Rubin (ed.) *The Politics of Terrorism: Terror as a State and Revolutionary Strategy*, Washington, DC: Foreign Policy Institute, 27–65.

Rude, G. (1959) *The Crowd in the French Revolution*, Oxford: The Clarendon Press.

Sacopulos, P. J. (1989) "Terrorism in Britain: Threat, Reality, Response," *Terrorism*, 12, 3: 153–65.

Saikia, J. (2002) "The ISI Reaches East: Anatomy of a Conspiracy," *Studies in Conflict and Terrorism*, 25, 3: 185–97.

Salla, M. E. (1994) "East Timor's Clandestine Resistance to Indonesian Integration," *Social Alternatives*, 13, 1: 44–7.

Samaranayake, G. (1997) "Political Violence in Sri Lanka: A Diagnostic Approach," *Terrorism and Political Violence*, 9, 2: 99–119.

—— (1999) "Patterns of Political Violence and Responses of the Government in Sri Lanka, 1971–1996," *Terrorism and Political Violence*, 11, 1: 110–22.

Sandler, S. (1997) "Religious Zionism and the State: Political Accommodation and Religious Radicalism in Israel," in B. Maddy-Weitzman and E. Inbar (eds) *Religious Radicalism in the Greater Middle East*, London: Frank Cass, 133–54.

Santina, P. (1998/9) "Army of Terror," *Harvard International Review*, 21, 1: 40–3.

Sayigh, Y. (1997) "The Armed Struggle and Palestinian Nationalism," in A. Sela and M. Ma'oz (eds) *The PLO and Israel: From Armed Conflict to Political Solution, 1964–1994*, New York: St. Martin's, 23–35.

Scherrer, C. P. (2002) *Genocide and Crisis in Central Africa: Conflict Roots, Mass Violence, and Regional War*, Westport, CT: Praeger.

Schmid, A. P. (1983) *Political Terrorism: A Research Guide to Concepts, Theories, Data Bases, and Literature*, New Brunswick, NJ: Transaction Books.

—— (1992a) "The Response Problem as a Definition Problem," *Terrorism and Political Violence*, 4, 4: 7–13.

—— (1992b) "Terrorism and Democracy," *Terrorism and Political Violence*, 4, 4: 14–25.

—— (2000) "Terrorism and the Use of Weapons of Mass Destruction: From Where the Risk?" in M. Taylor and J. Horgan (eds) *The Future of Terrorism*, London: Frank Cass, 106–32.

Schneider, J. and Schneider, P. (2002) "The Mafia and al-Qaeda: Violent and Secretive Organizations in Comparative and Historical Perspective," *American Anthropologist*, 104, 3: 776–82.

Schreiber, J. (1978) *The Ultimate Weapon: Terrorists and World Order*, New York: William Morrow.

Schuddekopf, O.-E. (1973) *Revolutions of Our Time: Fascism*, New York: Praeger Publishers.

Schulze, K. E. (2001) "The East Timor Referendum Crisis and Its Impact on Indonesian Politics," *Studies in Conflict and Terrorism*, 24, 1: 77–82.

Sciolino, E. (1991) *The Outlaw State: Saddam Hussein's Quest for Power and the Gulf Crisis*, New York: John Wiley & Sons.

Sederberg, P. C. (2003) "Global Terrorism: Problems of Challenge and Response," in C. W. Kegley, Jr (ed.) *The New Global Terrorism: Characteristics, Causes, Controls*, Upper Saddle River, NJ: Prentice Hall, 267–84.

Shabad, G., and Llera Ramo, F. J. (1995) "Political Violence in a Democratic State: Basque Terrorism in Spain," in M. Crenshaw (ed.) *Terrorism in Context*, University Park, PA: Pennsylvania State University Press, 410–69.

Shalom, S. R. (2001) "Genocide in Rwanda," in W. Dudley (ed.) *Genocide*, San Diego, CA: Greenhaven Press, 43–58.

Shapiro, J. and Suzan, B. (2003) "The French Experience of Counter-Terrorism," *Survival*, 45, 1: 67–98.

Shikaki, K. (2002) "Palestinians Divided," *Foreign Affairs*, 81, 1: 89–105.

Shirer, W. L. (1959) *The Rise and Fall of the Third Reich*, New York: MJF Books.

Shultz, R. H., Jr (1994) "Iranian Covert Aggression: Support for Radical Political Islamists Conducting Internal Subversion Against States in the Middle East/Southwest Asia Region," *Terrorism and Political Violence*, 6, 3: 281–302.

Shultz, R. H. and Vogt, A. (2002) "The Real Intelligence Failure on 9/11 and the Case for a Doctrine of Striking First," in R. D. Howard and R. L. Sawyer (eds) *Terrorism and Counterterrorism: Understanding the New Security Environment, Readings and Interpretations*, Guildford, CT: McGraw-Hill/Dushkin, 367–90.

Sick, G. G. (1990) "The Political Underpinnings of Terrorism," in C. W. Kegley, Jr (ed.) *International Terrorism: Characteristics, Causes, Controls*, New York: St. Martin's, 51–4.

Silke, A. (1999) "Rebel's Dilemma: The Changing Relationship between the IRA, Sinn Fein and Paramilitary Vigilantism in Northern Ireland," *Terrorism and Political Violence*, 11, 1: 55–93.

Silvestri, M. (2000) "'The Sinn Fein of India': Irish Nationalism and the Policing of Revolutionary Terrorism in Bengal," *Journal of British Studies*, 39, 4: 454–86.

Simmons, C. (2001) "Urbicide and the Myth of Sarajevo," *Partisan Review*, 68, 4: 624–30.

Simons, A. (1999) "Making Sense of Ethnic Cleansing," *Studies in Conflict and Terrorism*, 22, 1: 1–20.

Slack, J. A. and Doyon, R. R. (2001) "Population Dynamics and Susceptibility for Ethnic Conflict: The Case of Bosnia and Herzegovina," *Journal of Peace Research*, 38, 2: 139–61.

Slann, M. (1987) "The State as Terrorist," in M. Slann and B. Schechterman (eds) *Multidimensional Terrorism*, Boulder, CO: Lynne Reinner, 39–44.

Smith, B. L. (2000) "Moving to the Right: The Evolution of Modern American Terrorism," *Global Dialogue*, 2, 4: 52–63.

Smith, B. L., and Damphousse, K. R. (1998) "Two Decades of Terror: Characteristics, Trends, and Prospects for the Future of American Terrorism," in H. W. Kushner (ed.) *The Future of Terrorism: Violence in the New Millennium*, Thousand Oaks, CA: Sage, 132–54.

Snow, R. L. (1999) *The Militia Threat: Terrorists among Us*, New York: Plenum Trade.

Snyder, J. T. (2001) "The Moral Imperative," *Peace Review*, 13, 3: 441–8.

Sokolski, H. (2000) "Rethinking Bio-Chemical Dangers," *Orbis*, 44, 2: 207–19.

Sprinzak, E. (1995) "Right-Wing Terrorism in a Comparative Perspective: The Case of Split Delegitimization," in T. Bjorgo (ed.) *Terror from the Extreme Right*, London: Frank Cass, 17–43.

—— (2000) "Extremism and Violence in Israeli Democracy," *Terrorism and Political Violence*, 12, 3/4: 209–36.

Sprinzak, E. and Zertal, I. (2000) "Avenging Israel's Blood (1946)," in J. B. Tucker (ed.) *Toxic Terror: Assessing Terrorist Use of Chemical and Biological Weapons*, Cambridge, MA: MIT Press, 17–41.

Sproat, P. A. (1991) "Can the State be Terrorist?" *Terrorism*, 14, 1: 19–29.

Stein, D. and Ayotte, B. (1999) "East Timor: Extreme Deprivation of Health and Human Rights," *The Lancet*, 354, 9195: 2075.

Stern, J. (1993) "Will Terrorists Turn to Poison," *Orbis*, 37, 3: 393–410.

—— (1999) *The Ultimate Terrorists*, Cambridge, MA: Harvard University Press.

—— (2000a) "The Covenant, the Sword, and the Arm of the Lord (1985)," in J. B. Tucker (ed.) *Toxic Terror: Assessing Terrorist Use of Chemical and Biological Weapons*, Cambridge, MA: MIT Press, 139–57.

—— (2000b) "Pakistan's Jihad Culture," *Foreign Affairs*, 79, 6: 115–26.

—— (2002/3) "Dreaded Risks and the Control of Biological Weapons," *International Security*, 27, 3: 89–123.

Stohl, M. (2003) "The Mystery of the New Global Terrorism: Old Myths, New Realities," in C. W. Kegley, Jr (ed.) *The New Global Terrorism: Characteristics, Causes, Controls*, Upper Saddle River, NJ: Prentice Hall, 84–91.

Stone, M. (1997) *The Agony of Algeria*, New York: Columbia University Press.

Sydenham, M. J. (1961) *The Girondins*, Westport, CT: Greenwood Press.

—— (1966) *The French Revolution*, New York: Capricorn Books.

Szykowiak, K. and Steinhoff, P. G. (1995) "Wrapping Up in Something Long: Intimidation and Violence by Right-Wing Groups in Postwar Japan," in T. Bjorgo (ed.) *Terror from the Extreme Right*, London: Frank Cass, 265–98.

Tackett, Timothy (2000) "Conspiracy Obsession in Time of Revolution: French Elites and the Origins of the

Terror, 1789–1792," *American Historical Review*, Vol. 105, No. 3, pp. 691–713.

Tan, A. (2000) "Armed Muslim Separatist Rebellion in Southeast Asia: Persistence, Prospects, and Implications," *Studies in Conflict and Terrorism*, 23, 4: 267–88.

Taylor, B. (1998) "Religion, Violence and Radical Environmentalism: From Earth First! to the Unabomber to the Earth Liberation Front," *Terrorism and Political Violence*, 10, 4: 1–42.

Taylor, I. and Williams, P. (2002) "The Limits of Engagement: British Foreign Policy and the Crisis in Zimbabwe," *International Affairs*, 78, 3: 547–65.

Taylor, J. G. (1997) "Indonesian Terror in East Timor," in M. Crenshaw and J. Pimlott (eds) *Encyclopedia of World Terrorism*, Vol. 3, Armonk, NY: M. E. Sharpe, 659–60.

Taylor, M. and Horgan, J. (2000) "Future Developments of Political Terrorism in Europe," in Max. Taylor and John Horgan (eds) *The Future of Terrorism*, London: Frank Cass, 83–93.

Terrill, W. A. (1993) "Saddam's Failed Counterstrike: Terrorism and the Gulf War," *Studies in Conflict and Terrorism*, 16, 3: 219–32.

Testas, A. (2002) "The Roots of Algeria's Religious and Ethnic Violence," *Studies in Conflict and Terrorism*, 25, 3: 161–83.

Thompson, D. P. (1996) "Pablo Escobar, Drug Baron: His Surrender, Imprisonment, and Escape," *Studies in Conflict and Terrorism*, 19, 1: 55–91.

Thompson, Sir R. (1966) *Defeating Communist Insurgency: The Lessons of Malaya and Vietnam*, Studies in International Security 10, New York: Praeger.

Tracey, P. C. (2000) "Cherokee Gold in Georgia and California," *Journal of the West*, 39, 1: 49–55.

Traub, J. (2000) "Inventing East Timor," *Foreign Affairs*, 79, 4: 74–89.

Tucker, J. B. (1996) "Chemical/Biological Terrorism: Coping with a New Threat," *Politics and the Life Sciences*, 15, 2: 167–83.

—— (2000a) "Lessons from the Case Studies," in J. B. Tucker (ed.) *Toxic Terror: Assessing Terrorist Use of Chemical and Biological Weapons*, Cambridge, MA: MIT Press, 249–69.

—— (ed.) (2000b) *Toxic Terror: Assessing Terrorist Use of Chemical and Biological Weapons*, Cambridge, MA: MIT Press.

Tucker, J. B., and Pate, J. (2000) "The Minnesota Patriots Council," in J. B. Tucker (ed.) *Toxic Terror: Assessing Terrorist Use of Chemical and Biological Weapons*, Cambridge, MA: MIT Press, 159–83.

US Department of State (various years) *Patterns of Terrorism*, online at http://www.state.gov/s/ct/rls/pgtrpt.

Unnithan, N. P. (1995) "Explaining Collective Violence in India: Social Cleavages and their Consequences," *Studies in Conflict and Terrorism*, 18, 2: 93–109.

van Atta, D. (1998) "Carbombs & Cameras," *Harvard International Review*, 20, 4: 66–70.

van der Brug, M. F. and Tillie, J. (2000) "Anti-Immigrant Parties in Europe: Ideological or Protest Vote," *European Journal of Political Research*, 37, 1: 77–102.

van Every, D. (1966) *Disinherited: The Lost Birthright of the American Indian*, New York: William Morrow.

Veness, D. (2001) "Terrorism and Counterterrorism: An International Perspective," *Studies in Conflict and Terrorism*, 24, 5: 407–16.

Vickers, M. (1995) *The Albanians: A Modern History*, London: I. B. Tauris.

Wallace, P. (1995) "Political Violence and Terrorism in India: The Crisis of Identity," in M. Crenshaw (ed.) *Terrorism in Context*, University Park, PA: Pennsylvania State University Press, 352–409.

—— (1997) "Sikh Nationalist Terrorism in India," in M. Crenshaw and J. Pimlott (eds) *Encyclopedia of World Terrorism*, Vol. 2, Armonk, NY: M. E. Sharpe, 478–81.

Walters, E. G. (1993) *The Other Europe: Eastern Europe to 1945*, New York: Barnes and Noble.

Walton, J. (1984) *Reluctant Rebels: Comparative Studies of Revolution and Underdevelopment*, New York: Columbia University Press.

Watanabe, M. (1998) "Religion and Violence in Japan Today: A Chronological and Doctrinal Analysis of Aum Shinrikyo," *Terrorism and Political Violence*, 10, 4: 80–100.

Wege, C. A. (1991) "The Abu Nidal Organization," *Terrorism*, 14, 1: 59–66.

Weinberg, L. (1995) "Italian Neo-Fascist Terrorism: A Comparative Perspective," in T. Bjorgo (ed.) *Terror from the Extreme Right*, London: Frank Cass, 221–38.

—— (1996) "On Responding to Right-Wing Terrorism," *Terrorism and Political Violence*, 8, 1: 80–92.

Weinberg, L. and Eubank, W. (1998) "Terrorism and Democracy: What Recent Events Disclose," *Terrorism and Political Violence*, 10, 1: 108–18.

—— (2000) "Terrorism and the Shape of Things to Come," in M. Taylor and J. Horgan (eds) *The Future of Terrorism*, London: Frank Cass, 94–105.

Weiss, M. (2001) "The Body of the Nation: Terrorism and the Embodiment of Nationalism in Contemporary Israel," *Anthropological Quarterly*, 75,1: 37–62.

Welsh, D. (1995) "Right-Wing Terrorism in South Africa," in T. Bjorgo (ed.) *Terror from the Extreme Right*, London: Frank Cass, 239–64.

White, J. R. (1998) *Terrorism: An Introduction*, 2nd edn, Belmont, CA: Wadsworth.

White, R. W. (1993) "On Measuring Political Violence: Northern Ireland, 1969 to 1980," *American Sociological Review*, 58, 4: 575–85.

Whitsel, B. (1995) "Aryan Visions for the Future in the West Virginia Mountains," *Terrorism and Political Violence*, 7, 4: 117–39.

—— (2001) "Ideological Mutation and Millennial Belief in the American Neo-Nazi Movement," *Studies in Conflict and Terrorism*, 24, 2: 89–106.

Wieviorka, M. (1990) "French Politics and Strategy on Terrorism," in B. Rubin (ed.) *The Politics of Counterterrorism: The Ordeal of Democratic States*, Washington, DC: Foreign Policy Institute, 61–90.

Wilde, A. W. (1978) "Conversations among Gentlemen: Oligarchical Democracy in Colombia," in J. J. Linz and A. Stepan (eds) *The Breakdown of Democratic Regimes: Latin America*, Baltimore, MD: Johns Hopkins University Press, 28–81.

Wilkinson, P. (1995) "Violence and Terror and the Extreme Right," *Terrorism and Political Violence*, 7, 4: 82–93.

—— (1997) "The Media and International Terrorism," in M. Crenshaw and J. Pimlott (eds) *Encyclopedia of World Terrorism*, Vol. 3, Armonk, NY: M. E. Sharpe, 674–80.

—— (2000a) "Politics, Diplomacy and Peace Processes: Pathways out of Terrorism," in M. Taylor and J. Horgan (eds) *The Future of Terrorism*, London: Frank Cass, 66–82.

—— (2000b) *Terrorism versus Democracy: The Liberal State Response*, London: Frank Cass.

—— (2003) "Why Modern Terrorism? Differentiating Types and Distinguishing Ideological Motivations," in C. W. Kegley, Jr (ed.) *The New Global Terrorism: Characteristics, Causes, Controls*, Upper Saddle River, NJ: Prentice Hall, 106–38.

Willems, H. (1995) "Development, Patterns and Causes of Violence against Foreigners in Germany: Social and Biographical Characteristics of Perpetrators and the Process of Escalation," in Tore Bjorgo (ed.) *Terror from the Extreme Right*, London: Frank Cass, 162–81.

Willis, M. (1997) *The Islamist Challenge in Algeria: A Political History*, New York: New York University Press.

Wilson, J. S. (1992) "Turmoil in Assam," *Studies in Conflict and Terrorism*, 15, 4: 251–66.

Woodworth, P. (2001) "Why Do They Kill? The Basque Conflict in Spain," *World Policy Journal*, 18, 1: 1–12.

Wynia, G. W. (1986) *Argentina: Illusions and Realities*, New York: Holmes & Meier.

Yaeger, C. H. (1990) "Menia Muria: The South Moluccans Fight in Holland," *Terrorism*, 13, 3: 215–26.

—— (1991) "Sikh Terrorism in the Struggle for Khalistan," *Terrorism*, 14, 4: 221–31.

Zirakzadeh, C. E. (2002) "From Revolutionary Dreams to Organizational Fragmentation: Disputes over Violence within ETA and Sendero Luminoso," *Terrorism and Political Violence*, 14, 4: 66–92.

Zunes, S. (2000) "East Timor's Tragedy and Triumph," *Peace Review*, 12, 2: 329–35.

Films

Battle of Algiers (1965)
State of Siege (1973)

Index

Abdullah, King of Jordan 212
abortion, opposition to 65, 66, 214, 247, 252
Abu Nidal 52, 53, 56, 231, 251
Abu Sayyaf 85, 251
Aceh 102, 103, 213, 251
Aden 3, 83, 265
Afghanistan 68, 79, 82, 83–4, 85, 86, 168, 169, 226, 230, 232, 233, 264
African National Congress (ANC) 191, 230, 251
Akali Dal 76, 77, 251
Albania 105, 106
Albanians 51, 95, 103, 105–7, 112, 113, 194, 202, 212, 231, 247, 248, 258
Alexander, King of Yugoslavia 15–16, 52, 251
ALF *see* Animal Liberation Front
Algeria 3, 28, 56, 70, 73, 78–80, 84, 86, 87, 91, 93, 111, 112, 226, 229, 230, 231, 235, 236, 238, 246, 254, 257
al Qaeda *see* Qaeda, al
Ambion 213
American Revolution 90, 96, 111, 112
Amritsar 76, 77, 255, 261
anarchism 16, 118–20, 122, 139, 145, 214, 251, 262, 265
ANC *see* African National Congress
Angola 9, 200, 239
Animal Liberation Front (ALF) 124, 137–9, 251, 252
Animal Rights Militia (ARM) 138–9, 236, 251–2
anthrax 3, 29–30, 31, 252
Anti-Liberation Terrorism Group (GAL) 99, 252
April 19 Movement 180, 181, 234, 252
Arafat, Yassir 107, 108, 110, 126, 255, 261
Argentina 70, 132–5, 140, 141, 191, 209, 210, 224, 230, 237, 254, 259
ARM *see* Animal Rights Militia

Armenia 93, 94, 192; genocide in 94, 169, 192, 252
Armenian Secret Army for the Liberation of Armenia (ASALA) 94, 252
Army of God 66, 252
Aryan Nations 153, 154, 252
Asahara, Shoku 81–2, 252
Assam 214, 252
assassination 11, 34, 40, 41, 46, 47, 50, 52, 53, 54, 60, 67, 69, 105, 109, 110, 117, 119, 167, 233, 237, 252, 253, 258, 265; of Abdullah, King 212; of Alexander, King 15–16, 52, 251; of Alexander II, Tsar 119, 122, 265; in Algeria 76, 79; and anarchists 119–20, 139, 214; in Argentina 133, 134; of Bernadotte, Count Folke 91, 253; and Bush, President George 53, 54; in Colombia 180, 181; of Franz Ferdinand 48, 253; in Germany 125, 147, 151; in Greece 131; of Ghandi, Indira 76, 77, 255; of Ghandi, Rajiv 219, 255–6; of Gracchus, Tiberius and Gaius 144, 256; in India 69, 76, 77, 78, 79, 219, 255–6; in Iran 136; in Ireland 176, 177; in Israel/Palestine 52, 67–8, 91, 212, 233, 253, 262; in Italy 129, 130, 152, 167; in Japan 122, 147; in Kosovo 105; of McKinley, President William 119, 244; of Moro, Aldo 129, 259; of Mountbatten, Lord 34, 177, 260; in Peru 172, 173; of Rabin, Yitzak 67–8, 212; in Spain 99; in Sri Lanka 216, 217, 220; of Somoza, Anastacio 57, 61, 264; in Yugoslavia 51, 105; by Zealots 73
Assassins 67, 68, 233, 246–7, 252
Athens 48, 130, 131, 132
AUC *see* Self Defense Forces of Colombia
Aum Shinrikyo 73, 80–2, 85, 86, 87, 116, 238, 239, 252, 263
Australia 147
Austria 47, 93, 126, 145, 147

Austria-Hungary 18, 48–9, 51, 93, 111, 119
authoritarian systems 19, 37–8, 40–41, 52, 56, 57, 59, 60, 78, 102, 105, 130, 142, 145, 146, 148, 162, 175, 188, 201, 221, 222, 228, 229, 232, 239, 240, 247, 253, 257
axis of evil 59
Ayoda 213, 252
Azerbaijan 93, 95

Baader-Meinhof Gang 124, 125, 127, 245, 252; see also Red Army Faction
Ba'ath Party 52, 189, 253
Bakhtiar, Shahpur 54, 253
Bali bombing 36, 83, 213
Balkans Wars 18, 50, 51
Basque region 95, 98–100, 221, 229, 236, 240, 245, 246, 247, 255
Beer Hall Putsch 149, 253
Bekaa Valley 55, 253
Belgium 126, 141, 146, 205, 206, 254, 260
Bernadotte, Count Folke 91, 253
Bharatiya Janata Party 69, 253
Bhindranwale, Sant Jarnail Singh 76, 77, 253
Biafra 71, 92, 253, 256
biological weapons 24, 29, 30,54, 62, 81, 82, 124, 156, 227, 238, 252
Black Hand 48, 253
Black Hundred 145
Black International 152, 253
Black September 46, 109, 253, 260
Bologna 152, 163, 253
Bosnia 51, 73, 84, 93, 103, 107, 159, 202, 209, 210, 212, 221, 236; and ethnic cleansing 194, 202–4, 209, 212, 229
Boston Tea Party 95–6, 214, 244
Branch Davidians 156, 157, 253
Buddhism 156, 215, 216, 220
Bulgaria 15–16, 46, 50, 51, 52, 147, 156, 193, 212
Burghers 215, 253
Burundi 93, 204, 206, 256, 265
Bush, President George 53, 54

Canada 92, 154, 221, 240
casualties 2, 12, 20–1, 26, 27, 29–32, 33, 34, 38–40, 62, 72, 81, 84, 86, 146, 156, 157, 163–4, 168, 171, 177, 209, 213, 217, 238, 239, 265
CCC see Communist Combat Cells
Central Intelligence Agency see CIA
Chechens 92, 95, 168, 253–4
Chechnya 3, 37, 84, 168, 234, 254
chemical weapons 24, 29, 30, 54, 62, 81–2, 84, 125, 156, 238
Cherokees 194, 196–8, 208, 209, 210, 214, 229, 255
China 19, 72, 83, 120, 122, 171, 172, 184, 225

Christian Identity 155–6, 254
Christianity 65, 71, 72–3, 74, 84, 85, 116, 213; and terrorism 65, 66, 115
CIA 19–20, 42, 46, 57, 61, 130–1, 225, 226, 254
civil liberties 36, 37–8, 60, 141, 197, 229, 240
clash of civilizations 72–3, 86–7
Cold War 12, 19–20, 26, 46, 61, 83, 93, 170, 218, 225, 230, 244
Colombia 170, 173, 179–182, 183, 184, 185, 191, 229, 234, 238, 252, 254, 259, 260, 262, 265
colons 91, 254
Communist Combat Cells (CCC) 146, 254
concessions 4, 24, 35, 100, 121, 123, 161, 163, 229, 232, 235–6, 237, 239, 245
Confucianism 72
Congo-Kinshasa (Zaire) 94
Continuity IRA 178, 231, 254
Contras 50, 56–9, 61, 227, 248, 254
Covenant, the Sword and the Arm 156
Croatia 15–16, 51, 52, 61, 70, 92, 93, 103, 107, 193, 202, 203, 212, 221; and genocide 193
Cromwell, Oliver 193
Cuba 9, 57, 59, 92, 141, 180, 181, 183, 230, 252
Cyprus 91–2, 93, 96, 111, 236, 246
Czechoslovakia 47, 93, 95, 129, 141, 147
Czech Republic 95, 147

Dayaks 100, 102–3, 112, 213, 236, 245, 247, 254
death squads 188, 190–1, 192, 194, 208, 209, 245; in Argentina 134, 191, 230, 254; in Colombia 182, 191; in East Timor 199, 229, 230; in India 77–8, 191, 214, 230, 232, 262; in Indonesia 213; in Rwanda 206, 208, 229; in El Salvador 191, 230; in South Africa 191, 230; in Spain 252; in Sri Lanka 220; in Uruguay 122, 230
democracies 17, 60, 102, 121, 122, 151, 158, 220, 228–9, 232, 235, 239, 240, 247; vulnerability of 24, 36–42, 102, 121, 130, 145, 148, 213, 214, 221, 228, 240, 245
Denmark 90, 161
Diplock Courts 177, 240, 254
disappeared ones 134, 254
drug trade 167, 168, 169–70, 173, 175, 181–2, 183, 184, 218, 227, 228
Duvalier, Francois 37, 254

East Germany 124, 127, 141, 159
East Timor 102, 194, 198–200, 204, 209, 210, 213, 229, 230
economic sanctions 200, 230–1, 232
Egypt 19, 36, 37, 46, 47, 56, 66, 70, 84, 92, 107, 109, 233, 234
El Al 108, 109
ELN see National Liberation Army (Colombia)

empires: colonial 18, 68, 69, 90–1, 92, 94, 95–6, 112, 120, 166, 221; dissolution of 18, 37, 50–1, 91, 93, 94, 111–12, 221, 244, 245
Engels, Frederich 117, 254
environmentalism 123–4, 140, 141
EPL *see* Popular Liberation Army
Escobar, Pablo 181, 254
ETA *see* Euzkadi ta Askatasuna
ethnic cleansing 4, 188, 192–4, 202, 203, 204, 208, 209, 218, 244, 245, 254
Euzkadi ta Askatasuna (ETA) 98–100, 112, 113, 212, 221, 231, 236, 240, 245, 247, 252, 254, 255
extradition 13–14, 50, 237

FARC *see* Revolutionary Armed Forces of Colombia
Fascism 69, 145, 147, 148, 162, 193, 247, 253, 255, 260; in Italy 127, 145, 151, 162, 248, 255, 260
Fatah 107, 108, 112, 113, 126, 255
Feltrinelli, Franco 128, 227, 255
FIS *see* Islamic Salvation Front
foreign interests; as targets 25, 32, 35–6, 40, 41, 72, 79–80, 84, 99–100, 118
France 15–16, 17, 27, 28, 50, 51, 52, 83, 99, 100, 117, 119, 126, 141, 208–9, 226, 240, 241; and Algeria 28, 78, 80, 91, 226, 230; and Reign of Terror 194–6, 209
Franco, Francisco 98, 99, 255
Franz Ferdinand, Archduke 48
French Revolution 90, 111, 117, 144, 194, 196, 208, 209, 210, 236, 256, 257, 259, 262, 265
Fujimoro, Alberto 173, 255
furores 98, 255

GAL *see* Anti-Liberation Terrorism Group
Gaza Strip 55, 66, 107, 108, 109, 110, 255, 260
genocide 163, 188, 192, 193, 199, 207, 208, 255; in Armenia 94, 169, 192, 252; and Nazi Germany 192, 209; in Rwanda 204, 207–8, 209, 244, 256
Georgia Guard 197, 198, 255
Germany 4, 17, 18, 30, 50, 52, 65, 93, 111, 117, 140, 141, 144, 147, 151, 161, 162, 163, 164, 177, 189, 190, 193, 205, 206, 209, 214, 221, 233, 234, 240, 248, 249; and Baader-Meinhof Gang 32, 123, 124–7, 140, 146, 229, 245, 252; and neo-Nazis 148, 158–160, 214, and stormtroopers 148–51, 160, 190
Germany, East *see* East Germany
Germany, West, *see* Germany: Baader-Meinhof Gang
Gestapo 189, 255
Ghandi, Indira 76, 77, 218, 255
Ghandi, Rajiv 219, 255
GIA *see* Islamic Army Group
Girondins 195, 256
globalization 5, 17–18, 33, 71, 84, 87, 144, 147, 161, 236
Golan Heights 107
Goldstein, Baruch 66, 67, 69

Gracchus, Gaius 144, 256
Gracchus, Tiberias 144, 256
Greece 19, 48, 91, 124, 130–2, 140, 141, 152, 166, 221, 226, 229, 249, 263
Green Jackets (Denmark) 161
guerrilla tactics 57, 60, 91, 111, 139, 140, 246; in Afghanistan 79; in Algeria 91, 246; in Argentina 133; in Chechnya 168, 253, 254; in Colombia 180, 181; in East Timor 199, 229; in Greece 130; in India 9, 73, 191, 257; in Indonesia 102; in Iraq 54; in Ireland 175; in Kenya 97, 246; in Kosovo 105; in Malaya 171, 246; in Nicaragua 58, 254 in Palestine 107, 108; in Peru 172, 173, 175; in Rwanda 229; in El Salvador 59; in Southern Rhodesia 200, 266; in Sri Lanka 31, 215, 217, 219, 220, 247, 259
Guinea 94
Gush Emunim 66, 256
Guzman, Abimael 173, 256
Gypsies 106, 147, 190, 192, 193, 214

Haiti 37, 254
Hamas (Islamic Resistance Movement) 55, 69, 70, 107, 108, 110, 212, 233, 239, 256
Hearst, Patricia 121
hijacking 2, 4, 13, 25, 26, 28, 32, 46, 80, 108, 109, 123, 125, 132, 141, 224, 235
Hinduism 69–70, 72, 73, 74, 76, 77, 78, 87, 213–14, 262; and terrorism 69–70, 78, 213–14, 248, 252
Hinduvata 69, 77, 78, 256
Hitler, Adolf 17, 93, 144, 149, 150, 151, 160, 162, 190, 253, 256, 260, 263, 264
Hizballah 32, 55, 56, 70, 85, 167, 224, 231, 246, 256
Holocaust 30, 149, 192, 193, 209, 214, 256; denial 158, 192
Hungary 145, 147; and Yugoslavia 50–2, 61, 193, 212
Hussein, Saddam 37, 53–4, 55, 131, 189, 232, 237, 256
Hutu 194, 204, 206–8, 209, 256, 265

Ibos 71, 92, 256
imperialism 16, 125
Impuza Mugambi 206, 256
India 3, 27, 49, 61, 69–70, 72, 73, 112, 142, 191, 193, 213–14, 215, 218, 221, 227, 230, 232, 240, 251, 252, 253, 257; and Sikhs 73, 74, 76, 86, 191, 213; and Sri Lanka 214, 218–19, 220, 230
Indonesia 3, 53, 71, 93, 95, 100, 103, 112, 159, 190, 213, 221, 236, 251, 254, 256, 258, 264; and East Timor 102, 194, 198–200, 209, 213
INLA *see* Irish National Liberation Army
Inquisition 193
intelligence gathering 36, 42, 46, 49, 53, 97, 130, 225–7, 228, 229, 232, 233, 238, 239
Interahamwe 206, 256

international law 13, 59, 237
internet; use by terrorists 82, 160, 161
intifada 110, 126, 212, 256
IRA *see* Irish Republican Army
Iraq 9, 18, 37, 52–4, 61, 79, 84, 85, 86, 92, 107, 131, 169, 189, 230, 231, 232, 247, 253, 258; and Iran 50, 53, 61, 136, 141, 256, 260; and weapons of mass destruction 29, 32, 46–7, 54
Iran 9, 54–6, 61, 62, 68, 124, 135–7, 140, 167, 227, 230, 231, 253, 258, 260, 263; and Iraq 50, 53, 54, 55, 56, 61, 136, 231, 237, 260
Ireland 34, 97, 175, 176, 179, 193–4
Irian Jaya 102, 103, 213, 256
Irish National Liberation Army (INLA) 178, 183, 257
Irish Republican Army (IRA) 28, 34, 49, 170, 175–9, 182, 183, 184, 227, 228, 229, 234, 236, 240, 247, 248, 254, 257, 260, 262
Islam 62, 67, 68, 69, 71, 7, 73, 74, 76, 116, 156, 183; and terrorism 36, 68, 69, 71, 79–80, 83, 85, 168, 213, 236
Islamic Army Group (GIA) 70, 79, 87, 257
Islamic Jihad (Palestine) 55, 70, 108, 110, 212, 257
Islamic Movement Army (MIA) 79, 257
Islamic Movement of Uzbekistan 168
Islamic Salvation Front (FIS) 79, 80, 86, 236, 257
Israel 3, 4, 28, 50, 52, 55, 61, 66, 67, 69, 70, 72, 73, 84, 86, 91, 107–10, 123, 125, 156, 167, 212, 224, 226, 229, 234, 235, 236, 240, 253, 256; and retaliation 46, 61, 230, 231, 233, 239
Italy 18, 28, 50, 119, 126, 140, 141, 163, 164, 169; and Fascism 146, 162, 214, 248; and neo-Fascists 148, 151–3, 162, 163, 214; and Red Brigades 124, 127–30, 140, 152, 163, 190, 229, 244; and Yugoslavia 50–2, 61, 193, 212, 229

Jackson, Andrew 197
Jacobin Clubs 195, 257
Jammu and Kashmir *see* Kashmir
Janatha Vimukthi Peramuna (JVP) 215, 219–220, 221, 257
Japan 3, 29, 30, 31, 72, 86, 122, 123, 126, 147, 170, 226, 232; and Aum Shinrikyo 73, 80–2, 238, 239
Japanese Red Army (JRA) 60, 123, 126, 18, 257
Jewish extremists 3, 65–8, 69, 71–2, 91, 212, 227, 246, 253
Jewish Revolt 73–4, 85–6
jihad 68, 257
Jordan 107, 109, 113, 212, 230
JRA *see* Japanese Red Army
Judea and Samaria (West Bank) 66, 256, 257
June 2nd Movement 124, 257
Justice Commandos of the Armenian Genocide (JCAG) 94, 257
JVP *see* Janatha Vimukthi Peramuna

Kahane, Meir 66–7, 257
Kashmir 9, 49, 191, 193, 213, 221, 230, 257
Kenya 3, 40, 83, 93, 169, 258; and Mau Mau 95, 96–8, 111, 112, 246, 259
KGB 19–20, 46, 61, 141, 189, 227, 258
Khalistan 76, 85, 258
Khomeini, Ayatollah 53, 135, 140, 258, 260
kidnappings 10, 24, 26, 40, 41, 76, 100, 122, 125, 128, 130, 131, 133, 134, 167, 168, 171, 180 217, 225; of Aldo Moro 129
Kikuyu 96, 97, 258
KKK *see* Ku Klux Klan
KLA *see* Kosovo Liberation Army
kneecapping 24, 128, 131, 177, 258
Korea, North 9, 29, 50, 59–61, 62
Korea, South 50, 59, 60
Kosovo 95, 103, 105–6, 107, 112, 131, 170, 194, 209, 212, 221, 231, 247, 248, 258
Kosovo Liberation Army (KLA) 105, 106, 113, 170, 248, 258
Ku Klux Klan (KKK) 147–8, 154, 155, 161, 162, 214, 258
Kurds 15, 28, 32, 54, 92, 136, 169, 230, 248, 258
Kurdish Workers Party 32, 69, 70, 169, 248, 258, 260
Kuwait 53, 54, 70, 79, 84, 109

bin Laden, Osama 3, 28, 30, 73, 82–5, 86, 87, 213, 227, 233, 238, 239, 244, 247, 251, 258, 264
Laskar Jihad 213, 258
leaderless resistance 12, 66, 139, 148, 154, 155, 163, 226, 232, 252, 258–9
Lebanon 27, 32, 55, 61, 62, 67, 69, 70, 84, 107, 113, 152, 166, 182, 183, 230, 246, 247, 253
Lenin, Vladimir 18, 117, 120, 127, 259
Liberation Tigers of Eelam (LTTE) 70, 216–19, 220, 221, 259
Liberia 94
Libya 9, 47, 52, 61, 179, 230, 231, 233, 253
LTTE *see* Liberation Tigers of Eelam

M-19 *see* April 19 Movement
Maccabees 73
Macedonia 95, 103, 105, 106–7, 112, 212, 221, 231, 247, 259
McVeigh, Timothy 157, 229, 259, 260
Madurese 100, 102–3, 213, 236, 247
Major, John 28, 178
Malaya 170–2, 182, 183, 184, 246
Malaysia 171, 213
Mao Tse-tung (Mao Zedong) 117, 120, 139, 259
Marx, Karl 117–18, 120, 145, 254, 259
Mau Mau 95, 96–8, 111, 246, 258, 259
Medellin Cartel 181, 254, 259
media 19, 25, 33, 41, 42, 67, 91, 108, 138, 180, 200, 204, 248; as target 29, 34, 79, 125, 130, 149, 160, 167, 220

MIA *see* Islamic Movement Army
militia movement 148, 153–7, 163, 226
Milosevic, Slobodan 105, 106, 107, 212, 259
Minnesota Patriots Council 156, 227, 259
MKO *see* Mujahedin-e-Khalq
modernization 5, 17–18, 33, 42, 71, 78, 144, 236, 245
Moluccas 71, 102, 213, 234
Montagnards 195, 196, 259
Montenegro 50–1, 103, 105
Montoneros 124, 132–5, 139, 140, 141, 173, 191, 247, 259
Moro, Aldo 129, 259
Mountbatten, Lord 34, 177, 260
Mozambique 9, 200, 205
MRTA *see* Tupac Amaru Revolutionary Movement
Mugabe, Robert 200–1, 210, 260, 266
Mujahedin-e-Khalq (MKO) 53, 54, 61, 136–7, 141, 260
Munich Olympics 4, 46, 50, 109, 233, 234, 244, 260
Murrah Federal Office Building 2, 153, 157, 259, 260
Mussolini, Benito 52, 127, 145, 151, 152, 162, 214, 255, 260

Namibia 9, 200, 230
Napoleanic Wars 18
narcoterrorism 170, 183, 260
National Liberation Army (ELN)—Colombia 180, 181, 260
National Liberation Army (NLA)—Iran 53, 260
National Liberation Army—Macedonia 106
National Socialist Democratic Workers Party (Nazis) 9, 17, 30, 47, 125, 147, 149–50, 151, 158, 160, 161, 162, 190, 214, 248, 249, 255, 260, 264
Naxalites 214
neo-Nazis 32, 148, 157–62, 163, 214, 236
Netherlands 94, 112, 126, 160, 198, 215, 234
Nicaragua 50, 56–9, 227, 230, 248, 254, 263, 264
Nichols, Terry 157, 260
Nigeria 71, 73, 92, 253, 256
Nivelles Group 146, 260
NKVD 189, 260
NLA *see* National Liberation Army (Iran)
Noraid 179, 228, 260
Northern Ireland 3, 27, 170, 175–9, 183, 184, 185, 234, 240, 244, 247
Norway 90
nuclear weapons 4, 24, 29, 31, 54, 61, 62, 84, 238

Ocalan, Abdullah 169, 260
Occupied Territories (West Bank and Gaza) 53, 55, 66, 67, 68, 108, 109, 110, 126, 209, 212, 229, 256, 260–1
Official IRA 176, 178, 261
Oklahoma City 2, 21, 27, 40, 148, 153, 157, 162, 163, 214, 244, 259, 260

Operation Black Thunder 77, 261
Operation Blue Star 76, 261
Order, the 155, 261
Ottoman Empire 18, 93, 103, 111, 192, 202

Pakistan 9, 28, 49, 61, 68, 70, 74, 78, 83, 86, 112, 221, 230
Palestine 3, 52, 55, 61, 67, 68, 69, 84, 91, 93, 95, 96, 107–10, 112, 113, 125, 152, 184, 190, 212, 227, 229, 231, 233, 235, 236, 240, 247
Palestine Liberation Army 52
Palestinian Authority 110, 236, 255, 261
Palestinian Liberation Organization (PLO) 32, 49, 50, 52, 61, 107–10, 112, 113, 126, 135, 166, 179, 212, 227, 231, 233, 236, 246, 247, 253, 255, 256, 261, 262
Pan-American Flight 103 47, 61
Pavelich, Ante 52, 193, 261
Peloponnesian Wars 48
Pentagon 2, 32, 33, 40, 83, 225, 248
Peoples Revolutionary Army (ERP) 133, 134, 261
Peron, Evita 132
Peron, Isabel 134, 140, 261
Peron, Juan 132–3, 134, 140, 247, 259, 261
Peru 4, 173, 182–3, 184, 234, 238, 265; and Shining Path 170, 172–3, 175, 184
Philippines 85, 213, 246, 251
Pierce, William 154, 155, 261, 265
PFLP *see* Popular Front for the Liberation of Palestine
PFLP-GC *see* Popular Front for the Liberation of Palestine-General Command
PLO *see* Palestinian Liberation Organization
Poland 190
Popular Front for the Liberation of Palestine (PFLP) 108, 110, 123, 126, 141, 261
Popular Front for the Liberation of Palestine-General Command (PFLP-GC) 55, 261
Popular Liberation Army (EPL) 180, 262
Portugal 152, 198, 200, 205, 215
Posse Comitatus 153, 262
propaganda of the deed 119, 133, 140, 145, 262
propaganda of the word 119 262
Provisional IRA 176, 262; *see also* IRA
Provos *see* Provisional IRA
Punjab 76, 77, 78, 191, 213, 238, 251, 258
"Punjab" solution 191, 262

Qaeda, al 28, 32, 53, 70, 73, 82–5, 86, 163, 168, 169, 213, 226, 227, 228, 230,232, 233, 236, 238, 244, 245, 251, 254
Quebec 92, 221
Quebec Liberation Front 92, 262

Rabin, Yitzak 67–68, 212, 262
Radio Free Europe 46

rape 58, 80, 204
Rashtriya Swayamsevak Sangh 69, 70, 262
Real IRA 178, 231, 262
Red Army Faction 32, 123, 124, 139, 140, 141, 146, 160, 229, 252, 262; *see also* Baader-Mienhof Gang
Red Brigades 123, 124, 127–30, 139, 140, 141, 152, 173, 190, 226, 229, 244, 255, 258, 259, 262
Red Cells 124, 262
Reign of Terror 117, 194, 195, 208, 209, 259, 262
Rejectionist Front 126, 262
retaliation 46, 47, 62, 91, 230–2, 233, 234, 236, 238, 239
Revolutionary Armed Forces of Colombia (FARC) 180–2, 183, 185, 191, 229, 262–3
Revolutionary Guards 55, 56, 263
Rhodesia *see* Zimbabwe
ricin 46, 156, 227, 259, 263
Romania 69, 145, 147, 190
Rome 48, 73–4, 85–6, 117, 144, 263, 266
Ruby Ridge 156, 263
Russia 18, 69, 81, 92, 93, 111, 119–20, 122, 145, 147, 167, 168, 192, 226, 234, 266
Rwanda 4, 93, 194, 204–8, 209, 229, 244, 256, 265

SA—*see* Sturmabteilunger
El Salvador 57, 59, 191, 230
Sandinistas 56–9, 248, 254, 263, 264
sans-culottes 195, 236
sarin 3, 30, 80, 81, 238, 263
Saudi Arabia 54, 55, 83, 84, 109, 247
Schutzstaffel (SS) 30, 149, 263
SDS *see* Students for a Democratic Society
Self Defense Forces of Colombia (AUC) 182, 263
Sendero Luminosa *see* Shining Path
September 11th , 2001 2, 3, 4, 19, 20, 33, 157, 168, 224, 238, 240, 244, 247, 248, 258
Serbia 48–9, 50–1, 103, 105, 106, 202, 203, 221
17 November Organization 124, 130–2, 140, 166, 221, 226, 229, 263
Sharait 68–9, 70, 71, 84, 263
Shia 54, 55, 56, 61–2, 67, 68, 135, 166, 167, 252, 253, 263
Shining Path 170, 172–3, 175, 255, 256, 263
Shintoism 72
Sicarri 73, 263
Sierra Leone 94
Sikhs 73, 74, 76–8, 85, 86, 87, 184, 191, 210, 213, 251, 253, 258, 262, 263
Singapore 170, 171, 213
Sinhalese 215, 216, 217, 218, 220
Sinn Fein 247
skinheads 158, 160, 163, 263
SLA *see* Symbonese Liberation Army
Slovakia 95
Somoza, Anastacio 56, 57, 61, 263, 264

Sons of Liberty 95
South Africa 9, 93, 191, 200, 230, 251
Spain 18, 98, 126, 133, 141, 152; and Basques 95, 98–100, 112, 212, 221, 236, 240, 245, 246, 247, 252, 254
Sparta 48, 69
Special Air Services Regiment (SAS) 177, 234–5, 240, 264
Sri Lanka 3, 28, 31, 69, 70, 159, 212, 214–21, 229, 235, 238, 240, 244, 247, 248, 253, 255, 257, 259
Stalin 168, 189, 249, 260, 264
SS—*see* Schutzstaffel
Stern Gang 91, 264
Students for a Democratic Society (SDS) 120, 264, 265
Sturmabteilunger (SA) 148, 149–51, 160, 190, 264
Sudan 9, 55–6, 62, 68, 73, 194
Suharto 102, 213, 264
suicide attacks 3, 8, 27, 28, 31, 69, 80, 86, 90, 123, 136, 169, 219, 265; in Israel 53, 69, 212, 224, 227, 231, 240, 256; in Sri Lanka 69, 217, 248
Sulawesi 102, 103, 213
Sunni 55, 68, 166, 167, 264
surface-to-air missiles 27–8, 207
Sweden 90, 126, 160, 190
Symbionese Liberation Army (SLA) 120, 121, 264
Syria 9, 37, 52, 55, 56, 61, 85, 107, 109, 113, 167, 230, 231, 258

Taliban 68, 84, 86, 168, 230, 232, 264
Tamil Nadu 214, 215, 219, 264
Tamils 215, 216, 217, 218–19, 220, 230, 235, 247
Tamil Tigers 214, 216–19, 226, 229, 240, 248, 264; *see also* Liberation Tigers of Tamil Eelam
Tanzania 3, 40, 83
totalitarian systems 36–7, 40, 41, 188, 222, 228, 229, 240
tourists as targets 34–5, 83, 99, 213
Trotsky, Leon 120, 215, 264–5
Tupac Amaru Revolutionary Movement (MRTA) 172, 175, 183, 234, 255, 265
Tupamaros 122, 133, 139, 209, 210, 265
Turkey 15, 32, 56, 70, 92, 94, 169, 230, 248, 252, 258, 260
Turner Diaries 154, 261, 265
Tutsi 194, 204, 206–8, 209, 256, 265

Uganda 125, 126, 235, 265
Ukranian nationalists 49, 227
Unabomber 11–12, 265
Uruguay 122, 133, 140, 209, 210, 230, 237
USS Cole 3, 83, 265
Utashe 52, 193, 212
Union of Soviet Socialist Republics (USSR) 3, 9, 19, 29, 37, 41, 47, 49, 56, 57, 58, 59, 61, 94, 95, 109, 111–12, 120, 123, 126, 127, 141, 151, 159, 167, 168, 189, 221,

244, 249; and Afghanistan 68, 79, 83; and Cold War 19, 46, 49, 58, 61, 83, 93, 170, 225, 230; and nuclear weapons 29, 84; state support of terrorism 9, 19–20, 109, 120, 124, 127, 184

United Kingdom 17, 42, 49, 51, 61, 64, 90, 92, 119, 124, 130, 134, 137, 200, 201, 205, 215, 221, 226, 236, 237, 240, 251; and American Revolution 95–6; and Cyprus 91–2, 236, 246; and Kenya 95, 96–8, 246; and Malaya 170–2, 184, 246; and Northern Ireland 28, 34, 175–9, 229, 236, 240, 245, 247; and Palestine 91, 107, 212, 236, 246, 264

United States 2–3, 9, 17, 27, 29–30, 33, 40, 46, 49, 54, 56, 57, 62, 65, 66, 83–4, 86, 105–6, 109, 110, 118, 119, 120, 121, 123, 124, 127, 130, 131, 147, 151, 158, 162, 173, 179, 214, 226, 227, 228, 229, 230, 231, 232, 233, 234, 236, 237, 238, 240, 244, 247, 248, 252, 258, 264; and Afghan rebels 28, 83, 230; and Cherokees 197, 198, 214; and Cold War 19–20, 46, 49, 57, 61, 83, 93, 225, 230; and Contras 50, 56–9, 61, 227, 230; and Iraq 53–4; and militias 148, 153–7, 163, 226; and vulnerability 40, 41–2

Vendée 144, 265
Vietnam 120, 127, 139, 214, 264
Violencia, La 179–80, 183, 265

weapons of mass destruction 24, 29–32, 54, 61, 62, 84, 168, 238–9, 265

weapons of mass disruption 29, 265
Weathermen 120, 139, 214, 265
West Bank 55, 66, 107, 108, 109, 110, 235, 256, 260; *see also* Judea and Samaria
Will of the People 119, 265
World Trade Center 2, 20, 27, 28, 32, 33, 39–40, 83, 157, 225, 248
World War I 18, 48, 50, 51, 94, 111, 148, 149
World War II 12, 21, 52, 107, 111, 120, 130, 149, 151, 170

Yugoslavia 4, 15–16, 37, 50–2, 61, 92, 95, 103, 105, 107, 111–12, 117,131, 193, 194, 202–3, 204, 212, 221, 251, 259

ZANU(PF) *see* Zimbabwean African National Union (Popular Front)
ZAPU *see* Zimbabwean African Peoples Union
Zealots 73–4, 85, 86, 87, 245, 246, 266
Zhirinorsky, Vladimir 147, 266
Zimbabwe 194, 200–2, 208, 209, 210, 229, 260
Zimbabwean African National Union (ZANU) 200, 201, 208, 266
Zimbabwean African Peoples Union (ZAPU) 200, 266
Zionist Occupation Government (ZOG) 154, 155, 156, 157, 160, 162, 266
Zionists 212, 266
ZOG—*see* Zionist Occupation Government

Essential Reading

The Dictionary of Terrorism
2nd edition
Richard Thackrah   Freelance writer on security issues, UK
Routledge
Hb: 0–415–29820–2
Pb: 0–415–29821–0

The Terrorism Reader
2nd edition
David Whittaker   Formerly of University of Teeside, UK
Routledge
Hb: 0–415–30101–7
Pb: 0–415–30102–5

Global Responses to Terrorism
9/11, Afghanistan and Beyond
Mary Buckley and Rick Fawn   Royal Holloway and UK University of
St Andrews, UK (respectively)
Routledge
Hb: 0–415–31429–1
Pb: 0–415–31430–5

War without End
The Rise of Islamist Terrorism and Global Response
Dilip Hiro   Freelance journalist
Routledge
Hb: 0–415–28801–0
Pb: 0–415–28802–9

Information and ordering details
For price availability and ordering visit our website www.tandf.co.uk

Alternatively our books are available from all good bookshops.